P9-ARY-059

Passing the PMP® Exam

Assessing the 21st Century Skills

Passing the PMP® Exam
How to Take It and Pass It

Rudd McGary, Ph.D., PMP

Contributors:
Jim Blaylock, PMP
Karl Kill, PMP
Karen Tate, PMP

PRENTICE
HALL
PTR

Upper Saddle River, NJ • Boston • Indianapolis • San Francisco
New York • Toronto • Montreal • London • Munich • Paris • Madrid
Capetown • Sydney • Tokyo • Singapore • Mexico City

CARL CAMPBELL BRIGHAM LIBRARY
EDUCATIONAL TESTING SERVICE
PRINCETON NJ 08541

Many of the designations used by manufacturers and sellers to distinguish their products are claimed as trademarks. Where those designations appear in this book, and the publisher was aware of a trademark claim, the designations have been printed with initial capital letters or in all capitals.

PMP and the PMP Logo are certification marks of the Project Management Institute, which are registered in the United States and other nations.

PMI is a service and trademark of the Project Management Institute, Inc., which is registered in the United States and other nations.

PMBOK is a trademark of the Project Management Institute, Inc., which is registered in the United States and other nations.

PMI did not participate in the development of this publication and has not reviewed the content for accuracy. PMI does not endorse or otherwise sponsor this publication and makes no warranty, guarantee, or representation, expressed or implied, as to its accuracy or content. PMI does not have any financial interest in this publication and has not contributed any financial resources.

The authors and publisher have taken care in the preparation of this book, but make no expressed or implied warranty of any kind and assume no responsibility for errors or omissions. No liability is assumed for incidental or consequential damages in connection with or arising out of the use of the information or programs contained herein.

The publisher offers excellent discounts on this book when ordered in quantity for bulk purchases or special sales, which may include electronic versions and/or custom covers and content particular to your business, training goals, marketing focus, and branding interests. For more information, please contact:

> U. S. Corporate and Government Sales
> (800) 382-3419
> corpsales@pearsontechgroup.com

For sales outside the U. S., please contact:

> International Sales
> international@pearsoned.com

Visit us on the Web: www.phptr.com

Library of Congress Catalog Number: 2005925815

Copyright © 2006 Pearson Education, Inc.

All rights reserved. Printed in the United States of America. This publication is protected by copyright, and permission must be obtained from the publisher prior to any prohibited reproduction, storage in a retrieval system, or transmission in any form or by any means, electronic, mechanical, photocopying, recording, or likewise. For information regarding permissions, write to:

> Pearson Education, Inc.
> Rights and Contracts Department
> One Lake Street
> Upper Saddle River, NJ 07458

ISBN 0-13-186007-0

Text printed in the United States on recycled paper at R.R. Donnelley in Crawfordsville, Indiana.
First printing, July 2005

This book is dedicated to Sharon, Clayton, and Carter,
the three most important people in my life.

Table of Contents

Preface

There is no profession more interesting or challenging than modern project management. Because of the nature of projects, the project manager will be working in environments where change is occurring, where there is uniqueness to the management, and where time constraints guide the work to be done. Project management has been used for thousands of years with almost all of the projects including some aspect of building. From the pyramids of Egypt to the great cathedrals of Europe, projects involving thousands of people and sometimes hundreds of years have been completed.

While there were de facto project managers all throughout history, the formalization of project management did not really begin until the second half of the twentieth century. As large organizations, such as the U.S. military, began to run larger and more expensive projects, there was a need for the discipline and common knowledge base that is the hallmark of a profession. Some sort of passing on of best practices and common language that would make each successive generation of project managers able to have much the same skill set and background information as the previous one was needed to make project management professional.

In 1969, a group was formed that was dedicated to making project management a profession. The Project Management Institute (PMI) was formed in that year and later brought out a book, the Project Management Body of Knowledge or PMBOK, that began to codify information concerning the various unique factors of project management.

A validation of the status of the PMBOK came in the year 2000 when the American National Standards Institute declared the PMBOK the official publication of project management and the work was set up as the standard for project management in this country.

PMI instituted a certification test so that there would be a standardization of information and a knowledge base that could be transferred and used by people coming into the project management arena. Because of its very nature, project management is a job that is serendipitous. Most people come to it by chance, not by planned education or career path intention. So the one place that all aspiring project managers can go that has been accepted by ANSI is the PMI certification test leading to the designation PMP, or Project Management Professional.

The aim of this book is twofold. First, the book and CD-ROM are designed to help anyone taking the certification examination to pass it. (See Appendix C for details about the CD.) This is the driving force of the book. However, the manner in which the book is presented is also useful for information that can be used long after passing the exam. Anyone who has been a project manager will recognize the two uses of the book. It is both a primer for the exam and a textbook for project managers to use as they project manage.

I am often asked what the key to taking the exam is, and the best answer is "Know the material." Taking this exam is not about knowing answers to questions; it is about having the depth of knowledge that will be useful in future endeavors. If you have the knowledge base, you will pass the exam. I have enjoyed writing this book because of the dual nature of both passing the exam and then being a professional project manager. As you use the book, I hope that it is helpful in both ways and that when you pass the exam, you understand you are starting, not finishing, your education in project management. The project management profession is ongoing and can be fascinating, demanding a large range of skills for its practitioners. If this book helps people find new careers and challenges, then it will be worthwhile.

Good luck on the exam and in being a project manager.

Rudd McGary
Columbus, OH
April, 2005

Acknowledgments

First, to my wife Sharon, without whom nothing I do would be worthwhile. The encouragement she gave is the reason this book was written. To my sons, Clayton and Carter, for their support during the writing of the book and staying out of the way when I was writing. The work of Paul Petralia and Michelle Vincenti at Prentice Hall has been invaluable, and they made it possible to bring this book to its final shape. To Lori Lyons and Ben Lawson of Prentice Hall, thank you for your hard work in keeping me on track and making the book as professionally done as possible; it is a pleasure to work with people who do their job so well. Tim Bolwerk helped me get into the project management area and always was helpful during our long talks about the practice of project management. For Karen, Karl, and Jim, the contributors to the book, thank you for all your professional hard work; it makes the book better. And finally, to all of you who have been colleagues and students in the area of project management, thank you for helping me gain an understanding of what it means to be a professional project manager.

About the Author

Rudd McGary, Ph.D., PMP, lives in Columbus, Ohio, with his wife Sharon, and sons Clayton and Carter. As an educator, practitioner, and writer in project management, McGary has helped countless people as they have worked on and studied about project teams and project management. He continues that tradition with this book, which will aid people interested in passing the PMI certification examination to become familiar with the various areas of interest and study that make up project management.

About the Contributors

Jim Blaylock, PMP, has more than thirty years experience leading projects in IT, Logistics, Distribution, Manufacturing, and Transportation. While in the Navy, he successfully managed organizations having in excess of 200 people and projects that ranged from $5 million to $75 million in value. Since retirement from the Navy, he has concentrated primarily on commercial projects, successfully leading ones for Sherwin Williams, Caterpillar, Fel-Pro, Toyota, Vauxhall, Federal Express, Home Shopping Network, Reynolds and Reynolds, Cincinnati Bell, Bloomingdales-By-Mail, and the State of Ohio. Jim holds a BS in Chemistry and an MS in Computer Systems Management and is a graduate of the Crosby Quality College. Certified as a PMP since 1993, he has served on the Board of Directors of the SWOHIO Chapter of PMI for more than eight years and is currently Director of Best Practices for the Chapter. He is a frequent speaker at seminars related to project management and in his spare time, Jim serves as an adjunct professor at the Williams College of Business at Xavier University in Cincinnati, teaching Operations Management for MBA candidates.

Karl Kill, PMP, is a Senior Project Manager with CheckFree Corporation. Karl has more than seventeen years of project management experience in a wide variety of industries, both private and public sectors. He has directed multidiscipline teams for the planning, development, implementation, and deployment of several large Information Technology projects. In addition, he has been a PMP-certified project manager since 1999 and is facilitating a PMP exam study group at CheckFree Corporation, helping others to become certified.

Karen Tate, PMP, President of The Griffin Tate Group, Inc., is the coauthor of *The Project Management Memory Jogger, A Pocket Guide for Project Teams, Getting Started in Project Management, A Step By Step Approach to Risk Assessment, Triz: An Approach to Systematic Innovation*, and *The McGraw-Hill 36 Hour Course in Project Management*. Ms. Tate has been working with projects and project teams for more than twenty years. Prior to forming The Griffin Tate Group, Inc., she managed programs and projects of all types and sizes, in a variety of industries. She has consulted and trained with organizations throughout the U.S., South Africa, China, Europe, Asia, Australia, and New Zealand.

Ms. Tate has earned her Project Management Professional Certification (PMP) from the Project Management Institute (PMI), and she has an MBA from Xavier University. She lives in Cincinnati, Ohio, with her sons and her husband, Andy, also a PMP. Ms. Tate is a Senior Life member of the Society of Women Engineers (SWE) and serves as the Chair of the External Relations and Volunteer Involvement Committee of the Board of Directors of Project Management Institute.

CHAPTER ONE

Introduction

It is nine o'clock in the morning wherever you are. You have arrived at a learning center and are about to take the Project Management Institute Certification exam for Project Management Professional (PMP). You have two pencils, a few clean sheets of paper, and a four-function calculator. You also have just about enough adrenaline flowing to go out and run a marathon. Before that marathon, though, you have the little matter of a certification exam to take.

You have a tendency for short-term memory loss when you're filled with adrenaline. So, do not get up early in the morning and try to cram in a few more minutes of stressed-out study; it will not help you. Finish studying the night before, get some sleep, and then wake up ready to take the test.

After you receive authorization from PMI, you can schedule your own exam. The examination is done at learning centers, all of which offer just about the same facilities. You can choose the time of day that you take the exam, so you need to know when your best test time-taking hours of the day are. Having taught at several universities over the years, my experience has been that morning test takers generally do better than people who take the test later in the day. Of course, this is not true for everyone, so make a decision when you will be the most comfortable. Remember to take as much charge as you can of the environment and time of the test.

Repeat after me: "I am not here to take this test, I'm here to **pass it**."

Onward.

The PMBOK

The official definition of project management from the Project Management Body of Knowledge, the PMBOK® (pronounced "pimbok"), is "The application of knowledge, skills, tools, and techniques to project activities to meet the project requirements." Much of the writing in the PMBOK is like that—rather terse, with lots of information in a single sentence. It is a key to passing this exam to get comfortable with the style of writing in the PMBOK and to know the definitions that are specific to the PMI. The best place to find the definitions is in the Glossary section of PMBOK. It is a good idea to learn these definitions exactly as they are written because they will be given in the test, and the key to being successful on this examination is to understand what is wanted by PMI. You may have had extensive experience in project management and have your own vocabulary, but for this examination, the Glossary definitions are the ones you should use.

> **Q.** The _____ is the official text for the PMI examination.
>
> ❏ A. Dictionary   ❏ B. Thesaurus
>
> ❏ C. PMI Lexicon   ❏ D. PMBOK

The answer is D. Make sure that you have a copy, which you can buy through the PMI website. If there is any question as to the correctness of an answer, the answer should conform to materials found in the PMBOK.

The questions on the exam always have four answers. An important fact to remember is that there are instances on the examination where two answers shown are potentially correct. It is your task to make sure that you pick the answer that is found in the PMBOK. Here is an example of a question where anyone who has read through the PMBOK knows that C, project management, is the answer. A person coming to the test from another discipline might answer B, management systems. You answer the questions according to the PMBOK.

> **Q.** The application of knowledge, skills, tools, and techniques to project activities to meet the project requirements is:
>
> ❏ A. Project Administration   ❏ B. Management systems
>
> ❏ C. Project Management   ❏ D. Common knowledge

The answer is C. This is the exact quote from the PMBOK. You now have gotten one question correct on the exam.

Q. There will be questions where _____ answers appear to be correct.

    ☐ A. Four   ☐ B. Three

    ☐ C. No   ☐ D. Two

The answer is D. Be careful when you are taking the exam. If two answers look correct, then you should answer with the PMBOK in mind. The final reference for the correctness of answers lies in knowing how the answer was explained in the PMBOK.

    First big rule for taking the certification examination:

    Look at all the answers before you answer the question.

The test is given on a computer. You are given a chance to see how the mouse works and what your questions look like on the screen, and this is done without taking any time off of your test-taking time. Then you begin the examination. As you see the questions come up, you will have three options. First, you can click on the correct answer if you are certain of it. If there is no doubt in your mind, click on it and go on to the next one.

The second option is to mark an answer but not to finalize it at that time. Instead, you can choose to come back to the question after you have gone through the test. Generally, the answer you choose first is going to be the answer that you should use, so click on one of the answers if you have a feeling about what is correct, but you do not have to make a final decision right at that time.

The third option is to go past the question and come back to it later. If the question is confusing, if you don't know the answer, or if the answers that are shown are not what you were expecting, go past the question. This point cannot be stressed enough. You do not need to spend time at the beginning of the exam on questions that you do not feel comfortable with. Go through the examination and get the questions that you are certain you know. Usually there will be one hundred or more questions that you can answer comfortably.

Because you need one hundred and forty answers to be correct, you start with a good step up with one hundred questions that are correct. The next forty questions are the ones you should take time with and the ones that will determine how you do on the examination.

> **Q.** **Which of these is not an option when taking the PMP certification examination?**
>
> ❑　A.　Leaving questions blank and finishing the test.
>
> ❑　B.　Clicking on the correct answer the first time you see the question.
>
> ❑　C.　Leaving questions blank and then coming back to answer them.
>
> ❑　D.　Clicking on the answer you think may be correct but not making that your final answer at the time.

The answer is A. You must pick an answer for all of the questions on the test before you are allowed to finish.

> **Q.** **You should always:**
>
> ❑　A.　Click on the first answer that seems correct.
>
> ❑　B.　Never click on any answer but come back later.
>
> ❑　C.　Read all the answers carefully before clicking on one.
>
> ❑　D.　Expect to get several answers wrong in any case.

The answer is C. Take time to read all the answers, even if you are sure that the answer under the letter A is the correct one. You may find that there will be an even better answer in the four-part list.

How Much Time Do I Have?

You will have four and a half hours to take the exam, although you can't start to take it, stop, and then come back later. Most people finish the exam within three hours; two and a half seems to be the mean. In other words, you've got plenty of time to do the exam, and this is particularly true if you use the tips throughout this book. There is no need to rush or panic.

Each question on this exam is worth exactly as much as the next. The very simple ones and the more complex ones are not weighted against each other; all are the same weight. So if you do not want to deal with a question that you do not understand at first, do not. You must answer all the questions on the examination before you can complete it. If you come to the end of the exam and there are still a few questions that you cannot figure out, simply choose a letter and click. You will have at least one chance in four of getting the correct answer. You must finish all the questions before finishing the exam. When you click on the finish button, you will get your score almost immediately. When you pass the exam, the learning center will give you a certificate, and you will be PMP certified. Within two weeks, you will receive your certificate from PMI. Frame it; you earned it.

One question, one point—all questions are worth the same value.

These are some of the types of hints you should keep in mind when preparing for the exam. You do not have to answer all the questions to do well; this is a simple pass/fail exam.

> **Q. All the questions on the examination are worth _____.**
> - ❑ A. The square root of the difficulty of the question.
> - ❑ B. The importance given to the question by the PMBOK committee.
> - ❑ C. The same.
> - ❑ D. The degree of difficulty given to the question by a panel of international judges.

The answer is C. No matter how complex the question, it does not get you any more points than the simplest question. Remember this as you take the examination. Although you may get some satisfaction from working out a complex question, the simple definition of a project is worth just as much.

Project Management and Projects

Many of the most famous projects in history involved construction or engineering of some sort. The pyramids of ancient Egypt were built over hundreds of years but are still considered projects. Notre Dame Cathedral in Paris took roughly 200 years to build and had dozens of what we would now call project managers, although that term was not in use during these two massive projects.

The important information concerning any project is in the definition we give for projects. PMBOK suggests that **A project is a temporary endeavor undertaken to create a unique product, service, or result.** Memorize this. You will certainly be asked about it on the exam.

Let's look at what this definition means to us as project managers. First, the fact that a project is temporary means that the management of the project is very different from managing a standard operating organization. Resource needs, financial considerations, quality concerns, risk management, and communication needs are all concerns that arise because a project has a specific beginning and ending.

Q. A project is a _____ endeavor undertaken to create a unique product, service, or result.

- ❑ A. Difficult
- ❑ B. Complex
- ❑ C. Critical
- ❑ D. Temporary

The answer is D. Although all of the other answers may be true, the temporary nature of the project is one of the major defining characteristics of a project.

Many organizations have difficulties in placing project managers because projects do not continue to be managed year after year as do the operations of a standard organization, so there may be slack or down time for the project manager. This "on the beach" or "on the bench" time is when project managers like you can help with other tasks in the organization such as responding to RFPs (Request for Proposal), or you can use the time to learn new skills that will help you on your next project. However, during this time, you are not actually project managing, and that is difficult for some organizations to defend—having someone on the payroll who is not actually doing the job for which he or she was hired.

For the most part, project managers become project managers because the organization needs someone to manage a project, and that need is often filled with someone who did not come to the organization as a project manager. There are very, very few organizations that have planned paths that lead to project management positions as a part of their overall HR strategy. Before 1969, there was no governing body to define the role of a project manager and no tests that could certify someone as a project manager. There were many good project managers working in a variety of industries, but there was no single certification or examination that would be accepted universally. The Department of Defense was one of the leaders in this area because it needed project managers for much of the construction it did as well as major projects such as those done by NASA. But the training given in the DoD was not the single international standard for project management, and that changed in 1969.

In 1969, the Project Management Institute was formed, and topics were discussed and material was written on the topic of project management. These early offerings gave way to the Project Management Body of Knowledge, the PMBOK. The PMBOK that we are referencing in this book is one that has gone through major revisions as project management becomes more and more a major type of management in our modern era.

A second event further codified the standards for project management when in 2000 ANSI (American National Standards Institute) declared that the standard for project management literature would be the PMBOK. This action changed the project management world. The PMBOK is now the official book to read, and the materials from it make up the official exam that qualifies the test taker as a Project Management Professional, or PMP.

Q. PMI was founded in:

❑ A. 1954 ❑ B. 1969

❑ C. 1970 ❑ D. 2000

The answer is B. PMI was founded in the late sixties.

Q. In 2000, _____ certified the PMBOK as the standard for project management literature.

❑ A. American Academy ❑ B. Ohio State

❑ C. ANSI ❑ D. Sorbonne

The answer is C. The American National Standards Institute is the body that governs standardization of information in the U.S. This is important because this is the first time that any document or book has been accepted as the single standard for project management in the United States.

One of the problems, albeit a small one, with the PMBOK is that there are several different writing styles within the book because it has multiple authors. This means that you will see slightly different styles of explanation. Throughout this book, we'll make sure that the questions and explanations you see conform to PMI and are explained as clearly as possible.

Two Different Models of Approaching the Study of Project Management

The Phase Approach

Within the structure of a project, there are five phases: Initiation, Planning, Execution, Control, and Closing. Some people study for the exam by using each phase as a separate study area, looking at the key components from initiation, planning, and so on. Although this works well when looking at a project from its inception, it becomes very difficult to place management actions only in one phase. For instance, you will be doing project risk management throughout the entire project. You do not simply do a risk plan once and leave it. Risk is managed in every phase, and so are many other project plans.

> **Q. Planning and Closing are two parts of a _____ approach to project management.**
>
>   ❑ A. Tactical   ❑ B. Phase
>
>   ❑ C. Methodical   ❑ D. Practical

The answer is B. The phase approach is one of the ways in this book used to prepare for the examination.

What is helpful in managing a project with the phase approach as your model is that you can see the dependencies that occur throughout an entire phase as well as the entire project, and you are able to see the different ways in which certain things will interact during the project. Working through and planning the project phases is the best way to manage an actual project, and the phase approach of study will help to explain how the actual flow of a project occurs.

In this book, we will discuss the five phases, and we will tie two phases together because phases overlap during a project. So Initiation and Planning are the topic of one chapter, Planning and Execution are the topic of another, and so on. It is impossible to actually manage a project without overlapping phases.

One other reason that the phase approach is used is that some topics do not fit exactly into one knowledge area from the PMBOK. These are the topics that are discussed in the phase part of the book. Although there is some redundancy between phase topics and knowledge areas in terms of content, looking at the topics from different viewpoints will help you with the examination.

The Knowledge Area Approach

This is the way the PMBOK is structured. There are nine separate areas of study: Integration, Scope, Cost, Time, Quality, HR, Communications, Risk, and Procurement. Each knowledge area is given a chapter in the PMBOK that explains the facts that PMI thinks are important in the study of the particular topic. Most of the chapters are fairly short. The problem is not how long or short the knowledge area chapters are in the book; it's the fact that there is so much to learn in each topic that each chapter could be a doctoral dissertation area. This book will give you the knowledge that is required in a certain study area to satisfy testing requirements and also will link it to the rest of the areas because there are constant interactions between knowledge groups when a project is actually going on.

Because PMBOK is structured by knowledge areas, it would seem that you should study this model. Actually, if you only had one way to look at the exam and actual project management performances, that would be true. But the PMBOK doesn't give you everything you need to know about passing the test, nor does it have depth in more demanding project management practice areas. So it will be one of the learning models we will concentrate on for the test, but it is not the only model for preparing for the test.

Each knowledge area has several processes within it. These are subdivided into three categories: Inputs, Tools and Techniques, and Outputs. An example is the process areas found within the Scope Management Chapter of PMBOK. These five process areas are listed in the PMBOK as Scope Planning, Scope Definition, Create WBS, Scope Verification, and Scope Change Control. Within each of these are Inputs, Tools and Techniques, and Outputs. Some people like to memorize every one of the processes, and this can be helpful. The processes are detailed in Chapter 3 of the PMBOK. This chapter, titled "Project Management Processes," is a good one to read to understand how the processes fit into the phases. Make sure you read the first three chapters of PMBOK in depth. They help to explain how the entire project management process is linked together with all its sub-processes.

> **Q. Each knowledge area is divided into _____ areas.**
>
>   ❑ A. Tactical   ❑ B. Process
>
>   ❑ C. Project management   ❑ D. Strategic

The answer is B. Each of the knowledge areas has several subdivisions that are process areas.

> **Q. Each process is divided into:**
>
> ❏ A. Inputs, Tactics, and Strategy
>
> ❏ B. Inputs, Outputs, and Tactics
>
> ❏ C. Inputs, Tools and Techniques, and Tactics
>
> ❏ D. Inputs, Tools and Techniques, and Outputs

The answer is D. It is helpful to know what the three areas are in each of the processes, and this can be found in the third chapter of PMBOK.

> **Q. Which is the best model for studying for the PMI examination?**
>
> ❏ A. The Phase Model ❏ B. The Knowledge Area model
>
> ❏ C. Both models ❏ D. The DoD model

The answer is C. Use parts of both the Phase and the Knowledge Area model. In this book we will be offering various ways to approach the knowledge you need to pass the test. For some people, one model fits their cognitive process; for other people, another model is best. In this book you get a variety of ways to understand, memorize, and use information for the exam in the future. By using a combination of the two, we think you'll have the best chance of passing the exam and going on to become a PMP.

How Is the Test Constructed?

The test consists of 200 questions over the nine knowledge areas and the five phases. According to PMI, here are the percentages of questions asked by phase.

Phase	Percentage
Initiation	4
Planning	37
Execution	24
Control	28
Closing	7

Note that the Planning/Execution/Control phases comprise 89% of the test and that Planning has the most questions of all on the examination. Concentrate on these areas because that is how the examination is written.

> **Q. The single phase that has the most questions about it on the examination is the _____ phase.**
>
> ☐ A. Closing   ☐ B. Initiation
>
> ☐ C. Planning   ☐ D. Control

The answer is C. On the examination, 37% of the questions will focus on planning.

Questions You Should Not Answer

There are questions on the examination that you should not take the time to answer, at least on the first reading of the examination. These may be questions that are extremely complex, questions that are outside of your comfort zone from your study, or questions where you really have no idea of the answer when you first encounter them. Taking this exam consists of being aware of how much time you have, strengths in your study, and ways to pass the exam, not trying to get 100%. I have had many people tell me that the first few questions were confusing to them. There are going to be some confusing questions in all examinations. The best way to get rid of this stress is very simple. Keep on going through the questions until you find one whose answer you know for certain. Answer it and go on with the exam. By going through and finding questions that you understand, your stress level will come down, and later you can go back to questions that may have been daunting at first. Remember ONE QUESTION, ONE POINT. Let the exam "come to you" by working with questions that are in your strengths. Do not worry even if you have to go to the fifteenth question before you see one about which you're certain. Go there, get started, and you will find yourself relaxing, which is a key to test taking.

Why Do People Fail This Exam?

There are many reasons people fail an exam. The most common reason is that they didn't study enough. There are many good books available on the PMI examination that basically consist of a list of potential questions. These are very helpful in getting used to the styles of questions, and they help get the test taker more comfortable with the exam.

However, this type of studying comes apart if you memorize answers to specific questions instead of learning the content of the material. This book will give questions because questions are a good learning aide. But there will also be discussion about the answers so that the test taker understands what both the question and the answer mean. Do not just learn long lists of questions; learn the topic.

Another reason people fail a test of this type is that they fail to read all of the answers. There are several questions on the exam that have two answers that are very close. Your job is to understand the answer that PMI wants and use it. By failing to read all of the questions, your answer may not be the one that PMI is looking for. Within this book, we'll be looking at the questions through the eyes of the PMBOK.

People come up to me all the time and say, "I've been a project manager for more than 20 years. Do I need to study for the exam?" The answer is a resounding yes. I've known excellent PMs who weren't certified and who took the exam without a class and without using a book like this. Most of them failed to pass. It may be that the experience is there but learning the style of the PMBOK is critically important. So use this book as a platform to understand what is expected of you for the PMP exam.

Q. **What is the best time to sit for the examination?**

❑ A. Immediately after taking the course

❑ B. When you feel comfortable

❑ C. When the teacher tells you to do so

❑ D. Whenever your organization thinks it is time

The answer is A. You have the best short-term memory right after the course, so you should take the test as soon as possible after you have finished the course. The longer you wait, the more studying you will have to do to pass the exam.

What Do I Need for the Exam?

First, you need your authorization letter from PMI. Bring it to the testing center. Also, bring a four-function calculator. Any calculators that are programmable will be taken away from you. The testing center will give you scrap paper and pencils. You should turn these in at the end of the test.

(One quick aside: if there are formulas that you want to remember, write them down immediately when you are in the examination room. This is the best way to make sure you have them down correctly. This procedure is in compliance with the test.)

You will be given a 15-minute computer tutorial, and then you will begin the test. When you have answered all the questions and signified you are finished, the computer will tell you whether you have passed right then and there, and a certificate will be printed out. This is a nice moment, at least for the many students I have talked with after they passed the examination. (If you do not pass, inquire what needs to be done to reschedule. Do not take too long to reschedule because you will begin to forget short-term memory materials.)

When Should I Apply to Sit for the Exam?

As soon as you have finished studying and you feel ready. When teaching the exam for PMI, I wanted the students to have their test dates scheduled at least half way through the class so that they would be taking the exam only a week or two after finishing. This is the standard way you have tests scheduled in an academic setting. It would be highly unusual for a school to schedule an examination covering a course that you had a half a year ago. You do not need a lot of extra study time after you've taken a course. The time immediately after taking a course is the time when the information is at the front of your consciousness. Submit your request by email (not snail mail) and be ready to go and pass the exam.

Style of the Book

This book will include questions in the body of text. This is done to reinforce specific pieces of information that are important for the examination. Many of the questions come right after the discussion of the topic, as you have already seen in this chapter. This will help you focus on the information and also will give you an idea of the way in which the questions are found in the examination. There are also questions that are part of the teaching process, so you should pay careful attention to any and all questions found in this book.

The two models of project management in the PMBOK are the Phase model and the Knowledge Area model. Both are used and discussed in this book. There are overlaps between the two, and the redundancy in information is intended. Certainly you should know that if a topic is explained in both the phase and knowledge areas of the book that the topic is important and will be examined on the test.

There may be several discussions throughout the book of a single topic. This is done to offer different ways of understanding the topic to the reader. One of the explanations may be easier to comprehend than another. The reader can choose the explanation that makes the most sense to him or her, although all explanations are intended to help the reader get a grasp of the basic information.

At the end of each chapter, there will be a list of questions that have been used throughout the text of the chapter. This time, the answers will be separate so that you can use each chapter as a test on the materials. The answers and explanations of the answers if necessary will also be found at the end of the chapter.

There will be a mid-book test of one hundred and nine questions. This is done after the phases are taught. Use this mid-book exam to see how you are doing up to that point. You will get a good feel about your progress from how you are scoring on the mid-book exam. You should take no more than one and a half minutes as an average for each question. Because you will have already seen most of the questions in the mid-book exam, you should not need too long to get the correct answer. The questions in the mid-book exam are mixed, whereas the questions at the end of other chapters are focused specifically on the chapter that precedes them.

This first chapter gives you basic ideas about how to pass the examination and some basic terms. The following chapters will be on specific project management techniques and practices that you can use in you professional life as well as when preparing for the PMP certification examination.

Questions from Chapter One   ?

1. The _____ is the official text for the PMI examination.

- ❑ A. Dictionary
- ❑ B. Thesaurus
- ❑ C. PMI Lexicon
- ❑ D. PMBOK

2. The application of knowledge, skills, tools, and techniques to project activities to meet the project requirements, is:

- ❑ A. Project Administration
- ❑ B. Management systems
- ❑ C. Project Management
- ❑ D. Common knowledge

3. There will be questions where _____ questions appear to be correct.

- ❑ A. Four
- ❑ B. Three
- ❑ C. No
- ❑ D. Two

4. Which of these is not an option when taking the PMP certification examination?

- ❑ A. Leaving questions blank and finishing the test.
- ❑ B. Clicking on the correct answer the first time you see the question.
- ❑ C. Leaving questions blank and then coming back to answer them.
- ❑ D. Clicking on the answer you think may be correct but not making that your final answer at the time.

5. You should always:

- ❑ A. Click on the first answer that seems correct.
- ❑ B. Never click on any answer but come back later.
- ❑ C. Read all the answers carefully before clicking on one.
- ❑ D. Expect to get several answers wrong in any case.

6. All the questions on the examination are worth _____.

- ❑ A. The square root of the difficulty of the question.
- ❑ B. The importance given to the question by the PMBOK committee.
- ❑ C. The same.
- ❑ D. The degree of difficulty given to the question by a panel of international judges.

7. A project is a _____ endeavor undertaken to create a unique product, service, or result.

  □ A. Difficult   □ B. Complex

  □ C. Critical   □ D. Temporary

8. PMI was founded in:

  □ A. 1954   □ B. 1969

  □ C. 1970   □ D. 2000

9. In 2000, _____ certified the PMBOK as the standard for project management literature.

  □ A. American Academy   □ B. Ohio State

  □ C. ANSI   □ D. Sorbonne

10. Planning and Closing are two parts of a _____ approach to project management.

  □ A. Tactical   □ B. Phase

  □ C. Methodical   □ D. Practical

11. Each knowledge area is divided into _____ areas.

  □ A. Tactical   □ B. Process

  □ C. Project management   □ D. Strategic

12. Each process is divided into:

  □ A. Inputs, Tactics, and Strategy

  □ B. Inputs, Outputs, and Tactics

  □ C. Inputs, Tools and Techniques, and Tactics

  □ D. Inputs, Tools and Techniques, and Outputs

13. Which is the best model for studying for the PMI examination?

  □ A. The Phase model   □ B. The Knowledge Area model

  □ C. Both models   □ D. The DoD model.

14. The single phase that has the most questions about it on the examination is the
_____ phase.

   ❑ A. Closing   ❑ B. Initiation

   ❑ C. Planning   ❑ D. Control

15. What is the best time to sit for the examination?

   ❑ A. Immediately after taking the course

   ❑ B. When you feel comfortable

   ❑ C. When the teacher tells you to do so

   ❑ D. Whenever your organization thinks it is time

Answers from Chapter One

1. **The answer is D.** Make sure that you have a copy, which you can buy through the PMI website. If there is any question as to the correctness of an answer, the answer should conform to materials found in the PMBOK.

2. **The answer is C.** This is the exact quote from the PMBOK. You now have gotten one question correct on the exam.

3. **The answer is D.** Be careful when you are taking the exam. If two look correct, then you should answer with the PMBOK in mind. The final reference for the correctness of answers lies in knowing how the answer was explained in the PMBOK.

4. **The answer is A.** You must pick an answer for all of the questions on the test before you are allowed to finish.

5. **The answer is C.** Take time to read all the answers even if you are sure that the answer under the letter A is the correct one. You may find that there will be an even better answer in the four-part list.

6. **The answer is C.** No matter how complex the question, it does not get you any more points than the simplest question. Remember this as you take the examination. Although you may get some satisfaction from working out a complex question, the simple definition of a project is worth just as much.

7. **The answer is D.** Although all of the other answers may be true, the temporary nature of the project is one of the major defining characteristics of a project.

8. **The answer is B.** PMI was founded in the late sixties.

9. **The answer is C.** The American National Standards Institute is the body that governs standardization of information in the U.S. This is important because this is the first time that any document or book has been accepted as the single standard for project management in the United States.

10. **The answer is B.** The phase approach is one of the ways in this book used to prepare for the examination.

11. **The answer is B.** Each of the knowledge areas has several subdivisions that are process areas.

12. **The answer is D.** It is helpful to know what the three areas are in each of the processes, and this can be found in the third chapter of PMBOK.

13. **The answer is C.** Use parts of both. In this book we will be offering various ways to approach the knowledge you need to pass the test. For some people, one model fits their cognitive process; for other people, another model is best. In this book you get a variety of ways to understand, memorize, and use information for the exam in the future. By using a combination of the two, we think you'll have the best chance of passing the exam and going on to become a PMP.

14. **The answer is C.** On the examination, 37% of the questions will focus on planning.

15. **The answer is A.** You have the best short-term memory right after the course, so you should take the test as soon as possible after you have finished the course. The longer you wait, the more studying you will have to do to pass the exam.

CHAPTER TWO

Initiation and Planning

The entire project management process can be divided up into five different phases: Initiation, Planning, Execution, Control, and Closing. The diagram shows that the different phases come at specific parts of the project. However, in reality there are many overlaps between the phases, and seldom do you see one phase completely finished before the next begins. For the purpose of studying for the exam, we will combine Initiation and Planning. Later we will look at the Planning and Execution phases together, the Execution and Control phases, and finally the Control and Closing phase.

The Five Phases of the Project

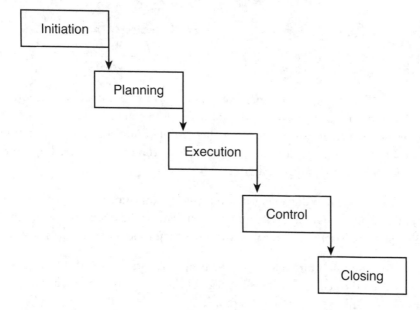

Initiation and Planning occur before Execution and Control, and much of what you need to know about project management can be made simpler by combining two sections. **The first of these phases, Initiation, is the time when someone or some organization specifically authorizes beginning and executing a project.** Actually, Initiation is often the most overlooked of all the phases. Along with Closing, it seems to fall by the wayside in a lot of organizations.

Although the authorizing of resources may seem to be absolutely necessary, it is surprising how many times projects begin without specific authorization from one person. You must have one person to authorize all the resources, and that one person must have control of the project. This means that only one person is authorizing materials, money, and people. In many organizations, a department or a group of people approves projects. This can cause problems. Without a single point of responsibility for the project, there is a major issue of accountability floating through this process. Only when you have a single source for accountability can you be truly certain that one person is watching the project and is responsible in the end for the final outcome of the project.

Note that the person who authorizes the project is *not* the project manager. This person is called the sponsor. A question about this would come in the form:

> **Q.   The person in the organization who authorizes the commencement of a project is the:**
>
> ❑   **A. Senior Manager**   ❑   **B. Project Manager**
>
> ❑   **C. Sponsor**   ❑   **D. Project Specialist**

The answer is C. The project manager executes the project but does not authorize the project. The project manager's duties do not begin until someone within the organization has authorized resources. He or she is then brought into the process of planning and controlling the entire project. Let's look at the document that is used to begin a project; this document is called a Charter.

The Charter is the written document that releases organizational resources to the project and assigns accountability for the project. This is the document where the sponsor's signature is found. There are two other major parts of the document.

First, the business reason for conducting the project is determined. If the project doesn't fit within the general business strategy of the company, it shouldn't be started. This reason should be stated in the Charter.

Second, the project manager is assigned. The best possible situation is for a project manager to be chosen at the beginning of the project and then manage the project through to its conclusion. As most of us know, that doesn't always happen. It doesn't mean that it shouldn't, just that it doesn't.

Is a Charter created every time a project is started? Hardly. On major engineering projects and large construction projects, there will be some kind of Charter. (It's not good form to start building a bridge without someone first authorizing resources.) But on some smaller projects, particularly ones found in organizations that do not have project management practices in place, projects are often started simply by writing down a request on a napkin in the company cafeteria. It's a good idea for everyone involved to get a written Charter. It protects everyone and gives the project manager his or her first general guidelines from which to work.

Here are some Charter questions.

Q. The document that authorizes the release of organizational resources to the project is the:

❑ A. Statement of Work   ❑ B. Project Design Plan

❑ C. WBS   ❑ D. Charter

The answer is D. The Charter is the document that formalizes the project. Without a Charter, you may be in deep yogurt as the project goes on because you will be using organizational resources and someone above you in the organization must authorize it. It seems obvious, but often is not the case, that the person who is authorizing the work must have the authority to do so.

Q. The project manager is assigned in the:

❑ A. Charter   ❑ B. Project Plan

❑ C. SOW   ❑ D. Management Plan

The answer is A. Failure to get a project manager assigned early in the project can lead to delays and problems as the project is executed.

> **Q.** **Without a _____ the project cannot go forward.**
>
> ☐ A. Leader ☐ B. Charter
>
> ☐ C. Project Administrator ☐ D. WBS

The answer is B. This question is a good example of why you want to look over questions and answers carefully. In this case the reason that Charter (B) is the correct answer is that it precedes everything else. There can be no leader or WBS without a Charter. When you take the test, be sure to look through the exam and determine what the *best* answer is. Two answers may look correct, but find the one that PMI is looking for. That's what we are doing in this book.

Let's go back to the question of whether Charters are always created. The answer is that you find perfect documentation and perfect projects only in theory; in real life, a lot of projects begin without a formal document. This doesn't mean that you should not try to create one; it simply means that reality often dictates that one isn't forthcoming. You do need to know what a Charter is for the test.

Initiation and Feasibility

Although project managers do not generally get involved in the feasibility part of choosing a project, it's important to note why a project is handed to a project manager in the first place.

Organizations must change to survive, and projects are the main mechanism for achieving change. The question of why to do a project is left to the senior management, and the following are some of the issues that senior management must consider in order to come to a conclusion about where money should be spent for various projects.

New projects either make money or save money. In the case of a product introduction, the project is designed to attract more revenue to the company through an offering to consumers. The senior managers charged with funding projects must look at how well the individual project will attract revenue in relation to other projects that are proposed. The project that forecasts out to be the most profitable for the organization is usually the one that gets the funding. (Watch out for pet projects; more on this later.)

If the project is being done to replace some part of an existing infrastructure, it is being done to save money. A new inventory system will save time and therefore money. The project is authorized because the organization must upgrade its capacity to control inventory in order to remain competitive.

It's often harder to get funding for this type of project than for new product introductions; this type of project is just as important for the organization, but it doesn't have the public component that makes product introduction exciting.

A third type of project comes from reaction to outside sources. Take for example HIPPA, the Health Insurance Portability and Accountability Act of 1996. This act mandates certain ways in which medical information must be transferred and stored. If you have an organization that deals with medical information, you will have already started complying with the new requirements given out by the government. This is an example of an outside force making your organization conduct a project that is not internally initiated. These projects are often both very complex and extremely crucial to the success of your organization.

Initiation is not where project managers live. It is the phase in which the project manager is assigned, but only after organization management has determined the reason for the project in the first place. **In the Initiation phase, the reason for the project is laid out, the sponsor releases resources to get the project done, and the project manager is chosen.**

The question on the exam pertaining to the Initiation phase most often looks like this:

Q. **A project manager is assigned to a project in the _____ phase of the project.**

❑ A. Management   ❑ B. Initiation

❑ C. Closing   ❑ D. Controlling

The answer is B. The sooner the project manager is selected, the better for the project manager and the project.

We will look at feasibility and the different models for feasibility in the Cost section of the knowledge areas later in the book. However, the key to remember is that although there are many models for choosing projects for an organization, the project manager is generally not the one who proposes a project and has to defend his or her proposal personally. The financial models that will be shown later are interesting, but often project managers do not have to deal with them.

Planning

The Planning phase of a project is where a project manager can utilize guidance from the PMBOK in order to professionally control the overall planning of the project. This means learning what documents are needed as well as forming a cohesive project plan.

Because this phase is so important, we are going to look at it several times in the book. The other times will be in relationship to knowledge areas. In this section, we are going to examine some key documents you need to produce and the relationship between them. Without these key planning documents, it is almost impossible for a project manager to maintain control over time. It's possible to leave out a few of the documents we are going to discuss, but we will focus on the ones that absolutely, positively must be done for project success. These are also the ones that are most commonly covered on the exam, and you will see why as we go through this chapter.

Scope Statement

The Charter is the first major document that is produced in the Initiation phase. After the Charter, the next important document in sequence is the Scope Statement. According to the PMBOK, "Project Scope Management includes the processes required to ensure that the project includes all the work required, and only the work required, to complete the project successfully." The key phrase in this definition is meant to ensure that you aren't adding anything to the project that shouldn't be there. When the definition says, "only the work required," it means that you as the project manager know the boundaries of the project, and in fact the scope of the project. The process is called Project Scope Management; the major document is the Scope Statement.

You should note that there are actually two types of scope: product scope and project scope. Product scope determines the features and functions of the output of the project. Project scope determines the work to be done in order to deliver that output. The exam will have questions on both, so it is necessary to have these two clear in your mind before you take it.

Q. _____ scope determines the features and functions of the output of the project.

❑ A. Management
❑ B. Control
❑ C. Project
❑ D. Product

The answer is D. The Product Scope is written confirmation of what the output of the project is going to be. It then shows the features and functions, or in other words, the scope of the output.

And:

Q. **The work that needs to be done to produce a product/service is included in the:**

❑ A. Execution Plan   ❑ B. Product Scope

❑ C. Project Scope   ❑ D. SOW

The answer is C. Be sure to be able to differentiate between Product Scope and Project Scope. One describes the features and functions (Product Scope), and one defines the work that must be done for the project to be completed (Project Scope).

Make sure you know the difference between the two; they will be on the exam.

In the Planning phase, you begin with a scope statement that is built from the original Charter. You will have a list of high-level deliverables that will determine whether you have successfully completed the project. PMBOK 3rd edition defines a deliverable as "any unique and verifiable product, result, or capability to perform a service that must be produced to complete a process, phase, or project." You need to know this definition for the exam. The key to this particular phase is that there must be a single final deliverable that signifies that the project is finished. Without this, the project can go on interminably. This is discussed at length in Chapter 5, "Control and Closing."

It's important to note that there are several different levels of deliverables. In a project lasting for six months, you may find that you have deliverables for each week or for every two weeks. Certainly you do not want to have only one big deliverable for the project because you can't manage six months of time without something against which to measure progress. So you should always manage deliverables—that is, you should be focusing on intermediate deliverables that you can manage and measure. Doing this will make it easier on you as the project manager, and easier on the sponsor and the project team as well.

Q. **The tangible measurement or outcome that must be produced to complete a part of a project or the project itself is called a:**

❑ A. Work Statement   ❑ B. RFP

❑ C. Deliverable   ❑ D. Project Plan

The answer is C. Having deliverables formally stated throughout the project is one of the traits of a well-run project.

> **Q.   A description of the final deliverable is one of the best ways to make sure that you are in control of the project in the _____ phase.**
>
> ❏   A. Initiation   ❏   B. Closing
>
> ❏   C. Execution   ❏   D. Planning

The answer is B. You should formally describe the final deliverable of the project at the beginning of the project. This way, there is formal acceptance of the final output of the project, and you can measure the project's progress against that goal.

The Scope Statement describes what the final output of the project will be, and just as importantly, it states what will be left out. A common mistake for first-time project managers is to accept changes to the scope after it has been finalized and put under version control. What happens in this case is known as Scope Creep. We will discuss this further in Chapter 4, "Execution and Control," but it's never too early to make sure that you are working only on the product or service that was defined first in the Charter and again in the Scope Statement. The most common mistake is to accept small changes in the scope without changing the version number. You will soon find that just a few small changes will add up to make a completely different project output. Beware—you won't be the first project manager to be approached by management and asked if you would be willing to make "just a small change" in the scope. Do not do it.

The Work Breakdown Structure (WBS)

Of all the documents used in project management, none is more important than the Work Breakdown Structure (WBS). It is this document that determines how you will manage all the aspects of the project, and this document is absolutely necessary if you want to be a professional project manager.

The WBS comes after the Scope Statement, and it "decomposes" (sic) the scope statement into tasks that form the basis for all the work on the project. The breakdown structure actually takes the larger sections of a project and breaks them into smaller tasks so that the project manager can control and manage the project.

You can do a WBS with one of two methods. The first method is to use yellow sticky notes that are given to the team members. The project team meets in a room and begins by putting together a tree-like diagram. Each level of the diagram represents more detail about the task above it. The visuals vary as the breakdown structures vary, but in general it looks something like Figure 2-1.

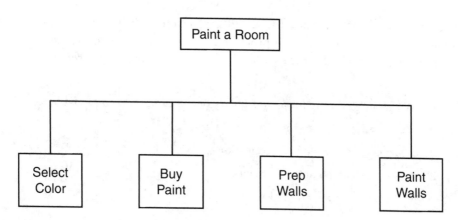

FIGURE 2-1: A task structure diagram.

This is a very simple WBS for painting a room. The second task level begins to break down what the project manager will have to do to get the room painted. To more clearly establish the project needs, you will probably need breakdowns in the second level, too. For instance, under the task "Prep Walls," you could have the subtasks to "Clean Walls," "Sand Walls," and "Apply Primer."

The more detail you have for project tasks, the better off you are. I have worked with dozens, even hundreds of different people who prepared a WBS for a given project. One thing you should *not* do is to get too detailed. Usually four or five levels of tasks are sufficient to give the project manager a complete view of the work to be done. Detail beyond this level is usually not helpful. Using common sense is a good idea. Also using someone who has done WBS before can be helpful.

Remember that the WBS is written by the team and comes after the scope statement is delivered to the team. In the systems approach that is used in PMBOK, 3rd edition, the place where a scope statement is constructed is in section 5.1, titled "Scope Planning." The section where the WBS is detailed is in section 5.2, titled "Scope Definition." The section where major stakeholders accept the WBS is section 5.4, titled "Scope Verification." And finally, for the scope process, the last section, numbered 5.5, is "Scope Change Control." We will deal with these in more detail in the knowledge area section of this review book.

Q. The Work Breakdown Structure is done by:

- ❑ A. The Sponsor
- ❑ B. Senior Management
- ❑ C. The Project Manager
- ❑ D. The Project team

The correct answer, D, indicates that the building of the WBS is an important part of the initial bringing together of your project team. This is the first action that the team can complete together and is the basis for building a team on the project.

> **Q. The WBS is done during Scope Definition; Scope Definition comes between:**
> ❏ A. Scope Planning and Scope Change Control
> ❏ B. Scope Verification and Scope Change Control
> ❏ C. Scope Planning and Scope Verification
> ❏ D. Scope Management and Scope Planning

The answer is C. Scope Planning and Scope Verification are sections that you will see in the PMBOK. It is not necessary to memorize all of the sections, but there are ones that often are asked about on the exam. We will note those. We will also look at the knowledge areas using the systems explanations in the PMBOK so that you will be familiar with them as they pertain to the exam.

There are several different ways to develop the WBS with your team. One of the most common is to use yellow sticky notes on a board to make sure everyone has a chance to participate. Make people write down their ideas for tasks to be included in the WBS and get them up on the board. It doesn't matter at first pass how right or wrong the WBS is. You are certainly going to make several versions before putting the WBS under version control, so at the beginning, let everyone have input. If one dominant person is controlling the conversation, you can ask everyone to write down their ideas on the notes, put them up on the board in silence, and only then allow people to critique ideas. By doing this, everyone has an equal chance of showing their concepts about the project and the tasks in which they will be involved.

Here are the key parts so far of developing a WBS:

- Everyone is involved.

- No one person dominates.

- The PM doesn't dominate but rather leads the group through the task at hand.

- There are no bad ideas at the beginning.

- In order to make sure tasks do not slip through the cracks, you need to get everyone thinking about their own tasks.

- Doing this one time isn't enough.

This last point is extremely important. Some first-time PMs go through the WBS process with the team once and believe they have a complete, working WBS. This is usually not true, particularly if the project team hasn't worked together before. Many times, only the major tasks are identified. It may take several days until all of the subtasks are recognized and remembered. A project team with many veterans will probably be able to do a WBS in a shorter period than a team doing something like this for the first time.

> **Q. Most projects need _____ meeting(s) to do a good WBS.**
>
> ❑ A. One   ❑ B. Multiple
>
> ❑ C. Long   ❑ D. Interactive

The answer is B. It is very rare that a good WBS can be written in one meeting. I have found it is often best to give the team some time to think about the WBS after the first meeting. There are often omissions and misunderstandings that clear up with follow-up meetings.

One of the techniques is to develop the WBS on a whiteboard with the team and then let it sit for a day or two. Perhaps even have a scribe write out what is on the board and then take down the WBS. This means that any new ideas about tasks will be allowed to come out at the next meeting. Remember that each project is unique, so it is extremely important to think and rethink those tasks that will be unique to the project at hand. If everything on your new project is the same as one before it, you do not have a project at all. It is the changes that make the project a project.

Another major consideration is the final format of your WBS. People on the team should be able to see the WBS and request changes to it, and it should be portable enough so that people do not have to walk to the same place to look at it. The answer to this question is simple.

Microsoft Project is the program of choice for most people working on a breakdown structure. Other excellent ones are available for engineering and construction, such as Primavera. For the standard practicing PM, though, MS Project is the best choice.

So after you have had your team together to create a WBS and put it up on the board, the scribe needs to translate that into MS Project, which isn't a very hard task. Because this is electronic, you can email it to all of the team, changes can be recorded, and version control can be maintained. Not only can version control be maintained—it must be.

We will look at this topic again when we cover the Time knowledge area, but here are some questions that will appear on the test.

> **Q. A good WBS:**
>
> ❏ A. Helps pull the team together ❏ B. Is a roadmap for the project
>
> ❏ C. Defines the scope ❏ D. All of the above

The answer is D. There are multiple uses for a WBS, and all of them help a project manager gain control of his or her project and manage it professionally.

> **Q. Getting the WBS done is the responsibility of:**
>
> ❏ A. Senior Management ❏ B. The Project Team
>
> ❏ C. The Project Manager ❏ D. The Sponsor

The answer is C. Although the project team helps do the WBS, the responsibility for getting it done lies with the project manager.

In the Planning phase of a project, the single major deliverable is the project plan. This will be discussed in the chapters on the knowledge areas because the project plan includes: Schedule, budget, quality plan, procurement plan, risk management plan, change control plan, communication plan, HR plan, and others that will be discussed within the knowledge sections of this book.

The important first parts of planning are to have a clear scope statement and a comprehensive WBS. With these two documents you can begin to control how the project is to be managed and have the most important information about the project in front of you.

Here are some other questions to be considered.

> **Q. The project team is created in the _____ phase.**
>
> ❏ A. Initiation ❏ B. Control
>
> ❏ C. Execution ❏ D. Planning

The answer is D. Although you do not always have everyone on the project team participating on the planning, the sooner the team members can be brought together, the better for the project.

> **Q.** **The document that shows the tasks needed to complete the project in detail is the:**
>
> ❏ A. Statement of Work   ❏ B. Schedule
>
> ❏ C. WBS   ❏ D. Network diagram

The answer is C. This is your road map and your bible. Failure to do a WBS almost always means a schedule failure of some sort. The detail in the WBS lets you manage a project professionally.

> **Q.** **The single most important position for completing a project successfully is the:**
>
> ❏ A. President of the company   ❏ B. Sponsor
>
> ❏ C. Project Manager   ❏ D. Scribe

The answer is C. The default answer for PMI is almost always the project manager. If you see it on the test, use it as the answer. Project managers are apparently wondrous people who can do just about anything. Hooray for project managers!

One key for preparing for the test:

Do not just learn the answers to questions; learn what the questions mean.

Most of the questions on the test will look something like the questions you see in this book, but they are not going to be exactly the same. If you know the material, you will be able to do very well on the test. Study the material, not the questions.

In the next chapter, we will look at different issues concerning the Planning and Execution phases of projects. Remember, we will look at projects and questions for the exam from various perspectives. By the time you finish this book, you should be able to walk in and pass the test. Let's keep going.

Questions from Chapter Two ?

1. The person in the organization that authorizes the commencement of a project is the:
   - ❑ A. Senior Manager
   - ❑ B. Project Administrator
   - ❑ C. Sponsor
   - ❑ D. Project Specialist

2. The document that authorizes the release of organizational resources to the project is the:
   - ❑ A. Statement of Work
   - ❑ B. Project Design Plan
   - ❑ C. WBS
   - ❑ D. Charter

3. The project manager is assigned in the:
   - ❑ A. Charter
   - ❑ B. Project Plan
   - ❑ C. SOW
   - ❑ D. Management Plan

4. Without a _____ the project cannot go forward.
   - ❑ A. Leader
   - ❑ B. Charter
   - ❑ C. Project Administrator
   - ❑ D. WBS

5. A project manager is assigned to a project in the _____ phase of the project.
   - ❑ A. Management
   - ❑ B. Initiation
   - ❑ C. Closing
   - ❑ D. Controlling

6. _____scope determines the features and functions of the output of the project.
   - ❑ A. Management
   - ❑ B. Control
   - ❑ C. Project
   - ❑ D. Product

7. The work that needs to be done to produce a product/service is included in the:
   - ❑ A. Execution Plan
   - ❑ B. Product Scope
   - ❑ C. Project Scope
   - ❑ D. SOW

8. The tangible measurement or outcome that must be produced to complete a part of a project or the project itself is called a:

   ❏ A. Work Statement   ❏ B. RFP

   ❏ C. Deliverable   ❏ D. Project Plan

9. A description of the final deliverable is one of the best ways to make sure that you are in control of the project in the _____ phase.

   ❏ A. Initiation   ❏ B. Closing

   ❏ C. Execution   ❏ D. Planning

10. **The Work Breakdown Structure is done by:**

    ❏ A. The Sponsor   ❏ B. Senior Management

    ❏ C. The Project Manager   ❏ D. The Project team

11. **The WBS is done during Scope Definition; Scope Definition comes between:**

    ❏ A. Scope Planning and Scope Change Control

    ❏ B. Scope Verification and Scope Change Control

    ❏ C. Scope Planning and Scope Verification

    ❏ D. Scope Management and Scope Planning

12. **Most projects need _____ meeting(s) to do a good WBS.**

    ❏ A. One   ❏ B. Multiple

    ❏ C. Long   ❏ D. Interactive

13. **A good WBS:**

    ❏ A. Helps pull the team together   ❏ B. Is a roadmap for the project

    ❏ C. Defines the scope   ❏ D. All of the above

14. **Getting the WBS done is the responsibility of:**

    ❏ A. Senior Management   ❏ B. The Project Team

    ❏ C. The Project Manager   ❏ D. The Sponsor

15. **The project team is created in the _____ phase.**

    ❏ A. Initiation   ❏ B. Control

    ❏ C. Execution   ❏ D. Planning

16. The document that shows the tasks needed to complete the project in detail is the:

❑ A. Statement of Work   ❑ B. Schedule

❑ C. WBS   ❑ D. Network diagram

17. The single most important position for completing a project successfully is the:

❑ A. President of the company   ❑ B. Sponsor

❑ C. Project Manager   ❑ D. Scribe

Answers from Chapter Two

1. **The answer is C.** The project manager executes the project but does not authorize the project.

2. **The answer is D.** The Charter is the document that formalizes the project. Without a Charter, you may be in deep yogurt as the project goes on because you will be using organizational resources and someone above you in the organization must authorize it. It seems obvious, but often is not the case, that the person who is authorizing the work must have the authority to do so

3. **The answer is A.** Failure to get a project manager assigned early in the project can lead to delays and problems as the project is executed.

4. **The answer is B.** This question is a good example of why you want to look over questions and answers carefully. In this case the reason that Charter (B) is the correct answer is that it precedes everything else. There can be no leader or WBS without a Charter. When you take the test, be sure to look through the exam and determine what the **best** answer is. Two answers may look correct, but find the one that PMI is looking for. That's what we are doing in this book.

5. **The answer is B.** The sooner the project manager is selected, the better for the project manager and the project.

6. **The answer is D.** The Product Scope is written confirmation of what the output of the project is going to be. It then shows the features and functions, or in other words, the scope of the output.

7. **The answer is C.** Be sure to be able to differentiate between Product Scope and Project Scope. One describes the features and functions (Product Scope), and one defines the work that must be done for the project to be completed (Project Scope).

8. **The answer is C.** Having deliverables formally stated throughout the project is one of the traits of a well-run project.

9. **The answer is B.** You should formally describe the final deliverable of the project at the beginning of the project. This way, there is formal acceptance of the final output of the project, and you can measure the project's progress against that goal.

10. **The correct answer, D,** indicates that the building of the WBS is an important part of the initial bringing together of your project team. This is the first action that the team can complete together and is the basis for building a team on the project.

11. **The answer is C.** Scope Planning and Scope Verification are sections that you will see in the PMBOK. It is not necessary to memorize all of the sections, but there are ones that often are asked about on the exam. We will note those. We will also look at the knowledge areas using the systems explanations in the PMBOK so that you will be familiar with them as they pertain to the exam.

12. **The answer is B.** It is very rare that a good WBS can be written in one meeting. I have found it is often best to give the team some time to think about the WBS after the first meeting. There are often omissions and misunderstandings that clear up with follow-up meetings.

13. **The answer is D.** There are multiple uses for a WBS, and all of them help a project manager gain control of his or her project and manage it professionally.

14. **The answer is C.** Although the project team helps do the WBS, the responsibility for getting it done lies with the project manager.

15. **The answer is D.** Although you do not always have everyone on the project team participating on the planning, the sooner the team members can be brought together, the better for the project

16. **The answer is C.** This is your road map and your bible. Failure to do a WBS almost always means a schedule failure of some sort. The detail in the WBS lets you manage a project professionally.

17. **The answer is C.** The default answer for PMI is almost always the project manager. If you see it on the test, use it as the answer. Project managers are apparently wondrous people who can do just about anything. Hooray for project managers!

CHAPTER THREE

Planning and Execution

Just as the Planning phase and Initiation phase are linked, so too are the Planning and Execution phases. The old cliché "Plan the work, work the plan" becomes a truism and a way of life for a project manager. Without a plan, the project can be executed, but there is little chance of knowing how successful the project is at a given time unless there is a plan against which to measure it.

The Planning phase is the phase with the least risk attached. Only planning resources are being used at this point, and in fact the ways in which resources will be used are in question until the project plan is actually finalized. On the exam, you will likely see a question like:

Q. **Which phase of a project has the least risk?**

☐ A. Closing ☐ B. Controlling

☐ C. Planning ☐ D. Execution

Because you have not committed the major part of your resources, C (Planning) is the correct answer.

At the same time, the Execution phase of the project is when you are using your resources at their highest level and when expenditures and risk are at their highest. Some might argue that risk increases the closer to the end of the project you are, but the reality is that the Execution phase is where you have the most operating functions going on, which makes it the most risky.

> **Q.** **The document that describes the objectives, work content, deliverables, and end product of a project is the:**
>
> ❏ A. Project charter   ❏ B. WBS
>
> ❏ C. SOW   ❏ D. Scope Statement

The answer is D. The Scope Statement controls pretty much everything that goes on in execution. All the rest of the plans are done based on the content of the scope plan, and it is the document that supplies information about what is to be done and what isn't. If you don't look at your Scope Statement often, it's likely you'll have added or subtracted something from the original project plan. Keep it easily accessible.

IT and Engineering

Although all projects follow basic phases, it's important to note that IT projects and engineering projects differ, for a few simple reasons. First, engineering is a discipline that is taught with very rigid standards that have been gathered for thousands of years. In fact, as you go through an engineering school, you will be taught project management implicitly because engineering projects are conducted according to well-designed plans. You don't start building a bridge without something written down. It just won't work.

IT, however, has a very different feel to it. Many of the people I meet each day in IT didn't start in the area and were not trained in it. Instead, they had extraordinary skills of some sort, and they often began as coders—that is, writers of the language for the machines. They then continued up the corporate ladder but often topped out as a group leader or lead technical person. For many, the next step is project management, and because most people don't take anything like project management topics in their undergraduate studies, PMI offers a way to become aware of and then competent in Project Management Practices.

Another major consideration in IT is that often a single "build" is done and then sent to the sponsor for approval. This means that often it is difficult to write a complete project plan because rework or sponsor input sometimes change the original schedule. This issue causes consternation among those who want project management to be a rigid science, as in the engineering realm. But in fact there is a major divide between IT and engineering that should be acknowledged even as we teach for the exam. The notion of an "agile" programming process originated conceptually as a response to the more rigid building standards of engineering, and it is becoming more and more important in the IT world. For this exam, most of the model describes a plan that is written at the beginning and followed to completion of the project. The original writers of PMBOK seem to have had an engineering frame of reference, and the book reflects it. Remember this point if you want to pass the exam, no matter what your area of project management.

Each of the Knowledge Areas has a plan within it that is a part of the overall project plan. Here is a list of the various parts of the project plan as explained in the PMBOK:

- Project Scope Management Plan
- Schedule Management Plan
- Cost Management Plan
- Quality Management Plan
- Process Improvement Plan
- Staffing Management Plan
- Communications Management Plan
- Risk Management Plan
- Procurement Management Plan
- Major Milestones and Target Dates
- Resource Calendar
- Schedule Baseline
- Cost Baseline
- Quality Baseline
- Risk Register

Q. Which one of these comes first in the project plan?
- ❏ A. Scope Statement
- ❏ B. WBS
- ❏ C. Risk Management Plan
- ❏ D. Quality Plan

The answer is A. You have to have a Scope Statement before doing any other parts of the plan.

As you can see, a full-blown project plan is a major undertaking. Planning can be one of the longest phases in a project because project management consists of being able to forecast and control actions that will occur during the project itself. The more detail that goes into the planning, the more control the project manager will have during the execution of the project.

Do all of these plans get written on every project? No. But it is still a good idea to know what they are and how they need to be managed, even without writing down all the details.

A question on the project plan might have this form:

> **Q.** **Which of these plans is *not* done during the writing of a project plan?**
>
> ❑ A. Risk Management ❑ B. Quality Management
>
> ❑ C. Procurement Management ❑ D. Executive Communication

The answer is D, Executive Communication. There are two aspects of this question that you should consider. First, be careful when the questions are phrased in the negative. Second, although Executive Communication might be a part of your overall communication process, it is also the name of a plan that is found in the PMBOK. It is important that you know the parts of the project plan. As we go through the knowledge areas later in the book, we will look at each of these plans in much more detail.

> **Q.** **Who is responsible for the formation of the final project plan?**
>
> ❑ A. Project Team ❑ B. Sponsor
>
> ❑ C. Project Manager ❑ D. Team Leader

The answer is C, the project manager. I say again, usually on this exam if there is a chance to pick "project manager" as the answer to a question, do it. Because this entire exam is about project managers, it stands to reason that they will be the answer to several questions.

Organizational Design

As you begin to work in various organizations, one of the major factors of project success is the way in which the organization is organized and managed. For the purposes of this exam, consider that there are three major types of organizational structures. The first type is titled "Functional." This is also known as line management. The working person is in one group type, such as marketing or accounting, and the members within that group report to their superiors, who then report to their superiors, and so on. It is the classic business pyramid. It looks like Figure 3-1.

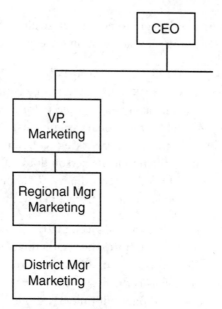

FIGURE 3-1: The classic business pyramid.

In this functional diagram, the marketing department is set up with a hierarchy that starts with a district manager reporting to a regional manager, who reports to a VP Marketing, who then reports in turn to the CEO. Each person in the marketing area of this company reports directly up to only one person. How does this translate into project management systems? First, the PM has no control over anyone in the marketing department, so although the marketing people may be included in the project team, they report to someone in the structure of the marketing department. Given a project team that has a marketing component, an accounting component, a sales component, and a technical component, each of these project team members will report to a superior who is not on the project team. If these people report to their superiors within their group, then the project manager has little or no authority and is often a part-time person who is called a project administrator or coordinator. Thus, the functional structure is the weakest of all from the project management viewpoint.

Q. **What is another name for functional structure?**

❑ A. Matrix   ❑ B. Strict

❑ C. Line   ❑ D. Developmental

The answer is C, line structure. Be sure to note when reading if there is more than one word to describe the answer. You may see both on the exam.

The next type of structure to consider is the "Matrix" organization. According to the PMBOK, these range from a very weak matrix to a strong configuration. In the weak matrix, the team members are only assigned to projects for 25% or less of their time. The rest of the time, they go back to functional assignments. The project manager is a part-time function and has part-time staff working with him or her. In fact, in the weak matrix, you will find most often that the person does not use the title "project manager" but rather uses something like "coordinator," "administrator," or "leader." This is still not a very strong position from a project management standpoint.

The next matrix to consider is called the balanced matrix. This is the structure in which the PM has low to moderate authority but starts to get more personnel who are assigned full-time to project work. Up to 60% of the project team in a balanced matrix structure are full-timers. This is the first of the structures we are discussing where a project manager is assigned on a full-time basis, but usually support staff is part-time rather than being fully dedicated to the project.

In a strong matrix structure, the percentage of people on the project team assigned and dedicated to a single project may run as high as 90%. The project manager is assigned full-time and has a full-time support staff. Even though most of the people are assigned to the project full-time, they still have dual reporting lines, with both their functional managers and the project manager giving input into their work.

Any type of matrix (weak, balanced, or strong) indicates that the people on the project have at least two masters. This means that the project manager does not have *complete* control of the team members.

> **Q.** **Which of these types of matrix structure gives the project manager the most control?**
>
> ❑ A. Strong   ❑ B. Weak
>
> ❑ C. Product focused   ❑ D. Balanced

The answer is A, strong. Next to a projectized form of organization, a strong matrix gives the most authority to the project manager.

The type of organizational structure in which the project manager does have the highest authority is called **projectized.** This means that the organization is structured around projects rather than around ongoing standard operations. Construction companies are companies where this type of configuration might be found. In this case the project manager has authority over the people on the project team and is a full-time manager for the project. In the construction company there may be two or three construction projects going on at the same time. If the same project manager is managing multiple projects, the title is actually program manager.

With all three of these organizational types, it is possible to use project management skills and techniques to gain control of different projects. It is important to remember that for the most part, project managers do not have complete control over all aspects of the project in most companies. This is why communication skills and general management skills are so useful to a successful project manager.

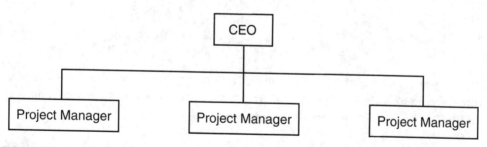

FIGURE 3-2: A projectized organization.

Below the project manager and reporting directly to him or her will be the staff for the particular project. Note that the project managers report directly to the CEO and that the projects are the focus of the organization. Once again, a structure like this is possible in major construction companies, which can have several ongoing projects.

Here are some of the types of questions you can encounter in the exam on this subject:

Q. **Three types of organizational structure discussed in PMBOK are:**

❑ A. Matrix, line, departmental

❑ B. Functional, matrix, product driven

❑ C. Matrix, functional, projectized

❑ D. Projectized, departmental, functional

The answer is C, matrix, functional, projectized.

Q. **The type of organization where the project manager has the *least* authority is:**

❑ A. Developmental ❑ B. Matrix

❑ C. Functional ❑ D. Projectized

The answer is C, functional.

Q. **You can use project management skills in which of the following structural organizations?**

❑ A. Functional ❑ B. Projectized

❑ C. Matrix ❑ D. All of the above

The answer is D, all of the above. Although different types of organizational structures offer more or less authority to a project manager, project management skills can and should be used in a variety of environments.

Q. **The title of a manager who is responsible for more than one project is:**

❑ A. Team Leader ❑ B. General Manager

❑ C. Project Manager ❑ D. Program Manager

The answer is D. A program manager manages multiple projects and project managers.

Q. **Communication in a matrix environment is usually classified as:**

- ☐ A. Simple
- ☐ B. Complex
- ☐ B. Direct
- ☐ D. Relational

The answer is C, complex. This is because the project team members may have reporting lines to more than one person, which causes very complex communication and authority issues.

Q. **A project team member working in a functional organization reports to:**

- ☐ A. The Project Manager
- ☐ C. The Functional Manager
- ☐ B. The Team Leader
- ☐ D. Anyone he can contact

The answer is C, the Functional Manager.

Even when you are in the Planning phase, it is important to know what type of organization you will be in as a project manager. It is certainly easier to manage a project in a projectized structure than it is in a functional structure. As you go from the Planning phase to the Execution phase, you need to be certain of the authority you have and the people to whom your project team needs to report in order to have a successful project. Being a project manager would be much simpler if all organizations were projectized.

Stakeholders

According to the PMBOK, project stakeholders are "persons and organizations such as customers, sponsors, performing organization and the public, that are actively involved in the project, or whose interests may be positively or negatively affected by execution or completion of the project." As a project manager beginning to plan and execute a project, there is no more valuable information than to know who is a stakeholder for the project. This information will help determine who will be on the project team, manage it, sponsor it, and use the output of the project when it is completed. Communication with stakeholders is a constant task of a project manager. On all successful projects, this is one of the most important tasks possible. Here are various stakeholders you will find on all projects.

- **Project Manager**—The person who has the responsibility for the outcome of the project.

- **Team Members**—The project team that does the actual work on the project.

- **Sponsor**—The person or group that allocates resources to the project.

- **Customer**—The individual or organization that will use the output of the project. Other names for this stakeholder may be "client" or "user."

All these people or organizations need to be constantly informed about the progress of the project itself. This communication will ultimately determine the overall success of the project.

Here are questions concerning stakeholders:

Q. The person or group having the responsibility for the outcome of a project is:

❑ A. The Project Team

❑ B. The Project Manager

❑ C. The Executive Management

❑ D. The Sponsor

The answer is B. For the most part, if you see the choice "Project Manager" in any question on the exam, choose it. PMI is very strong on the importance of project managers, and that is evident in the exam.

Q. Which one of these types is generally *not* a stakeholder?

❑ A. Project Manager   ❑ B. Sponsor

❑ C. Project Observer   ❑ D. Project Team Member

The answer is C. The Observer is not a stakeholder, whereas the other three clearly are.

Q. Stakeholders are important because:

❑ A. Their intense interest in the workings of the project gives the project energy.

❑ B. Their interests may be positively or negatively affected by the project.

❑ C. Their knowledge of important product information helps the project manager.

❑ D. They know whom to talk to in order to get things done.

The answer is B, even though it would really be handy to have people who knew exactly whom to talk to in order to get things done.

Communication in the Execution Phase

During the Planning phase, the project manager constructs the communication plan for the project. In a survey in which I participated, more than 90% of the PMs suggested that communication during the Execution phase was the number one priority action for the successful project manager. However, even knowing that communication is a major priority, most of the time, project managers don't write out a formal communication plan. Part of the reason is that it isn't very clear exactly what should be in the plan. Here are some of the communication components that are important for the success of the project.

Channels

There are two aspects concerning communication channels that you need to know for the exam. First, there is a formula that you should remember for the test. It determines how many channels are involved with any number of people. The formula is:

$N(N-1)/2$, where N=the number of people

The final answer will tell you how many channels are in the communication pattern. Here are two examples.

Q. If there are 2 people in the communication system, how many channels will there be?

❑ A. 2

❑ B. 4

❑ C. 1

❑ D. 3

The correct response in this case is 1, or the answer C. The formula filled in looks like this with two people in the communication:

$2(2-1)/2 = 1$ or $2(1)/2 = 1$

Two people can have only one channel between them.

A communication diagram between two people is really simple and would look like this with Bob and Ellen being the two people.

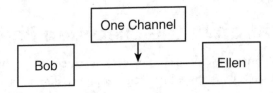

FIGURE 3-3: A communication channel between two people.

Q. If there are 4 people in the communication system, how many channels will there be?

☐ A. 3   ☐ B. 6

☐ C. 4   ☐ D. 8

The correct answer is B, or 6. Here is how the formula fills out:

4(4–1)/2 = 6 or 4(3)/2 = 6

Four people have six possible channels between them.

The diagram for four people looks like this.

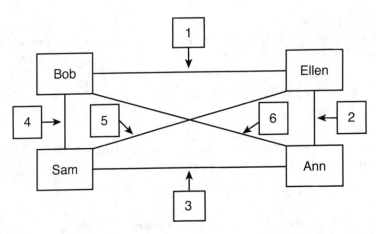

FIGURE 3-4: There are six possible communication channels between four people.

For the test, you should be able to answer a question that is posed like this:

Q. What is the difference in the number of channels between 5 people and 8 people?

❑ A. 18

❑ B. 3

❑ C. 14

❑ D. 6

A, 18, is the correct answer to the question.

Here is how to work this out. Remember the formula $N(N-1)/2$.

$5(5-1)/2 = 10$ or $5(4)/2 = 10$ and $8(8-1)/2 = 28$ or $8(7)/2 = 28$.

Subtract 10 from 28, and you get 18.

Q. What is the difference in communication channels between 6 and 9 people?

❑ A. 3

❑ B. 21

❑ C. 36

❑ D. 15

The answer to the problem is B, 21.

Using $N(N-1)/2$,

$6(6-1)/2 = 15$ or $6(5)/2 = 15$ and $9(9-1)/2 = 36$ or $9(8)/2 = 36$.

Again you subtract, this time 15 from 36, and the answer to the problem is 21.

Use a variety of numbers to practice. This type of problem is on the test. Just remember the formula $N(N-1)/2$, and you should have no problem.

When you go into the test, you can take a four-function calculator. Test administrators will supply you with blank paper and pencils to do any calculations. The first thing you should do is to write down formulas you are going to use on a piece of paper. You obviously can't write them down before you go in, but it is a good test-taking procedure to make sure you write down all the formulas you will need to have. The number of channels of communication is one of those formulas you need. Write it down as soon as you are sitting in the testing room. Other formulas will be mentioned in this book, and we'll tell you whether you need them for the test.

Baseline

In the Planning phase of the project, you set the Baseline for the project. In the Execution phase of the project, you measure how well the project is going against the Baseline. For some, it seems that the word "Baseline" is difficult to conceptualize. The definition of a baseline is simply "the original approved plan." That is it. Thus, when you are in the Execution phase of the project, you will be executing against the Baseline (usually these are modified by the type of plan, for instance, the Cost Baseline is the approved plan for Cost, and the Schedule Baseline is the original approved Schedule).

> **Q. What are you measured against during the Execution phase of the project?**
>
> ❏ **A.** Statement of Work ❏ **B.** Project Baseline
>
> ❏ **C.** Management Objectives ❏ **D.** Engineering Design

You might argue for C or D, but in the project world and as a project manager, you are going to be measured against a baseline, or B.

Status Meetings

As you go through the project, one of the important actions that you take is to set up status meetings for the project team. In these meetings, you look at the project baseline and discuss the project's status, or in other words, how well you have kept to the original plan. You will have a Schedule and a WBS at a very minimum. Even if you don't create formal plans for other areas (which will happen in some cases, particularly in fairly short projects), you must have a Schedule and a WBS to manage a project.

For many organizations, it seems that meetings take the place of working. Don't let this happen on your projects. First, you should write down and formalize who is going to attend the status meetings. This simple information is part of the communication plan. Who should go to the meetings? That depends on who needs information to get the project done. On long projects, there may be people who won't be involved at the beginning of the project but who will do important tasks later. There is no, I repeat, no good reason to ask those people to be at the early status meetings. You can talk to them by phone, keep them up to date, email them, but they do not need to sit in meetings where the discussion doesn't directly affect them. If their tasks begin five months from now, you shouldn't demand that they sit through early status meetings unless they actually want to do so. If they find it helpful to be there, people will ask to be informed about when your status meetings are held. If they find it painfully boring to sit through status meetings that give them no useful information for their particular part of the project, you will see their eyes glaze over during your meetings. Let them out. They will be appreciative.

Q. Who should go to status meetings?

  ❑ A. The Project Team

  ❑ B. The people in the communication plan

  ❑ C. The Project Team and Sponsor

  ❑ D. Stakeholders

The answer is B, the people listed in the communication plan. It is easy to get too many people involved in status meetings. Put a list of necessary people in the communication plan and stick to it.

How long should status meetings last? If you can't keep a status meeting under one hour, you will have some very unhappy people. The only time a status meeting may go longer is when major changes in the original plan have been approved and everyone needs to know. However, if you are prepared for a status meeting, there isn't really much that cannot be said or conveyed within an hour.

How often should status meetings be held? At least once a week is the PMI suggestion, and it is sound project management practice. There may be times just after the project is launched when you meet more than once a week; sometimes every day is a good idea. But you certainly shouldn't go longer than a week in between. In order to control the project, information needs to be available on a timely basis. Keeping people in the dark about how the project is going is not a recommended way to manage a project.

Q. Status meetings should be held at least:

  ❑ A. Once a year

  ❑ B. Once a week

  ❑ C. Every day

  ❑ D. As little as possible

The answer is B, once a week. If you space meetings out any longer than this, you might overlook problems that need to be handled promptly. The only time that daily meetings are required may be at the beginning of the project when the project team members are getting to know each other.

How do you prepare for a status meeting? First, and absolutely necessarily for running a meeting on time, you should put out an agenda. Every major item that will be discussed should be on that agenda. This forces both you and your project team to think through what needs to be done at the status meeting. Send the agenda out to the participants before the meeting. Ask people to reply to you by email if they want additional topics discussed in the status meeting. Then send out a final agenda and ask the people to bring it to the meeting.

On the agenda, list the amount of discussion time for each status item. Then stick to it in your first status meeting, and you will be in control of the amount of time the meeting takes. As the project manager, and with the agenda in front of everybody, just go down the list, and as you do, mention how much time is allotted to that topic. Stop talking about the topic when the time is up. If you write down a topic will take ten minutes, stop the discussion in ten minutes. This will shock some people the first time you do it, particularly in an organization that is used to long meetings, but do it anyway. People who go through this type of status meeting recognize how much time you are saving, and everyone with whom I have worked appreciates not having to be in long, boring meetings. Remember that you are managing your project off of a schedule and a WBS, both of which are timed. Run your meetings like you run your project.

Q. **The most important document for running a status meeting professionally is:**

- ❑ A. The WBS
- ❑ B. The Scope Statement
- ❑ C. An agenda
- ❑ D. SOW

The answer is C, an agenda. It is your most important tool for keeping a meeting on track.

During the status meeting, someone should act as a scribe and take notes for the meeting. Sometimes this person will be the project manager. On large projects, it may be someone from the staff. It is important to take notes. It is more important to get those notes out to the people who attended the meeting. Ask for corrections. If no corrections are sent back to you, file the notes.

One way of making sure that you are discussing every important item is to record the meeting. I have known several good project managers who had a recording function on their laptop computers. When the meeting was over, they would go through the recording to make sure that what they wrote down was actually what was said. It may seem a bit laborious, but it works, and it helps ensure that the people in the team are getting a good representation of what was said at the meetings.

And, oh yes, keep the notes short. You are not transcribing every word of the status meeting, just giving highlights. During the meeting, you should note if an action item occurs. An action item is something that needs to be done by someone on the project team. Make sure during the meeting that someone takes responsibility for each action item. List action items at the end of the meeting notes and also list who is responsible for each item. Also make sure that each action item has a time frame. They should not be left open. Just as each item in your WBS has a time attached to it, so should your action items from a status meeting.

> **Q.** **The person writing down meeting notes for a project status meeting is called a:**
>
> ❏ A. Bookkeeper   ❏ B. Secretary
>
> ❏ C. Scribe   ❏ D. Project Manager

The answer is C, scribe. The scribe may or may not be the project manager. It depends on the size of the project and the staff.

General Comments on Planning and Execution

More than 90% of a project manager's job is done in the Planning and Execution phases. Planning is where you create the roadmap you are going to follow to the end of the project, and Execution is where you make it happen. Which is more important? Neither and both. If you are not a very good planner, then problems will occur in the Execution phase because you probably will be "winging" it at some point, which is not very good project management. At the same time, you can save projects during execution even if the first planning was less than excellent.

Although the project manager must be able to do "workarounds" for unexpected problems, if you have planned well, there will be few of these. You will not, repeat not, have a project that goes exactly as planned from day one to the end of the project. That happens only in theory. If you are using people on your project (or I guess animals too), something will happen that is unexpected. But plan for the best.

There are also cases where projects aren't planned completely, but a good project manager manages to bring the project in close to time and cost. This is not recommended procedure, but all of us have had to do it. Sometimes the organization is ready to start at a certain date and does not build in the necessary planning time. My only hope is that they are fortunate enough to have a professional project manager in place and that he or she can draw on enough intelligence and experience to bring it off.

So, having a project manager who can handle workarounds or any type of unexpected action taking place, and who understands the various organizational structures in which he/she finds him/herself, means that the Execution phase of the project is one where the actual project management skills of the project manager can make or break a project. Planning and Execution are too closely linked to be thought of as completely separate phases in a project.

Q. **What are the actions called that are done in response to unexpected problems?**

❑ A. Stopgaps   ❑ B. Patches

❑ C. Hail Marys   ❑ D. Workarounds

The answer is D, workarounds.

Q. **Which is more important, Planning or Execution?**

❑ A. Neither   ❑ B. Both

❑ C. Planning   ❑ D. Execution

The answer is B, both.

As we go through the phases, topics will be discussed that also belong in the knowledge areas of the PMBOK. We will revisit them when we discuss the topic area later in the book, but I think it is important to put several topics in the phases in which they occur in addition to describing them as separate entities in the knowledge areas part of the book.

Questions from Chapter Three   **?**

1. Which phase of a project has the least risk?

❑ A. Closing

❑ B. Controlling

❑ C. Planning

❑ D. Execution

2. The document that describes the objectives, work content, deliverables, and end product of a project is the:

❑ A. Project charter

❑ B. WBS

❑ C. SOW

❑ D. Scope Statement

3. Which one of these comes first in the project plan?

❑ A. Scope Statement

❑ B. WBS

❑ C. Risk Management Plan

❑ D. Quality Plan

4. Which of these plans is *not* done during the writing of a project plan?

❑ A. Risk Management

❑ B. Quality Management

❑ C. Procurement Management

❑ D. Executive Communication

5. Who is responsible for the formation of the final project plan?

❑ A. Project Team

❑ B. Sponsor

❑ C. Project Manager

❑ D. Team Leader

6. What is another name for functional structure?

❑ A. Matrix

❑ B. Strict

❑ C. Line

❑ D. Developmental

7. Which of these types of matrix structure gives the project manager the most control?

❑ A. Strong

❑ B. Weak

❑ C. Product focused

❑ D. Balanced

8. **Three types of organizational structure discussed in PMBOK are:**

   ❑ A. Matrix, line, departmental

   ❑ B. Functional, matrix, product driven

   ❑ C. Matrix, functional, projectized

   ❑ D. Projectized, departmental, functional

9. **The type of organization where the project manager has the *least* authority is:**

   ❑ A. Developmental   ❑ B. Matrix

   ❑ C. Functional   ❑ D. Projectized

10. **You can use project management skills in which of the following structural organizations?**

   ❑ A. Functional   ❑ B. Projectized

   ❑ C. Matrix   ❑ D. All of the above

11. **The title of a manager who is responsible for more than one project is:**

   ❑ A. Team Leader   ❑ B. General Manager

   ❑ C. Project Manager   ❑ D. Program Manager

12. **Communication in a matrix environment is usually classified as:**

   ❑ A. Simple   ❑ B. Direct

   ❑ C. Complex   ❑ D. Relational

13. **A project team member working in a functional organization reports to:**

   ❑ A. The Project Manager   ❑ B. The Team Leader

   ❑ C. The Functional Manager   ❑ D. Anyone he can contact

14. **The person or group having the responsibility for the outcome of a project is:**

   ❑ A. The Project Team

   ❑ B. The Project Manager

   ❑ C. The Executive Management

   ❑ D. The Sponsor

15. **Which one of these types is generally *not* a stakeholder?**

    ❏ A. Project Manager   ❏ B. Sponsor

    ❏ C. Project Observer   ❏ D. Project Team Member

16. **Stakeholders are important because:**

    ❏ A. Their intense interest in the workings of the project gives the project energy.

    ❏ B. Their interests may be positively or negatively affected by the project.

    ❏ C. Their knowledge of important product information helps the project manager.

    ❏ D. They know whom to talk to in order to get things done.

17. **What is the difference in the number of channels between 5 people and 8 people?**

    ❏ A. 18   ❏ B. 3

    ❏ C. 14   ❏ D. 6

18. **What is the difference in communication channels between 6 and 9 people?**

    ❏ A. 3   ❏ B. 21

    ❏ C. 36   ❏ D. 15

19. **What are you measured against during the Execution phase of the project?**

    ❏ A. Statement of Work   ❏ B. Project Baseline

    ❏ C. Management Objectives   ❏ D. Engineering Design

20. **Who should go to status meetings?**

    ❏ A. The project team   ❏ B. The people in the communication plan

    ❏ C. The project team and sponsor   ❏ D. Stakeholders

21. **Status meetings should be held at least:**

    ❏ A. Once a year   ❏ B. Once a week

    ❏ C. Every day   ❏ D. As little as possible

22. **The most important document for running a status meeting professionally is:**

    ❑ A. The WBS   ❑ B. The Scope Statement

    ❑ C. An Agenda   ❑ D. SOW

23. **The person writing down meeting notes for a project status meeting is called a:**

    ❑ A. Bookkeeper   ❑ B. Secretary

    ❑ C. Scribe   ❑ D. Project Manager

24. **What are the actions called that are done in response to unexpected problems?**

    ❑ A. Stopgaps   ❑ B. Patches

    ❑ C. Hail Marys   ❑ D. Workarounds

25. **Which is more important, Planning or Execution?**

    ❑ A. Neither   ❑ B. Both

    ❑ C. Planning   ❑ D. Execution

As we go through the phases, topics will be discussed that also belong in the knowledge areas of the PMBOK. We will revisit them when we discuss the topic area later in the book, but I think it is important to put several topics in the phases in which they occur in addition to describing them as separate entities in the knowledge areas part of the book. The questions at the end of the chapter need to be learned in random order, they are not separated by knowledge area. Learn them this way and the sections on knowledge areas should be much easier.

Answers from Chapter Three

1. **The answer is C**, Planning, because you have not committed the major part of your resources.

2. **The answer is D**, or the Scope Statement. The document that describes the objectives, work content, deliverables and the end product. The Scope Statement controls pretty much everything that goes on in execution. All the rest of the plans are done based on the content of the scope plan, and it is the document that supplies information about what is to be done and what isn't. If you don't look at your Scope Statement often, it's likely you'll have added or subtracted something from the original project plan. Keep it easily accessible.

3. **The answer is A.** You have to have a Scope Statement before doing any other parts of the plan.

4. **The answer is D**, Executive Communication. There are two aspects of this question that you should consider. First, be careful when the questions are phrased in the negative. Second, although Executive Communication might be a part of your overall communication process, it is the name of a plan that is found in the PMBOK. It is important that you know the parts of the Project Plan. As we go through the knowledge areas later in the book, we will look at each of these plans in much more detail.

5. **The answer is C**, the project manager. I say again, usually on this exam if there is a chance to pick "project manager" as the answer to a question, do it. Because this entire exam is about project managers, it stands to reason that they will be the answer to several questions.

6. **The answer is C**, line structure. Be sure to note when reading if there is more than one word to describe the answer. You may see both on the exam.

7. **The answer is A**, strong. Next to a projectized form of organization, a strong matrix gives the most authority to the project manager.

8. **The answer is C**, matrix, functional, projectized.

9. **The answer is C**, functional.

10. **The answer is D**, all of the above. Although different types of organizational structures offer more or less authority to a project manager, project management skills can and should be used in a variety of environments.

11. **The answer is D.** A program manager manages multiple projects and project managers.

12. **The answer is C**, complex. This is because the project team members may have reporting lines to more than one person, which causes very complex communication and authority issues.

13. **The answer is C**, the functional manager.

14. **The answer is B.** For the most part, if you see the choice "Project Manager" in any question on the exam, choose it. PMI is very strong on the importance of project managers, and that is evident in the exam.

15. **The answer is C.** The observer is not a stakeholder, whereas the other three clearly are.

16. **The answer is B**, even though it would really be handy to have people who knew exactly whom to talk to in order to get things done.

17. **The answer is A**, 18.

    Here is how to work this out. Remember the formula N (N–1)/2.

    5(5–1)/2 = 10 or 5(4)/2 = 10 and 8(8–1)/2 = 28 or 8(7)/2 = 28. Subtract 10 from 28, and you get 18.

18. **The answer is B**, 21.

    Using N(N–1)/2,

    6(6–1)/2 = 15 or 6(5)/2 = 15 and 9(9–1)/2 = 36 or 9(8)/2 = 36. Again you subtract, this time 15 from 36, and the answer to the problem is 21.

19. **The answer is B.** You might argue for C or D, but in the project world and as a project manager, you are going to be measured against a baseline.

20. **The answer is B**, the people listed in the communication plan. It is easy to get too many people involved in status meetings. Put a list of necessary people in the communication plan and stick to it.

21. **The answer is B**, once a week. If you space meetings out any longer than this, you might overlook problems that need to be handled promptly. The only time that daily meetings are required may be at the beginning of the project when the project team members are getting to know each other.

22. **The answer is C**, an agenda. It is your most important tool for keeping a meeting on track.

23. **The answer is C**, scribe. The scribe may or may not be the project manager. It depends on the size of the project and the staff.

24. **The answer is D**, workarounds.

25. **The answer is B**, both.

Execution and Control

Just as the Planning and Execution phases of a project are closely linked, so too are the Execution and Control phases. In fact, the two phases are simultaneous, with control being a major function that the project manager uses in the execution of the project. It is almost impossible to go through a project of any significant length without some changes occurring. In addition, control of information to and from the project team is extremely important. Let's look first at Scope Change Control.

When you begin the project, one of the first documents that you create is a Scope Statement. This statement outlines the actions and tasks that must be done in order to produce the output of the project, and it is the baseline for all further work. Any work that is requested outside of your Scope Statement needs to be controlled through some system of change control. You should be particularly concerned with any requested actions that will change the schedule of your project and cause you not to meet the baseline schedule that you have prepared.

In order to keep your changes under control, you must first determine that a change has occurred. Then you need to make sure that an appropriate management group agrees to the changes that are created. (It may just be one person if the changes are small. If only one person is accepting changes, that person should be the project manager.) The role of the project manager is then to manage the changes as they become part of the overall project execution.

> **Q.** One of the functional managers wants to make a major scope change during the execution of the project. The project manager's action should be to:
>
> ☐ A. Refuse the change.
>
> ☐ B. Complain to the sponsor.
>
> ☐ C. Detail the impact of the change for the functional manager.
>
> ☐ D. Make the change and go on.

The answer is C. This is often one of the most difficult parts of a project manager's job. To let a manager know what will happen, you have to make sure you have all of the information you need to go to a manager and discuss the requested changes. You must also make sure that you get the person requesting the change to understand that most changes are going to add time or cost to the project. Many times the person requesting the change does not have a full understanding of what the change will mean to the project schedule. Even with proof, it is sometimes difficult to get across how much a requested change will alter the outcome of a project.

As the Scope changes are approved, a new baseline emerges. However, you can't change the original baseline; it remains throughout the project if done correctly. You can change the plan so that it reflects additions to your original baseline. Keep the original to show everyone involved what the starting plan looked like. Your job as the project manager is to make sure that you make the appropriate changes to the project plan and that everyone involved with the project is alerted to these changes. It is extremely important to make everyone aware of the changes. Having even one member who is not aware of changes can cause severe problems as the project goes on.

If the changes are major, you need to rewrite the project Scope Statement and get it out to everybody. It is certainly worth a status meeting when major changes occur because these changes will affect the entire project team. This should be done as quickly as possible after any major scope change. For your own sanity, and for the history of the project, you should keep the first or original plan throughout the course of the project. You need to be able to see the changes to the original, to track when the changes were accepted, and to point out all of these facts to people who want to know why the project is not proceeding as designed in the original project plan.

As PMBOK puts it, a Scope Change Control system "defines the procedures by which the project scope and product scope can be changed." One of the assumptions in this definition of scope control is that the project manager is working to make sure that the changes are beneficial for the project. Instead of being reactive to changes, the project manager should be proactive and seek out help on keeping the scope changes under basic control. For instance, if one of the subsidiary plans created after the Scope Statement isn't complete, such as the risk plan, the project manager should actively work with the person or persons responsible to get that plan finished so that it can be locked down under version control as the project goes on.

> **Q.** **In Scope Change Control, the project manager must make sure that:**
>
> ❏ A. The team is involved ❏ B. The changes are beneficial
>
> ❏ C. Schedules do not change ❏ D. The sponsor takes charge

The answer is B. When changes are requested, the first task of the project manager is to make sure that the changes would benefit the project as the project is outlined in the Scope Statement. If not, the project manager should note this and relay the information to the person requesting the change.

> **Q.** **As changes are brought forward, the project manager should always:**
>
> ❏ A. Refuse to consider the change
>
> ❏ B. Install the change immediately
>
> ❏ C. Consider the impact of the change
>
> ❏ D. Stall until given further instructions

The answer is C. When a change is requested, the first task of the manager is to analyze the impact of the change on the project. This information is valuable to the people who request changes and to the project team.

Change Control System and Change Control Board

A change control system (PMBOK 3rd edition) "includes the documentation, tracking systems, and approval levels necessary for authorizing changes. It includes the paperwork, tracking systems, processes, and approval levels necessary for authorizing changes." In practice, this describes a way of determining how the project manager will deal with changes and also a way of tracking whether the changes have been accepted. If you don't write the changes down and make them a permanent part of the project record, problems will probably occur later. Make sure you keep track of changes. If you do not have the information about how you, the project manager, should deal with changes, then meet with functional managers and the sponsor to get this information recorded.

One of the systems that you need to put in place immediately upon beginning the execution of a planned project is a Change Control Board. This group is the one through which all changes to the project are channeled. It is not always necessary to have a CCB, particularly on fairly small projects. But as the projects get larger, it is important to have a board that controls changes.

Who is on the CCB? The first person on the CCB is always the project manager of the project. You do not want to have changes going on as a project manager without the capacity to give input into how the changes will affect the project. If possible, you should include the sponsor. This may be problematic if the sponsor is a high-ranking manager in the organization who does not really have the time to look at each change. In that case, get someone to represent the sponsor. It is also possible that a project manager may be able to sign off on changes up to a certain dollar amount or a certain time span. If the change in question goes above the approved dollar or time amount, the sponsor or the sponsor's representative should be on the CCB.

Often technical experts are included on a CCB. For an IT project, several functions are needed to complete a project. You may choose someone from marketing or someone from development to sit on your CCB if his or her particular expertise is useful. You are looking for someone who can evaluate the impact of the requested change on the project—in particular, someone who can explain how the change will impact his or her specific functional area during the project.

Q. **The one function that must be on the CCB is the:**

❑ A. Sponsor ❑ B. Executive manager

❑ C. Team lead ❑ D. Project manager

The answer is D. Once again, the project manager is an indispensable part of the whole project process. Hooray for project managers!

You do not want to have a massive CCB that moves slowly. Much of the time, the requested changes impact the project immediately. Failure to have a CCB that is available to act quickly on change requests can back up a project and frustrate everyone working on the project. After the change request is approved, you immediately need to inform the project team. How to do this is discussed more in the information control sections. If the change request is denied, you should save the request anyway. Note who was on the CCB and what the reasons were that the request was turned down. It is possible that the same request may be resubmitted later, in which case it is helpful to have some historical perspective on what happened the first time. It is also possible that the request will be accepted the second time it goes past the CCB. Again, it is helpful for the project manager to keep records of change requests so that he or she can refer to them throughout the project.

One of the major parts of a change control system is a formal system of accepting or rejecting change requests. One of the most insidious problems a project manager can have is a series of small changes that are done without formal recognition. This may happen when one of the team members is meeting with his or her manager and agrees to make a small change in the baseline. Often this is done verbally. (I do not know why, but these small changes always seem to be requested in the company cafeteria.)

What happens when you have one small change that isn't recognized formally? Well, actually not too much. But the problem is compounded when dozens of "small" changes are made to the project without formal acknowledgment. This is known as "Scope Creep," and it can cause the project to fail as much as any other factor. Every change must be formally requested and noted. Unless this is done, you will find that lack of control, either using a CCB or doing Scope control by yourself, will cause you problems.

Finally, it is extremely important that whoever is on your Change Control Board is flexible in handling change requests. This means that they have the authority to act for the organization on major changes to the project and are available to consider the changes. Nothing is quite so frustrating as having a CCB without authority, where from time to time someone says, "I must take this to my boss." If this happens, reconstruct your CCB to get the necessary authority in the meeting. It also means that CCB members should be available on short notice for reviewing changes. Change requests can come at any time during the project, so the CCB, if you have one, has to be able to react quickly.

Q. After a change request has been denied, you should:

    ❑ A. Record it and save it   ❑ B. Get on with the next request

    ❑ C. Forget it   ❑ D. Tell the project team

The answer is A. Keeping track of all change requests is valuable as the project goes on.

Q. Change requests are made against the:

❑ A. Charter ❑ B. SOW

❑ C. Executive summary ❑ D. Project baseline

The answer is D. All change requests are made against a project plan that has the project baseline. If a change is desired in the baseline, a change request should be submitted.

Q. Change requests should be:

❑ A. Formal ❑ B. Timely

❑ C. Interesting ❑ D. Long

The answer is A. This makes the process the same time after time and gives a record of changes requested.

Q. If change requests are not done formally, this often leads to:

❑ A. Management excellence ❑ B. A new scope statement

❑ C. Scope creep ❑ D. Information creep

The answer is C. Track everything that changes your original planning. Scope creep is a killer as the project goes on. It can also bring the project to a grinding halt.

Q. The Change Control Board should:

❑ A. Be flexible ❑ B. Have appropriate authority

❑ C. Include the project manager ❑ D. All of the above

The answer is D. All of the questions in this section point out that the control of changes is one of the major tasks of a professional project manager. Here is a question that reflects the reality of having a senior manager making change requests without going through a system.

Q. The CEO comes into your office (cubby). He or she asks for changes to be made in the scope of the project but doesn't have enough time to go through a formal procedure, and because everyone on the project actually reports to him or her, it is expected that you get these things done. You should:

- ❑ A. Run like hell.
- ❑ B. Make sure the project team knows you are important enough to talk to the president.
- ❑ C. Determine what will happen if the change is made and then report that to the president.
- ❑ D. Run like hell.

I know that A and D are the same, but it is a human reaction to want to get out of a bad situation. The answer is C. At least make an attempt to let the CEO know what his or her change requests will do to the project. That is about the most you can do. Unless you have another job waiting, that is.

Project Management Information System (PMIS)

Although this topic gets little explanation in the PMBOK 3rd edition, it turns up on the exam, so it is a good idea to understand it. According to the PMBOK 2nd edition, a PMIS consists of "the tools and techniques used to gather, integrate, and disseminate the outputs of project management processes." In this case, there is a formalized understanding of the various means of getting information about the project, putting it together, and sending it out to the appropriate people on the project. Although the concept is good, it often isn't done formally but rather becomes a de facto part of running a project.

You can use either electronic documents or paper to implement this system. For the most part, today people keep documents in electronic form, particularly on IT projects. If you are working on large construction projects with paper blueprints, then some of your management systems will be on paper.

Q. The tools and techniques used to gather, integrate, and disseminate the outputs of project management processes are called a:

- ❑ A. SOW
- ❑ B. Scope Statement
- ❑ C. Management system
- ❑ D. PMIS

The answer is D. This is an example of two answers that are alike. You could argue that a PMIS is in fact a management system, and it is. However, you are going to take the exam, so remember the definition of a PMIS.

Version Control

As much as Scope Change Control is important to running a project smoothly, so too is having version control of the documents used on the project. Recently I was in a meeting with eight people, and we were all looking at a WBS done in MS Project. The problem was that the manager running the meeting failed to ask for a specific version to be used at the meeting, so three versions of the same document were being used at the same time.

It didn't take very long to ascertain that there were different versions, and the meeting leader made a good decision when she had all the documents collected, copied the latest version, and distributed it to everybody at the meeting. All of us were on the same page (literally), and the meeting ran well.

This incident highlights several issues. First, several versions of documents will be created during the course of a project. It is necessary to change the version number every time the content changes. So it is possible to have several versions of a single document going on at the same time, particularly when the changes made to the document are coming fast and furious. Second, when a meeting is being held, the chair of the meeting (in many cases the project manager) should specify the version number to be discussed at the meeting.

When this type of control is first implemented in an organization, many people fail to understand the importance of version control. Much like with Scope Change Control, small incremental changes are left out at the beginning of an organization's attempts at project management techniques and processes. But just like Scope Change Control, version change control will be a great help in the Controlling Phase of the project. This is particularly true when you are using documents in meetings. You will be getting the latest information to various people on the project team, which they can discuss with confidence.

After a document is finalized in the project plan, it should be locked down under version control. That is, the baseline form of the document is version 1.0. Any changes, repeat, *any* changes made in the document from that time on warrant a version change. This may seem like much ado about nothing, but as with scope creep, you will have "version creep" if you do not note all changes. It is very hard to inculcate this technique into an organization when its people are accustomed to version creep.

If you go to one meeting where people are using different versions, that is one problem. It is just as much of a problem if there is only one version but people on the project team have been making additions and deletions to a document without changing the version number. You only have to go to one meeting that gets muddled down with people asking "What line did you say that was?" to realize that having the same document in front of everyone is a key to holding a successful meeting. It is even more difficult if you are having a phone meeting. Make sure that you keep documents under control.

Q. **The baseline version number of a document is:**

❑ A. 2.0   ❑ B. 2.1

❑ C. 1.0   ❑ D. 1.a

The answer is C, 1.0. Every version change starts with this baseline number.

In order to implement version control, you start at your baseline with the number 1.0. After this, if the document retains most of its original material, you simply increase the number after the decimal point for each version. The next document is 1.1; after that, the next is 1.2. If the document has entirely new content, the version number begins at 2.0 and then goes up when numbers are added after the decimal point. So a new version of a document, which might be brought about because of an accepted scope change, will be 2.0.

The point of version control is that a good project manager will be able to control documentation in a project. Unfortunately I have been around acting project managers who let documentation change without noting the changes. It takes a lot of unnecessary patience to manage a project when people are looking at different versions of the project. The project manager must take charge of the project, and usually people who learn about how to use version control are willing to use it. Get them use to it at the beginning of a project, and the project will go much more smoothly.

Q. **Version control numbers should change when:**

❑ A. Major changes are made   ❑ B. Scope change is involved

❑ C. Any change occurs   ❑ D. The sponsor says so

The answer is C. Although it is true that a scope change will cause version changes in documents, a professional project manager keeps control of the versions and notes any change that occurs.

> **Q.   Version control helps make meetings easier because:**
>
> ❑   A.   People like it
>
> ❑   B.   It keeps everyone on the same page
>
> ❑   C.   It is easy
>
> ❑   D.   It is a predecessor to a SOW

The answer is B. If everyone is going to be involved in a discussion of a certain document, it is necessary for control to have the same version of the document in front of the entire meeting.

Work Authorization System

Yet another way to control a project is through a work authorization system (I find it unusual that this term didn't get a three-letter acronym). The PMBOK defines a work authorization system as "a collection of formal documented procedures that defines how project work will be authorized to ensure the work is done by the identified organization, at the right time, and in the proper sequence." This is most often a written authorization to begin a specific activity or work package that is part of the project plan.

PMBOK suggests that determining whether to use a formal work authorization system is a question of balancing cost against use. If putting a formal system in place will take too long or will actually be a cost that the project must support, there certainly will be times when verbal authorization will be used. Verbal authorization is used most often in smaller projects where a formal work authorization system may be too costly or complex to install.

The work authorization system can easily be confused with other procedures and systems. The question will be phrased something like this:

> **Q.   A formal procedure for sanctioning project work is a:**
>
> ❑   A.   Charter   ❑   B.   Scope Statement
>
> ❑   C.   Statement of Work   ❑   D.   Work authorization

The answer is D. Notice that the key words are "formal procedure." The document that allocates work is actually the Charter. But the procedure is called a work authorization system. This is a case of memorizing the definition. You will see it on the test.

Statement of Work (SOW)

Although this document is usually described in the procurement knowledge area, it can also be seen as a major part of control that is needed in the project. It will be discussed again in the procurement area, but here is an explanation of the SOW.

According to the PMBOK, the SOW is "a narrative description of products, services, or results to be supplied." The SOW is extremely important on projects that will use materials and items from outside vendors. The better the description in the SOW, the better the vendor will be at offering an item that fits the needs of the project.

The SOW should be done in sufficient detail so that all collateral services are also included in the description. For instance, if you are planning an IT project that involves outside vendors who will do the actual code development, you should explain the product of the development you expect as well as how you want the vendor to report the progress on this part of the project.

The SOW is often seen with a Request for Proposal. For most government projects, an RFP is sent out to a list of authorized bidders. But a Request for Proposal doesn't give detail on the specific items. That is in the SOW. This is a thin line for many projects, but in PMBOK, the SOW is a specific document that you can use to control the costs of the project and to give various vendors as much information as possible about the type of items you want to purchase for your product.

Q. Verbal authorization of project work is most often seen in _____ projects.

   ❑ A. Smaller   ❑ B. Strange

   ❑ C. Large   ❑ D. Important

The answer is A. A formal procedure might be too costly or time-consuming for a smaller project.

> **Q.** **Procurement items are detailed in the:**
>
> ❑ A. WBS   ❑ B. SOW
>
> ❑ C. Charter   ❑ D. Scope Statement

The answer is B. This is the document that will give bidders the detail they need to determine whether they should be bidding on a certain item or task.

Earned Value

This is one part of the Control phase that is unique to projects. It is also questioned on the examination, so it is a good idea to know it well. Having taught this concept for many classes, I find that if you can get the general concept, it is fairly easy to understand and use the various formulas for earned value. Understand that this concept is project-oriented and that if you discuss it with the accounting department at your firm, they will often look at you with glazed eyes, or even worse, with a slightly demeaning smile. Earned value is not taught in standard accounting, and the concepts, although simple, are not a part of the vocabulary of an accountant. Let us go gently into the good night that is earned value.

When you do standard corporate accounting, for the most part you look at one year at a time. This becomes the grade card against which the company is measured and the standard by which the managers are analyzed and compensated. When you do a project that takes a six-month period or a fourteen-month period, the way you analyze and control the information about the project changes.

Earned value analysis is simply the analysis of what has actually been done so far on the project. Think of a six-month project. You are now at the end of the third month. By looking at the plan, you will see how far along you should be at this point. You will also see how much money you were supposed to have spent by the end of the third month.

All you do is measure what was in the plan against what you actually have done at the end of the third month. If you were scheduled to be 50% done with all your tasks by the end of the third month and you find that you are only 45% done, then you are behind the original schedule. If you were to have spent 55% of the funds for the project by the end of the third month and you have only spent 50% of the funds, you are under the budget at this time. There are formulas to explain these calculations.

Two sets of acronyms are used on the exam. The old ones were used through the 1996 edition of the PMBOK, and the new ones came out with the 2000 edition of the same book and are used in the 3rd edition. Most people, myself included, think that the new acronyms are much easier to use. (On the exam, both sets are shown at the same time.) They are easy to comprehend. Here are the acronyms.

EV=Earned Value. This is the value of the work on the project that is actually completed. The old acronym was BCWP, or Budgeted Cost of Work Performed. EV and BCWP mean the same thing.

PV=The new abbreviation (PMBOK 2000), which stands for Planned Value. This means that PV equals what you have in your plan for the project. It was your baseline and also your best estimate of what resources would be needed and used for the activities in a given time frame.

PV is the new abbreviation. The old one (PMBOK 1996) for the concept was BCWS or Budgeted Cost of Work Scheduled. PV and BCWS are the same thing with different letters.

OK so far? Here are the new and old acronyms:

The new acronym is EV. The old acronym is BCWP. These are the same concept and mean the same thing.

The new acronym is PV. The old acronym is BCWS. These are the same concept and mean the same thing.

AC=Actual Cost. This is the new abbreviation, which is the amount actually spent during the period of the project you want to analyze. Let's say that you have an eight-month project and that you have finished the fourth month of that project. You need to take the amount of money that you have actually spent and measure that against what you thought you were going to spend in your plan. If you have spent less than you planned, you are under budget. If you have spent more than you planned, you are over budget.

The old designation for actual cost was the four-letter acronym ACWP: Actual Cost of Work Performed. AC and ACWP mean the same thing.

The new acronym is AC. The old acronym is ACWP. These are the same concept and mean the same thing.

Here are several questions on the acronyms.

Q. **The acronym for the value of the work already completed on the project is:**

❏ A. PV   ❏ B. AC

❏ C. EV   ❏ D. AM

The answer is C, EV. Learn this definition for Earned Value.

Q. **EV, or Earned Value, is the same as:**

❏ A. ALCS   ❏ B. BCWP

❏ C. NLCS   ❏ D. ACWP

The answer is B, BCWP. This stands for Budgeted Cost of Work Performed.

Q. **PV is the same as:**

❏ A. BCWS   ❏ B. BCWP

❏ C. IPRG   ❏ D. ALCS

The answer is A. This stands for Budgeted Cost of Work Scheduled.

Here come the formulas. Memorize these; you will be using them for the exam. There are also a few other acronyms you need to know.

CV=Cost Variance. This is your measurement of how you are doing compared to the expected cost. The actual amount in dollars that your project varies from what you planned is represented by the formula EV-AC. So you have the earned value and the actual cost. You subtract the Actual Cost from the Earned Value, and you will have the dollar variance.

Let's do one to find the Cost Variance of your project.

Q. **If your AC = $25,000 and your EV = $20,000, how are you doing?**

❏ A. Over Budget $5,000   ❏ B. No variance

❏ C. Under Budget $5,000   ❏ D. You are in deep yogurt

A is the correct answer. Fill in the numbers in the formula, EV-AC. $20,000 – $25,000 = –$5,000. If the number is negative, you are over budget.

Here is another.

> **Q. If your AC = $3,000 and your EV = $3,400, how are you doing?**
>
> ❑ A. –$400   ❑ B. No variance
>
> ❑ C. +$400   ❑ D. Here's that yogurt again

The answer is C. Fill in the numbers in the formula. $3,400 – $3,000 = $400. This means that you planned to spend $3,400 and only spent $3,000, so you are under budget.

CPI=Cost Performance Index. This is used as a measurement to determine the cost efficiency of your project. The formula is simple: EV/AC. You divide the Earned Value by the Actual Cost. The final answer comes out as a decimal.

Let's do one.

> **Q. Your Earned Value is $10,000 and your Actual Cost is $8,000. That means that your CPI is:**
>
> ❑ A. Incomprehensible   ❑ B. .80
>
> ❑ C. 1.25   ❑ D. 80

The answer is C. Fill in the numbers. $10,000 is divided by $8,000. This gives us 1.25 as your Cost Performance Index. If the CPI is above the number 1, as it is in this case, this means that you are doing better than the planned budget.

Here is another example.

> **Q. Your Earned Value is $10,000 and your Actual Cost is $12,000. What is your CPI?**
>
> ❑ A. 1.20   ❑ B. 2.0
>
> ❑ C. .80   ❑ D .83

The answer is D. Fill in the numbers. $10,000 is divided by $12,000. This gives you .83 as your Cost Performance Index. If the CPI is lower than one, as it is in this case, it means that you are over budget at this time.

SPI=Schedule Performance Index. This is sometimes used with the CPI. The formula for this is simple: SPI=EV/PV. Here is an example.

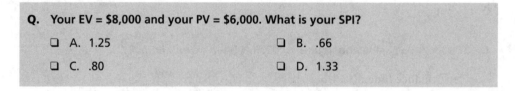

Q. **Your EV = $8,000 and your PV = $6,000. What is your SPI?**

   ❑ A. 1.25   ❑ B. .66

   ❑ C. .80   ❑ D. 1.33

The answer is D. Fill in the numbers. EV = 8,000, PV = 6,000. 8,000/6,000 = 1.33.

Here is another example.

Q. **Your EV = $500 and your PV = $600. What is your SPI?**

   ❑ A. .83   ❑ B. 1.25

   ❑ C. .66   ❑ D. 1.20

The answer is A. Let's fill in the numbers. EV=500, PV=600. 500/600=.83.

The only way to learn these is to memorize them. They aren't difficult to do from a math standpoint, and the only part that takes some time is learning the various formulas. These are examples of formulas that you would want to write down immediately at the beginning of the exam. You can't take them into the exam with you, but you can write them down immediately upon starting the exam. This is a best practice for passing the exam.

Earned Value Acronyms and Formulas

This chapter has several formulas that you need to memorize. Because they are so important, they are included here again. These mathematical formulas are not hard; you simply have to know them and apply them to a set of questions. These formulas deal with earned value. They will be shown here and again later in the book because of their importance on the test.

Both the old and new acronyms are shown here; the new ones are used on the test, but the old ones are included here for completeness. The new ones are much clearer and make more sense.

EV = Earned Value. The value of the work on the project that is already complete.

PV = Planned Value. What you show in your plan for the project.

AC = Actual Cost. The actual cost of performing the work on the project.

Cost Variance (CV) = Earned Value-Actual Cost. In acronyms, EV-AC.

Cost Performance Index (CPI) = Earned Value divided by Actual Cost, or EV/AC.

Schedule Performance Index (SPI) = Earned Value divided by Planned Value, or EV/PV.

In the CD at the back of the book, you will find an electronic version of these formulas. I recommend printing them out and keeping them handy because you will need to know them for the exam.

The earned value section of the exam can be found in different sections of the PMBOK. It was put in the Execution and Control phases of this book because it belongs there. Your knowledge of earned value and how to use it can be very helpful in explaining how a project is being conducted.

I should mention again that in many cases, doing an accurate job of earned value analysis is extremely difficult. Most of the time in projects, the preciseness that we present in theory is not as clear as it is in a book. However, you need to do some sort of analysis on variances as you execute and control the project, and earned value is another tool with which you can work.

Questions from Chapter Four ?

1. **One of the functional managers wants to make a major scope change during the execution of the project. The project manager's action should be to:**

   ❑ A. Refuse the change.

   ❑ B. Complain to the sponsor.

   ❑ C. Detail the impact of the change for the functional manager.

   ❑ D. Make the change and go on.

2. **In Scope Change Control, the project manager must make sure that:**

   ❑ A. The team is involved

   ❑ B. The changes are beneficial

   ❑ C. Schedules do not change

   ❑ D. The sponsor takes charge

3. **As changes are brought forward, the project manager should always:**

   ❑ A. Refuse to consider the change

   ❑ B. Install the change immediately

   ❑ C. Consider the impact of the change

   ❑ D. Stall until given further instructions

4. **The one function that must be on the CCB is the:**

   ❑ A. Sponsor

   ❑ B. Executive manager

   ❑ C. Team lead

   ❑ D. Project manager

5. **After a change request has been denied, you should:**

   ❑ A. Record it and save it

   ❑ B. Get on with the next request

   ❑ C. Forget it

   ❑ D. Tell the project team

6. **Change requests are made against the:**

   ❑ A. Charter

   ❑ B. SOW

   ❑ C. Executive summary

   ❑ D. Project baseline

7. Change requests should be:

   ❑ A. Formal   ❑ B. Timely

   ❑ C. Interesting   ❑ D. Long

8. If change requests are not done formally, this often leads to:

   ❑ A. Management excellence   ❑ B. A new scope statement

   ❑ C. Scope creep   ❑ D. Information creep

9. The Change Control Board should:

   ❑ A. Be flexible   ❑ B. Have appropriate authority

   ❑ C. Include the project manager   ❑ D. All of the above

10. The CEO comes into your office (cubby). He or she asks for changes to be made in the scope of the project but doesn't have enough time to go through a formal procedure, and because everyone on the project actually reports to him or her, it is expected that you get these things done. You should:

   ❑ A. Run like hell.

   ❑ B. Make sure the project team knows you are important enough to talk to the president.

   ❑ C. Determine what will happen if the change is made and then report that to the president.

   ❑ D. Run like hell.

11. The tools and techniques used to gather, integrate, and disseminate the outputs of project management processes are called a:

   ❑ A. SOW   ❑ B. Scope Statement

   ❑ C. Management system   ❑ D. PMIS

12. The baseline version number of a document is:

   ❑ A. 2.0   ❑ B. 2.1

   ❑ C. 1.0   ❑ D. 1.a

13. Version control numbers should change when:

   ❑ A. Major changes are made   ❑ B. Scope change is involved

   ❑ C. Any change occurs   ❑ D. The sponsor says so

14. Version control helps make meetings easier because:

- ❑ A. People like it
- ❑ B. It keeps everyone on the same page
- ❑ C. It is easy
- ❑ D. It is a predecessor to a SOW

15. A formal procedure for sanctioning project work is a:

- ❑ A. Charter
- ❑ B. Scope Statement
- ❑ C. Statement of Work
- ❑ D. Work authorization

16. Verbal authorization of project work is often seen in _____ projects.

- ❑ A. Smaller
- ❑ B. Strange
- ❑ C. Large
- ❑ D. Important

17. Procurement items are detailed in the:

- ❑ A. WBS
- ❑ B. SOW
- ❑ C. Charter
- ❑ D. Scope Statement

18. The acronym for the value of the work already completed on the project is:

- ❑ A. PV
- ❑ B. AC
- ❑ C. EV
- ❑ D. AM

19. EV, or Earned Value, is the same as:

- ❑ A. ALCS
- ❑ B. BCWP
- ❑ C. NLCS
- ❑ D. ACWP

20. PV is the same as:

- ❑ A. BCWS
- ❑ B. BCWP
- ❑ C. IPRG
- ❑ D. ALCS

21. If your AC = $25,000 and your EV = $20,000, how are you doing?

- ❑ A. Over Budget $5,000
- ❑ B. No variance
- ❑ C. Under Budget $5,000
- ❑ D. You are in deep yogurt

22. **If your AC = $3,000 and your EV = $3,400, how are you doing?**

❑ A. –$400

❑ B. No variance

❑ C. +$400

❑ D. Here's that yogurt again

23. **Your Earned Value is $10,000 and your Actual Cost is $8,000. That means that your CPI is:**

❑ A. Incomprehensible

❑ B. .80

❑ C. 1.25

❑ D. 80

24. **Your Earned Value is $10,000 and your Actual Cost is $12,000. What is your CPI?**

❑ A. 1.20

❑ B. 2.0

❑ C. .80

❑ D .83

25. **Your EV = $8,000 and your PV = $6,000. What is your SPI?**

❑ A. 1.25

❑ B. .66

❑ C. .80

❑ D. 1.33

26. **Your EV = $500 and your PV = $600. What is your SPI?**

❑ A. .83

❑ B. 1.25

❑ C. .66

❑ D. 1.20

Answers from Chapter Four

1. **The answer is C.** This is often one of the most difficult parts of a project manager's job. To let a manager know what will happen you have to make sure you have all of the information you need to go to a manager and discuss the requested changes. You must also make sure that you get the person requesting the change to understand that most changes are going to add time or cost to the project. Many times the person requesting the change does not have a full understanding of what the change will mean to the project schedule. Even with proof, it is sometimes difficult to get across how much a requested change will alter the outcome of a project.

2. **The answer is B.** When changes are requested, the first task of the project manager is to make sure that the changes would benefit the project as the project is outlined in the Scope Statement. If not, the project manager should note this and relay the information to the person requesting the change.

3. **The answer is C.** When a change is requested, the first task of the manager is to analyze the impact of the change on the project. This information is valuable to the people who request changes and to the project team.

4. **The answer is D.** Once again, the project manager is an indispensable part of the whole project process. Hooray for project managers!

5. **The answer is A.** Keeping track of all change requests is valuable as the project goes on.

6. **The answer is D.** All change requests are made against a project plan that has the project baseline. If a change is desired in the baseline, a change request should be submitted.

7. **The answer is A.** There will be times when a line manager meets you in the company cafeteria and asks you for a "small" scope change. Maybe he or she even writes it down on a paper napkin. You must have formal processes or else you will have massive "scope creep."

8. **The answer is C.** Track everything that changes your original planning. Scope creep is a killer as the project goes on. It can also bring the project to a grinding halt.

9. **The answer is D.** The Change Control Board also has to be available.

10. **The answer is C.** I know that A and D are the same, but it is a human reaction to want to get out of a bad situation. At least make an attempt to let the CEO know what his or her change requests will do to the project. That is about the most you can do. Unless you have another job waiting, that is.

11. **The answer is D**. This is an example of two answers that are alike. You could argue that a PMIS is in fact a management system, and it is. However, you are going to take the exam, so remember the definition of a PMIS.

12. **The answer is C**, 1.0. Every version change starts with this baseline number.

13. **The answer is C**. Although it is true that a scope change will cause version changes in documents, a professional project manager keeps control of the versions and notes any change that occurs.

14. **The answer is B**. If everyone is going to be involved in a discussion of a certain document, it is necessary for control to have the same version of the document in front of the entire meeting.

15. **The answer is D**. Notice that the key words are "formal procedure." The document that allocates work is actually the Charter. But the procedure is called a work authorization system. This is a case of memorizing the definition. You will see it on the test.

16. **The answer is A**. A formal procedure might be too costly or time-consuming for a smaller project.

17. **The answer is B**. This is the document that will give bidders the detail they need to determine whether they should be bidding on a certain item or task.

18. **The answer is C**, EV. Learn this definition for Earned Value .

19. **The answer is B**, BCWP. This stands for Budgeted Cost of Work Performed.

20. **The answer is A**. This stands for Budgeted Cost of Work Scheduled.

21. **A is the correct answer**. Fill in the numbers in the formula, EV-AC. $20,000-$25,000 = –$5,000. If the number is negative, you are over budget.

22. **The answer is C**. Fill in the numbers in the formula. $3,400-$3,000 = $400. This means that you planned to spend $3,400 and only spent $3,000, so you are under budget.

23. **The answer is C**. Fill in the numbers. $10,000 is divided by $8,000. This gives us 1.25 as your Cost Performance Index. If the CPI is above the number 1, as it is in this case, this means that you are doing better than the planned budget.

24. **The answer is D**. Fill in the numbers. $10,000 is divided by $12,000. This gives you .83 as your Cost Performance Index. If the CPI is lower than one, as it is in this case, it means that you are over budget at this time.

25. **The answer is D**. Fill in the numbers. The formula is EV/OV = SPI. (The Schedule Performance Index) EV=8,000, PV=6,000. 8,000/6,000= 1.33

26. **The answer is A**. Let's fill in the numbers. EV=500, PV=600. 500/600=.83.

CHAPTER FIVE

Control and Closing

J ust as the previous phases overlapped, so too do the Control and Closing phases. Several controlling actions are done throughout the project that are key to a successful closing, and two distinct areas are dealt with only in the Closing phase. Let's look at these from the standpoint of a professional project manager.

Everyone with whom I have talked describes some project they have been on where it seemed that the project never ended. Even if they were switched to another project, the initial project seemed to go on and on of its own volition. Almost everyone called this a part of their "project from hell." There are many reasons why projects don't end. Some projects can go on and on because of funding issues. In many companies, it is easier to get funds to do a project than it is to get operating funds. Even when the project is actually complete, it is sometimes easier to request ongoing funds even though the product of the project is completed. *When the project has been done and the actions have become a part of the operating system, the project is over.* It is not unusual for a group of people or a segment of a company to want to continue the process they have started, but in fact it doesn't help the company to continue to call an operating process a project.

How do you stop this? At the beginning of the project planning process, the project manager needs to work with all of the stakeholders to get agreement on what a complete project is. There must be a well defined deliverable that is the final output of the project. Failure to define project completion will cause the project to drag on and on. In one organization for which I consulted, several so-called "projects" had been running for years. In fact, the projects were part of the overall operating system and required some maintenance, but they weren't *true* projects.

By defining the final deliverable, you give strength to the Scope Statement as well as the initial Charter. Without this definition, you cannot ever run a successful project because there will be no closure, which is the sign of a troubled organization, or at least one that does not recognize the differences that make project management a specialized type of management.

Q. You define the end of the project by defining the:

   ❑ A. Scope Statement   ❑ B. Charter

   ❑ C. Final deliverable   ❑ D. Schedule

The answer is C. Only with this will you have a project that will have closure.

Q. The phase in which you define the final deliverable is:

   ❑ A. Planning   ❑ B. Execution

   ❑ C. Closing   ❑ D. Control

The answer is A. If you define your final deliverable any later than this, you may find that you have a moving target, and you are back in the "project from hell."

You should first get a clear definition of the final deliverable for the project and then put it on your wall. Often projects are changed by outside forces, and those forces actually change the final deliverable. Because you, as the project manager, are responsible for the execution of the project, keep your goal clearly in view at all times. Every now and then, it is a good idea to make sure that all the stakeholders agree on the final deliverable. It is surprising how many times projects get changed and people forget to change the final deliverable. It is the responsibility of the project manager to have complete accord on the final deliverable. Without that, deep yogurt looms.

The longer the project, the harder it is in some organizations to focus on the original final deliverable. This issue goes back to change control, and it is clearly within the function of the project manager to make sure that changes to anything in the project are recorded and agreed to by the stakeholders.

Q. The person who has the responsibility for keeping the final deliverable clear to all stakeholders is the:

   ❑ A. Sponsor   ❑ B. Technical lead

   ❑ C. Team member   ❑ D. Project manager

The answer is D. Surprised?

Administrative Closure

In the 3rd edition of the PMBOK, Administrative Closure is not discussed in depth. However, it is an extremely important part of project management, so it is covered here. Administrative Closure is, according to PMBOK, 2nd ed., pg 117, "the generating, gathering, and disseminating information to formalize a phase or project." Note that if you are doing a project in multiple phases, you will do Administrative Closure at the end of each phase, not only at the end of the overall project. Administrative Closure includes "collecting project records; ensuring that they reflect final specifications; analyzing project success, effectiveness, and lessons learned; and archiving such information for future use" (PMBOK 2nd ed., pg 125).

The way to begin Administrative Closure of a project or project phase is to review all of the various performance measurement tools for the project. This includes your planning documents such as the Scope Statement, the WBS, and the schedule. By comparing what has happened against what was planned, you can see how the project has been executed. Remember that although you should always keep your baseline available, you will measure the efficiency of the project based on how well you met with the final approved plan, which includes any approved changes that have occurred during the project.

This is why change control is so important—not only because changes alter the original plan but also because good change control records why the changes were made and how the project is expected to be impacted by the changes.

> **Q. Administrative Closure should occur:**
>
> ❑ A. Only at the end of a project   ❑ B. Every week
>
> ❑ C. At the end of each phase   ❑ D. On Thursdays

The answer is C. We need to review and close each phase, not only the project. This is particularly true if the project is run in multiple phases.

One of the most important tasks of the project manager during the Execution and Control phases of the project is the management of information. The first determination you need to make as a project manager is how much information you need to keep the project on track and how much information other stakeholders need to be current and aware of their roles in executing the project.

Q. **Information needs to go to:**

❑ A. Everyone on the team

❑ B. The sponsors

❑ C. The stakeholders

❑ D. Everyone in the communication plan

The answer is D. This is another example where there are several answers to the question included in the list. However, the communication plan is where you list people that are going to get information and the type they get. Although A, B, and C are all correct, D is actually more inclusive.

Here are basic documents you need to have to control the project and to report on the project. The first document you need to have and manage is your project Charter. This document sets down what the purpose of the project is and who is responsible for release of resources to get it done, and it assigns a project manager. Although you can't change any of these as the project manager, you should make sure that nothing is changed in the Charter as you go through the project.

As you go into the Administrative Closure of the phase or project, you should also look at your original Scope Statement. First, this tells you what was intended at the beginning of the project's life. If changes have been made, and usually they will be, you should be able to document who accepted the changes and what effect the changes had on the overall cost, schedule, and quality of the project.

Remember that anything that isn't in the Scope Statement isn't in the project. Often, when doing analysis of a project to determine how effectively and efficiently the project was run, it is revealing to look at the original Scope Statement and then to look at scope changes as they occurred during the execution of the project. If these were managed and controlled, then you will have a complete understanding of how the project was managed. If scope itself changes during the project but there is no mechanism that tracks the scope change, then the strictness of the project's management is in question. So make sure that you revisit the Scope Statement at Administrative Closure.

Q. **As you make approved changes to the original scope, you should:**

❑ A. Save the old versions   ❑ B. Shred the old versions

❑ C. Amend the SOW   ❑ D. Do a completely new WBS

The answer is A. You should save any versions that you have and make sure that each version is put under version control as it comes out. You do not have to do a completely new WBS unless the approved change actually changes the entire project.

The next document that needs to be examined in the Administrative Closure part of the project is the Work Breakdown Structure. What you are looking for is the variance between what was planned and what actually happened. In fact you can do this in MS Project. The variance is one of the most important pieces of information that you have for the project. It shows how well you either planned or managed. Because one of the final outputs of Administrative Closure is a project archive, it is extremely important that you are able to analyze what went on during the project, and using a WBS to look at variance is a valuable action to take.

There is some question among professional project managers about what constitutes "good" variance from the plan. In other words, what is an acceptable percentage from the original plan? In general, 10% is usually "acceptable." It is not something that you consciously shoot for when you begin. Saying that you are going to hit the project numbers within 10% may be realistic, but sponsors do not like to hear it. What they want and what you are supposed to do with a project plan is to conform to the schedule, the cost plan, and the quality plan as closely as possible.

Getting the project done well under budget and well ahead of schedule are not good things. You want to make the project come in at the cost that was planned and with the schedule as planned. Saying that you have brought the project in four weeks ahead of schedule may look good to certain parts of management, but as a project manager, it means that your planning was not very good. So the project manager that comes closest to the approved plan is the project manager that is doing the best job.

Q. **If your project comes in 20% ahead of schedule and 25% under budget, you should:**

❑ A. Reward yourself

❑ B. Demand a raise and throw a party

❑ C. Be proud

❑ D. Find out why there was such a variance from the original plan

The answer is D. What you are trying to do as a project manager is to make a plan and then stick to it. Even if you are able to do the project for less money and take less time than you planned, this does not help the organization. It is very hard to plan anything if time and money are not controlled.

It is likely, or at least should be likely, that you will know how you are doing during the project. The final Administrative Closure for the project is when you look at the complete project and determine what variances occurred from the original plan. It is at this time that your final lessons learned need to be archived. This is the overall view of everything that happened in the project, and by putting all of this information into an archive, future project managers will have the opportunity to look at how the project did and what actions they can take to make their projects successful.

Project Archives

The definition in PMBOK 2nd ed. of "project archives" is "A complete set of indexed project records for archiving by the appropriate parties." Note that this set is indexed, which is not true of lessons learned. Be careful not to confuse the two on the exam. The question will look something like this:

> **Q.** **A complete set of indexed project records is called:**
>
> ❑ A. Project history ❑ B. Project archives
>
> ❑ C. The index ❑ D. The SOW

The answer is B. The key word to get this question correct is "indexed." If you see that word, you are talking about project archives.

When you finish a project, particularly a large and complex project, you should make sure that all financial records are archived. It is always possible that years later, people will want to see the financial part of the project; this is increasingly true as financial responsibility becomes important for good management. The archives must be put in a secure place and kept available for years. It is surprising how often people conduct accounting analysis only after periods of years. There should not be a time limit for storing the records, although there may be some statute of limitations that applies.

The project archives are generally stored in some type of database. If any changes occur after the project has been closed, such as someone making a claim for a service performed, you should be able to find the information quickly. It is acceptable to have the records in paper if killing trees is your idea of fun, but an electronic database is much more useful.

Project Closure

Project closure means that the organization or people who set up the requirements for the product of the project agree that the project team has delivered the product. When you started the project, there should have been formal approval of the project plan. When the project ends, you need to get confirmation that the project team met the requirements of the project. If the customers formally checked the requirements at the beginning of the project, then you need the customers to formally OK the final project output. It is extremely important to make this a formal document because you do not want to be arguing with a customer years after the project has been closed.

As the project manager, you also need to make sure that the requirements of your own organization have been met for project closure to occur. Any reports, such as performance evaluation, budgets, and lessons learned, that are required by the delivering organization should be filed and formal acceptance sought. Formal acceptance may simply consist of the appropriate manager initialing the final reports, but you should still establish some formal way of closing the project and making sure that you have done all the appropriate tasks for your organization.

Q. Acceptance of the product of the project should be:

❑ A. Formal   ❑ B. Fast

❑ C. Consistent   ❑ D. Personal

The answer is A. The acceptance should be formal.

Q. Formal acceptance includes:

❑ A. High praise   ❑ B. Written acceptance

❑ C. Dialectic   ❑ D. Verbal acceptance

The answer is B. If you do not have written acceptance, you do not have formal acceptance. You need to have something that is permanent. Verbal is not enough. Written acceptance is the only type that will give you the permanent record you need for any future discussions.

> **Q.** The _____ is the person/organization that gives project acceptance.
>
>   ❑ A. Sponsor   ❑ B. Project team
>
>   ❑ C. Delivering organization   ❑ D. Customer

The answer is D. As with most things in business, the customer must be satisfied before work is complete. You may need to get project acceptance from various people in your organization, but the final acceptance always comes from the customer.

> **Q.** The project manager must comply with the requirements of both the customer and:
>
>   ❑ A. His own organization   ❑ B. The functional managers
>
>   ❑ C. The line manager   ❑ D. Executive management

The answer is A. If there are tasks to be done for Administrative Closure that pertain to the delivering organization, these must be finished before complete Administrative Closure is possible.

Contract Closeout

Although Administrative Closeout will occur on every project, Contract Closeout occurs only when a formal contract has been written. For instance, there may be no formal contract if you are doing the project as part of an internal system for an organization. In this case, it is unusual to have a formal contract.

However, if you are a delivering organization outside of the one where the project is being done, then it is likely that you will have a contract with specific terms and specifications. This means that you will have contract documentation that you will need to conform to in order to fulfill the obligations as written in the contract itself.

The PMBOK also mentions procurement audits as a part of Contract Closeout. A procurement audit is "a structured review of the procurement process from procurement planning through contract administration." Procurement audits are prevalent in government contracting, although more and more private businesses use procurement audits on their projects. Usually, procurement audits are not controlled by the project manager but rather are conducted by a separate individual or organization.

Q. A _____ must be written in order to require Contract Closeout.

- ❑ A. WBS
- ❑ B. Formal contract
- ❑ C. SOW
- ❑ D. Scope Statement

The answer is B. Without a formal contract, there is no real need for Contract Closeout.

Q. A(n) _____ performs the procurement audit.

- ❑ A. Project manager
- ❑ B. Project team
- ❑ C. Sponsor
- ❑ D. Outside individual/organization

The answer is D. Otherwise the inmates are running the asylum, and we know where that has gotten us with some of the financial misdoings in large companies that have been a major part of the news lately.

Lessons Learned

After the project is finished, the project manager should set up an archive that contains lessons learned. PMBOK 3rd ed. defines these as "the learning gained from the process of performing the project." Lessons learned happen throughout the project and are a major part of what you should record to help the next project manager. The lessons are neither good nor bad, but for the most part, they are simply actions that occurred that were influential on the outcome of the project. By recording these during and after the project, you will be helping the next project manager who has a project that includes tasks like the ones you have had on your project.

In reality, there are lots of times when lessons learned are not gathered at a formal meeting held after the project has been executed, particularly when you have a short project that goes fairly well. The lessons learned from these projects reside in the heads of the people who were on the project team as well as the stakeholders for the project.

Although the lessons learned often are not formally recorded, they should be. Lessons learned are a valuable part of project management. Often, when asking another project manager what happened on his or her past project, the responses are actually lessons learned. Recording lessons learned is very useful for any type of management, but it's required in project management.

Here are some ideas that will help you become a better project manager; they are also included on the test in some form. First, lessons learned do not have to be a major epiphany for the project team and yourself. Lessons learned can be as simple as making sure that you contact a certain vendor at least ten days before delivery because you have learned in the past that the vendor has a tendency to be late. Note this in your lessons learned, and it will help the project move along more smoothly.

If you word it correctly, you might also include lessons learned concerning how the organization works or how individual managers work with projects. If you note that one manager wants reports in a certain format, this is good information to pass along to future project managers in the company.

Lessons learned should be written down at the time they occur, not only at a meeting done after the project. I have been involved with organizations that do lessons learned but record them at a formal meeting at the close of a project. Although this does capture some of the lessons learned, it certainly will not capture all of the important information. During a project, you should set aside some time for lessons learned at each status meetings. If the lessons learned are simple, you can record them at the meeting. If they are more complex, you might want to get everyone together to discuss what information they have that they feel would be valuable to pass along to the entire team.

For the most part, make sure you write down lessons learned when they happen or closely thereafter. Even writing them down does not ensure that you will get them correct or that you will remember what you meant when you wrote them. So write down each lesson learned when it happens, and if it needs elaboration, do it then.

A frequently asked question is where to write down and store the lessons learned. The ideal answer is that you should have room on a server somewhere that is reserved for lessons learned. Very few organizations do this, so I find it a good idea to keep a file of lessons learned for the project on my own computer. At the end of a project, I send the file out and ask for comments and additions. After this, I schedule a lessons learned meeting but only after everyone has had a chance to write comments on lessons learned and add their input. Lessons learned need to be gathered from everyone on the team. Valuable information can slip through the cracks if only a few people record the lessons learned.

I also keep my lessons learned in my project logbook. This is a hardcover book that I use to record daily events, major meetings, and lessons learned throughout the project. After you get into the habit of using one of these, you will find that it is easy to keep track of the project and what is happening during it. Lessons learned are always noted as such, and I find that sending them out at least once a month helps keep people thinking about information that is valuable to the team in the form of lessons learned.

Finally, encourage everyone on your team to keep his or her own lessons learned. The one caveat I should mention is that personal issues can surface as lessons learned. This is where you need all your skills as a project manager. Make sure the lessons learned focus on the project and what can be done to make projects more successful in the future. By doing this, you will be helping the organization and your fellow project managers in the future.

Q. What information goes into lessons learned?

□ A. Everything that happens

□ B. Only major concerns

□ C. Only minor concerns

□ D. Information that will help future project managers

The answer is D. Lessons learned should be useful to any future project manager and his or her project team.

Q. When do you discuss lessons learned?

□ A. Once a month

□ B. At a formal meeting after the project

□ C. At regular status meetings

□ D. At the New Year's party

The answer is C. You should be monitoring and discussing lessons learned throughout the project.

Q. Lessons learned should be:

□ A. Written down

□ B. Carried around in the project team's head

□ C. Chiseled in stone

□ D. Only done at the end of the project

The answer is A. Do not depend on memory to keep track of lessons learned. By writing down the lessons learned, you have a permanent record of them and can show them to others as well as store them for future reference.

Q. Lessons learned are valuable to:

- ❏ A. Project managers
- ❏ C. Stakeholders
- ❏ B. Project teams
- ❏ D. All of the above

The answer is D. There are many people who benefit from having lessons learned formally written down and distributed.

Q. Who is responsible for keeping a lessons learned log?

- ❏ A. The project manager
- ❏ C. Team members
- ❏ B. The sponsor
- ❏ D. Stakeholders

The answer is A. Once again the value of the project manager is proven.

The majority of projects on which I worked did not have a lessons learned meeting. People dispersed to other projects and otherwise were not able to attend the meeting. On large projects, the opposite was true. The more formal the organization, the more likely that there will be formal closure. The project manager can facilitate getting lessons learned into permanent form. By doing so, he or she will be helping the organization save valuable information about the current project and will be giving valuable guidance to people working on upcoming ones.

Formal Acceptance

After the project is closed, the project manager has to complete a contract file. All contracts used on the project go into a set of indexed records. This gives the project manager and the delivering organization a formal set of records about who delivered the work on the project and when it was delivered.

It should be obvious that you will have contracts on major projects where vendors are helping do the work of the project. On projects that are done internally, particularly small projects, it is unlikely that you will have contracts to index. Some organizations use contracts between divisions when a project is performed. Mostly this becomes an accounting function. These contracts should be saved, too.

> **Q. The contract file consists of _____ records.**
>
> ❑ A. All   ❑ B. Good
>
> ❑ C. Indexed   ❑ D. Accounting

The answer is C. If you simply put all the contracts in a big file without an index, you will have nightmarish times trying to find a specific contract three years after the project has been completed.

As a project manager, there is one other factor to consider when contracts are involved between an outside vendor and the organization desiring the project. With many vendors, sub-contractors will be doing various parts of the overall work for the project. You want to be sure that all the subs are paid before the primary vendor is paid. This alleviates potential problems after the project is closed.

> **Q. Before the main vendor is paid, be sure that _____ are paid.**
>
> ❑ A. Employees   ❑ B. Sub-contractors
>
> ❑ C. Sponsors   ❑ D. Developers

The answer is B. It is important to get the subs paid. The project manager can check on this or make it a requirement of the vendor.

The closing phase of a project is extremely important. You cannot be successful unless you know how to close a project. By stating a final deliverable and then going through both Administrative Closure and Contract Closeout, you will be ensuring that all the work done on the project has been finished. The better a project manager is at closing the project, the more often that project manager will have satisfied stakeholders, which is an important factor in being a professional project manager.

Questions from Chapter Five   **?**

1. You define the end of the project by defining the:

□ A. Scope Statement   □ B. Charter

□ C. Final deliverable   □ D. Schedule

2. The phase in which you define the final deliverable is:

□ A. Planning   □ B. Execution

□ C. Closing   □ D. Control

3. The person who has the responsibility for keeping the final deliverable clear to all stakeholders is the:

□ A. Sponsor   □ B. Technical lead

□ C. Team member   □ D. Project manager

4. Administrative Closure should occur:

□ A. Only at the end of a project   □ B. Every week

□ C. At the end of each phase   □ D. On Thursdays

5. Information needs to go to:

□ A. Everyone on the team

□ B. The sponsors

□ C. The stakeholders

□ D. Everyone in the communication plan

6. As you make approved changes to the original scope, you should:

□ A. Save the old versions   □ B. Shred the old versions

□ C. Amend the SOW   □ D. Do a completely new WBS

7. If your project comes in 20% ahead of schedule and 25% under budget you should:

□ A. Reward yourself

□ B. Demand a raise and throw a party

□ C. Be proud

□ D. Find out why there was such a variance from the original plan

8. A complete set of indexed project records is called:

- ❑ A. Project history
- ❑ B. Project archives
- ❑ C. The index
- ❑ D. The SOW

9. Acceptance of the product of the project should be:

- ❑ A. Formal
- ❑ B. Fast
- ❑ C. Consistent
- ❑ D. Personal

10. Formal acceptance includes:

- ❑ A. High praise
- ❑ B. Written acceptance
- ❑ C. Dialectic
- ❑ D. Verbal acceptance

11. The _____ is the person/organization that gives project acceptance.

- ❑ A. Sponsor
- ❑ B. Project team
- ❑ C. Delivering organization
- ❑ D. Customer

12. The project manager must comply with the requirements of both the customer and:

- ❑ A. His own organization
- ❑ B. The functional managers
- ❑ C. The line manager
- ❑ D. Executive management

13. A _____ must be written in order to require Contract Closeout.

- ❑ A. WBS
- ❑ B. Formal contract
- ❑ C. SOW
- ❑ D. Scope Statement

14. A(n) _____ performs the procurement audit.

- ❑ A. Project manager
- ❑ B. Project team
- ❑ C. Sponsor
- ❑ D. Outside individual/organization

15. What information goes into lessons learned?

- ❑ A. Everything that happens
- ❑ B. Only major concerns
- ❑ C. Only minor concerns
- ❑ D. Information that will help future project managers

16. **When do you discuss lessons learned?**

    ❑ A. Once a month

    ❑ B. At a formal meeting after the project

    ❑ C. At regular status meetings

    ❑ D. At the New Year's party

17. **Lessons learned should be:**

    ❑ A. Written down

    ❑ B. Carried around in the project team's head

    ❑ C. Chiseled in stone

    ❑ D. Only done at the end of the project

18. **Lessons learned are valuable to:**

    ❑ A. Project managers   ❑ B. Project teams

    ❑ C. Stakeholders   ❑ D. All of the above

19. **Who is responsible for keeping a lessons learned log?**

    ❑ A. The project manager   ❑ B. The sponsor

    ❑ C. Team members   ❑ D. Stakeholders

20. **The contract file consists of _____ records.**

    ❑ A. All   ❑ B. Good

    ❑ C. Indexed   ❑ D. Accounting

21. **Before the main vendor is paid, be sure that _____ are paid.**

    ❑ A. Employees   ❑ B. Sub-contractors

    ❑ C. Sponsors   ❑ D. Developers

Answers from Chapter Five

1. **The answer is C**. Only with this will you have a project that will have closure.

2. **The answer is A**. If you define your final deliverable any later than this, you may find that you have a moving target, and you are back in the "project from hell."

3. **The answer is D**. Surprised?

4. **The answer is C**. We need to review and close each phase, not only the project. This is particularly true if the project is run in multiple phases. The project manager must have acceptance, formal acceptance, for each milestone, and these occur at the end of each phase. If you don't have acceptance for all phases you will find that there are major arguments about the final outcome of the overall project.

5. **The answer is D**. This is another example where there are several answers to the question included in the list. However, the communication plan is where you list people that are going to get information and the type they get. Although A, B, and C are all correct, D is actually more inclusive.

6. **The answer is A**. You should save any versions that you have and make sure that each version is put under version control as it comes out. You do not have to do a completely new WBS unless the approved change actually changes the entire project.

7. **The answer is D**. What you are trying to do as a project manager is to make a plan and then stick to it. Even if you are able to do the project for less money and take less time than you planned, this does not help the organization. It is very hard to plan anything if time and money are not controlled.

8. **The answer is B**. The key word to get this question correct is "indexed." If you see that word, you are talking about project archives.

9. **The answer is A**. The acceptance should be formal.

10. **The answer is B**. If you do not have written acceptance you do not have a formal acceptance. You need to have something that is permanent. Verbal is not enough. Written acceptance is the only type that will give you the permanent record you need for any future discussions.

11. **The answer is D**. As with most things in business, the customer must be satisfied before work is complete. You may need to get project acceptance from various people in your organization, but the final acceptance always comes from the customer.

12. **The answer is A**. If there are tasks to be done for Administrative Closure that pertain to the delivering organization, these must be finished before complete Administrative Closure is possible. As important as the customer is, the project manager must make sure that he or she has formal acceptance from all of the pertinent parties.

13. **The answer is B**. Without a formal contract, there is no real need for Contract Closeout.

14. **The answer is D**. Otherwise the inmates are running the asylum, and we know where that has gotten us with some of the financial misdoings in large companies that have been a major part of the news lately.

15. **The answer is D**. Lessons learned should be useful to any future project manager and his or her project team.

16. **The answer is C**. You should be monitoring and discussing lessons learned throughout the project.

17. **The answer is A**. Do not depend on memory to keep track of lessons learned. By writing down the lessons learned, you have a permanent record of them and can show them to others as well as store them for future reference.

18. **The answer is D**. There are many people who benefit from having lessons learned formally written down and distributed.

19. **The answer is A**. Once again the value of the project manager is proven. Hooray for project managers.

20. **The answer is C**. If you simply put all the contracts in a big file without an index, you will have nightmarish times trying to find a specific contract three years after the project has been completed.

21. **The answer is B**. It is important to get the subs paid. The project manager can check on this or make it a requirement of the vendor.

CHAPTER SIX

Professional Conduct and Ethics

As project management enters the 21st century, the governing body, PMI, is working to make project management more professional. By publishing the PMBOK, PMI has given us a working body of knowledge that can be transferred from generation to generation of project managers. We also have a common vocabulary because of the PMBOK and the PMP exam. All of these actions help make project management a professional career.

The next step in the evolution of a profession is to establish rules of conduct and ethics. Professions such as medicine and architecture have had codes of conduct and ethics for years. PMI believes, and rightly so, that in order to make project management more of a profession, a standardized code should be published, and the various parts of the code of ethics and professional conduct should be tested on the PMP examination.

The first attempt at implementing this idea has been the publishing of a page on the PMI website (page 22 of the Project Management Institute Certification Handbook) that describes the basic concepts to be recognized as standards for the PMI member and the PMP candidates and certified project professionals. This has become a major part of the PMP certification exam, and we will use this chapter to help prepare you for this particular part of the exam. The code of professional ethics and conduct is more than theory; it is a workable delineation of how a project manager should conduct himself or herself in normal project management practice. As such, it is an extremely valuable part of preparing for the PMP exam and something that is usable each day in practicing project management.

The website divides the information concerning ethics and conduct into two sections. Each of those two sections is then subdivided. We will look at the area of conduct and ethics by using questions to show how the examination will ask about the topic. In many cases, ethics and conduct simply involve using common sense. One would hope that most people would use high standards in practicing project management, and the following shows you how PMI wants project managers to conduct themselves. We will look at each section and its subsections.

Responsibility to the Profession

This section of the code has several subsections.

Compliance with All Organizational Rules and Policies

The first section deals with the responsibility of the PMP project manager to make "accurate and truthful representations concerning all information…related to the PMI Certification Program." The PMP should have both knowledge of and an ability to convey information about all aspects of the PMP examination.

> **Q.** **You are a PMP-certified project manager who works for a company that is trying to get all its project managers certified. You are asked by some of your non-certified colleagues for guidance on how to take the exam. You should:**
>
> ❑ A. Refer them to the main library for project management information.
>
> ❑ B. Tell them that you are far too busy to help them right now.
>
> ❑ C. Write a short guide to taking the exam and hand it out to everyone.
>
> ❑ D. Give them guidance about the various resources available.

The answer is D. You don't have to write a guide to be helpful. A wide variety of resources are available for getting ready for the exam, including websites, books, magazines, and papers. Part of your responsibility after you pass the exam is to give help and guidance to those who are taking it after you. This is the way that a profession becomes stronger, and by this type of conduct, you can give back to the profession, which professionals can and should do.

The second section of "Compliance with All Organizational Rules and Policies" can be problematical for the practicing PMP. The PMP Code suggests that "upon a reasonable and clear factual basis, [PMPs] have the responsibility to report possible violations of the Code." Although this seems to be a good standard, care must be taken to ensure that you have all the facts available and that you know to whom you should report violations. It is not clear in the Code where to go with your information. That, combined with the stigma of being a "snitch," occasionally makes this a hard part of the Code to follow. However, you should not allow repeated violations of the PMP Code to go unchallenged. Sometimes the person who is violating the Code is not aware of that fact, in which case you must be circumspect in your handling of the problem.

> **Q.** **You have been with the organization for a short time, and you find what you think are clear violations of the PMP Code that occur with frequency. As a PMP, you should:**
>
>   ❑ A. Move to another company.
>
>   ❑ B. Write down the infractions, discuss them discreetly with other PMPs, and decide how to handle the situation.
>
>   ❑ C. Confront the other PMPs in the hall and make sure that you do it loudly and often.
>
>   ❑ D. Let the situation take care of itself.

The answer is B. This is not an easy situation to be in. This is also a time when asking other PMPs for input will be extremely useful. As with anything where you will be accusing someone of infractions of the rules, make sure you have your facts straight before going to anyone. There is always the possibility that you do not have an understanding of the actual situation. This is a good time to be professional and circumspect in how you handle the problem. Gather up all the information you can to make sure of what you are doing.

> **Q.** **In this same organization, you constantly hear rumors about a certain PMP failing to live up to the PMP Code. You should:**
>
>   ❑ A. Confront him or her immediately.
>
>   ❑ B. Ignore the rumors.
>
>   ❑ C. Gather as much information as you can before proceeding.
>
>   ❑ D. Make sure you pass the rumors along.

The answer is C. The more information you have, the more you can plan for dealing with the problem, if there is one.

> **Q.** You should _____ the information you have so that you can present it to others if that becomes necessary.
>
> ❑ A. Write down
>
> ❑ B. Memorize
>
> ❑ C. Modify
>
> ❑ D. Hide

The answer is A. The more written information you have, the better off you are. If you only have verbal information, you probably shouldn't proceed.

This is a very difficult situation in which to find yourself. You have a responsibility to the PMP Code and also a responsibility to the individuals with whom you are dealing. There is no single way of handling this well, and you must balance the need for adhering to the Code with the need for protecting the rights of the person or persons you might report. This is not easy.

The PMP Code of Professional Conduct states that "[you have the] responsibility to cooperate with PMI concerning ethics violations and the collection of related information." This statement complicates the debate. As PMI clarifies how to handle infractions, it will be easier for the practicing PMP project managers to be compliant with PMI procedures.

The final section under "Compliance with All Organization Rules and Policies" states that the PMP has the "responsibility to disclose to clients, customers, owners, or contractors, significant circumstances that could be construed as a conflict of interest or an appearance of impropriety." This statement contains the same issues as are found in all the sections of the Code.

> **Q.** You believe you have found someone who is not disclosing all of the costs involved with an upcoming project. Rather, this PMP is constructing a WBS that does not include all the tasks necessary to get the project done. You should:
>
> ❑ A. Ignore it because the PMP is a friend of yours.
>
> ❑ B. Call PMI home headquarters.
>
> ❑ C. Confront the other project manager immediately.
>
> ❑ D. Talk to the PMP about the WBS to see if you can rework it to reflect actual costs of the project.

The answer is D. By working with this PMP, you may be able to avoid a serious conflict. If he or she refuses to change the WBS, you have a responsibility to go to stakeholders and voice your concerns. How you do that depends in great part on your personality. In any case, you should construct a WBS that more fully shows all the tasks involved in the project in question and make sure of their accuracy before going to any stakeholders.

Candidate/Certificate Holder Professional Practice

According the Code of Professional Conduct, the PMP or candidate is responsible for "provid[ing] accurate, truthful advertising and representations concerning qualifications, experience and performance of services." A part of being professional is truthfully representing yourself in print and verbally. This means that you cannot claim to have had experiences you have not had, nor can you claim education that you have not received.

There have been several cases in the sports world recently of coaches who misrepresented themselves in their resumes, and as a result, they were let go from the colleges that hired them. As a project manager, it is important that you keep your resume up to date and correct. As you add experience to your career, this should be reflected in updated material in the resume. It is also important to note that some people are better at writing resumes than others. There are also companies available that will help you prepare a professional-looking resume. Some advice for resume writing: if you didn't do something, don't even think of putting it on your resume. There will only be trouble if you do.

> **Q.** You are looking for classes that will help you professionally. There are a series of one-day seminars that you can take that will help you. This series is presented as a set with the tuition for the set of five inclusive of all of them. You are unable to attend one of the days of the set. The topic covered that day is important to you, and you have already taken the other four days. What should you do?
>
> ❑ A. Sign up for all five days again.
>
> ❑ B. Put it in your resume that you have attended the set.
>
> ❑ C. Put only the classes you have actually attended in your resume.
>
> ❑ D. Do self-learning about the class you missed.

The answer is C. This is another example where there is more than one correct answer. It would be good if you did self-study about the topics that you missed, but it would not give you permission to put it in your resume. Only show the classes you have taken and your actual experience.

When I was in the first days of studying for my PhD, a memo circulated around the department that told the sad story of a person who was a professor at a major university. He stole his dissertation from another person who actually had written the material in the 1930s. Because the topic was obscure and there was not a complete tracking of all dissertations written, he got away with his deception for more than 20 years. A young researcher had happened upon both dissertations, and when he found that they were the same word for word, he turned the information into the dean. The man who stole the dissertation was fired, even though he had tenure. No one mentioned what he was going to do in the future, but certainly he was ruined in the academic community. This memo went to everyone in the department without comment. We all understood what was being said.

Another major area of professional practice is the PMP responsibility to "comply with laws, regulations, and ethical standards governing professional practice in the state/province and/or country when providing project management services." This is a major issue when you work abroad. You must know and abide by all of the laws, regulations, and ethical standards of the place where you are working. Here is a question that reflects how difficult this can be.

Q. You have been assigned to a major project in another country. Before you go, you check with your providing organization to make sure you understand all of the constraints of working in the other country. When you get there, you settle into a routine and do excellent work, completing the project within 5% of the planned budget and schedule. To show their appreciation, the sponsors of the project, who are wealthy men in their own country, send you an expensive gift to, as they put it, "Say thank you for your hard work." It turns out that this is a fairly common practice in that country but is against both ethics and regulations in your own country. What should you do?

❑   A.   Send it back.

❑   B.   Take it and go home where you can enjoy the gift because you did such an outstanding job.

❑   C.   Say nothing but leave the gift in your hotel room when you leave the country.

❑   D.   Talk to your management about the problem and get them involved.

The answer is D. When there are conflicts between one culture and another, it is a good idea to get your own management involved. Do not try to resolve problems like this without telling your management. Although it may be acceptable in the country in which you worked to accept gifts, it may not be acceptable in your own country. Because your management already has some relationship with the sponsors, get them involved so that no one will be offended by the actions you take.

Advancement of the Profession

The PMP Code of Professional Conduct says that you have the "Responsibility to recognize and respect intellectual property developed or owned by others, and to otherwise act in an accurate, truthful and complete manner, including all activities related to professional work and research." This relates very closely to issues that have been discussed earlier. One of the most powerful tools to make sure that you are giving credit to others is the use of quotation marks whenever you are using someone else's material. This shows that the material is not yours and that someone else has done the writing and/or the research. Anything that someone else has published, either privately or in public domain, must be cited when using it. Failing to do so is called plagiarism and is not allowed when using the intellectual property of other people.

> **Q.** **You are writing an article about risk. In the middle of the article, you use a statistic from a well-known report that is the standard for explaining risk. Everyone writing in the area of risk knows the report. Because the report is so well known, you:**
>
> ❑ A. Assume that everyone knows where the statistic comes from.
>
> ❑ B. Hope nobody notices.
>
> ❑ C. Cite the report.
>
> ❑ D. Let someone complain.

The answer is C. No matter how well known the materials are, if they are someone else's, then you have the responsibility to cite the source.

The PMP Code of Professional Conduct also states under Advancement of the Profession that you have the "Responsibility to support and disseminate the PMP Code of Professional Conduct to other PMI [certificate holders]." Let other people know that page 22 of the Project Management Institute Certification Handbook has the complete Code, and you will have complied with this responsibility.

Responsibilities to Customers and the Public

This is the second major rubric of the Code of Professional Conduct.

Qualifications, Experience, and Performance of Professional Service

The Code of Professional Conduct states that a PMP has the "Responsibility to provide accurate and truthful representations to the public in advertising, public statements and in the preparation of estimates concerning costs, services and expected results." The key part of this statement that is new is the preparation of estimates. This is often a very difficult problem to handle and is something that sets apart a professional project manager.

The first task that a project manager must handle is ensuring that the correct Scope Statement is written. Even if no Charter is written, there must be a Scope Statement for the project to progress. This is where all the estimates start. The clearer the Scope Statement, the better the chance for making good estimates. All projects involve estimates because no project is exactly the same as another.

The issue of creating estimates and ways to make estimates closer to reality will be handled in Chapter 11, "Project Cost Management." The Code of Professional Conduct is not about how to do estimates but rather how to be professional in your work. On several occasions, I have been asked as a consulting project manager to look at estimates from outside vendors. Some vendors have a tendency to bid low and then, after receiving the contract for the work, immediately put in change requests. This type of conduct should not be happening if you are a PMP. Put in what is known and correct and be prepared to defend what you have written.

> **Q.   Offering an estimate that you know will be changed shortly after the contract is signed is:**
>
> ❑   A. Bad practice   ❑   B. Unprofessional practice
>
> ❑   C. Bad for both the buyer and seller ❑   D. All of the above

The answer is D. It is both bad and unprofessional to knowingly offer an estimate that is incorrect. It is bad for both the buyer and seller because the budget will be affected immediately by the changes. This makes it almost impossible to have good budget and schedule.

There is also a tendency among the people who are getting the estimates to think that the document in front of them is written in stone. You can write the word "estimate" in bold letters and highlight it, and people still expect the estimate to be the final budget. Estimates are just that: they are educated guesses at the correct number. There is a vast difference between submitting a number you know to be an estimate and failing to submit the correct numbers because you believe you will not get the job. The latter is a violation of professional conduct. It will eventually hurt both the vendor and the buyer, and it gives a bad image to the company that allows someone to behave in that fashion. Do not do it. Be a professional.

Q. Estimates are:

❑ A. Always correct   ❑ B. Written in stone

❑ C. Estimates   ❑ D. Easy to do

The answer is C. Estimates are just that, estimates. The Merriam-Webster Online Dictionary defines estimate as, "to judge tentatively or approximately the value, worth, or significance of." Unless the numbers used to make an estimate are known completely, you are getting an approximate value, not a concrete one.

Q. Estimates should:

❑ A. Never be changed after you write them

❑ B. Be the closest to correct as you can get

❑ C. Be forgotten as you get into the project

❑ D. Be changed immediately when a contract is signed

The answer is B. Given that estimates are roughly the correct number, your task as a PMP is to get as close as you can to the actual costs. This can often be difficult. You owe it to the project sponsor to make a concerted effort to get close to correct every time you do an estimate.

> **Q.** You have just been assigned to a project that has been ongoing for more than three months. In looking over the project plan, you see deliverables that seem to be impossible to deliver to the client in the specified time frame. You should:
>
> ☐ A. Stop everything until you have talked this problem over with your project team
>
> ☐ B. Keep on going
>
> ☐ C. Talk to the sponsor and explain your concerns for the accuracy of the schedule
>
> ☐ D. Write down your concerns and keep them in a project file

The correct answer is C. Most of the questions on the exam that are concerned with the code of ethics are like this one. They have several sentences in the explanation, basically a short case study, and then ask you to choose the correct answer. The best way to study for these questions is to go to the PMI Certification Handbook and completely familiarize yourself with the code of professionalism.

The second area of "Qualifications, Experience, and Performance of Professional Services" deals with the "Responsibility to maintain and satisfy the scope and objectives of professional services, unless otherwise directed by the customer." There are really two issues here. First, the overall scope of what you are offering to the customer should be set at the beginning of the engagement and kept throughout. Although services outside of the original scope may be added later in the project, if you are going to change the service scope, you should do so through the direction of the customer. This means that the service scope is under the same scope change control as the rest of the project. There should be some mechanism by which you can make changes, but no changes can be made without the agreement of the customer.

> **Q.** The final arbiter of any service scope change is the:
>
> ☐ A. Project manager   ☐ B. Project team
>
> ☐ C. Delivery managers   ☐ D. Customer

The answer is D. The customer has the final say over any service scope change. Without the signoff of the customer, do not make any changes.

> **Q.** When the project was begun, both the customer and the project manager understood that it was likely that some service scope changes would occur. A few weeks into the project, some services need to be added. Because you, as the project manager, and the customer already have talked over the possibility of this happening, you should follow standard scope change procedure that includes:
>
> ❏ A. A written request for service scope change
>
> ❏ B. A tacit understanding agreement so that you can make all appropriate changes
>
> ❏ C. A new SOW
>
> ❏ D. Verbal assurances that you will be able to make the scope service change quickly

The answer is A. Even if you have talked with the customer about the possibility of making a service scope change, when it occurs, you must go through a written trail to include in your project records. No changes should occur without having a permanent record of their occurrence.

The second part of this subsection of the Code of Professional Conduct deals with the project objectives. Everyone should agree to the project objectives at the beginning. If the objectives are changed, it should be because the customer wants the changes. The professional project manager manages against the objectives that should be set up as a group of deliverables, not only at the end of the project but also throughout the stages of the project. By agreeing to an objective with the customer at the beginning of the project, the project manager can be certain that what he or she is doing is with the express consent of the customer.

Although there is no specific writing about objective change control, it should be handled the same way as scope change control. The professional project manager always keeps the customer's understanding of project objectives in mind and works to make sure that those objectives are met. Although the objectives may be changed, they can only be changed by the customer and then only through some written system of change control that may include a Change Control Board. Project managers do not have the authority to change objectives by themselves.

> **Q.** The objectives of the project are agreed to in the _____ phase of the project.
>
> ❏ A. Execution   ❏ B. Planning
>
> ❏ C. Closing   ❏ D. Control

The answer is B. The customer and the project manager should be in agreement concerning the project objectives before executing the project plan. Thus, one of the first tasks of the project manager is to meet with the customer and make sure that there is agreement on the project objectives.

Q. If the objectives of the project are changed, these changes are accepted only with the consent of the _____.

❏ A. Project manager ❏ B. Stakeholders

❏ C. Customer ❏ D. Project team

The answer is C. This is another example of a question where there are two possible correct answers. The customer is also a stakeholder, but the correct answer is C, not B. The customer has the final say over any objective changes, and without buy-in from the customer, no changes should be allowed.

The final section of the heading "Qualifications, Experience, and Performance of Professional Services" deals with the "Responsibility to maintain and respect the confidentiality of sensitive information obtained in the course of professional activities or otherwise where a clear obligation exists." In some projects, a confidentiality agreement is signed if there is information sensitive enough to warrant one. This constitutes a legal agreement between both parties that forbids any party to give sensitive information to a third party.

In other projects, no such confidentiality agreement is signed, but PMI considers it a matter of professional conduct to maintain the confidentiality of sensitive information without having a written confidentiality agreement. If you are not sure whether the information you are passing on to someone else is confidential, it is better to check with other stakeholders to make sure. Most of the time, it will be made clear what information is sensitive and should not be passed on to others. Here is an example that puts the project manager in a difficult situation that nonetheless can be worked out if all parties are flexible.

> **Q.** You are a project manager sitting in a meeting with executives of the company for which you work as a contract manager. These executives include the president of the company, who begins the meeting by specifically stating, "What is said in this room at this meeting stays in this room. There are no exceptions to this." This is a clear statement from the president, so you do not report on some issues discussed in the meeting when you file your weekly report to your manager. The manager calls you, asking why you have not filed a complete report, and you reply that the president specifically said that no one outside of the people in the room should hear the information. Your manager replies that both parties have signed a confidentiality agreement, so it is OK for you to report. What do you do to keep both parties satisfied?
>
> ❑ A. Tell your manager whatever he or she wants to know.
>
> ❑ B. Have a major lapse of memory.
>
> ❑ C. Get written permission from the president to give out the information.
>
> ❑ D. Stall as long as you can, hoping that your manager will forget the whole thing.

The answer is C. If you were invited to the meeting in the first place, it is highly likely that the president knows whom you are. Email him or her, explaining that your manager would like more information, and request a reply. Usually this can get done more quickly if you call the president's assistant and explain what you are trying to do. But do not in any case go against the express wishes of the president of a client company.

If you are not sure whether the information you get may be disseminated, always ask the person giving the information. Doing so is a safeguard against giving out proprietary information that should not be made public.

Conflict of Interest Situations and Other Prohibited Professional Conduct

The Code of Conduct states that a PMP has the "Responsibility to ensure that conflict of interest does not compromise legitimate interests of a client or customer, or influence/interfere with professional judgments."

Sometimes a project manager is put into a position where conflicts of interest arise. These may be found in many different scenarios, including that of a contract project manager or even in conflicts between divisions within a single organization. These conflicts are always hard to resolve. This is one of the rare cases where the answer to a question is not automatically, "the customer is always right." When dealing with conflicts of interest, the customer is not always right.

> **Q.** **You are a contracted PM and are working within an organization. The sponsor of the project comes to you and asks you for some extra work not within the agreed project plan. She makes it clear that she expects it to be done without a change in cost and that this is something that happens often in projects that she sponsors, even suggesting that your company will be removed from the project if you do not comply. Now what?**
>
> ❑   A.   There is no single answer to this question.
>
> ❑   B.   Give in because if you do not, you may lose the project.
>
> ❑   C.   Check with your engagement manager before doing anything else.
>
> ❑   D.   Run.

The answer is all of them, except perhaps D. (Running is an option in fight-or-flight response theory but not very often in corporate life.) There is no simple answer to this. The best is C. Check with your own manager. But there are situations where even that is not possible. So, this is one that you have to work out by yourself, considering the situation and the people. I wish it were easier than that. But real life in the project management lane is sometimes uncomfortable. We are not paid for doing the easy parts of the job, only the hard ones. Anyone who tells you differently has not been a project manager.

The last section in the Code states that a PMP has the "Responsibility to refrain from offering or accepting inappropriate payments, gifts or other forms of compensation for personal gain, unless in conformity with applicable laws or customs of the country where project management services are being provided." This issue arose in an earlier question. If you are traveling abroad, make sure you understand as much as you can about local customs concerning scenarios in which you might find yourself. As mentioned earlier, in certain countries, gifts are given to show gratitude for a job well done. To refuse these can be seen as a minor insult. However, in most places that you work, the people who are sponsoring the project will be aware of the country of your origin and also will be aware of acceptable compensation practices in that country.

Much of the problem is based on the size of the gift. If someone buys you lunch, that is acceptable in most countries. If someone gives you a loaded Volvo, that is another issue. In any case, any gifts or extra compensation that seem excessive probably are. It does not take too much awareness on your part about the size of the gift to know whether it is out of line or crosses into the area of prohibited personal conduct.

The second area concerns the giving of gifts. This follows the same basic rules as those just mentioned. If a gift appears to be excessive, it probably is. Here is a scenario that occurred when I was working in the U.S. with a major overseas company.

> **Q. The president of a major international firm had just arrived in our city. During our first meetings to go over project expectations, the conversation turned to his favorite sports, and the one that he followed was soccer (European football). It just so happened that the U.S. national team was playing a World Cup qualifying game in our city that evening. I bought tickets and drove him to the game, which he enjoyed immensely. He said it was good to see his home country's sport and was gracious in his thanks. Was I right or wrong to do this?**
>
> ❑ A. Even by revealing this now I should be flayed and sent to jail.
>
> ❑ B. Because nothing was gained except an enjoyable experience, it was acceptable.
>
> ❑ C. One little gift could lead to another.
>
> ❑ D. Did the U.S. win?

The answer is B. The tickets were not particularly expensive, cheaper than those of our football (U.S.) team. There was no intent to influence the man's actions, and in any case, the contract was already signed for the project. He later bought me a lunch, and we were even. I also believe it made him more comfortable with our city and the people in it, and that is good for both sides. (Yes, the U.S. national team did win.)

The issue keeps coming back to the cost of the gift as well as the intent of the gift. When a vendor has offered an inappropriate gift, it should be easy to say no. It may be tempting to accept such a gift sometimes, but we must behave professionally to protect the profession at all times.

I believe that the Code of Professional Conduct is an excellent addition to the overall understanding of how to be a PMP. The Code is still being formulated and will certainly need more depth, but any attempt to show how to act professionally as well as ethically and how to protect the profession will strengthen the profession. In fact, the Code makes project management more of a profession and less of a job.

For the examination, you should memorize the various parts of the Code of Professional Conduct. Some of the questions can be quite long, so there are opportunities for you to reason out the answers. Make sure you read the entire question before answering it. The short narratives that are used as questions will give you clues as to the best answer.

Questions from Chapter Six ?

1. **You are a PMP-certified project manager who works for a company that is trying to get all its project managers certified. You are asked by some of your non-certified colleagues for guidance on how to take the exam. You should:**

   ☐ A. Refer them to the main library for project management information.

   ☐ B. Tell them that you are far too busy to help them right now.

   ☐ C. Write a short guide to taking the exam and hand it out to everyone.

   ☐ D. Give them guidance about the various resources available.

2. **You have been with the organization for a short time, and you find what you think are clear violations of the PMP Code that occur with frequency. As a PMP, you should:**

   ☐ A. Move to another company.

   ☐ B. Write down the infractions, discuss them discreetly with other PMPs, and decide how to handle the situation.

   ☐ C. Confront the other PMPs in the hall and make sure that you do it loudly and often.

   ☐ D. Let the situation take care of itself.

3. **In this same organization, you hear rumors constantly about a certain PMP failing to live up to the PMP Code. You should:**

   ☐ A. Confront him/her immediately.

   ☐ B. Ignore the rumors.

   ☐ C. Gather as much information as you can before proceeding.

   ☐ D. Make sure you pass the rumors along.

4. **You should _____ the information you have so that you can present it to others if that becomes necessary.**

   ☐ A. Write down

   ☐ B. Memorize

   ☐ C. Modify

   ☐ D. Hide

5. **You believe you have found someone who is not disclosing all of the costs involved with an upcoming project. Rather, this PMP is constructing a WBS that does not include all the tasks necessary to get the project done. You should:**

   - ❑ A. Ignore it because the PMP is a friend of yours.

   - ❑ B. Call PMI home headquarters.

   - ❑ C. Confront the other project manager immediately.

   - ❑ D. Talk to the PMP about the WBS to see if you can rework it to reflect actual costs of the project.

6. **You are looking for classes that will help you professionally. There are a series of one-day seminars that you can take that will help you. This series is presented as a set with the tuition for the set of five inclusive of all of them. You are unable to attend one of the days of the set. The topic covered that day is important to you and you have already taken the other four days. What should you do?**

   - ❑ A. Sign up for all five days again.

   - ❑ B. Put it in your resume that you have attended the set.

   - ❑ C. Put only the classes you have actually attended in your resume.

   - ❑ D. Do self-learning about the class you missed.

7. **You have been assigned to a major project in another country. Before you go, you check with your providing organization to make sure you understand all of the constraints of working in the other country. When you get there, you settle into a routine and do excellent work, completing the project within 5% of the planned budget and schedule. To show their appreciation, the sponsors of the project, who are wealthy men in their own country, send you an expensive gift to, as they put it, "Say thank you for your hard work." It turns out that this is a fairly common practice in that country but is against both ethics and regulations in your own country. What should you do?**

   - ❑ A. Send it back.

   - ❑ B. Take it and go home where you can enjoy the gift because you did such an outstanding job.

   - ❑ C. Say nothing but leave the gift in your hotel room when you leave the country.

   - ❑ D. Talk to your management about the problem and get them involved.

8. **You are writing an article about risk. In the middle of the article, you use a statistic from a well-known report that is the standard for explaining risk. Everyone writing in the area of risk knows the report. Because the report is so well known, you:**

   ❑ A. Assume that everyone knows where the statistic comes from.

   ❑ B. Hope nobody notices.

   ❑ C. Cite the report.

   ❑ D. Let someone complain.

9. **Offering an estimate that you know will be changed shortly after the contract is signed is:**

   ❑ A. Bad practice   ❑ B. Unprofessional practice

   ❑ C. Bad for both the buyer and seller   ❑ D. All of the above

10. **Estimates are:**

    ❑ A. Always correct   ❑ B. Written in stone

    ❑ C. Estimates   ❑ D. Easy to do

11. **Estimates should:**

    ❑ A. Never be changed after you write them

    ❑ B. Be the closest to correct as you can get

    ❑ C. Be forgotten as you get into the project

    ❑ D. Be changed immediately when a contract is signed

12. **You have just been assigned to a project that has been ongoing for more than three months. In looking over the project plan, you see deliverables that seem to be impossible to deliver to the client in the specified time frame. You should:**

    ❑ A. Stop everything until you have talked this problem over with your project team.

    ❑ B. Keep on going.

    ❑ C. Talk to the sponsor and explain your concerns for the accuracy of the schedule.

    ❑ D. Write down your concerns and keep them in a project file.

13. **The final arbiter of any service scope change is the:**

    ❑ A. Project manager   ❑ B. Project team

    ❑ C. Delivery managers   ❑ D. Customer

14. When the project was begun, both the customer and the project manager understood that it was likely that some service scope changes would occur. A few weeks into the project, some services need to be added. Because you, as the project manager, and the customer already have talked over the possibility of this happening, you should follow standard scope change procedure that includes:

❏ A. A written request for service scope change

❏ B. A tacit understanding agreement so that you can make all appropriate changes

❏ C. A new SOW

❏ D. Verbal assurances that you will be able to make the service scope change quickly

15. The objectives of the project are agreed to in the _____ phase of the project.

❏ A. Execution

❏ B. Planning

❏ C. Closing

❏ D. Control

16. If the objectives of the project are changed, these changes are accepted only with the consent of the _____.

❏ A. Project manager

❏ B. Stakeholders

❏ C. Customer

❏ D. Project team

17. You are a project manager sitting in a meeting with executives of the company for which you work as a contract manager. These executives include the president of the company who begins the meeting by specifically stating, "What is said in this room at this meeting stays in this room. There are no exceptions to this." This is a clear statement from the president, so you do not report on some issues discussed in the meeting when you file your weekly report to your manager. The manager calls you, asking why you have not filed a complete report, and you reply that the president specifically said that no one outside of the people in the room should hear the information. Your manager replies that both parties have signed a confidentiality agreement, so it is OK for you to report. What do you do to keep both parties satisfied?

❏ A. Tell your manager whatever he or she wants to know.

❏ B. Have a major lapse of memory.

❏ C. Get written permission from the president to give out the information.

❏ D. Stall as long as you can, hoping that your manager will forget the whole thing.

18. You are a contracted PM and are working within an organization. The sponsor of the project comes to you and asks you for some extra work not within the agreed project plan. She makes it clear that she expects it to be done without a change in cost and that this is something that happens often in projects that she sponsors, even suggesting that your company will be removed from the project if you do not comply. Now what?

    ❑ A. There is no single answer to this question.

    ❑ B. Give in because if you do not, you may lose the project.

    ❑ C. Check with your engagement manager before doing anything else.

    ❑ D. Run.

19. The president of a major international firm had just arrived in our city. During our first meetings to go over project expectations, the conversation turned to his favorite sports and the one that he followed was soccer (European football). It just so happened that the U.S. national team was playing a World Cup qualifying game in our city that evening. I bought tickets and drove him to the game, which he enjoyed immensely. He said it was good to see his home country's sport and was gracious in his thanks. Was I right or wrong to do this?

    ❑ A. Even by revealing this now I should be flayed and sent to jail.

    ❑ B. Because nothing was gained except an enjoyable experience, it was acceptable.

    ❑ C. One little gift could lead to another.

    ❑ D. Did the U.S. win?

Answers from Chapter Six

1. **The answer is D**. You don't have to write a guide to be helpful. A wide variety of resources is available for getting ready for the exam, including websites, books, magazines, and papers. Part of your responsibility after you pass the exam is to give help and guidance to those who are taking it after you. This is the way that a profession becomes stronger, and by this type of conduct, you can give back to the profession, which professionals can and should do.

2. **The answer is B**. This is not an easy situation to be in. This is also a time when asking other PMPs for input will be extremely useful. As with anything where you will be accusing someone of infractions of the rules, make sure you have your facts straight before going to anyone. There is always the possibility that you do not have an understanding of the actual situation. This is a good time to be professional and circumspect in how you handle the problem. Gather up all the information you can to make sure of what you are saying about another person. There may be nothing worse in business life than to accuse someone or be accused of wrongdoing. Great care and sensitivity is needed in this case.

3. **The answer is C**. The more information you have, the more you can plan for dealing with the problem, if there is one. This is a constant and natural theme when you are gathering information concerning potential conflicts. Get as much information as you can. When you think you have enough, get some more.

4. **The answer is A**. The more written information you have, the better off you are. If you only have verbal information, you probably shouldn't proceed. There is nothing quite as awkward as confronting someone and then having to go through an "I said, you said" type of meeting. Make sure that everything you are going to discuss is available in written form and shows dates of the activities about which you are going to talk.

5. **The answer is D**. By working with this PMP, you may be able to avoid a serious conflict. If he or she refuses to change the WBS, you have a responsibility to go to stakeholders and voice your concerns. How you do that depends in great part on your personality and your relationship with the other project manager. In any case you should construct a WBS that more fully shows all the tasks involved in the project in question and make sure of their accuracy before going to any stakeholders.

6. **The answer is C**. This is another example where there is more than one correct answer. It would be good if you did self-study about the topics that you missed, but it would not give you permission to put it in your resume. Only show the classes you have taken and your actual experience.

7. **The answer is D**. When there are conflicts between one culture and another, it is a good idea to get your own management involved. Do not try to resolve problems like this without telling your management. Although it may be acceptable in the country in which you worked to accept gifts, it may not be acceptable in your own country. Because your management already has some relationship with the sponsors, get them involved so that no one will be offended by the actions you take.

8. **The answer is C**. No matter how well known the materials are, if they are someone else's, then you have the responsibility to cite the source. It is not only a conduct violation to fail to cite another person's work; it is a professional discourtesy. If they worked hard to prepare the research, give them the credit.

9. **The answer is D**. It is both bad and unprofessional to knowingly offer an estimate that is incorrect. It is bad for both the buyer and seller because the budget will be affected immediately by the changes. This makes it almost impossible to have good budget and schedule.

10. **The answer is C**. Estimates are just that, estimates. The Merriam-Webster Online Dictionary defines estimate as, "to judge tentatively or approximately the value, worth, or significance of." Unless the numbers used to make an estimate are known completely, you are getting an approximate value, not a concrete one.

11. **The answer is B**. Given that estimates are roughly the correct number, your task as a PMP is to get as close as you can to the actual costs. This can often be very difficult. You owe it to the project sponsor to make a concerted effort to get close to correct every time you do an estimate.

12. **The correct answer is C**. Most of the questions on the exam that are concerned with the code of ethics are like this. They have several sentences in the explanation, basically a short case study, and then ask you to choose the correct answer. The best way to study for this is to go to the PMI Certification Handbook and completely familiarize yourself with the code of professionalism.

13. **The answer is D**. The customer has the final say over any service scope change. Without the signoff of the customer, do not make any changes.

14. **The answer is A**. Even if you have talked with the customer about the possibility of making a service scope change, when it occurs, you must go through a written trail to include in your project records. No changes should occur without having a permanent record of their occurrence.

15. **The answer is B**. The customer and the project manager should be in agreement concerning the project objectives before executing the project plan. Thus, one of the first tasks of the project manager is to meet with the customer and make sure that there is agreement on the project objectives.

16. **The answer is C.** This is another example of a question where there are two possible correct answers. The customer is also a stakeholder, but the correct answer is C, not B. The customer has the final say over any objective changes, and without buy-in from the customer, no changes should be allowed.

17. **The answer is C.** If you were invited to the meeting in the first place, it is highly likely that the president knows whom you are. Email him or her, explaining that your manager would like more information, and request a reply. Usually this can get done more quickly if you call the president's assistant and explain what you are trying to do. But do not in any case go against the express wishes of the president of a client company.

18. **The answer is all of them**, except perhaps D. (Running is an option in fight-or-flight response theory but not very often in corporate life.) There is no simple answer to this. The best is C. Check with your own manager. But there are situations where even that is not possible. So, this is one that you have to work out by yourself, considering the situation and the people. I wish it were easier than that. But real life in the project management lane is sometimes uncomfortable. We are not paid for doing the easy parts of the job, only the hard ones. Anyone who tells you differently has not been a project manager.

19. **The answer is B.** The tickets were not particularly expensive, cheaper than those of our football (U.S.) team. There was no intent to influence the man's actions, and in any case, the contract was already signed for the project. He later bought me a lunch, and we were even. I also believe it made him more comfortable with our city and the people in it, and that is good for both sides. (Yes, the U.S. national team did win.)

CHAPTER SEVEN

Mid-Book Exam

The book is divided into discussions of topics as they appear in the phases of a project and into the knowledge areas. The project phases are now finished, and this is the midpoint of the book. To find out how you are doing in remembering the topics and questions presented in the first part of the book, the mid-book practice examination follows.

There are 108 questions. The questions come from the text, but their order is completely changed. After the questions, you will find a complete set of answers. This information is also on the CD.

The practice test should take no more than two hours, and for most people, it will take a lot less. You can also take it in sections by answering a smaller number of questions. You can break it up any way you want. The best way to record your answers is by printing your answers on a yellow pad.

The questions are random; there is no set of questions on a specific topic. This way you will see how you encounter the questions on the PMP exam where the questions are also in random sequence.

If you get to a question that has you stumped, forget it and go on. You can always come back to it later. Answer the questions you are sure of and then come back to ones that you do not know. In order to make this work you should write out the numbers of the questions you are going to practice with on the yellow pad and go back to the ones you do not answer at a later time. This is also a technique that will stand you in good stead with the actual PMP exam.

Time yourself. When two hours is up, stop. Most of you will have already finished the practice exam. When you are finished, go to the answers section to check how you did. It is a good idea to read the explanations with the answers again. It will reinforce the answers for you.

Good luck.

Mid-Term ?

1. **The person in the organization who authorizes the commencement of a project is the:**

   ❑ A. Senior manager ❑ B. Project administrator

   ❑ C. Sponsor ❑ D. Project specialist

2. **Which phase of a project has the least risk?**

   ❑ A. Closing ❑ B. Controlling

   ❑ C. Planning ❑ D. Execution

3. **One of the functional managers wants to make a major scope change during the execution of the project. The project manager's action should be:**

   ❑ A. Refuse the change

   ❑ B. Complain to the sponsor

   ❑ C. Detail the impact of the change for the functional manager

   ❑ D. Make the change and go on

4. **You define the end of the project by defining the:**

   ❑ A. Scope Statement ❑ B. Charter

   ❑ C. Final deliverable ❑ D. Schedule

5. **You have been with an organization for a short time, and you find what you think are clear violations of the PMP Code that occur frequently. As a PMP, you should:**

   ❑ A. Move to another company.

   ❑ B. Write down the infractions, discuss them discreetly with other PMPs, and decide how to handle the situation.

   ❑ C. Confront the PMP in the hall and make sure that you do it loudly and often.

   ❑ D. Let the situation take care of itself.

6. **The document that authorizes the release of organizational resources to the project is the:**

   ❑ A. Statement of Work ❑ B. Project Design Plan

   ❑ C. WBS ❑ D. Charter

7. **The document that describes the objectives, work content, deliverables, and end product of a project is the:**

   ❑ A. Project Charter   ❑ B. WBS

   ❑ C. SOW   ❑ D. Scope Statement

8. **In scope change control, the project manager must make sure that:**

   ❑ A. The team is involved   ❑ B. The changes are beneficial

   ❑ C. Schedules do not change ❑ D. The sponsor takes charge

9. **The phase in which you define the final deliverable is:**

   ❑ A. Planning   ❑ B. Execution

   ❑ C. Closing   ❑ D. Control

10. **You are a PMP-certified project manager and work for a company that is trying to get all its project managers certified. You are asked by some of your non-certified colleagues for guidance on how to take the exam. You should:**

    ❑ A. Refer them to the main library for project management information.

    ❑ B. Tell them that you are far too busy to help them right now.

    ❑ C. Write a short guide to taking the exam and hand it out to everyone.

    ❑ D. Give them guidance about the various resources available.

11. **The project manager is assigned in the:**

    ❑ A. Charter   ❑ B. Project Plan

    ❑ C. SOW   ❑ D. Management Plan

12. **Which one of these comes first in the project plan?**

    ❑ A. Scope Statement   ❑ B. WBS

    ❑ C. Risk Management Plan   ❑ D. Quality Plan

13. **As changes are brought forward, the project manager should always:**

    ❑ A. Refuse to consider the change

    ❑ B. Install the change immediately

    ❑ C. Consider the impact of the change

    ❑ D. Stall until given further instructions

14. **The person who has the responsibility for keeping the final deliverable clear to all stakeholders is the:**

    ❑ A. Sponsor   ❑ B. Technical lead

    ❑ C. Team member   ❑ D. Project manager

15. **In your organization, you hear rumors constantly about a certain PMP failing to live up to the PMP Code. You should:**

    ❑ A. Confront him or her immediately

    ❑ B. Ignore the rumors

    ❑ C. Gather as much information as you can before proceeding

    ❑ D. Make sure you pass the rumors along

16. **Without a _____, the project cannot go forward.**

    ❑ A. Leader   ❑ B. Charter

    ❑ C. Project administrator   ❑ D. WBS

17. **Which of these plans is *not* done during the writing of a project plan?**

    ❑ A. Risk Management   ❑ B. Quality Management

    ❑ C. Procurement Management   ❑ D. Executive Communication

18. **The one function that must be on the CCB is the:**

    ❑ A. Sponsor   ❑ B. Executive manager

    ❑ C. Team lead   ❑ D. Project manager

19. **The project manager should work with all of the _____ to get agreement on a final deliverable.**

    ❑ A. Team members   ❑ B. Sponsors

    ❑ C. Stakeholders   ❑ D. Line managers

20. **You should _____ the information you have so that you can present it to others if necessary.**

    ❑ A. Write down   ❑ B. Memorize

    ❑ C. Modify   ❑ D. Hide

21. **A project manager is assigned to a project in the _____ phase of the project.**

    ❑ A. Management

    ❑ B. Initiation

    ❑ C. Closing

    ❑ D. Control

22. **Who is responsible for the formation of the final project plan?**

    ❑ A. Project team

    ❑ B. Sponsor

    ❑ C. Project manager

    ❑ D. Team leader

23. **After a change request has been denied, you should:**

    ❑ A. Record it and save it

    ❑ B. Get on with the next request

    ❑ C. Forget it

    ❑ D. Tell the project team

24. **Administrative Closure should occur:**

    ❑ A. Only at the end of a project

    ❑ B. At the end of each phase

    ❑ C. Every week

    ❑ D. On Thursdays

25. **You believe you have found a PMP who is not disclosing all of the costs involved with an upcoming project. Instead, this person is constructing a WBS that does not include all the tasks necessary to get the project done. You should:**

    ❑ A. Ignore it because this PMP is a friend of yours.

    ❑ B. Call PMI home headquarters.

    ❑ C. Confront this PMP immediately.

    ❑ D. Talk to this PMP about the WBS to see if you can rework it to reflect actual costs on the project.

26. **_____ scope determines the features and functions of the output of the project.**

    ❑ A. Management

    ❑ B. Control

    ❑ C. Project

    ❑ D. Product

27. **What is another name for functional structure?**

    ❑ A. Matrix

    ❑ B. Strict

    ❑ C. Line

    ❑ D. Developmental

28. **Change requests are made against the:**

    ❑ A. Charter
    ❑ B. SOW
    ❑ C. Executive summary
    ❑ D. Project baseline

29. **Information needs to go to:**

    ❑ A. Everyone on the team
    ❑ B. The sponsors
    ❑ C. The stakeholders
    ❑ D. Everyone in the communication plan

30. **You are looking for classes that will help you professionally. A helpful five-day seminar is available, but you are unable to attend one of the days. The topic covered that day is important to you, and you have already taken the other four days. What should you do with respect to your resume?**

    ❑ A. Sign up for all five days again
    ❑ B. Put it in your resume that you have attended the set
    ❑ C. Put only the classes you have actually attended in your resume
    ❑ D. Do self-learning about the class you missed

31. **The work that needs to be done to produce a product or service is included in the:**

    ❑ A. Execution Plan
    ❑ B. Product Scope
    ❑ C. Project Scope
    ❑ D. SOW

32. **Which of these types of matrix structures gives the project manager the most control?**

    ❑ A. Strong
    ❑ B. Weak
    ❑ C. Product-focused
    ❑ D. Balanced

33. **Change requests should be:**

    ❑ A. Formal
    ❑ B. Timely
    ❑ C. Interesting
    ❑ D. Long

34. **As you make approved changes to the original scope, you should:**

    ❏ A. Save the old versions   ❏ B. Shred the old versions

    ❏ C. Amend the SOW   ❏ D. Do a completely new WBS

35. **You are writing an article about risk. In the middle of the article, you include a statistic that comes from a well-known report that is the standard for explaining risk. Everyone writing in the area of risk knows the report. Because the report is so well known, you:**

    ❏ A. Assume that everyone knows where the statistic comes from

    ❏ B. Hope nobody notices

    ❏ C. Cite the report

    ❏ D. Let someone complain

36. **The tangible measurement or outcome that must be produced to complete part of a project or the project itself is called a:**

    ❏ A. Work Statement   ❏ B. RFP

    ❏ C. Deliverable   ❏ D. Project Plan

37. **Three types of organizational structures discussed in PMBOK are:**

    ❏ A. Matrix, line, departmental

    ❏ B. Functional, matrix, product driven

    ❏ C. Matrix, functional, projectized

    ❏ D. Projectized, departmental, functional

38. **If change requests are not done formally, this often leads to:**

    ❏ A. Management excellence   ❏ B. A new Scope Statement

    ❏ C. Scope creep   ❏ D. Information creep

39. **If your project comes in 20% ahead of schedule and 25% under budget, you should:**

    ❏ A. Reward yourself

    ❏ B. Demand a raise and throw a party

    ❏ C. Be proud

    ❏ D. Find out why there was such a variance from the original plan

40. You have been assigned to a major project in another country. Before you go, you check with your providing organization to make sure you understand all of the constraints of working in the other country. When you get there, you settle into a routine and are doing excellent work, bringing the project in within 5% of the planned budget and schedule. To show their appreciation, the sponsors of the project, who are wealthy men in their own country, send you an expensive gift to, as they put it, "Say thank you for your hard work." It turns out that this is a fairly common practice in that country but is against both ethics and regulations in your own country. What should you do?

- ❑ A. Talk to your management about the problem and get them involved.
- ❑ B. Take it and go home where you can enjoy the gift because you did such an outstanding job.
- ❑ C. Say nothing but leave the gift in your hotel room when you leave the country.
- ❑ D. Send it back.

41. A description of the final deliverable is one of the best ways to make sure that you are in control of the project in the _____ phase.

- ❑ A. Initiation
- ❑ B. Closing
- ❑ C. Execution
- ❑ D. Planning

42. You can use project management skills in which of the following structural organizations?

- ❑ A. Functional
- ❑ B. Projectized
- ❑ C. Matrix
- ❑ D. All of the above

43. The Change Control Board should:

- ❑ A. Be flexible
- ❑ B. Have appropriate authority
- ❑ C. Include the project manager
- ❑ D. All of the above

44. A complete set of indexed project records is called:

- ❑ A. Project archives
- ❑ B. Project history
- ❑ C. The index
- ❑ D. The SOW

45. Offering an estimate that you know will be changed shortly after the contract is signed is:

- ❑ A. Bad practice
- ❑ B. Unprofessional practice
- ❑ C. Bad for both the buyer and seller
- ❑ D. All of the above

46. The Work Breakdown Structure is done by:

☐ A. The sponsor

☐ B. Senior management

☐ C. The project manager

☐ D. The project team

47. The title of a manager who is responsible for more than one project is:

☐ A. Team leader

☐ B. General manager

☐ C. Project manager

☐ D. Program manager

48. The CEO comes into your office (cubby). He or she asks for changes to be made in the scope of the project but doesn't have enough time to go through a formal procedure, and because everyone on the project actually reports to him or her, it is expected that you get these things done. You should:

☐ A. Run like hell.

☐ B. Make sure the project team knows you are important enough to talk to the CEO.

☐ C. Determine what will happen if the change is made and then report that to the CEO.

☐ D. Run like hell.

49. The best form to save the project archives in is:

☐ A. Log book

☐ B. Electronic database

☐ C. Yellow pads

☐ D. Excel

50. Estimates are:

☐ A. Always correct

☐ B. Written in stone

☐ C. Estimates

☐ D. Easy to do

51. The WBS is done during Scope definition, which comes between:

☐ A. Scope Planning and Scope Change Control

☐ B. Scope Verification and Scope Change Control

☐ C. Scope Planning and Scope Verification

☐ D. Scope Management and Scope Planning

52. **Communication in a matrix environment is usually classified as:**

   - ❑ A. Simple
   - ❑ B. Direct
   - ❑ C. Complex
   - ❑ D. Relational

53. **The tools and techniques used to gather, integrate, and disseminate the outputs of project management processes are called a:**

   - ❑ A. SOW
   - ❑ B. Scope Statement
   - ❑ C. Management system
   - ❑ D. PMIS

54. **Acceptance of the product of the project should be:**

   - ❑ A. Formal
   - ❑ B. Fast
   - ❑ C. Consistent
   - ❑ D. Personal

55. **Estimates should:**

   - ❑ A. Never be changed once you write them
   - ❑ B. Be as close to actual costs as you can get
   - ❑ C. Be forgotten as you get into the project
   - ❑ D. Be changed immediately when a contract is signed

56. **A good WBS:**

   - ❑ A. Helps pull the team together
   - ❑ B. Is a roadmap for the project
   - ❑ C. Defines the scope
   - ❑ D. All of the above

57. **A project team member working in a functional organization reports to:**

   - ❑ A. The project manager
   - ❑ B. The team leader
   - ❑ C. The functional manager
   - ❑ D. Anyone he can contact

58. **The baseline version number of a document is:**

   - ❑ A. 2.0
   - ❑ B. 2.1
   - ❑ C. 1.0
   - ❑ D. 1.a

59. **Formal acceptance includes:**

   - ❑ A. High praise
   - ❑ B. Written acceptance
   - ❑ C. Dialectic
   - ❑ D. Verbal acceptance

60. You have just been assigned to a project that has been ongoing for more than three months. In looking over the project plan, you see deliverables that seem to be impossible to deliver to the client in the specified time frame. You should:

    ❏ A. Stop everything until you have talked this problem over with your project team

    ❏ B. Keep on going

    ❏ C. Talk to the sponsor and explain your concerns for the accuracy of the schedule

    ❏ D. Write down your concerns and keep them in a project file

61. Getting the WBS done is the responsibility of:

    ❏ A. Senior management   ❏ B. The project team

    ❏ C. The project manager   ❏ D. The sponsor

62. The person having the responsibility for the outcome of a project is:

    ❏ A. The project team

    ❏ B. The project manager

    ❏ C. The executive management

    ❏ D. The sponsor

63. Version control numbers should change when:

    ❏ A. Major changes are made   ❏ B. Scope change is involved

    ❏ C. Any change occurs   ❏ D. The sponsor says so

64. The _____ is the person/organization that gives project acceptance.

    ❏ A. Sponsor   ❏ B. Project team

    ❏ C. Delivering organization   ❏ D. Customer

65. The final arbiter of any service scope change is the:

    ❏ A. Project manager   ❏ B. Project team

    ❏ C. Delivery managers   ❏ D. Customer

66. Most projects need _____ meeting(s) to do a good WBS.

    ❏ A. One   ❏ B. Multiple

    ❏ C. Long   ❏ D. Interactive

67. Which of the following is generally *not* a stakeholder?

 ❏ A. Project manager   ❏ B. Sponsor

 ❏ C. Project observer   ❏ D. Project team member

68. Version control helps make meetings easier because:

 ❏ A. People like it   ❏ B. It puts everyone on the same page

 ❏ C. It is easy   ❏ D. It is a predecessor to a SOW

69. The project manager must comply with the requirements of both the customer and:

 ❏ A. His own organization   ❏ B. The functional managers

 ❏ C. The line manager   ❏ D. Executive management

70. When the project was begun, both the customer and the project manager understood that it was likely that some type of service scope changes would occur. A few weeks into the project, some services need to be added. Because you, as the project manager, and the customer already have talked over the possibility of this happening, you should follow standard scope change procedure, which includes:

 ❏ A. A written request for service scope change

 ❏ B. A tacit understanding agreement so that you can make all appropriate changes

 ❏ C. A new SOW

 ❏ D. Verbal assurances that you will be able to make the service scope change quickly

71. The project team is created in the _____ phase.

 ❏ A. Initiation   ❏ B. Control

 ❏ C. Execution   ❏ D. Planning

72. Stakeholders are important because:

 ❏ A. Their intense interest in the workings of the project gives the project energy.

 ❏ B. Their interests may be positively or negatively affected by the project.

 ❏ C. Their knowledge of important product information helps the project manager.

 ❏ D. They know whom to talk to in order to get things done.

73. **A formal procedure for sanctioning project work is a:**

  ❑ A. Charter   ❑ B. Scope Statement

  ❑ C. Statement of Work   ❑ D. Work authorization system

74. **A _____ must be written in order to require contract closeout.**

  ❑ A. WBS   ❑ B. Formal contract

  ❑ C. SOW   ❑ D. Scope Statement

75. **The objectives of the project are agreed to in the _____ phase of the project.**

  ❑ A. Execution   ❑ B. Planning

  ❑ C. Closing   ❑ D. Control

76. **The document that shows the tasks needed to complete the project in detail is the:**

  ❑ A. Statement of Work   ❑ B. Schedule

  ❑ C. WBS   ❑ D. Network diagram

77. **What is the difference in the number of channels between 5 people and 8 people?**

  ❑ A. 18   ❑ B. 3

  ❑ C. 14   ❑ D. 6

78. **Verbal authorization of project work is often seen in _____ projects.**

  ❑ A. Smaller   ❑ B. Strange

  ❑ C. Large   ❑ D. Important

79. **A(n) _____ performs the procurement audit.**

  ❑ A. Project manager   ❑ B. Project team

  ❑ C. Sponsor   ❑ D. Outside individual/organization

80. **If the objectives of the project are changed, these changes are accepted only with the consent of the _____.**

  ❑ A. Project manager   ❑ B. Stakeholders

  ❑ C. Customer   ❑ D. Project team

81. **The single most important position for completing a project successfully is the:**

    ❑ A. President of the company   ❑ B. Sponsor

    ❑ C. Project manager   ❑ D. Scribe

82. **What is the difference in communication channels between 6 and 9 people?**

    ❑ A. 3   ❑ B. 21

    ❑ C. 36   ❑ D. 15

83. **Procurement items are detailed in the:**

    ❑ A. WBS   ❑ B. SOW

    ❑ C. Charter   ❑ D. Scope Statement

84. **What information goes into lessons learned?**

    ❑ A. Everything that happens

    ❑ B. Only major concerns

    ❑ C. Only minor concerns

    ❑ D. Information that will help future project managers

85. **You are a project manager and are sitting in a meeting with executives of the company for which you project manage as a contract manager. These executives include the president of the company, who begins the meeting by specifically stating, "What is said in this room at this meeting stays in this room. There are no exceptions to this." This is a clear statement from the president, so you do not report on some issues discussed in the meeting when you file your weekly report to your manager. The manager calls you, asking why you have not filed a complete report, and you reply that the president specifically said that no one outside of the people in the room should hear the information. Your manager replies that both parties have signed a confidentiality agreement, so it is OK for you to report. What do you do to keep both parties satisfied?**

    ❑ A. Tell your manager whatever he or she wants to know

    ❑ B. Have a major lapse of memory

    ❑ C. Get written permission from the president to give out the information

    ❑ D. Stall as long as you can, hoping that your manager will forget the whole thing

86. The acronym for the value of the work already completed on the project is:

    ❏ A. PV   ❏ B. AC

    ❏ C. EV   ❏ D. AM

87. When do you discuss lessons learned?

    ❏ A. Once a month

    ❏ B. At a formal meeting after the project

    ❏ C. At regular status meetings

    ❏ D. At the New Year's party

88. You are a contracted PM and are working within an organization. The sponsor of the project comes to you and asks you for some extra work not within the agreed project plan. She makes it clear that she expects it to be done without a change in cost and that this is something that happens often in projects that she sponsors, even suggesting that your company will be removed from the project if you do not comply. Now what?

    ❏ A. There is no one answer to this question.

    ❏ B. Give in because if you do not, you may lose the project.

    ❏ C. Check with your engagement manager before doing anything else.

    ❏ D. Run.

89. Who should be going to status meetings?

    ❏ A. The project team

    ❏ B. The people in the communication plan

    ❏ C. The project team and sponsor

    ❏ D. Stakeholders

90. If your AC = $25,000 and your EV = $20,000, how are you doing?

    ❏ A. Over budget $5,000   ❏ B. No variance

    ❏ C. Under budget $5,000   ❏ D. You are in deep yogurt

91. If your AC = $3,000 and your EV = $3,400, how are you doing?

    ❏ A. −$400   ❏ B. No variance

    ❏ C. +$400   ❏ D. Here's that yogurt again

92. **Lessons learned should be:**

   ❑ A. Written down

   ❑ B. Carried around in the project team's head

   ❑ C. Chiseled in stone

   ❑ D. Only done at the end of the project

93. **The president of a major international firm had just arrived in our city. During our first meetings to go over project expectations, the conversation turned to sports, and he said that his favorite was soccer (European football). It just so happened that the U.S. national team was playing a World Cup qualifying game in our city that evening. I bought tickets and drove him to the game, which he enjoyed immensely. He said it was good to see his home country's sport and was gracious in his thanks. Was I right or wrong to do this?**

   ❑ A. Even by revealing this now I should be flayed and sent to jail.

   ❑ B. Because nothing was gained except an enjoyable experience, it was acceptable.

   ❑ C. One little gift could lead to another.

   ❑ D. Did the U.S. win?

94. **Status meetings should be held at least:**

   ❑ A. Once a year   ❑ B. Once a week

   ❑ C. Every day   ❑ D. As little as possible

95. **Your Earned Value is $10,000 and your Actual Cost is $8,000. That means that your CPI is:**

   ❑ A. Incomprehensible   ❑ B. .80

   ❑ C. 1.25   ❑ D. 80

96. **Here is another example. Your EV is $10,000 and your AC is $12,000. What is your CPI?**

   ❑ A. 1.20   ❑ B. 2.0

   ❑ C. .80   ❑ D. 83

97. **The most important document for running a status meeting professionally is:**

   ❑ A. The WBS   ❑ B. The Scope Statement

   ❑ C. The agenda   ❑ D. SOW

98. **Lessons learned are valuable to:**

   ❑ A. Project managers
   ❑ B. Project teams
   ❑ C. Stakeholders
   ❑ D. All of the above

99. **The person writing down meeting notes for a project status meeting is called a:**

   ❑ A. Bookkeeper
   ❑ B. Secretary
   ❑ C. Scribe
   ❑ D. Project manager

100. **The sum of all individual EV budgets divided by the sum of all individual ACs is:**

   ❑ A. Cumulative EVs
   ❑ B. Cumulative CPI
   ❑ C. Cumulative SPI
   ❑ D. GNP

101. **A projection tool for looking at project costs at the completion of a project is:**

   ❑ A. WBS
   ❑ B. Cumulative CPI
   ❑ C. Baseline Schedule
   ❑ D. SOW

102. **Who is responsible for keeping a lessons learned log?**

   ❑ A. The project manager
   ❑ B. The sponsor
   ❑ C. Team members
   ❑ D. Stakeholders

103. **What are the actions called that are done in response to unexpected problems?**

   ❑ A. Stopgaps
   ❑ B. Patches
   ❑ C. Hail Marys
   ❑ D. Workarounds

104. **Your EV = $8,000 and your PV = $6,000. What is your SPI?**

   ❑ A. 1.25
   ❑ B. .66
   ❑ C. .80
   ❑ D. 1.33

105. **The contract file consists of _____ records.**

   ❑ A. All
   ❑ B. Good
   ❑ C. Indexed
   ❑ D. Accounting

106. Which is more important, Planning or Execution?

- ❏ A. Neither
- ❏ B. Both
- ❏ C. Planning
- ❏ D. Execution

107. Your EV = $500 and your PV = $600. What is your SPI?

- ❏ A. .83
- ❏ B. 1.25
- ❏ C. .66
- ❏ D. 1.20

108. Before the primary vendor is paid, be sure that _____ are paid.

- ❏ A. Employees
- ❏ B. Sub-contractors
- ❏ C. Sponsors
- ❏ D. Developers

Mid-Term Answers

1. **The answer is C.** The project manager executes the project but does not authorize the project.

2. **The answer is C,** Planning, because you have not committed the major part of your resources.

3. **The answer is C.** This is often one of the most difficult parts of a project manager's job. To let a manager know what will happen, you have to make sure you have all of the information you need to discuss the requested changes. You must also make sure that you get the person requesting the change to understand that most changes are going to add time or cost to the project. Many times, the person requesting the change does not have a full understanding of what the change will mean to the project schedule. Even with proof, it is sometimes difficult to get across how much a requested change will alter the outcome of a project.

4. **The answer is C.** Only with this will you have a project that will have closure.

5. **The answer is B.** This is not an easy situation to be in. This is also a time when asking other PMP project managers for input will be extremely useful. As with anything where you will be accusing someone of infractions of the rules, make sure you have your facts straight before going to anyone. There is always the possibility that you do not have an understanding of the actual situation. This is a good time to be professional and circumspect in how you handle the problem. Gather up all the information you can to make sure of what you are saying about another person. There may be nothing worse in business life than to accuse someone or be accused of wrongdoing. Great care and sensitivity are needed in this case.

6. **The answer is D.** The Charter is the document that formalizes the project. Without a Charter, you may be in deep yogurt as the project progresses because you will be using organizational resources, and someone above you in the organization must authorize it. It seems obvious, but often is not the case, that the person who is authorizing the work must have the authority to do so.

7. **The answer is D,** the Scope Statement. The Scope Statement controls pretty much everything that goes on in execution. All the rest of the plans are done based on the content of the Scope Statement, and it is the document that supplies information about what is to be done and what isn't. If you don't look at your Scope Statement often, it's likely you'll have added or subtracted something from the original project plan. Keep it easily accessible.

8. **The answer is B.** When changes are requested, the first task of the project manager is to make sure that the changes would benefit the project as the project is outlined in the Scope Statement. If not, the project manager should note this and relay the information to the person requesting the change.

9. **The answer is A**. If you define your final deliverable any later than this, you may find that you have a moving target, and you are back in the "project from hell."

10. **The answer is D**. You don't have to write a guide to be helpful. A wide variety of resources are available for the person getting ready for the exam. Part of your responsibility after you pass the exam is to give help and guidance to those who are taking it after you. This is the way that a profession becomes stronger, and by this type of conduct, you can give back to the profession, which professionals should want to do. Referring them to the main library or the PMI website is an excellent start. I also believe that you should be willing to give up some of your time to help interested parties to understand the profession. This occurs in most professions. It should in ours, too.

11. **The answer is A**. Failure to get a project manager assigned early in the project can lead to delays and problems as the project is executed.

12. **The answer is A**. You have to have a Scope Statement before doing any of the other parts of the plan.

13. **The answer is C**. When a change is requested, the first task of the manager is to analyze the impact of the change and the project. This information is valuable to the people who request change and to the project team.

14. **The answer is D**. Surprised?

15. **The answer is C**. The more information you have, the more you can plan for dealing with the problem, if there is one. This is a always a good idea when you are gathering information concerning potential conflicts. Get as much information as you can. When you think you have enough, get some more.

16. **The answer is B**. This question is a good example of why you should look over questions and answers carefully. In this case, B, Charter, is the correct answer because it precedes everything else. There can be no leader or WBS without a Charter. When you take the test, be sure to look through the exam and determine what the *best* answer is. Two answers may both appear to be correct. Find the one that PMI is looking for. That's what we are doing in this book.

17. **The answer is D**, Executive Communication. There are two parts of this question that you should consider. First, be careful when the questions are phrased in the negative. Second, although Executive Communication might be a part of your overall communication plan, it is the name of a plan that is found in the PMBOK. It is important that you know the parts of the project plan. As we go through the knowledge areas later in the book, we will look at each of these plans in much more detail.

18. **The answer is D**. Once again, the project manager is an indispensable part of the whole project process. Hooray for project managers!

19. **The answer is C.** You can work with all of the people listed as answers, but you need to get agreement from all of your stakeholders. Until you have everyone on the same page, you may find it very difficult to get agreement at the end of the project that the project is actually finished.

20. **The answer is A.** The more written information you have, the better off you are. If you only have verbal information, you probably shouldn't proceed. There is nothing quite as awkward as confronting someone and then having to go through the "I said, you said" meeting. Make sure that everything you are going to discuss is available in written form and that it shows dates of the activities about which you are going to talk.

21. **The answer is B.** The sooner the project manager is selected, the better for the project manager and the project.

22. **The answer is C**, the project manager. I say again, usually on this exam, if there is a chance to pick "project manager" as the answer to a question, do it. Because this entire exam is about project managers, it stands to reason that they will be the answer to several questions.

23. **The answer is A.** Keeping track of all change requests is valuable as the project goes on.

24. **The answer is** B. We need to review and close each phase, not only the project. This is particularly true if the project is run in multiple phases. The project manager must have formal acceptance for each milestone, which occur at the end of each phase. If you don't have acceptance for all phases, major arguments will occur about the final outcome of the overall project.

25. **The answer is D.** By working with this PMP, you may be able to avoid a serious conflict. If he or she refuses to change the WBS, you have a responsibility to go to stakeholders and voice your concerns. How you do that depends in great part on your personality and your relationship with the other project manager. In any case, you should construct a WBS that more fully shows all the tasks involved in the project in question and make sure of their accuracy before going to any stakeholders.

26. **The answer is D.** The product scope is written confirmation of what the output of the project will be. It then shows the features and functions, or in other words, the scope of the output.

27. **The answer is C**, line structure. Be sure to note when reading if more than one word describes the answer. You may see both on the exam.

28. **The answer is D.** All change requests are made against a project plan that has the project baseline. If a change is desired in the baseline, a change request should be submitted.

29. **The answer is D**. This is another example where several answers to the question are included. However, the communication plan is where you list people that should receive information and the type of information they will receive. Although A, B, and C are all correct, D is actually more inclusive.

30. **The answer is C**. This is another example where there is more than one correct answer. It would be good to do self-study about the topics that you missed. However, this would not give you permission to put it in your resume. Only show the classes you have taken and your actual experience.

31. **The answer is C**. Be sure to be able to differentiate between product scope and project scope. One describes the features and functions (product scope), and one defines the work that must be done for the project to be completed (project scope).

32. **The answer is A**, strong. Next to a projectized form of organization, a strong matrix gives the most authority to the project manager.

33. **The answer is A**. There will be times when a line manager meets you in the company cafeteria and asks you for a "small" scope change. Maybe he or she even writes down the request on a paper napkin. You must have formal processes in place, or else you will have massive scope creep.

34. **The answer is A**. You should save any versions that you have and make sure that each version is put under version control as it comes out. You do not have to do a completely new WBS unless the approved change actually changes the entire project.

35. **The answer is C**. No matter how well known the materials are, if they are someone else's, then you have the responsibility to cite the source. It is not only a conduct violation to fail to cite another person's work; it is also a professional discourtesy. If that person worked hard to prepare the research, give him or her the credit.

36. **The answer is C**. Having deliverables formally stated throughout the project is one of the traits of a well-run project.

37. **The answer is C**, matrix, functional, projectized.

38. **The answer is C**. Track everything that changes your original planning. Scope creep is a killer as the project goes on. It can also bring the project to a grinding halt.

39. **The answer is D**. It does not matter if the project is ahead or behind schedule, above or below cost. Whenever there is variance from the plan, you should work to ascertain how it came about.

40. **The answer is A**. When there are conflicts between one culture and another, it is a good idea to get your own management involved. Do not try to resolve problems like this without telling your management. Although it may be acceptable in the country in which you worked to accept gifts, it may not be acceptable in your own country. Because your management already has some relationship with the sponsors, get them involved so that no one will be offended by the actions you take.

41. **The answer is B**. You should formally describe the final deliverable of the project at the beginning of the project. This way, there is formal acceptance of the final output of the project, and you can manage against it.

42. **The answer is D**, all of the above. Although different types of organizational structures offer more or less authority to a project manager, project management skills can and should be used in a variety of environments.

43. **The answer is D**. The Change Control Board also has to be available.

44. **The answer is A**. The key word to get this question correct is "indexed." If you see that word, you are talking about project archives.

45. **The answer is D**. It is both bad and unprofessional to knowingly offer an estimate that is incorrect. It is bad for both the buyer and seller because the budget will be affected immediately by the changes. This makes it almost impossible to have good budget and schedule. It is also unethical to state information that is incorrect if you know it to be so.

46. **The correct answer, D**, indicates that the building of the WBS is an important part of the initial bringing together of your project team. This is the first action that the team can complete together and is the basis for building a team on the project.

47. **The answer is D**. A program manager manages multiple projects and project managers.

48. **The answer is C**. I know that A and D are the same, but it is a normal reaction to want to get out of a bad situation. At least make an attempt to let the CEO know what his or her change requests will do to the project. That is about the most you can do. Unless you have another job waiting, that is.

49. **The answer is B**. By saving your project archives in an electronic database, you can call up records as you need them. It is possible that some of the records you are saving do not come to you in electronic form. In that case, you can use your good old filing system. In any case, save your materials.

50. **The answer is C**. Estimates are just that, estimates. The Merriam-Webster Online Dictionary defines estimate as "to judge tentatively or approximately the value, worth, or significance of." Unless the numbers used to make an estimate are known completely, you are getting an approximate value, not a concrete one.

51. **The answer is C**. Scope Planning and Scope Verification are sections that you will see in the PMBOK. It is not necessary to memorize all of the sections, but there are ones that are often asked about on the exam. We will note those. We will also look at the knowledge areas using the systems explanations in the PMBOK so that you will be familiar with them as they pertain to the exam.

52. **The answer is C**, complex. This is because the project team members may have reporting lines to more than one person, which causes very complex communication and authority issues.

53. **The answer is D**. This is an example of two answers that are alike. You could argue that a PMIS is in fact a management system, and it is. However, you are going to take the exam, so remember the definition of a PMIS.

54. **The answer is A**. The acceptance should be formal.

55. **The answer is B**. Given that estimates are roughly the correct number, your task as a PMP is to get as close as you can to the actual costs. This can often be very difficult. You owe it to the project sponsor to make a concerted effort to get close to actual costs every time you do an estimate.

56. **The answer is D**. There are multiple uses for a WBS, and all of them help a project manager gain control of his or her project and manage it professionally.

57. **The answer is C**, the functional manager.

58. **The answer is C**, 1.0. Every version change starts with this baseline number.

59. **The answer is B**. If you do not have written acceptance, you do not have formal acceptance. You need to have something that is permanent. Verbal is not enough. Written acceptance is the only type that will give you the permanent record you need for any future discussions.

60. **The answer is C**. Most of the questions on the exam that are concerned with the code of ethics are like this one. They have several sentences in the explanation, briefly describing a situation, and then they ask you to choose the correct answer. The best way to study for these questions is to go to the PMI Certification Hand-book and completely familiarize yourself with the code of professionalism.

61. **The answer is C**. Although the project team helps to create the WBS, the responsibility for getting it done lies with the project manager.

62. **The answer is B**. For the most part, if you see the choice "Project Manager" in any question on the exam, choose it. PMI is very strong on the importance of project managers, and this is evident in the exam.

63. **The answer is C**. Although it is true that a scope change will cause version changes in documents, a professional project manager keeps control of the versions and notes any change that occurs.

64. **The answer is D**. As with most things in business, the customer must be satisfied before work is complete. You may need to get project acceptance from various people in your organization, but the final acceptance always comes from the customer.

65. **The answer is D**. The customer has the final say over any service scope change. Without the signoff of the customer, do not make any changes.

66. **The answer is B**. It is very rare that a good WBS can be written in one meeting. I have found it is often best to give the team some time to think about the WBS after the first meeting. There are often omissions and misunderstandings that clear up with follow-up meetings.

67. **The answer is C**. The observer is not a stakeholder, whereas the other three clearly are.

68. **The answer is B**. If everyone is going to be involved in a discussion of a certain document, it is necessary to have the same version of the document in front of the entire meeting.

69. **The answer is A**. If there are tasks for Administrative Closure that pertain to the delivering organization, these must be finished before complete Administrative Closure is possible. As important as the customer is, the project manager must make sure that he or she has formal acceptance from all of the pertinent parties.

70. **The answer is A**. Even if you have talked with the customer about the possibility of making a service scope change, when it occurs, you must create a written trail to include in your project records. No changes should occur without having a permanent record of their occurrence.

71. **The answer is D**. Although you do not always have everyone on the project team participating in the planning, the sooner the team members can be brought together, the better for the project.

72. **The answer is B**, even though it would really be handy to have people who knew exactly whom to talk to in order to get things done.

73. **The answer is D**. Notice that the key words are "formal procedure." The document that allocates work is actually the Charter, but the procedure is called a work authorization system. This is a case of memorizing the definition. You will see it on the test.

74. **The answer is B**. Without a formal contract, there is no real need for contract closeout.

75. **The answer is B**. The customer and the project manager should be in agreement concerning the objectives of the project before executing the project plan. That means that one of the first tasks of the project manager is to meet with the customer and make sure that there is agreement on the objectives to be reached at the closing of the project.

76. **The answer is C**. This is your road map and your bible. Failure to create a WBS almost always means a schedule failure of some sort. The details in the WBS enable you to manage a project professionally.

77. **The answer is A**, 18.

    Here is how to work this out. Remember the formula N (N–1)/2.

    5(5–1)/2 = 10 or 5(4)/2 = 10 and 8(8–1)/2 = 28 or 8(7)/2 = 28 Subtract 10 from 28, and you get 18.

78. **The answer is A**. A formal procedure might be too costly or time-consuming for a smaller project.

79. **The answer is D**. Otherwise the inmates are running the asylum, and we know where that has gotten us with some of the financial misdoings in large companies that have been a major part of the news lately.

80. **The answer is C**. This is another example of a question where there are two possible correct answers. The customer is also a stakeholder, but the correct answer is C, not B. The customer has the final say over any objective changes, and without buy-in from the customer, no changes should be allowed.

81. **The answer is C**. The default answer for PMI is almost always the project manager. If you see it on the test, use it as the answer. Project managers are apparently wondrous people who can do just about anything. Hooray for project managers!

82. **The answer to the problem is B**, 21.

    Using N (N–1)/2,

    6 (6–1)/2 = 15 or 6 (5)/2 =15 and 9 (9–1)/2 = 36 or 9 (8)/2 = 36. Again you subtract, this time 15 from 36, and the answer to the problem is 21.

83. **The answer is B**. This is the document that will give bidders the detail they need to determine if they should be bidding on a certain item or task

84. **The answer is D**. Lessons learned should be useful to any future project manager and his or her project team.

85. **The answer is C**. If you were invited to the meeting in the first place, it is highly likely that the president knows whom you are. Email him or her, explaining that your manager would like more information and request a reply. Usually this can get done more quickly if you call the president's assistant and explain what you are trying to do. But do not in any case go against the express wishes of the president of a client company.

86. **The answer is C**, EV.

87. **The answer is C**. You should be monitoring and discussing lessons learned all throughout the project.

88. **The answer is all of them**, except perhaps D. (Running is an option in fight-or-flight response theory but not very often in corporate life.) There is no simple answer to this. The best is C. Check with your own manager. But there are situations where even that is not possible. So, this is one that you have to work out by yourself, considering the situation and the people. I wish it were easier than that. But real life in the project management lane is sometimes uncomfortable. We are not paid for doing the easy parts of the job, only the hard ones. Anyone who tells you differently has not been a project manager.

89. **The answer is B**, the people listed in the communication plan. It is easy to get too many people involved in status meetings. Put a list of necessary people in the communication plan and stick to it.

90. **A is the correct answer**. Fill in the numbers in the formula, EV-AC. $20,000 – $25,000 = –$5,000. If the number is negative, you are over budget.

91. **The answer is C**. Fill in the numbers in the formula. $3,400 – $3,000 = $400. This means that you planned to spend $3,400 and only spent $3,000, so you are under budget.

92. **The answer is A**. Do not depend on memory to keep track of lessons learned. By writing down the lessons learned, you have a permanent record of them, and you can show them to others and store them for future reference.

93. **The answer is B**. The tickets were not particularly expensive, cheaper than those of our football (US) team. There was no intent to influence the man's actions, and in any case, the contract was already signed for the project. He later bought me a lunch, and we were even. I also believe it made him more comfortable with our city and the people in it, and that is good for both sides. (Yes, the US national team did win.)

94. **The answer is B**, once a week. Any longer than this, and problems might arise that aren't dealt with promptly. The only time that daily meetings are needed may be at the beginning of the project when the project team is getting to know each other.

95. **The answer is C**. Fill in the numbers. $10,000 is divided by $8,000. This gives us 1.25 as your cost performance index. If the CPI is above the number 1, as it is in this case, this means that you are doing better than the planned budget.

96. **The answer is D**. Fill in the numbers. $10,000 is divided by $12,000. This gives you .83 as your cost performance index. If the CPI is lower than one, as it is in this case, it means that you are over budget at this time.

97. **The answer is C**, the agenda. It can be your most important tool in keeping a meeting on track.

98. **The answer is D**, all of the above.

99. **The answer is C**, scribe. The scribe may or may not be the project manager. It depends on the size of the project and the staff.

100. **The answer is** B. This is something you should memorize for the test.

101. **The answer is** B. Memorize, memorize, memorize.

102. **The answer is A**. Again proving how valuable a project manager is.

103. **The answer is D**, workarounds.

104. **The answer is D**. Fill in the numbers. The formula is EV/OV = SPI (Schedule Performance Index). EV=8,000, PV=6,000. 8,000/6,000= 1.33

105. **The answer is C**. If you simply put all the contracts in a big file without an index, you will have nightmarish times trying to find a specific contract three years after the project has been completed.

106. **The answer is B**, both.

107. **The answer is A**. Let's fill in the numbers. EV=500, PV=600. 500/600=.83

108. **The answer is B**. It is important to get the subs paid. The project manager can check on this or make it a requirement of the vendor.

CHAPTER EIGHT

Project Integration Management

The first half of this book deals with the phases of a project. The final half will deal with the knowledge areas as they are found in the PMBOK. The various knowledge areas permit you to study specific topics in depth, while the phases deal with topical areas that occur throughout a project.

The nine knowledge areas of PMBOK all use the same format. The sections to be studied are in sequence as they would happen in a project. For instance, in the Integration knowledge section, there are seven sections or processes through which you go to execute and manage a project. They are: Develop Project Charter, Develop Preliminary Project Scope Statement, Develop Project Management Plan, Direct and Manage Project Execution, Monitor and Control Project Work, Integrated Change Control, and Close Project.

Within each of these sections are Inputs, Tools and Techniques, and Outputs. This organization greatly corresponds to systems theory, where Inputs are transformed into Outputs by use of throughput. In the PMBOK version, Tools and Techniques are the transformation mechanisms to go from Inputs to Outputs.

Because PMBOK is set up this way, and in order to make it easy to use this book with PMBOK, the Inputs, Tools and Techniques, and Outputs formats will be followed. If there is something that does not fit exactly within these three areas, it will be explored, but only if it is going to be on the exam. So we start the knowledge area section of the book. By studying both sections of this book, you will have a better understanding of the exam topics and different ways to approach them.

Develop Project Charter

This is the first of the processes within this chapter. (The various processes found in Project Integration Management sometimes overlap during a project.) Certainly, as you saw in Chapter 4, "Execution and Control," there are constant overlaps as the project is changed during its execution. So although the various processes always seem discrete on paper, very few projects are so neatly or clearly delineated.

Q. **The processes required to ensure that the various elements of the project are coordinated are called:**

❑   A. Work breakdown methodology

❑   B. SOW

❑   C. Project Integration Management

❑   D. Tactical planning

The answer is C. The entire chapter deals with this topic.

The Charter is the document that gives authority and resources to start the project. As discussed when talking about the Charter in the Initiation phase (Chapter 2, "Initiation and Planning"), the project to be managed must fit in with the overall objectives, strategies, and operations of the organization. This is an example of integration of the project with functions outside of the project itself. The organization and its management must release resources to get the project done.

Project scope and product scope must also be integrated. These topics were discussed in the Planning phase in Chapter 2 and will be discussed again in the Scope section of the knowledge areas (Chapter 9, "Project Scope Management"). This is another example of integration.

Q. **The document that begins the process of integrating the project with organizational goals is called the:**

❑   A. Charter   ❑   B. Schedule

❑   C. Scope Statement   ❑   D. SOW

The answer is A. This is the first document that integrates the project itself with the organizational strategies and objectives.

The Project Plan

The actual project plan that you will manage flows from the normal way an organization determines its activities, goals and objectives for the future. The strategic planning conducted by an organization's management determines which projects will be sponsored in order to achieve the organizational goals. For many companies, strategic planning is a formal process through which the top management goes in order to utilize the assets of the company in the best possible way for the shareholders. In later chapters, we will look at various tools and techniques for determining the selection of projects to be funded, but in this chapter, suffice it to say that the organizational management team determines in some fashion that certain projects will bring about better results for the organization than others. These are the projects that get chosen and funded.

Q. **The first planning that occurs when doing the organizational process of choosing projects is:**

☐ A. Project planning ☐ B. Tactical planning

☐ C. Scheduling ☐ D. Strategic planning

The answer is D. The beginning of total organizational planning should be strategic planning. Only after a goal and objectives have been set can management determine which projects would be the best to execute.

After a project is selected, the project plan development process begins. The importance of a coherent clear project plan cannot be overstated. Several uses of a project plan are listed in PMBOK. The first and most important is that the project plan is the road map for the execution of the project.

Project management deals with making a plan and then managing actual results as compared to the plan. The overall project plan is the one place where all types of sub-plans are gathered and the one plan that must be followed in order for the project to be successful. The project plan is seldom created in one session. Most of the time, multiple sessions concerning the various parts of the plan and the sub-plans go into the making of the overall plan.

PMBOK suggests that the project plan is the place where all project planning assumptions are documented. This is the way it should be. Unfortunately, it is not the way that it usually is. First of all, assumptions often do not get documented. This is where the trouble begins. If you make assumptions concerning any facet of the project, you should create some sort of note saying what the assumptions are. The definition of "assumption" found on yourDictionary.com is "Something taken for granted or accepted as true without proof." PMBOK describes assumptions as "factors that, for planning purposes, are considered to be true, real, or certain." The key aspect of assumptions lies in the first definition, and the key words are "without proof." As a project manager, one of the phrases you should commit to memory and use often is "Prove it." You should be constantly trying to use as few assumptions as possible and instead use proven facts.

However, it is not always possible to document and verify assumptions used in the planning process. Best practices suggest that at the very least, you should note assumptions and be aware that they are not facts. Everyone who has worked on a project knows that there are times when assumptions are made, if for no other reason than the fact that each project is unique. Because nothing quite like a given project has been done before, assumptions are made. Be sure to manage them. Assumptions can come back and bite you in the middle of a project if they are the only factors that you use in building a plan.

Q. **Assumptions are factors that, for planning purposes, are considered to be:**

   ❑ A. True, real, or certain   ❑ B. Certain and defensible

   ❑ C. Easy to use   ❑ D. True, real, or interesting

The answer is A. This is the PMBOK definition, and you will see it on the exam.

Q. **Assumptions in the project plan should be:**

   ❑ A. Copious   ❑ B. Understandable

   ❑ C. Easy to defend   ❑ D. Written down

The answer is D. Assumptions that are not written down are the most dangerous. In order to recognize statements in the project plan that are assumptions, document them as such and write them down. It does not mean that the assumptions will all prove to be true, real, or certain, but it does mean that you will understand which statements are assumptions and which are facts.

According to the PMBOK, the project plan will also show the decisions made regarding alternative suggestions from which the final plan was produced. This simply means that whatever is left in the project plan constitutes the final choices that will be used as guides for executing the project.

Because the finalized project plan is the document against which all progress will be measured, it is the document, according to PMBOK, that "defines how the project is executed, monitored, and controlled." The project plan shows the project scope and the breakdown of the tasks for achieving the deliverables within that scope. By sharing the project plan, you make all the project stakeholders aware of the project's goals. As such, the project plan becomes a valuable communication tool. Project managers create status reports to measure how the project is doing against the original project plan.

The project plan also determines when the status reports will be done and to whom the information will be sent. The majority of this information is developed in the communication part of the project plan, where status reports and reports of any type are discussed. Remember that you send information only to people who are included in the communication plan, not to everyone involved in the project. So the project plan, of which the communication plan is a part, is where you determine what to communicate, how much to communicate, with whom you will communicate, and when you will communicate.

Q. **The final choices about how to execute the project are found in the:**

❑ A. Scope Statement   ❑ B. Project Plan

❑ C. SOW   ❑ D. Charter

The answer is B. The project plan is the final document to be created before the execution of the project. As such, the final choices of the planning team are shown in it.

Q. **The project plan helps to facilitate:**

❑ A. Camaraderie   ❑ B. Good will

❑ C. Communication   ❑ D. Strict discipline

The answer is C. Because the project plan shows what should be done to execute the project, various team members can communicate about their progress on the project by referring to the project plan.

> **Q.** **The project plan determines what you will communicate, when you will communicate, how much you will communicate, and:**
>
>   ❑ A. Why you will communicate
>
>   ❑ B. With whom you will communicate
>
>   ❑ C. The language you will use to communicate
>
>   ❑ D. Correct grammar

The answer is B. Not only does the project plan say what, when, and how much you will communicate, but it also tells you with whom you will communicate during the project.

Finally, the project plan is your baseline for the project. The concept of the baseline was discussed in Chapter 3, "Planning and Execution," and the final place where you set your baseline for the project is the project plan.

It is important to remember that the project plan is not one large document that is written page after page after page. The various sub-plans are a part of the overall project plan and may be written in forms altogether different from other parts of the plan. The overall set of plans will be discussed later, but it's important to remember that the project plan is a set of plans and that you need to use all of the plans to effectively manage the project.

> **Q.** **The _____ is a part of the project plan.**
>
>   ❑ A. Baseline   ❑ B. Project Scope
>
>   ❑ C. Schedule   ❑ D. All of the above

The answer is D. The project plan contains the information you need to start to execute the project as well as to manage it.

Develop Preliminary Project Scope Statement

The inputs into developing this process are the project Charter, project statement of work, enterprise environmental factors, and organizational process assets according to the PMBOK. The Charter has been described previously. The project statement of work, or SOW, is created at this stage and contains narrative that describes the products or services that will be the output of the project. The SOW shows the business need for the project, which links it closely to the Charter. In addition, the scope definition gives the product requirements. Finally, the Charter has a clear link to the strategic plan of the organization. Because all projects support the organization's overall strategic vision, the strategic plan (or at least the main points in the strategy) should be part of the development of the early project scope statements.

One of the techniques of managing an organization or project is to manage the variance between what was planned and what actually occurs. This is also one of the tools and techniques found in project management methodology. We have already encountered one of the techniques used in project management through the use of earned value (EV), as discussed in Chapter 4. This technique measures the variance in projects and is an accounting form that is not often seen in general management. In Project Integration Management, the term used to describe the process of managing by variance is called Earned Value Management (EVM). EVM is a project integrating methodology, whereas EV is the technique. EVM is the way project management uses variance management to assess the state of the project. It measures performance against the project plan.

Q. The methodology that is used to measure variance in projects is:

   ❏ A. Earned Value (EV)   ❏ B. Accounting

   ❏ C. Scheduling   ❏ D. Earned Value Management (EVM)

The answer is D. The *methodology* is EVM; the *technique* is EV.

Q. EVM is generally not seen in:

   ❏ A. Big projects   ❏ B. Schedules

   ❏ C. Small projects   ❏ D. General management

The answer is D. (Be sure to note when the question is asked in the negative. This will occur on the exam.) Earned Value Management is a project management methodology. It is important to note this when you are reporting to a sponsor who does not understand what EVM is. You can try to use EVM with an explanation of what it represents, but you may have to rewrite your status reports so that you are expressing the variance between the plan and reality in terms that the sponsor understands. In some cases, the sponsor will learn new terminology, but in most cases, they will not want to do so. The professional project manager must make sure that he or she passes information to the sponsor and other stakeholders in forms that they understand.

EVM is an excellent methodology, but you probably will use it more for yourself and the project team than for stakeholders outside of the team.

Q. EVM is a methodology that deals with _____ management.

   ❑ A. Natural   ❑ B. General

   ❑ C. Variance   ❑ D. Customer

The answer is C. Although variance management is a common business technique, Earned Value Management is specific to projects.

The output of developing a preliminary Scope Statement is the document itself. Remember that everything is preliminary until you lock the Scope Statement under version control. As you do preliminary work, you look for as many inputs as you can find in order to finalize your baseline Scope Statement.

Developing the Project Plan

To begin the process of planning the project, it is necessary to gather as much information concerning the new project as you can. Because projects are not exactly the same time after time, you can get information from other projects that will at least give you guidelines to follow. These guidelines will not be plans that you can follow exactly because there are by definition differences between projects. But other plans used in the past can be valuable if you use them with the caveat that your project is not the same as what you are examining.

The first place to go for information is other project managers who have planned and executed projects like the one you are about to undertake. This is particularly true if these project managers are also PMPs. I have had many good conversations with other project managers about projects I was about to undertake, and I know that I saved a great deal of time by using other PMPs as a resource. If nothing else, I get a sounding board for my planning and also experience with a similar project. Ideas and tasks almost always come up that I had not thought about in any depth or at all. There is nothing quite like a conversation with another project manager about risks he or she overcame during the execution of his or her project.

You may also be able to find databases of formally recorded information. This information can include how the estimating was done as well as how the project was executed against its original baseline. Any information that has been kept on former projects can be very useful to you as you plan and execute yours.

A very valuable addition to your information can be the WBS of a previous project. These can be very helpful in defining tasks and sequencing. One of the problems with looking at a previous project's WBS, though, is the trap of using the numbers in the WBS you are examining. These were probably different people in a different time setting who almost certainly had deliverables other than those that your project has now. Although using a previous WBS for task identification on a current project is an excellent idea, remember that your project is unique, so there are likely to be significant differences in how your WBS is created.

Q. Past project plans should not be followed exactly because each project is:

  ❏ A. A mess   ❏ B. Unique

  ❏ C. Typical   ❏ D. Hard

The answer is B. Each individual project is unique and should be thought of as a new planning and execution problem. Although past project plans can be helpful, they are not the exact same plan that you will be using.

Q. Which of the following is useful in your current planning?

  ❏ A. Contact with former project managers

  ❏ B. Utilizing databases from past projects

  ❏ C. Reviewing WBSs from other projects

  ❏ D. All of the above

The answer is D. Using any information that will make your project run more effectively is a good idea. Other people and other information about previous projects that are similar to yours are all useful tools.

Another set of information used within a project plan is plans from other knowledge areas, such as a risk plan or quality plan. A very valuable figure to examine is Figure 3-7 from the third chapter of the PMBOK. Rather than reproduce it here, you should look at it in the PMBOK. There is relevant information around section 3.2.2 of the PMBOK that is well explained.

All of the planning done in preparing sub-plans of the project plan will be useful input to the overall project plan. These sub-plans will be created by subject matter experts in each planning area and will reflect the best thoughts on those knowledge areas. There are plans that need to be managed as well as the overall plan. The project manager's job is to integrate all of these plans into a coherent project plan so that the project can be managed as efficiently as possible.

Another topic that appears on the exam deals with the organizational policies as they relate to writing a project plan. As the organization becomes more complex, all major policies will need to become fixed. The major policies are written down, and they form a constraint on the project because they determine certain ways that the organization wants to handle operations. The policies may include personnel issues, quality issues, how controls are to be handled, and even how to dress in the organization. Policies tell anyone dealing with the organization how that organization expects different actions to be taken. If you are a project manager, your major project plan will be influenced by all the different policies the organization has.

Q.   Which of these is an example of an organizational policy?

❏ A. The project schedule   ❏ B. Hiring and firing guidelines

❏ C. Scope Statement   ❏ D. Company address book

The answer is B. The hiring and firing of employees and the way to handle these two extremely important tasks is a major part of organizational policy. This policy may affect whom you hire and the pool of people that you have to work with on your project. It is a good practice to understand any organizational policies that will affect your project before you start to formalize the project plan.

The PMBOK defines a constraint as "An applicable restriction that will affect the performance of the project." Many different types of constraints are involved in executing a project. Among the most obvious are the available budget, the time when the project is expected to be done, and the expected quality level. All three of these constraints are major considerations for a project manager. Certainly these constraints not only will act as inputs to the development of a project plan but also will become guidelines for you to follow throughout the project. As with organizational policy, constraints exist throughout the project, and understanding how they work and the ways in which they affect your project is a major task of the project manager.

Q. A _____ is an example of a constraint.

- ❑ A. SOW
- ❑ B. RFP
- ❑ C. Contract
- ❑ D. Sponsor

The answer is C. Any contract with another organization or individual has provisions that are constraints. All contracts should be cleared through your own legal department so that you can be certain that you are complying with the contract. The project manager is not expected to be a legal expert, so he or she should rely on professional help to understand the provisions of the contract.

Q. Risk plans, quality plans, and procurement plans are all _____ to the project plan.

- ❑ A. Agendas
- ❑ B. Assumptions
- ❑ C. Contingent
- ❑ D. Inputs

The answer is D. All of these sub-plans are used in the project plan and are important for the execution of the project.

In order to do project planning, it is necessary to have some type of methodology to follow. Some of the tools you use may be "hard" tools, such as project management software. Some may be "soft" tools, such as facilitated startup meetings. The quotation marks come from the PMBOK, and they indicate that software and mechanical tools are considered "hard," whereas human resource management is considered "soft." You may also use templates that are provided by your organization or forms that have become standard for project planning. These would all be a part of the organization's methodologies and can be useful to the project manager as he or she begins to do project plan development.

As mentioned in Chapter 2, "Initiation and Planning," the software that is most often used in the project management area is Microsoft Project. Specific types of management use other tools, such as Primavera, but MS Project is generally the electronic planning device that is found in most organizations.

Q. Project management software is an example of a _____ tool for project management methodology.

- ❑ A. Special
- ❑ B. Hard
- ❑ C. Soft
- ❑ D. Pliable

The answer is B. In the language of the PMBOK, mechanical tools are described as hard tools.

Q. **Templates and forms are a part of an organization's _____ for project plan development.**

   ❑ A. Constraints   ❑ B. Assumptions

   ❑ C. Methodology   ❑ D. Software

The answer is C. Any resource that can be reused as a useful tool is part of the total methodology of project planning. Templates are forms that an organization can use to plan a variety of projects. Each project manager can make up his or her own tools, but in general, standard tools will be available to use as a part of the project planning.

A second set of tools available to the project manager consists of the project stakeholders' skills and background. Each stakeholder will have some useful special skills or experience, and a good project manager should always work to get this information from the stakeholders into the project plan. A given stakeholder might have been on a similar project before, or he or she might have specific training or education that is useful for the rest of the project team. No matter what, the better the project manager is at getting the stakeholders' skills and knowledge revealed for the whole team to see, the better the chances for project success. These are the most overlooked tools in project management. The Asian cultures look to people with experience for help and guidance. We should do the same on a project. On the other hand, a person does not have to have many years of experience to be useful to the project team. Sometimes the fact that one of your stakeholders has not had a great deal of experience may be useful. These people think in different ways than people who have done the same types of projects over and over again. Young blood is just as necessary as more experienced people. A good project manager looks for skills and experience. The appropriate skills may be available from people of any age.

Q. **An engineer on a project participates in the Planning phase and makes considerable contributions to the technical planning. What type of skill/knowledge is this?**

   ❑ A. Stakeholder   ❑ B. Technical analysis

   ❑ C. Convergent thinking   ❑ D. Sponsor

The answer is A. The engineer is a stakeholder and a part of the project team. Using stakeholder skills is an important part of project success.

The Project Management Information System (PMIS) was discussed in Chapter 4. It is everything that you use to collect and disseminate information about the project. As with almost all the planning parts of a project, there are both manual and automated systems that you can use. PMIS is the system that supports the project from the Planning phase to the Closing phase.

> **Q. The PMIS has both _____ and _____ systems that are useful in project plan development.**
>
> ❏ A. Manual, automated   ❏ B. Small, large
>
> ❏ C. Hard, easy   ❏ D. Strange, wonderful

The answer is A. There are many useful types of systems in the Project Management Information System; some are manual, and others, such as software, are automated.

After you have gone through project plan development, the major output is the project plan itself. Here is a list of the parts of the plan. This comes from the PMBOK, page 89:

- Scope Management Plan
- Schedule Management Plan
- Cost Management Plan
- Quality Management Plan
- Process Improvement Plan
- Staffing Management Plan
- Communication Management Plan
- Risk Management Plan
- Procurement Management Plan

The project plan includes all of these different parts, and if you are doing a comprehensive project plan, you should include the items from this PMBOK list. The subsidiary plans will be discussed in each of their specific knowledge areas, so they will not be discussed here. The project plan therefore shows how work will be controlled and how change control will occur during the project. In addition, it includes the specific selected processes that will be used to manage the project. There are other parts to the project plan, and you should refer to page 88 of the PMBOK for more information.

The other output of project plan development is supporting detail. This includes a variety of information that is available in the sub-plans but not included in the project plan itself. The plan would become enormous if all the supporting detail was included. As the project manager, you should make sure you know where supporting detail is for the parts of the overall project plan. If there is insufficient detail to allow you to understand a particular sub-plan, go to the writers and get it. This information will help you understand how the various parts of the project plan have been put together.

Technical documentation should be part of the supporting detail as well. This means that the designs, requirements, and specifications for the project need to be placed in the plan. Finally, you need to include any relevant standards that will be used in executing the project as a part of your supporting material.

Supporting detail is just that, detail. You do not need to have all the detail in the main project plan, but it is good project management practice to have your detail organized so that you can use it as needed on the project.

> **Q.** **The supporting detail, which consists of requirements, designs, and specifications, is part of:**
>
> ☐ A. The Scope Statement ☐ B. SOW
>
> ☐ C. Technical documentation ☐ D. Charter

The answer is C. You should have detail concerning all of the three areas in order to refer to the baseline used as your technical guide.

Project Plan Execution

The inputs to project plan execution are the project plan itself, corrective action, preventive action, change requests, defect repair, and administrative closing procedure. The first three topics have been discussed already, but it is important to note the difference between preventive action and corrective action.

According to the PMBOK, preventive action is "anything that reduces the probability of potential consequences of risk events." This is a proactive type of management where the project manager considers the risk events that might occur that will in some way hinder the completion of the project. He or she then takes management actions that reduce or mitigate the risks on the project.

Corrective action is "anything done to bring expected future project performance in line with the project plan." Corrective action comes from the various control processes you will have on the project. It is reactive and comes after an event occurs. For the exam, it is a good idea to know the definitions of these two types of actions. They are close in definition, but they are not the same.

Q. Anything that reduces the probability of potential consequences of risk events is:

❑ A. A hassle

❑ B. Interesting

❑ C. Corrective action

❑ D. Preventive action

The answer is D. Reduction in "probability" is the key concept for this type of action.

Q. You are working on a project, and the status reports you are getting indicate that the project is slipping schedule. You bring the necessary parts of the project team together and map a course that you can use to bring the schedule back in line with the baseline of the project plan. This is an example of:

❑ A. A hassle

❑ B. Preventive action

❑ C. Corrective action

❑ D. Interesting action

The answer is C. Corrective action is taken after the variance in plan has occurred.

Make sure you have memorized these two definitions. They are found in the exam in some form or another.

Defect repair has two parts to it. The first is the request for correction of a defect, and the second is the notification that the repair has been done and is acceptable.

A project manager has a specialized set of skills that he or she brings to a project. Areas such as scope management, risk management, quality management, and all of the knowledge areas are specific to project management.

At the same time, the project manager must also have a standard set of skills that you would find with a general manager. It is possible that you will not have training in these particular management skills because many people come to project management from other areas. Some of these skills as finance, sales/marketing, research and development, and various planning types such as strategic and tactical. In addition, the motivational skills and all other HR skills such as team building, communication, leadership, conflict resolution, negotiating, and problem solving are also important to the project manager.

The project manager needs general management skills on almost every project. One of the ongoing problems for project management as an overall profession is that often project managers are elevated to the project manager position because of competency in a technical area. This does not help much in understanding the different skill sets found in general management, but there are certainly a great many resources to read about general management, which is highly recommended for anyone who wants to be as professional as possible.

Q. **Risk management, quality management, and scope management are examples of _____ skills.**

❑　A.　Project management　　　　❑　B.　General management

❑　C.　Team management　　　　❑　D.　Executive management

The answer is A. The specific knowledge areas in the PMBOK, such as scope and risk, are examples of project management skills.

Q. **Communication, leadership, and negotiation are examples of _____ skills.**

❑　A.　Project management　　　　❑　B.　General management

❑　C.　Team management　　　　❑　D.　Executive management

The answer is B. General management skills are extremely important for a project manager. A project manager should always continue learning about the aspects of general management that he or she will use almost every day in managing a project.

Product skills and knowledge are also part of the tools and techniques used in project plan execution. Subject matter experts help round out a project by providing specific technical knowledge. The project manager is not necessarily the person with the most knowledge about the technical areas of the project. This is a common mistake that general managers make when choosing a project manager. The job of the project manager is to bring the project to a successful conclusion, not to be a technical expert on all of the aspects of the project.

When putting together a project team, the project manager should always consider what information he or she lacks on the technical side and make sure that the staffing of the project includes one or more people who are technically proficient. But knowing how to project manage is not the same as being able to explain how something on the project works technically. This is an ongoing issue for all project managers. As project management itself is recognized as a profession, more and more organizations will choose project managers based on project management skill sets rather than technical skill sets. That is the reason why PMP is an important designation. It indicates that you have studied and understand project management as a topic by itself.

Q. Product skills and knowledge are brought to the project team by:

- ❑ A. Having the project manager go to school for 30 years so he or she knows everything about the project.
- ❑ B. Incredible good luck.
- ❑ C. Going through an incredibly long learning curve.
- ❑ D. Finding resources that bring the necessary skills and knowledge to the project.

The answer is D. No one person knows everything about a given project. It is a major function of putting together a project team to make sure that the various technical and product skills are available for the execution of the project. The more complex the project, the more likely it is that you will have many technical leads and experts working on the project. The project manager should know what kinds of skills are needed to complete the project successfully, but he or she is not responsible for having all of them.

The work authorization system is another tool that is used to execute the project plan. This has been discussed at length in Chapter 4, and you can refer back to that section if necessary. Here is a question concerning the work authorization system.

Q. The value of a work authorization system should be balanced with the _____ of the work authorization system.

- ❑ A. Length
- ❑ B. Size
- ❑ C. Cost
- ❑ D. Complexity

The answer is C. The cost of your work authorization system should be balanced by the value of the system to the project and the project manager. Some highly sophisticated work authorization systems are used in major, complex projects. The costs of these systems would not be balanced by the value they would provide to a small project. So as the project manager, you must balance value against cost.

Another extremely important tool in project plan execution is the status review meeting. Status review meetings will be discussed at some length in the communication knowledge area, but here are some of the ways you can make a status meeting more productive and useful.

The most important thing you can bring to a status meeting is a prepared agenda. The first step is to send out an email asking all the people scheduled to be at the meeting if they have specific topics that should be on the agenda. After you have gathered that information, you blend it with the topics that you were planning to discuss and send out an agenda a few days before the meeting.

The second step in preparing an agenda is to time every item on it. Give a finite time that will be allowed for discussion of a single topic. The first time you do this, you will get some pushback from people who are used to rambling and taking time to "explore" topics. So your job at the first timed agenda meeting is to cut off discussion after the allotted time has passed. The best way to do this is to give a five-minute warning before the topic is supposed to end. That way, everyone on the team knows that you are watching the time. The first time you do this is often problematic for people not used to time control and the discipline it takes to make meetings effective. But I guarantee that after the people in the status review meetings realize that they will be saving large amounts of time, they will like the control factor.

Not every stakeholder needs to be at every meeting. You may have weekly status meetings for the project core team and bring in other stakeholders only once a month. This helps speed up meetings and makes them effective at the same time.

> **Q.** After you have written an agenda, the next step is to _____ it.
>
> ❑ A. Time   ❑ B. Burn
>
> ❑ C. Correct   ❑ D. Publish

The answer is A. Putting in times will help you get control of the meeting.

According to PMBOK, the outputs from the project plan execution are work results and change requests. Work results are the "outcomes of the activities performed to accomplish the project." You hold your status meetings to discuss work results, and as usual, the work results are measured against the plan baseline. As the project manager, you will manage against the variances seen from the original plan.

Change requests happen during the execution of the project. The changes can be requested on many different parts of the project plan, such as scope, costs, and schedule times. Change requests are natural, and your job as a project manager is to make sure that change requests are kept under control.

> **Q.** **"The outcomes of the activities performed to accomplish the project" are:**
>
> ❑ A. Change requests   ❑ B. Important
>
> ❑ C. Varied   ❑ D. Work results

The answer is D. This definition comes directly from the PMBOK.

Integrated Change Control

Another major area of Project Integration Management is Integrated Change Control. According to the PMBOK, there are four major factors to consider: identifying that a change has occurred or needs to occur, making sure that only approved changes are implemented, reviewing and approving requested changes, and managing the actual changes when they occur. In order to do this, you must be able to delineate the original performance measure baselines. These are the standards you use to measure change. The baselines used to measure performance are written during the project plan development, and they can consist of a variety of sub-plans.

> **Q.** **Part of Project Integration Management is making sure that only _____ changes are implemented.**
>
> ❑ A. Approved   ❑ B. Good
>
> ❑ C. Tactical   ❑ D. Written

The answer is A. You must be careful to control changes and make sure that only approved changes enter into the new project plan.

> **Q.** **Ensuring that changes to the project are agreed upon, determining that a change has occurred, and managing changes when they occur is the definition of:**
>
> ❑ A. Project Management   ❑ B. Integrated Risk Management
>
> ❑ C. Integrated Change Control ❑ D. Scope Management

The answer is C. This is the full definition of Integrated Change Control. Learn it. It is on the exam.

> **Q. If you make changes in product scope, these changes should be reflected in your:**
> - ❏ A. Project Scope
> - ❏ B. Schedule
> - ❏ C. SOW
> - ❏ D. Quality Baseline

The answer is A. To keep your plan integrated, changes in one area of the project plan that affect other areas must be managed and reflected in those areas.

> **Q. Changes should be reflected across other _____ areas.**
> - ❏ A. Project
> - ❏ B. Scheduling
> - ❏ C. Standard
> - ❏ D. Knowledge

The answer is D. A change made in one area should not stand alone. Every affected knowledge area should be changed appropriately.

The major input to Integrated Change Control is the project plan. This is the baseline for the project and as such is where all changes will be made. By finishing a comprehensive project plan, you will be building a document that is your change control standard. All changes are requested against a baseline. You project plan is that baseline.

A second input to Integrated Change Control, which will be described more fully in the communication knowledge area, is that of performance reports, stated as work performance information. These reports are your scorecard and tell you how you are doing against the original plan. If variances between the baseline and the information appear on the performance reports, the entire project team should manage them. If there are negative trends in the performance reports, for instance one part of the project is falling further and further behind at every new performance report, you must make the necessary changes to bring performance back in line with the plan. This looks good theoretically but is very difficult to do on most projects. Being aware of the variance reported in performance reports at least gives you a "heads up" concerning the problems that are occurring and ones that may occur in the future.

Finally, change requests are an input into Integrated Change Control. PMBOK states that there are many forms of change requests: oral or written, direct or indirect, externally or internally initiated, and legally mandated or optional. An example of an externally initiated change request may come in the form of a government change in reporting laws that forces you to change when you report your status. This might also be an example of a legally mandated change. Anyone who has worked with HIPAA knows that legally mandated changes can occur at any time.

Q. The baseline for the project and the standard against which all changes will be measured is the:

❑ A. Scope Statement   ❑ B. Charter

❑ C. Project Schedule   ❑ D. Project Plan

The answer is D. The project plan is always your overall project baseline.

Q. "Legally mandated" and "optional" are types of:

❑ A. Legal problems   ❑ B. Change requests

❑ C. Scheduling options   ❑ D. Management styles

The answer is B. There are several types of change requests, including those that are legally mandated, usually by some form of government intervention, and optional change requests, which are just that—they are to be done at the option of the project stakeholders.

The tools and techniques for Integrated Change Control include the change control system that you put in place at the beginning of the project. This may include a Change Control Board (CCB) that has agreed-upon members. The members of the CCB are chosen by the sponsor and the project manager. The members evaluate and suggest inclusion or rejection of new changes. We've also discussed several other tools, such as the Technical Review Board (TRB), which may be the de facto Change Control Board. The change control system may also include changes that can be done at certain cost levels. For instance, under such a system, a change costing less than $5,000 may be approved only by the project manager, whereas a change costing more than $5,000 must be approved by a CCB.

Whatever procedures you use to bring about an approved change, the change control system should list as many as will be encountered in the project. This list should be written or recorded electronically and distributed to all the stakeholders so that the project manager can keep changes under his or her control.

> **Q. If a change can be approved only by the project manager, this is still part of the:**
>
>   ❑ A. Project Plan   ❑ B. Charter
>
>   ❑ C. Change Control System   ❑ C. Scope Statement

The answer is C. Any change requests must go through some sort of review. Any of the organizations or people who conduct the reviews should be listed in the change control system as well as the conditions under which they will be used.

One topic that seems to confuse people taking the exam is configuration management. It is a tool used in Integrated Change Control, and actually the concept is simple. Technical and administrative overviews are done in the configuration management section of Integrated Change Control. Configuration information may include the types of servers, software, and hardware that will be used and how all of these will be linked together. It is the technical part of the project and as such should be written in the project plan. You, as the project manager, need to know what hardware is going to be used on an IT project. This will be managed in the documents that are used for configuration management.

> **Q. Which of the following identifies the functional and physical characteristics of a system used on the project?**
>
>   ❑ A. SOW   ❑ B. Engineering plans
>
>   ❑ C. Technical outlines   ❑ D. Configuration management

The answer is D. Think of a schematic that explains how a building is going to be wired. This is an example of a document that is used in configuration management.

If a change request occurs and is approved, then additional planning will be necessary. Any modifications to the original plan will require the project manager and team to go through additional planning. This is common. However, you should make sure that all the appropriate people are informed of the change. There may be times when people affected by an approved change request are not in the meetings where the new request is reviewed and rescheduled. You need to inform them of the changes and make sure that a new version of the plan is made available to all appropriate parties so that the changes can be kept under control.

Q. Additional planning occurs when:

❑ A. Any change request is approved

❑ B. The project manager feels like it

❑ C. The sponsor says something

❑ D. A change is made in the project manager

The answer is A. Any change request that is approved requires a planning sequence in order to include the changes within an approved project plan. It does not matter if the change is small or large; it must be included in a new version of the project plan. Failure to do additional planning because the approved change request seems rather minor will result in serious problems if many small changes occur without being recorded.

The outputs from Integrated Change Control include project plan updates, corrective action, and lessons learned. The updates to the plan must be kept under version control so that any changes to the plan force a new version number to be used. In this way, anyone looking at the changed plan can easily reference the version number. It is a good idea to get team members to give you old versions of the plan so that you will have complete control over which plan is used. Failure to do this can result in a great deal of confusion that can be avoided with strict version control.

Lessons learned should be kept all throughout the project. Some organizations have a lessons learned meeting after the project is finished, and although this is a good idea, the way to make it an excellent idea is to list lessons learned quickly after they occur. That way, you and your project team won't have to rely on your memories of lessons learned from months or years ago.

Ideally, you will have a database for lessons learned. Many organizations do not bother with this, but if you are project managing, you should suggest that a database be kept. It is an excellent tool for future project managers and one that helps explain how a project was managed and issues that arose during all the phases of the project. It is a hard discipline to get used to, but one that is very valuable in the long term.

Close Project

The inputs into the close project process include the project management plan, contract documentation, enterprise environmental factors, organizational process assets, work performance information, and the deliverables. The project plan and contract documentation have been described several times already in this book.

The enterprise environmental factors include the organization's culture and structure. Standards, as established by the industry or government regulations, are also part of the enterprise environmental factors.

The people available for the project are a major part of the internal environmental factors, as are the personnel administration guidelines set up by the company. Another important internal environmental factor is the stakeholder risk tolerances, which will determine how you will manage the risks that occur in the execution of projects.

An external factor in the enterprise environment will be the marketplace conditions. These conditions are outside the control of the organization but will still influence how the project is executed and will probably influence whether the project is actually chosen in the first place.

The work performance information will come from the various performance reports that are done throughout the project, and your job, as outlined before, is to manage the variances between the planned and the actual in the execution of the project.

The outputs of the close project process are the administrative closure procedures. These will be the guidelines that are needed in order to bring full administrative closure to the project, and they should be clearly recorded and kept throughout the project. Without these, the project will go on and on and on... The procedures must be agreed upon early in the project, and then as the end of a project phase or the project itself approaches, the procedures should be implemented to make sure that the project is successfully closed from an administrative standpoint.

Q. **Marketplace conditions are an example of _____ enterprise environmental factors.**

□ A. Tactical   □ B. Strategic

□ C. External   □ D. Internal

The answer is C. These factors are not under the control of the organization and in turn the project manager. However, external factors have as much bearing on the ability to execute a project as internal factors.

Questions from Chapter Eight   **?**

1. The processes required to ensure that the various elements of the project are coordinated are called:

❏ A. Work breakdown methodology

❏ B. SOW

❏ C. Project Integration Management

❏ D. Tactical planning

2. The document that begins the process of integrating the project with organizational goals is called the:

❏ A. Charter   ❏ B. Schedule

❏ C. Scope Statement   ❏ D. SOW

3. The methodology that is used to measure variance in projects is:

❏ A. Earned Value (EV)   ❏ B. Accounting

❏ C. Scheduling   ❏ D. Earned Value Management (EVM)

4. EVM is generally not seen in:

❏ A. Big projects   ❏ B. Schedules

❏ C. Small projects   ❏ D. General Management

5. EVM is a methodology that deals with _____ management.

❏ A. Natural   ❏ B. General

❏ C. Variance   ❏ D. Customer

6. The first planning that occurs when doing the organizational process of choosing projects is:

❏ A. Project planning   ❏ B. Tactical planning

❏ C. Scheduling   ❏ D. Strategic planning

7. Assumptions are factors that, for planning purposes, are considered to be:

❏ A. True, real, or certain   ❏ B. Certain and defensible

❏ C. Easy to use   ❏ D. True, real, or interesting

8. Assumptions in the project plan should be:

    ❑ A. Copious   ❑ B. Understandable

    ❑ C. Easy to defend   ❑ D. Written down

9. The final choices about how to execute the project are found in the:

    ❑ A. Scope Statement   ❑ B. Project Plan

    ❑ C. SOW   ❑ D. Charter

10. The project plan helps to facilitate:

    ❑ A. Camaraderie   ❑ B. Good will

    ❑ C. Communication   ❑ D. Strict discipline

11. The project plan determines what you will communicate, when you will communicate, how much you will communicate, and:

    ❑ A. Why you will communicate

    ❑ B. With whom you will communicate

    ❑ C. The language you will use to communicate

    ❑ D. Correct grammar

12. Each project phase is marked by completion of one or more:

    ❑ A. Task oriented objectives

    ❑ B. Deliverables

    ❑ C. Inputs

    ❑ D. Product life cycles

13. You will show the _____ as a part of the project plan.

    ❑ A. Baseline   ❑ B. Project scope

    ❑ C. Schedule   ❑ D. All of the above

14. Past project plans should not be followed exactly because each project is:

    ❑ A. A mess   ❑ B. Unique

    ❑ C. Typical   ❑ D. Hard

15. Which of the following is useful in your current planning?

- ❑ A. Contact with former project managers
- ❑ B. Utilizing databases from past projects
- ❑ C. Reviewing WBSs from other projects
- ❑ D. All of the above

16. Which of these is an example of an organizational policy?

- ❑ A. The project schedule
- ❑ B. Hiring and firing guidelines
- ❑ C. Scope statement
- ❑ D. Company address book

17. A _____ is an example of a constraint.

- ❑ A. SOW
- ❑ B. RFP
- ❑ C. Contract
- ❑ D. Sponsor

18. Risk plans, quality plans, and procurement plans are all _____ to the project plan.

- ❑ A. Agendas
- ❑ B. Assumptions
- ❑ C. Contingent
- ❑ D. Inputs

19. Project management software is an example of a _____ tool for project management methodology.

- ❑ A. Special
- ❑ B. Hard
- ❑ C. Soft
- ❑ D. Pliable

20. Templates and forms are a part of an organization's _____ for project plan development.

- ❑ A. Constraints
- ❑ B. Assumptions
- ❑ C. Methodology
- ❑ D. Software

21. An engineer on a project participates in the Planning phase and makes considerable contributions to the technical planning. What type of skill/knowledge is this?

- ❑ A. Stakeholder
- ❑ B. Technical analysis
- ❑ C. Convergent thinking
- ❑ D. Sponsor

22. The PMIS has both _____ and _____ systems that are useful in project plan development.

❑ A. Manual, automated

❑ B. Small, large

❑ C. Hard, easy

❑ D. Strange, wonderful

23. The supporting detail, which consists of requirements, designs, and specifications, is part of:

❑ A. The Scope Statement

❑ B. SOW

❑ C. Technical documentation

❑ D. Charter

24. Anything that reduces the probability of potential consequences of risk events is:

❑ A. A hassle

❑ B. Interesting

❑ C. Corrective action

❑ D. Preventive action

25. You are working on a project, and the status reports you are getting indicate that the project is slipping schedule. You bring the necessary parts of the project team together and map a course that you can use to bring the schedule back in line with the baseline of the project plan. This is an example of:

❑ A. A hassle

❑ B. Preventive action

❑ C. Corrective action

❑ D. Interesting action

26. Risk management, quality management, and scope management are examples of _____ skills.

❑ A. Project management

❑ B. General management

❑ C. Team management

❑ D. Executive management

27. Communication, leadership, and negotiation are examples of _____ skills.

❑ A. Project management

❑ B. General management

❑ C. Team management

❑ D. Executive management

28. Product skills and knowledge are brought to the project team by:

❑ A. Having the project manager go to school for 30 years so he or she knows everything about the project.

❑ B. Incredible good luck.

❑ C. Going through an incredibly long learning curve.

❑ D. Finding resources that bring the necessary skills and knowledge to the project.

29. The value of a work authorization system should be balanced with the _____ of the work authorization system.

❑ A. Length   ❑ B. Size

❑ C. Cost   ❑ D. Complexity

30. After you have written an agenda, the next step is to _____ it.

❑ A. Time   ❑ B. Burn

❑ C. Correct   ❑ D. Publish

31. "The outcomes of the activities performed to accomplish the project" are:

❑ A. Change requests   ❑ B. Important

❑ C. Varied   ❑ D. Work results

32. Ensuring that changes to the project are agreed upon, determining that a change has occurred, and managing changes when they occur is the definition of:

❑ A. Project management   ❑ B. Integrated risk management

❑ C. Integrated Change Control ❑ D. Scope management

33. If you make changes in product scope, these changes should be reflected in your:

❑ A. Project scope   ❑ B. Schedule

❑ C. SOW   ❑ D. Quality baseline

34. Changes should be reflected across other _____ areas.

❑ A. Project   ❑ B. Scheduling

❑ C. Standard   ❑ D. Knowledge

35. The baseline for the project and the standard against which all changes will be measured is the:

❑ A. Scope Statement   ❑ B. Charter

❑ C. Project Schedule   ❑ D. Project Plan

36. "Legally mandated" and "optional" are types of:

❑ A. Legal problems   ❑ B. Change requests

❑ C. Scheduling options   ❑ D. Management styles

37. If a change can be approved by only the project manager, this is still a part of the:

❑ A. Project plan
❑ B. Charter
❑ C. Change control system
❑ D. Scope statement

38. Which of the following identifies the functional and physical characteristics of a system used on the project?

❑ A. SOW
❑ B. Engineering plans
❑ C. Technical outlines
❑ D. Configuration management

39. Additional planning occurs when:

❑ A. Any change request is approved
❑ B. The project manager feels like it
❑ C. The sponsor says something
❑ D. A change is made in the project manager

40. Marketplace conditions are an example of _____ enterprise environmental factors.

❑ A. Tactical
❑ B. Strategic
❑ C. External
❑ D. Internal

Answers from Chapter Eight

1. **The answer is C**. The entire chapter deals with this topic.

2. **The answer is A**. This is the first document that integrates the project itself with the organizational strategies and objectives.

3. **The answer is D**. The *methodology* is EVM; the *technique* is EV.

4. **The answer is D**. (Be sure to note when the question is asked in the negative. This will occur on the exam.) Earned Value Management is a project management methodology. It is important to note this when you are reporting to a sponsor who does not understand what EVM is. You may either have to rewrite your status reports so you are expressing the variance between plan and actual in terms that the sponsor understands, or you can try to use EVM with an explanation of what it represents. In some cases the sponsor will learn new terminology, in most they will not want to do so. The professional project manager must make sure that he/she is getting information to the sponsor and other stakeholders in forms that they understand. EVM is an excellent methodology but may be one that you will use more for yourself and the project team than for stakeholders outside of the team.

5. **The answer is C**. While management of variances is a common business technique, Earned Value Management is specific to projects.

6. **The answer is D**. The beginning of total organizational planning should be strategic planning. Only after a goal and objectives have been set can management determine which projects would be the best to execute.

7. **The answer is A**. This is the PMBOK definition, and you will see it on the exam.

8. **The answer is D**. Assumptions that are not written down are the most dangerous. In order to recognize statements in the project plan that are assumptions, document them as such and write them down. It does not mean that the assumptions will all prove to be true, real, or certain, but it does mean that you will understand which statements are assumptions and which are facts.

9. **The answer is B**. The project plan is the final document to be created before the execution of the project. As such, the final choices of the planning team are shown in it.

10. **The answer is C**. Because the project plan shows what should be done to execute the project, various team members can communicate about their progress on the project by referring to the project plan.

11. **The answer is B**. Not only does the project plan say what, when, and how much you will communicate, but it also tells you with whom you will communicate during the project.

12. **The answer is B**. Unless you have definite deliverables as your objective, it is hard to consider a phase completed.

13. **The answer is D**. The project plan contains the information you need to start to execute the project as well as to manage it.

14. **The answer is B**. Each individual project is unique and should be thought of as a new planning and execution problem. Although past project plans can be helpful, they are not the exact same plan that you will be using.

15. **The answer is D**. Using any information that will make your project run more effectively is a good idea. Other people and other information about previous projects that are similar to yours are all useful tools.

16. **The answer is B**. The hiring and firing of employees and the way to handle these two extremely important tasks is a major part of organizational policy. This policy may affect whom you hire and the pool of people that you have to work with on your project. It is a good practice to understand any organizational policies that will affect your project before you start to formalize the project plan.

17. **The answer is C**. Any contract with another organization or individual has provisions that are constraints. All contracts should be cleared through your own legal department so that you can be certain that you are complying with the contract. The project manager is not expected to be a legal expert, so he or she should rely on professional help to understand the provisions of the contract.

18. **The answer is D**. All of these sub-plans are used in the project plan and are important for the execution of the project.

19. **The answer is B**. In the language of the PMBOK, mechanical tools are described as hard tools.

20. **The answer is C**. Any resource that can be reused as a useful tool is part of the total methodology of project planning. Templates are forms that an organization can use to plan a variety of projects. Each project manager can make up his or her own tools, but in general, standard tools will be available to use as a part of the project planning.

21. **The answer is A**. The engineer is a stakeholder and a part of the project team. Using stakeholder skills is an important part of project success.

22. **The answer is A**. There are many useful types of systems in the Project Management Information System; some are manual, and others, such as software, are automated.

23. **The answer is C**. You should have detail concerning all of the three areas in order to refer to the baseline used as your technical guide.

24. **The answer is D**. Reduction in "probability" is the key concept for this type of action.

25. **The answer is C**. Corrective action is taken after the variance in plan has occurred.

26. **The answer is A**. The specific knowledge areas in the PMBOK, such as scope and risk, are examples of project management skills.

27. **The answer is B**. General management skills are extremely important for a project manager. A project manager should always continue learning about the aspects of general management that he or she will use almost every day in managing a project.

28. **The answer is D**. No one person knows everything about a given project. It is a major function of putting together a project team to make sure that the various technical and product skills are available for the execution of the project. The more complex the project, the more likely it is that you will have many technical leads and experts working on the project. The project manager should know what kinds of skills are needed to complete the project successfully, but he or she is not responsible for having all of them.

29. **The answer is C**. The cost of your work authorization system should be balanced by the value of the system to the project and the project manager. Some highly sophisticated work authorization systems are used in major, complex projects. The costs of these systems would not be balanced by the value they would provide to a small project. So as the project manager, you must balance value against cost.

30. **The answer is A**. Putting in times will help you get control of the meeting.

31. **The answer is D**. This definition comes directly from the PMBOK.

32. **The answer is C**. This is the full definition of Integrated Change Control. Learn it. It is on the exam.

33. **The answer is A**. Product scope should be reflected in your project scope.

34. **The answer is D**. A change made in one area should not stand alone. Every affected knowledge area should be changed appropriately.

35. **The answer is D**. The project plan is always your overall project baseline.

36. **The answer is B**. There are several types of change requests, including those that are legally mandated, usually by some form of government intervention, and optional change requests, which are just that—they are to be done at the option of the project stakeholders.

37. **The answer is C**. Any change requests must go through some sort of review. Any of the organizations or people who are conducting the reviews should be listed in the change control system as well as the conditions under which they will be used.

38. **The answer is D**. Think of a schematic that explains how a building is going to be wired. This is an example of a document that is used in configuration management.

39. **The answer is A**. Any change request that is approved requires a planning sequence in order to include the changes within an approved project plan. It does not matter if the change is small or large, it must be included in a new version of the project plan. Failure to do additional planning because the approved change request seems rather minor will result in serious problems if many small changes occur without being recorded.

40. **The answer is C**. These factors are not under the control of the organization and in turn the project manager. However, external factors have as much bearing on the ability to execute a project as internal factors.

CHAPTER NINE

Project Scope Management

We have already looked at scope as a part of the Planning phase of a project in Chapter 2, "Initiation and Planning." Some of the materials in this chapter will be redundant. This is intended. The Planning phase is important both to the practicing project manager and for the exam. If you read both of the chapters, you will examine scope management from two different viewpoints. This should help you to better understand the topic.

This chapter will focus solely on how to break down the tasks that are needed to "ensure that the project includes all the work required, and only the work required, to complete the project successfully" (PMBOK).

There are five process areas in scope management: Scope Planning, Scope Definition, Create WBS, Scope Verification, and Scope Change Control. Each one has its own inputs, tools and techniques, and outputs. Although you can memorize each of the processes, the key is to know when they occur in the scope sequence and what major parts of scope management occur in each of them.

Q. The features and functions of a product or service are considered _____, and the work that must be done to deliver a product or service as the output of the project is considered _____.

❑ A. Product development, project development

❑ B. Marketing-oriented, management-oriented

❑ C. Product scope, project scope

❑ D. Used to differentiate, a management system

The answer is C. These two types of scope are discussed in the PMBOK. They are on the exam and are helpful to the project manager in differentiating between tasks that he or she must do to be successful on a project. Without either of these scope types, the project is in trouble because what is expected of the project manager and project team is not clearly delineated.

Note also that a project results in a single product or service but that the product or service itself may include many components. You do not need to write a separate scope plan for each component, but they should be in your original project plan.

Q. Completion of the project scope is measured against the _____.

❏ A. Project Charter   ❏ B. SOW

❏ C. Scope Statement   ❏ D. Project plan

The answer is D. In order to complete a project, the entire project plan must be executed. It is not simply a matter of working with a Scope Statement. Completion of the project includes everything within the project plan.

Q. Completion of the product scope is measured against _____.

❏ A. Project requirements   ❏ B. Charter requirements

❏ C. Technical requirements   ❏ D. Product requirements

The answer is D.

Putting the two questions together may result in a question like this on the exam.

Q. Completion of the product scope is measured against _____, and completion of the project scope is measured against the _____.

❏ A. Charter requirements, Scope Statement

❏ B. Technical requirements, schedule

❏ C. Product requirements, project plan

❏ D. Project plan, project execution plans

The answer is C. It is helpful to know both of these definitions. You will see them on the test. Both scope types must be integrated to ensure successful completion of the project. This means that the product outlined in the product requirements is success-fully delivered against the schedule and full project plan.

Q. **The process of formally authorizing that an existing project should continue into its next phase is part of _____.**

  ❑ A. Project authorization   ❑ B. Project control

  ❑ C. Initiation   ❑ D. Management decision-making

The answer is C. This is a part of the scope management knowledge area.

Q. **Formal authorization of advancement to the next project phase is generally not found in:**

  ❑ A. Great Britain   ❑ B. Small projects

  ❑ C. The project plan   ❑ D. Large projects

The answer is B. For the most part, small projects do not include formal authoriza-tion of advancement to each phase as a part of the overall scope management of the project.

The project should be linked to the overall mission or vision of an organization. For certain projects, a formal analysis is done to determine the feasibility of the project and its link to the overall strategy of the organization. Some projects, particularly small internal ones, are initiated without a formal initiation for the most part. (How-ever, some internal projects may be so large that a formal initiation plan is needed from the very beginning.) No matter what the size of the project is, it is a good idea to get clear authorization before beginning to work on the project. Sometimes, such as in product development projects, some work will have to be done to establish the feasi-bility of a project, which may include preliminary work on the product itself. This is not generally thought of as work done on the project but rather work done to estab-lish that a project needs to be done.

Q. **Some type of authorization is needed on _____ projects.**

  ❑ A. All   ❑ B. Big

  ❑ C. Special   ❑ D. Small

The answer is A. Unless you are independently wealthy and enjoy paying for projects you work on, someone has to authorize the project. This someone has to have the authority to release resources to get the project done.

> **Q.** **A market demand, a technological advance, and a legal requirement are all examples of:**
>
> ❏ A. Incredible amounts of hard work
>
> ❏ B. Reasons for authorizing a project
>
> ❏ C. Management concerns in terms of corporate strategy
>
> ❏ D. Reasons to become a project manager

The answer is B. There are many reasons for authorizing a project. The PMBOK lists several others under section 5.1. Remember that the reasons for authorizing a project are most often market-driven and usually contain the constraints of cost and schedule. For instance, just because there is market demand for a particular product doesn't mean your organization should authorize a project to plan and build it if the product is not in the organization's strategic plan.

The product description itself is an important part of scope management. The description should include the requirements and as much detail as possible about the product. The more detail, the better the chance of the final project deliverable matching what was expected. The earlier you can include detail, the better off you are from a planning standpoint. Although it is likely that more and more detail will emerge as you go through the planning, it is the project manager's job to make sure that detail is sought as early as possible and that until the final product is clear in the Scope Statement, the team keeps working with the definition of the product.

> **Q.** **When should detail about the product of the project be given?**
>
> ❏ A. Before anything else happens in the project
>
> ❏ B. Before the project plan is put under version control
>
> ❏ C. As soon as possible in the project planning
>
> ❏ D. Whenever the sponsor requires it

The answer is C. Do not leave the details for a later date if you can get them early in the planning process. The more clarity you have about the details of the project's product, the better you will be at writing the overall plan. Answer A does not work because you can begin doing various types of planning, such as risk management planning, without knowing the complete details of the product itself.

As mentioned before, the product description should create a viable connection between the product or service being created by the project and the overall strategic considerations of the organization, and of course the choice of a project should always be in line with those considerations. Although it is true that the project manager will not generally be given responsibility for making strategic decisions for the organization, it is necessary for the project manager to have a clear understanding of why the project is being undertaken. This will help in his or her management of the project and will give guidance for handling various issues that may arise during the execution of the project.

If the project is outsourced to a vendor, the buyer of the services has the responsibility of providing the initial product requirements and descriptions. Failure to do this may result in misunderstanding between buyer and vendor. If you are the project manager for the vendor, it is always a necessity to get clear information concerning product description as soon as possible. One of the phrases you do not want to hear or say as project manager is, "But I thought you meant…" Do not guess. Ask for a clear product or service description, and you can save a great deal of grief as the project progresses.

Q. **A connection between the product being created and the overall strategy of the organization is created by the _____.**

❑ A. Sponsor requirements ❑ B. Project plan

❑ C. Quality plan ❑ D. Product description

The answer is D. Unless this connection is made, the project will almost always be unsuccessful.

Q. **The responsibility for a clear product description in a project where the project manager will be supplied by a vendor lies with the:**

❑ A. Buyer ❑ B. Seller

❑ C. General management ❑ D. Project manager

The answer is A. Before an organization engages an outside project manager, a clear product description should be constructed.

There are many different types of project selection criteria from which to choose a project. Some of them were listed earlier, such as market demand or legal requirements. Some projects are mandated, such as new changes in consumer laws, and some are done to gain market entrance or enlarge market share. Almost all projects are done with some kind of financial consideration about the cost of the project as it relates to the benefit of the project to the sponsoring organization. Usually the project manager is not a part of the group that determines why the project is being done. Rather, the project manager's responsibility is to make sure that the project is being done in accordance with the project plan.

Q. _____ considerations are always important to the sponsoring organization.

   ❑ A. Risk   ❑ B. Financial

   ❑ C. Procurement   ❑ D. Scope

The answer is B. All of the other answers may be important, but for most organizations, the justification of a project has to be done on a financial basis before considering other areas. The only instance where financial considerations are not the top consideration is when regulatory control forces a project to be done in order to comply with the law.

A variety of historical information gleaned from the results of previous projects that are like the current one to be undertaken is another helpful way to look at potential projects. Anything that gives the project manager information to measure his or her current project will be helpful.

Project selection methods are extremely important in the life of a project. In order to initiate the project, you can use a variety of methods to measure the value of the project to the organization. In some cases, these methods are exact and mathematical; in other cases, they are more subjective in nature when there are no exact measurements to be had. Either way, some type of selection process goes on before a project is authorized. (I have been in organization where "rogue" projects got started because of the talents or wishes of a group within the organization. Very seldom did these projects get finished.)

There are two broad categories of project selection. The first is the benefit measurement method. This method measures the potential benefits of executing the project against the potential benefits of other projects put before the organization. If benefit measurement is to take place, it usually is used to decide between two or more projects. Because organizations' resources are limited, deciding which projects to execute is one of the most important decisions that can be made for an organization. Some of the measurements can include contribution to the organization, individual scoring models, and economic models, which generally will show how the investment in the project will contribute to the organization for all choices of projects that are proposed.

Q. Contribution, scoring models, and economic models are all examples of:

  ❑ A. Management models   ❑ B. Benefit measurement models

  ❑ C. Execution measurement   ❑ D. Project models

The answer is B. Benefit measurement measures one project against another and gives the organization information with which to select projects by comparing the benefits of each. Only in the case of a mandated project is there little concern about the benefits derived from the project.

A second type of selection method is termed "constrained optimization models." The main techniques that have been proposed for solving constrained optimization problems are reduced-gradient methods, sequential linear and quadratic programming methods including the augmented Lagrangian/multiplier, and sequential quadratic programming methods. If you feel lost at this time, you are not alone. These types of models are in use only in certain types of projects and are not going to be used for simpler projects. There are several websites you can turn to if you want more information on constrained optimization models, but this book is not the place for lengthy explanation of a very difficult concept. These models, which can include decision trees and others, are among the most complicated of all project selection criteria and are used only in complex projects themselves. They can be very useful and are often found in major scientific projects such as those done by NASA.

Q. The most complex type of project selection method is called the:

  ❑ A. Random choice method

  ❑ B. Constrained methodology method

  ❑ C. Optimistic random method

  ❑ D. Constrained optimization methods

The answer is D. Although these are important methods only for a limited number of projects, they can be very valuable. You certainly do not have to know how to run these methods for the exam.

Another tool found in scope management is expert judgment. This type of judgment can be found internally and externally. The internal experts may be found among your own stakeholders or other divisions or units of your own organization. The external experts can be consultants, industry groups, technical associations, or professional groups. For instance, a technical association may have information on past projects that will help in determining which projects to choose for your organization. Whichever you use, internal or external, expert judgment is a valuable tool for any project manager. In general, it is much better to use expert judgment to make choices concerning the projects to execute than it is to use expert judgment to help correct mistakes made.

Q. Technical associations and consultants are two examples of:

- ❑ A. Expert judgment
- ❑ B. Internal resources
- ❑ C. Expensive additions
- ❑ D. Scope managers

The answer is A. Expert judgment is often the most effective way of dealing with questions concerning choices of projects. Experts should save time for you but will cost something. Use them; they are worth it.

Q. The project manager is assigned in the _____ section of scope management.

- ❑ A. Scope planning
- ❑ B. Initiation
- ❑ C. Scope definition
- ❑ D. Scope verification

The answer is B. The project manager should be assigned as early as possible so that control of the project begins immediately. There will be times when a project manager is not assigned until the project has started. Usually this means that someone is actually acting as the project manager but that the title and position are not filled. If you come into a project after it is started, look for as much documentation as you can. It is particularly important to understand the assumptions and constraints that are part of the project. It is also extremely important that you know the business reason for the selection of the project and how the project fits into the priorities of the organization.

Q. The first document produced on a project should be the:

- ❑ A. Scope Statement
- ❑ B. Risk management plan
- ❑ C. Project Charter
- ❑ D. Quality plan

The answer is C. As discussed previously, this document does not always get done. But the areas is it supposed to control are ones that a project manager should view and manage for the project to be successful.

Scope Planning

Scope planning is "creating a project scope management plan that documents how the project scope will be defined, verified, controlled, and how the WBS will be created and defined" (PMBOK). You begin doing the scope planning process by using the inputs that will give guidance to the project manager. The inputs to scope planning have been discussed elsewhere. They are enterprise environmental factors, organizational process assets, a project charter, preliminary Scope Statement, and the project management plan. All five of these are needed to begin doing scope planning.

The organizational process assets describe processes that are in place in the organization that will be useful in doing the scope planning. Any organizational policies and procedures that are already in place and pertain to scope planning and management are considered assets, as would be historical information about previous projects, according to the 3rd edition of the PMBOK. Historical information can be in the form of lessons learned, although historical information is available in many other formats, such as reports and requirement documentation from previous projects.

A word on the preliminary Scope Statement is necessary. The preliminary nature of the Scope Statement listed in this scope management process indicates that the preliminary Scope Statement is not the final Scope Statement to be used to manage the project. Be careful to understand that a Scope Statement is not final until it is locked under version control, and only then will it be the baseline for your project. This is an input in the scope planning, not the final Scope Statement.

The tools and techniques for scope planning include expert judgment and the various templates, forms, and standards that are useful in constructing a Scope Statement. The Scope Statement is your baseline and one of the most important documents you have on a project. The Scope Statement that is given to the project manager at the beginning of the project is the baseline of scope for the project. It should be put under change control, and any changes to the Scope Statement should require a new version number. Failure to control the Scope Statement carefully and rigorously will result in major problems as the project is executed.

The various templates, forms, and standards that are inputs into scope planning can come from a variety of places in a variety of forms. You should check with your organization to see which types they have for use.

The output of scope planning is the project scope management plan, not the Scope Statement itself. The scope management plan will list various processes, such as how to prepare a Scope Statement, how to create the WBS, how formal verification and acceptance are obtained, and how requests for changes will be processed (PMBOK).

Q. The scope management plan lists _____.

❑ A. Details   ❑ B. Processes

❑ C. Definitions   ❑ D. Overviews

The answer is B. This is the plan that describes the various processes used to manage the scope plan, not the scope plan itself.

Scope Definition

Scope definition is "developing a detailed project Scope Statement as the basis for future project decisions" (PMBOK). The breaking down of the scope into small components is known as decomposition. With decomposition, you end up getting better cost, duration, and resource figures to work with as estimates, and you will give clear responsibility assignments in the project. As you break down tasks into sub-tasks, each of the sub-tasks must have a person who is responsible for making it happen. In order for the project to be successful, it is necessary for one person to be responsible for his or her tasks throughout the project. Simply writing down a task on a breakdown sheet does not mean it will get done. By putting a person's name next to the task, it becomes clear who is the person to contact as the task is being done. This is a key to good project management.

Q. According to the PMBOK, which of the following is not a function of scope definition?

❑ A. Improving the accuracy of cost, duration, and resource estimates

❑ B. Improving the communication system between the project manager and the sponsor

❑ C. Defining a baseline for performance measurement and control

❑ D. Facilitating clear responsibility assignments

The answer is B. Although it is helpful to have clear scope definition so that you can talk intelligently with your sponsor, the other three choices are specific to scope definition.

Q. Each task must have _____ assigned responsibility to get it done.

  ❑ A. One person   ❑ B. A project manager

  ❑ C. The project team   ❑ D. A manager

The answer is A. Only one person can be held responsible for one task. Having multiple people responsible is a certain way to have problems in execution. You always want to be able to go to one person to discuss the handling and results of a task.

The inputs to scope definition have been discussed earlier. They are: organizational process assets, project Charter, preliminary Scope Statement, Scope Statement management plan, and approved change requests.

The tools and techniques for scope definition begin with a product analysis. This has already been discussed in this chapter. Alternatives identification is another of the techniques used in scope definition, and it is just what its name implies—a technique that will show alternative approaches to working on and executing the project. Alternatives identification may be formal or informal. Brainstorming with the project team is an example of informal alternatives identification.

Q. When looking at historical information, it is important to note _____ made in previous projects.

  ❑ A. Project decisions   ❑ B. Tactical considerations

  ❑ C. Errors and omissions   ❑ D. Strategic decisions

The answer is C. By looking at errors and omissions in previous projects, you may be able to avoid the same mistakes in your current project.

Q. Brainstorming different approaches to working on the project with the project team is an example of _____ alternatives identification.

  ❑ A. Current   ❑ B. Tactical

  ❑ C. Simple   ❑ D. Informal

The answer is D. Informal alternatives identification is often the most useful, particularly on smaller projects.

Expert judgment comes in many forms. You may find it within the organization both in your current department and elsewhere. Often if the project is being attempted for the first time, you can consider using consultants, people who are subject matter experts and who can help you plan and frame your project scope. As with almost any tool used in project planning, you should be aware that input from previous projects, although valuable, might not be the exact information you need. Be careful as you use expert judgment so that the expertise of these people pertains to your own current project.

Q. _____ **are a form of expert judgment.**

❏ A. Consultants ❏ B. Managers

❏ C. Sponsors ❏ D. Workers

The answer is A. Consultants contribute to the project scope definition because they have specialized information that is useful for scope planning.

The outputs of scope definition are the project Scope Statement itself, requested changes, and an updated project scope management plan. All of these are discussed at length in this chapter and elsewhere in the book.

The Scope Statement should include the following. (They can either be directly in the Scope Statement itself or found in other documents used on the project.) First, there should be a listing of the project objectives. The second part of a Scope Statement, according to the PMBOK, is a description of the product of the project, also called the product scope description. It should be brief. Supporting documentation and detail should not be put in the Scope Statement, although references to documents that give detail can be included.

Another part of the Scope Statement is the listing of the project deliverables that will be the outputs of the project and that make up the product or service of the project. Project acceptance criteria show the process for accepting the completed products. These are also part of the Scope Statement.

Finally, project constraints and assumptions are part of the project Scope Statement.

Q. **The project justification is found in the project Charter, which is a part of the:**

  ❏ A. Scope Statement   ❏ B. Planning cycle

  ❏ C. Management plan   ❏ D. Stakeholder guide

The answer is A. The project Charter is a separate document done before the Scope Statement, but its contents should be a part of the overall Scope Statement.

Q. **References to documents that give detail about the product of the project can be found in the:**

  ❏ A. Stakeholder guide   ❏ B. Sponsor plan

  ❏ C. Scope Statement   ❏ D. Management plan

The answer is C. The detail is not put directly into the Scope Statement itself. References to where the detail can be found should be in the Scope Statement, not the actual detail itself.

A tool that is useful in scope definition is benefit/cost analysis. This method is the same as the benefit measurement methodologies used in initiation. The organization must make choices about scarce resources, and by determining which project will give the best benefit to the organization from a cost analysis, the project has a better chance of being chosen for execution. There are several types of benefit/cost analysis, including Return on Investment (ROI), payback period, and other financial methods. If you will be asked to participate in assessing your own future project (and this is rare), you should understand how to use the various financial models. However, it is not likely that you will be asked to do the analysis. Others in the organization will do the analysis before assigning a project manager. I have seen organizations using these models incorrectly. They are not difficult, but they require some education. If you are not strong in financial analysis, do not offer to do it. The choosing of a project is done before the project manager is assigned, not after, so it is unlikely that you will be involved in the financial analysis that leads to choosing a project.

Q. **ROI and payback period are examples of _____ project analysis.**

  ❏ A. Financial   ❏ B. Management

  ❏ C. Professional   ❏ D. Quantitative

The answer is A. Although these are also quantitative types of analysis, the answer that is looked for on the exam is financial.

Q. If you are asked to think "outside the box," what type of identification are you being asked to do?

❏ A. Financial
❏ B. Quantitative
❏ C. Qualitative
❏ D. Alternatives

The answer is D. You are being asked to think of alternative possibilities rather than doing a project as proposed. This is a good exercise if it is controlled. Although at the beginning of brainstorming meetings, any suggestion should be noted and kept, there will be a time when reality sets in and the alternative suggestions must be justified by the person suggesting them.

Q. Function analysis is best done by:

❏ A. The project manager
❏ B. Professional engineers
❏ C. The project sponsor
❏ D. The project team

The answer is B. Only people trained in the major engineering types of product analysis should attempt to use these techniques to gain a better understanding of the product of the project. These techniques are not easily learned and require a good background in a variety of mathematical analytics. In other words, if you do not understand how to use them, do not even try.

Create WBS

The Work Breakdown Structure (WBS) is one of the most important documents in all of project management. It is a deliverable-oriented breakdown of the tasks to be done for the execution of the project. The project team works from the WBS and uses it as a guiding document throughout the project. As the WBS is broken down, each lower level gives detail to the task it is breaking down. The inputs, which have been previously discussed, are the organizational process assets, project Scope Statement, project Scope Statement plan, and approved changes requests.

The breaking down of the WBS is called decomposition. The verb used to describe this process is "to decompose." The purpose of WBS decomposition is to make the tasks listed manageable. For instance, if a listed task takes eight weeks, you do not have enough control over the task to make it happen on time. You need to decompose the task into smaller units. Generally, the largest unit you can actually manage is considered 40 hours or five days. So any task that is longer than that in your WBS should be broken down to give you control of the sub-tasks as you go through the project.

Identifying major deliverables of the project is another factor that comes from decomposing the WBS. If you are running the project with each major life cycle shown in your WBS, each phase of the life cycle will have deliverables against which you can measure your success. Give yourself clear deliverables that are manageable, and you will be able to control your project. Vague or unclear deliverables, particularly ones that are due a long time from where you are now, are almost certain to cause major problems as you manage the project.

Q. _____ is the breaking down of the WBS.

   ❑ A. Scope definition   ❑ B. Decomposition

   ❑ C. Scope verification   ❑ D. Scope management

The answer is B. Decomposition is the word used in the PMBOK to define the breaking down of the WBS.

Q. **Generally, the largest unit that you can manage in the WBS is _____ hours.**

   ❑ A. 10   ❑ B. 20

   ❑ C. 50   ❑ D. 40

The answer is D. If the tasks listed in the WBS are longer than this, it will be difficult to control them.

One tip. It is important to note the differences in tasks on your new WBS as well as the similarities with those that were already used. Although tasks that are the same in historical projects will work well for creating a WBS for a new project, it is the managing of the variances between any previous project and the current one that will determine how well you project manage. Always look for variances; these are the tasks that need to be controlled in order to execute a successful project.

When creating a WBS, you should always verify the correctness of the decomposition. Look for and work for clarity in the definitions of the items in the WBS. Also determine whether each of the tasks listed and decomposed is manageable. The other side of this issue is to look at whether too much detail has been done. It is just as injurious to the project to have too many tasks listed as it is to have too few. The tendency is to get into micromanagement of the project, and this almost always leads to delays in work. Managing sufficient detail is necessary for executing a successful project. Over-managing small details will waste time and cause unnecessary delays.

> **Q. When you decompose a WBS, you should have _____ results to measure.**
>
> ❑ A. Verifiable, tactical ❑ B. Tactical, concrete
>
> ❑ C. Verifiable, tangible ❑ D. Tangible, tactical

The answer is C. Always have these types of results, or else you will not have a good way of measuring whether the task has been done.

The inputs into the creation of WBS process are the organizational process assets, the project Scope Statement, the project management plan, and approved change requests.

The tools and templates for the creation of a WBS are templates of work breakdown structures, templates, and decomposition. WBS templates are tools that come from past projects. Because the definition of a project is a unique event, it is certain that no template will fit exactly for a new project. However, it is likely that some past templates will include tasks that are the same as the ones on a new project, and because they have already been done, they can serve as a guideline for your new WBS. Some WBS templates become standards in organizations and can be used again and again.

The outputs from creating a WBS are an updated project Scope Statement, a Work Breakdown Structure, a WBS dictionary, the scope baseline, an updated scope management plan, and requested changes.

The WBS is not the only kind of breakdown structure that can be found in project management. One of the other types of breakdown structures is the Organizational Breakdown Structure, or OBS. This document shows how the organizational structure is organized.

Another breakdown structure that may be found on projects is the Risk Breakdown Structure, or RBS. This shows the hierarchy of the various risks of the project.

Unfortunately, the Resource Breakdown Structure has the same initials: RBS. The Resource Breakdown Structure shows the hierarchy of the resources to be used on the project.

Finally, there is a Bill of Materials, or BOM. This shows the components needed to make a finished product or service.

Q. The letters RBS stand for both Resource Breakdown Structure and the _____ Breakdown Structure.

  ❏ A. Ratified   ❏ B. Real

  ❏ C. Risk   ❏ D. Random

The answer is C. Make sure you know which breakdown is being considered when you see the letters RBS.

The WBS dictionary is a document created in the WBS creation process that contains detailed information about the tasks and components found in the WBS. This document is not always created in every organization for every project. When it is created, a WBS dictionary can be as detailed or simple as needed for control of the project.

The scope baseline is just that. It is the final baseline to be used to begin the execution of the project. As an output of the WBS, it gives you a detailed look at all the tasks that are needed to execute the project successfully.

Q. Detailed information about the tasks and components found in the WBS can be stored in a _____.

  ❏ A. Scope Statement   ❏ B. WBS dictionary

  ❏ C. Scope database   ❏ D. Schedule database

The answer is B. The WBS dictionary is helpful in holding detail about the tasks listed in the WBS.

Scope Verification

Scope verification is "the process of obtaining the stakeholder's formal acceptance of the project scope and associated deliverables" (PMBOK). This is the process of verifying that the Scope Statement you have is the baseline for the upcoming project and getting agreement from all the stakeholders involved in the project that the scope is correct, and it is also the process where you look at the various deliverables in the project and match them up with work results as the execution of the project goes on.

The scope verification process means that all stakeholders have seen and formally accepted a version of the scope that becomes the scope baseline for the project and is put under scope change control so that no changes to the scope of the project can be done without going through the scope change control process. After this is done, and all throughout the project, scope verification means that work results and deliverables are reviewed to make sure that they meet with the scope definition that was accepted at the beginning of the project.

Quality control, which will be discussed in more detail in Chapter 12, "Project Quality Management," deals with the correctness of the scope, whereas scope verification deals with the acceptance of the scope. Quality control is mentioned here because it deals with work results as matched against deliverables, as does scope verification. However, the major difference is that quality control looks at how well the deliverables were done from the view of correctly finishing a deliverable, whereas during scope verification, the stakeholders formally accept the work result. These two definitions will certainly be a part of the examination.

> **Q. Scope verification deals with the _____ of the scope, whereas quality control deals with the _____ of the scope.**
>
> ❑ A. Acceptance, correctness   ❑ B. Correctness, acceptance
>
> ❑ C. Acceptance, quality   ❑ D. Quality, correctness

The answer is A. The stakeholders accept what is being done during scope verification, and the correctness of the results is determined during the quality control process.

The inputs to scope verification include the project Scope Statement, the WBS dictionary, the project scope management plan, and the deliverables (PMBOK).

It is important to have the various documents that describe the output of the overall project (or the project's product) available for review. These are described in total as the product documentation. There are many different types of documents to be used in this process, including specifications of the product, technical documentation, any drawings or blueprints, and other documentation that is used in defining the final project product.

The Work Breakdown Structure also functions as a major input into scope verification because it shows various tasks that go into delivering the final product and also shows the tasks that, when executed, will serve to deliver the deliverables.

The Scope Statement has been described in detail earlier. As an input into scope verification, it is the baseline for all later execution of the project, and all decisions on the project that concern deliverables should be determined by decomposing the Scope Statement into tasks that are tangible and verifiable.

Q. **The project Scope Statement, the WBS dictionary, the project scope management plan, and the deliverables are all _____ of scope verification.**

❏ A. Tools   ❏ B. Techniques

❏ C. Outputs   ❏ D. Inputs

The answer is D. These are all inputs into scope verification.

Q. **Specifications and technical documentation are part of _____.**

❏ A. Product documentation   ❏ B. Process documentation

❏ C. Scope definition   ❏ D. Formal planning

The answer is A. This question is, once again, an example of a question where there is more than one feasible answer. You need to know the definition according to PMBOK, which makes A the correct answer.

The tools and techniques of scope verification consist of one process: Inspection. This is the act of measuring, testing, reviewing, auditing, or any of the various ways that you determine whether what has actually occurred during the execution of the project matches the requirements and other planning for the project.

The output from scope verification is formal acceptance of the project or the deliverable within a given phase, the requested changes, and recommended corrective actions. When you are doing a long project, the actual acceptance may be conditional. When the project is over, there should be a formal acceptance when the final deliverable is done. Getting formal acceptance of the work in the project is one of the major tasks of a project manager. The better the project is documented and planned, the better the chance that you will get acceptance during and at the end of the project because all people involved will have the same understanding of why the project was undertaken.

> **Q. You can determine whether requirements have been met by using _____.**
>
> ❑ A. Templates   ❑ B. Inspection
>
> ❑ C. WBS   ❑ D. Scope Statement

The answer is B. Inspection tells you whether the requirements have been met or whether there is compliance with other planning documents.

Scope Change Control

This topic has already been discussed at length in Chapter 4, "Execution and Control." The parts of scope change control that are listed in PMBOK are: "a) influencing the factors that create scope changes to ensure that changes are agreed upon, b) determining that a scope change has occurred, and c) controlling the impact of the actual changes when and if they occur." A large part of getting agreement on scope changes is implementing a scope change control system to which all stakeholders agree and will adhere during the execution of the project.

To determine that a scope change has occurred, you must have done careful planning, and you must have documents that are agreed upon in scope verification. If this has happened, you should have a rather easy time of determining that a scope change has occurred. If the documents are sloppy or nonexistent, there is a good chance that you will go through a lot of scope change without having much control over what is being done. Planning well and documenting the plan is a key to good scope control.

Finally, the project manager must manage the changes that are finally accepted. Keeping track of the changes and managing them throughout the project should be the job of every professional project manager. Again, it starts with documentation and planning.

> **Q. The tool that defines the procedures by which project scope may be changed is _____.**
>
> ❑ A. The project plan   ❑ B. Scope change control
>
> ❑ C. WBS   ❑ D. Scope methodology

The answer is B. This procedure defines how project scope can be changed.

> **Q. The process that includes managing the actual changes if and when they occur is known as:**
>
> ❏ A. The project plan   ❏ B. Scope change control
>
> ❏ C. WBS   ❏ D. Scope methodology

The answer here is also B. Both the tool within the process and the process itself are called the same thing according to the PMBOK.

The inputs to scope change control are: WBS, WBS dictionary, an updated scope baseline, change requests, recommended corrective action, updated organizational process assets, and an updated project management plan. All of these have been mentioned several times. The key to thinking about these various inputs is that all of them give you a baseline from which to work.

The changing of scope in a project always affects the time and cost and may also affect the quality of the final product or service of the project. If the project scope is enlarged, it is almost certain to add cost and often time. There are certain types of projects, for instance in construction, where it is possible to add costs by adding more shifts of crews and getting a better timeline. In these types, cost is traded for time. In IT projects, it is often impossible to trade cost for time because getting fifteen coders doing the same thing as three coders does not give a five-fold return on investment. Actually, having too many people work on a particular set of tasks in a project is as problematical as not having enough to do the work.

The opposite of enlarging scope is called descoping. This can occur as you get nearer to a deadline that must be met. Y2K was an example of this. As the new year approached, many projects were descoped because of the deadline that was impossible to either ignore or miss. When you make the project smaller in scope, it does not guarantee that you will be able to hit deadlines any better than you had before descoping it. All changes in projects change the project timeline. Making a project smaller in scope is not necessarily the same as making it easier.

> **Q. If you change the scope of a project to make the final output less than the original baseline, you have _____ the project.**
>
> ❏ A. Rewritten   ❏ B. Crashed
>
> ❏ C. Truncated   ❏ D. Descoped

The answer is D. When you change the project plan by removing parts of the final deliverable, you have descoped the project.

The performance measurements that you use will measure variance between the original approved plan and the actual execution of that plan. These measurements will be your tool for scope control. Your job as a project manager is to decide what is causing the variances and to decide whether the variance is significant enough to warrant taking corrective action. One of the questions I am most often asked is, "How large a variation is actually significant?" One of the standard answers is that there can be a 10% tolerance in variation between execution and plan. However, I believe that you should look at all variations. It is difficult to give an exact answer to this question.

A final tool is additional planning or replanning. If you work on a complex project, there will almost always be some additional planning. If you are doing iterative processes, such as you would see in most IT projects, it is likely that you will have to do more than just one-time planning to construct the original plan. Additional planning is a way of life in project management. I have not met anyone who wrote out a complete project plan and managed it perfectly from the beginning to the end unless the project only took a day or two.

> **Q.** **As a project manager, one of your jobs is to determine whether variances between the plan and the actual execution are large enough to take _____.**
>
> ❑ A. Extra time   ❑ B. Time off
>
> ❑ C. Corrective action   ❑ D. A vacation

The answer is C. The project manager is the one who determines whether corrective action is taken. During the planning of the project, it is a good idea to get agreement on how much variance is acceptable. This is particularly true of the sponsor.

The outputs of scope change control are an updated project Scope Statement, the updated WBS, the updated WBS dictionary, the updated scope baseline, change requests, recommended corrective actions for the change requests, updates on organizational process assets, and updates to the project management plan. As you can see, except for the recommended corrective actions, all of these outputs are updates of topics covered before.

Questions from Chapter Nine ?

1. The features and functions of a product or service are considered _____, and the work that must be done to deliver a product/service as the output of the project is considered _____.

   ❑ A. Product development, project development

   ❑ B. Marketing oriented, management oriented

   ❑ C. Product scope, project scope

   ❑ D. Used to differentiate, a management system

2. Completion of the project scope is measured against the _____.

   ❑ A. Charter   ❑ B. SOW

   ❑ C. Scope Statement   ❑ D. Project plan

3. Completion of the product scope is measured against _____.

   ❑ A. Project requirements   ❑ B. Charter requirements

   ❑ C. Technical requirements ❑ D. Product requirements

4. Completion of the product scope is measured against _____, and completion of the project scope is measured against the _____.

   ❑ A. Charter requirements, Scope Statement

   ❑ B. Technical requirements, schedule

   ❑ C. Product requirements, project plan

   ❑ D. Project plan, project execution plans

5. The process of formally authorizing that an existing project should continue into its next phase is part of _____.

   ❑ A. Project authorization   ❑ B. Project control

   ❑ C. Initiation   ❑ D. Management decision-making

6. Formal authorization of advancement to the next project phase is generally not found in:

   ❑ A. Great Britain   ❑ B. Small projects

   ❑ C. The project plan   ❑ D. Large projects

7. Some type of authorization is needed on _____ projects.

   ❑ A. All   ❑ B. Big

   ❑ C. Special   ❑ D. Small

8. A market demand, a technological advance, or a legal requirement are all examples of:

   ❑ A. Incredible amounts of hard work

   ❑ B. Reasons for authorizing a project

   ❑ C. Management concerns in terms of corporate strategy

   ❑ D. Reasons to become a project manager

9. When should detail about the product of the project be given?

   ❑ A. Before anything else happens in the project

   ❑ B. Before the project plan is put under version control

   ❑ C. As soon as possible in the project planning

   ❑ D. Whenever the sponsor requires it

10. A connection between the product being created and the overall strategy of the organization is created by the _____.

   ❑ A. Sponsor requirements   ❑ B. Project plan

   ❑ C. Quality plan   ❑ D. Product description

11. The responsibility for a clear product description in a project where the project manager will be supplied by a vendor lies with the:

   ❑ A. Buyer   ❑ B. Seller

   ❑ C. General management   ❑ D. Project manager

12. _____ considerations are always important to the sponsoring organization.

   ❑ A. Risk   ❑ B. Financial

   ❑ C. Procurement   ❑ D. Scope

13. Contribution, scoring models, and economic models are all examples of:

   ❑ A. Management models   ❑ B. Benefit measurement models

   ❑ C. Execution measurement   ❑ D. Project models

14. The most complex type of project selection method is called the:

- ❏ A. Random choice method
- ❏ B. Constrained methodology method
- ❏ C. Optimistic random method
- ❏ D. Constrained optimization methods

15. Technical associations and consultants are two examples of:

- ❏ A. Expert judgment
- ❏ B. Internal resources
- ❏ C. Expensive additions
- ❏ D. Scope managers

16. The project manager is assigned in the _____ section of scope management.

- ❏ A. Scope planning
- ❏ B. Initiation
- ❏ C. Scope definition
- ❏ D. Scope verification

17. The first document produced on a project should be the:

- ❏ A. Scope Statement
- ❏ B. Risk management plan
- ❏ C. Charter
- ❏ D. Quality plan

18. ROI and payback period are examples of _____ project analysis.

- ❏ A. Financial
- ❏ B. Management
- ❏ C. Professional
- ❏ D. Quantitative

19. If you are asked to think "outside the box," what type of identification are you being asked to do?

- ❏ A. Financial
- ❏ B. Quantitative
- ❏ C. Qualitative
- ❏ D. Alternatives

20. Function analysis is best done by:

- ❏ A. The project manager
- ❏ B. Professional engineers
- ❏ C. The project sponsor
- ❏ D. The project team

21. The project justification is found in the Charter, which is a part of the:

- ❏ A. Scope Statement
- ❏ B. Planning cycle
- ❏ C. Management plan
- ❏ D. Stakeholder guide

22. References to documents that give detail about the product of the project can be found in the:

    ❏ A. Stakeholder guide   ❏ B. Sponsor plan

    ❏ C. Scope Statement   ❏ D. Management plan

23. A list of the summary-level subproducts whose full and satisfactory delivery marks completion of the project describes:

    ❏ A. Project scope   ❏ B. Project Charter

    ❏ C. Project management   ❏ D. Project deliverables

24. All deliverables are important, but the deliverable that will be the one that helps you finish the project is the _____ deliverable.

    ❏ A. Big   ❏ B. Important

    ❏ C. Final   ❏ D. Best

25. When looking at historical information, it is important to note _____ made in previous projects.

    ❏ A. Project decisions   ❏ B. Tactical considerations

    ❏ C. Errors and omissions   ❏ D. Strategic decisions

26. _____ is the breaking down of the WBS.

    ❏ A. Scope definition   ❏ B. Decomposition

    ❏ C. Scope verification   ❏ D. Scope management

27. Generally, the largest unit that you can mange in the WBS is _____ hours.

    ❏ A. 10   ❏ B. 20

    ❏ C. 50   ❏ D. 40

28. When you decompose a WBS, you should have _____ results to measure.

    ❏ A. Verifiable, tactical   ❏ B. Tactical, concrete

    ❏ C. Verifiable, tangible   ❏ D. Tangible, tactical

29. Scope verification deals with _____ of the scope while quality control deals with the _____ of the scope.

    ❏ A. Acceptance, correctness   ❏ B. Correctness, acceptance

    ❏ C. Acceptance, quality   ❏ D. Quality, correctness

30. Work results, product documentation, WBS, Scope Statement, and the project plan are all _____ of scope verification.

- ❏ A. Tools
- ❏ B. Techniques
- ❏ C. Outputs
- ❏ D. Inputs

31. Specifications and technical documentation are part of _____.

- ❏ A. Product documentation
- ❏ B. Process documentation
- ❏ C. Scope definition
- ❏ D. Formal planning

32. You can determine whether requirements have been met by using _____.

- ❏ A. Templates
- ❏ B. Inspection
- ❏ C. WBS
- ❏ D. Scope Statement

33. The tool that defines the procedures by which project scope may be changed is _____.

- ❏ A. The project plan
- ❏ B. Scope change control
- ❏ C. WBS
- ❏ D. Scope methodology

34. The process that includes managing the actual changes if and when they occur is known as:

- ❏ A. The project plan
- ❏ B. Scope change control
- ❏ C. WBS
- ❏ D. Scope methodology

35. If you change scope in a project to make the final output less than the original baseline, you have _____ the project.

- ❏ A. Rewritten
- ❏ B. Crashed
- ❏ C. Truncated
- ❏ D. Descoped

36. As a project manager, one of your jobs is to determine whether variances between the plan and the actual execution are large enough to take _____.

- ❏ A. Extra time
- ❏ B. Time off
- ❏ C. Corrective action
- ❏ D. A vacation

37. The letters RBS stand for both Resource Breakdown Structure and the _____ Breakdown Structure.

- ❏ A. Ratified
- ❏ B. Real
- ❏ C. Risk
- ❏ D. Random

38. The scope management plan lists _____.

❑ A. Details

❑ B. Processes

❑ C. Definitions

❑ D. Overviews

39. Detailed information about the tasks and components found in the WBS can be stored in a _____.

❑ A. Scope Statement

❑ B. WBS dictionary

❑ C. Scope database

❑ D. Schedule database

Answers from Chapter Nine

1. **The answer is C**. These two types of scope are discussed in the PMBOK. They are on the exam and are helpful to the project manager in differentiating between tasks that he or she must do to be successful on a project. Without either of these scope types, the project is in trouble because what is expected of the project manager and project team is not clearly delineated.

2. **The answer is D**. In order to complete a project, the entire project plan must be executed. It is not simply a matter of working with a Scope Statement. Completion of the project includes everything within the project plan.

3. **The answer is D**.

4. **The answer is C**. It is helpful to know both of these definitions. You will see them on the test. Both scope types must be integrated to ensure successful completion of the project. That means that the product outlined in the product requirements is successfully delivered against the schedule and full project plan.

5. **The answer is C**. This is a part of the scope management knowledge area.

6. **The answer is B**. For the most part, small projects do not include formal authorization of advancement to each phase as a part of the overall scope management of the project.

7. **The answer is A**. Unless you are independently wealthy and enjoy paying for projects you work on, someone has to authorize the project. This someone has to have the authority to release resources to get the project done.

8. **The answer is B**. There are many reasons for authorizing a project. The PMBOK lists several others under section 5.1. Remember that the reasons for authorizing a project are most often market-driven and usually contain the constraints of cost and schedule. For instance, just because there is a market demand for a particular product doesn't mean your organization should authorize a project to plan and build it if the product is not in the organization's strategic plan.

9. **The answer is C**. Do not leave the details for a later date if you can get them early in the planning process. The more clarity you have about the details of the project's product, the better you will be at writing the overall plan. Answer A does not work because you can begin doing various types of planning, such as risk management planning, without knowing the complete details of the product itself.

10. **The answer is D**. Unless this connection is made, the project will almost always be unsuccessful.

11. **The answer is A**. Before an organization engages an outside project manager, a clear product description should be constructed.

12. **The answer is B**. All of the other answers may be important, but for most organizations, the justification of a project has to be done on a financial basis before considering other areas. The only instance where financial considerations are not the top consideration is when regulatory control forces a project to be done in order to comply with the law.

13. **The answer is B**. Benefit measurement measures one project against another and gives the organization information with which to select projects by comparing the benefits of each. Only in the case of a mandated project is there little concern about the benefits derived from the project.

14. **The answer is D**. Although these are important methods only for a limited number of projects, they can be very valuable. You certainly do not have to know how to run these methods for the exam.

15. **The answer is** A. Expert judgment is often the most effective way of dealing with questions concerning choices of projects. Experts should save time for you but will cost something. Use them; they are worth it.

16. **The answer is B**. The project manager should be assigned as early as possible so that control of the project begins immediately. There will be times when a project manager is not assigned until the project has started. Usually this means that someone is actually acting as the project manager but that the title and position are not filled. If you come into a project after it is started, look for as much documentation as you can. It is particularly important to understand the assumptions and constraints that are part of the project. It is also extremely important that you know the business reason for the selection of the project and how the project fits into the priorities of the organization.

17. **The answer is C**. As discussed previously, this document does not always get done. But the areas is it supposed to control are ones that a project manager should view and manage for the project to be successful.

18. **The answer is A**. Although these are also quantitative types of analysis, the answer that is looked for on the exam is financial.

19. **The answer is D**. You are being asked to think of alternative possibilities rather than doing a project as proposed. This is a good exercise if it is controlled. Although at the beginning of brainstorming meetings, any suggestion should be noted and kept, there will be a time when reality sets in and the alternative suggestions must be justified by the person suggesting them.

20. **The answer is B**. Only people trained in the major engineering types of product analysis should attempt to use these techniques to gain a better understanding of the product of the project. These techniques are not easily learned and require a good background in a variety of mathematical analytics. In other words, if you do not understand how to use them, do not even try.

21. **The answer is A**. The Charter is a separate document done before the Scope Statement, but its contents should be a part of the overall Scope Statement.

22. **The answer is C**. The detail is not put directly into the Scope Statement itself. References to where the detail can be found should be in the Scope Statement, not the actual detail itself.

23. **The answer is D**. Deliverables are the mark of a controlled project and as such should be planned early on in the project.

24. **The answer is C**. Take charge of a project by writing down the final deliverable early and you will be much more able to close the project.

25. **The answer is C**. By looking at errors and omissions in previous projects, you may be able to avoid the same mistakes in your current project.

26. **The answer is B**. Decomposition is the word used in the PMBOK to define the breaking down of the WBS.

27. **The answer is D**. If the tasks listed in the WBS are longer than this, it will be very difficult to have control over them.

28. **The answer is C**. Always have these types of results, or else you will not have a good way of measuring whether the task has been done.

29. **The answer is A**. The stakeholders accept what is being done during scope verification, and the correctness of the results is determined during the quality control process.

30. **The answer is D**. These are all inputs into scope verification.

31. **The answer is A**. This question is, once again, an example of a question where there is more than one feasible answer. You need to know the definition according to PMBOK, which makes A the correct answer.

32. **The answer is B**. Inspection tells you whether the requirements have been met or whether there is compliance with other planning documents.

33. **The answer is B**. This procedure defines how project scope can be changed.

34. **The answer here is also B**. Both the tool within the process and the process itself are called the same thing according to the PMBOK.

35. **The answer is D**. When you change the project plan by taking out some parts of the final deliverable, you have descoped the project.

36. **The answer is C**. The project manager is the one who determines whether corrective action is taken. During the planning of the project, it is a good idea to get agreement on how much variance is acceptable. This is particularly true of the sponsor.

37. **The answer is C**. Make sure you know which breakdown is being considered when you see the letters RBS.

38. **The answer is B**. This is the plan that describes the various processes used to manage the scope plan, not the scope plan itself.

39. **The answer is B**. The WBS dictionary is helpful in holding detail about the tasks listed in the WBS.

CHAPTER TEN

Project Time Management

According to the PMBOK, 3rd edition, Project Time Management consists of the "processes required to accomplish timely completion of the project." Although the chapter topic title is time management, this chapter is more about schedule management and the processes necessary to complete and control a working schedule for a project. The process areas listed in the PMBOK are: Activity Definition, Activity Sequencing, Activity Resource Estimating, Activity Duration Estimating, Schedule Development, and Schedule Control.

The document you start with for this whole process is the Scope Statement, discussed in the previous chapter. Because the overall scope of the project is included in the Scope Statement, this document will be your guide for all of the work to be done in the Project Time Management area. Not only the work to be done, but also what is to be left out of the project. Thus, the Scope Statement includes all that is needed to be done to execute the project and ensures that tasks not relevant to the particular project are left out.

Once you have a Scope Statement, you begin to break down the tasks needed to execute the project, and this process is called decomposition. After you have completed breaking down or decomposing the Scope Statement into the Work Breakdown Structure (WBS), you then need to break the WBS into individual work packages so that you can start developing the project schedule. Some people think the project plan is the same thing as the schedule. However, the project plan is much more than just the project schedule. The project plan contains all the management plans and processes used during the execution of the project. So the project plan and the schedule are not the same. In fact, the schedule is only one part of the project plan.

Q. The _____ is the document that starts the entire Project Time Management process.

   ❑ A. Charter   ❑ B. SOW

   ❑ C. RFP   ❑ D. Scope Statement

The answer is D. The Scope Statement is the base for all decisions you make about acquiring and utilizing resources during the execution of the project.

Q. Decomposition of the Scope Statement results in the _____.

   ❑ A. Project plan   ❑ B. WBS

   ❑ C. SOW   ❑ D. Schedule

The answer is B. The WBS is the document that you use to begin the definition of activities you will need to do in order to successfully complete the project.

Q. You break down the WBS into smaller _____ to get detail so that you can construct a schedule.

   ❑ A. Work packages   ❑ B. Time components

   ❑ C. Sections   ❑ D. Issues

The answer is A. The work packages give you the detail you need to construct a schedule.

Activity Definition

The first process in Time Management is activity definition. In executing the process of activity definition, you identify the activities that need to be done to complete the project, and the inputs to do this are: enterprise environmental factors, organizational process assets, the project Scope Statement, the Work Breakdown Structure (WBS), a WBS dictionary, and the overall project management plan.

The organizational process assets, which are listed throughout the PMBOK, are processes that already exist within the organization and that can be used to complete the task at hand. In the case of activity definition, there may be formal planning-related policies and guidelines that will help in developing activity definitions. In some cases, these will be informal processes. If there is help available that has been useful in the past to other project managers, it makes sense to use whatever the organization has that can be a guide for doing tasks on new projects.

In order to identify the activities necessary to complete the project, you may need to do a further breakdown of the WBS into a list of activities that are needed to complete each of the work packages. During this breakdown, you might break a work package into smaller and smaller pieces to create manageable activities. For instance, if you have a task that will take longer than 40 hours, you should break it down so that you can control the activities when they occur during the project. Two major mistakes can be made at this point. The first is not having sufficient information to break down the WBS enough to have a schedule that you can control. The second is the exact opposite, where you have so much detail that you drown in the act of micromanaging the project.

During the initial phase of a project, insufficient project scope for future activities might not allow breakdown of the WBS to detailed work packages. If this occurs, then you will have a planning component as the most detailed level of your WBS. (The planning component is a tool found in the activity definition process.) You leave this planning component in place until you can get sufficient information to create detail. So a planning component is simply a high-level task in the breakdown structure and does not offer detail enough to really flesh out a schedule. In some cases, it is like a placeholder for information to be entered later.

There are two planning components. These are controlling the account and the planning package. Control accounts are management control points of specific components at selected levels of the WBS. These components will be higher-level components and are less detailed than the work package level (PMBOK, p. 129). A planning package can be found under the control account but above the work package. The planning package is used to plan work that is known but about which you do not have enough detail yet to do a schedule. Remember that the work package is going to be your lowest level of breakdown.

Rolling wave planning is a form of progressive elaboration (PMBOK 3rd edition, p. 128). Rolling wave planning is where early activities are detailed and future activities are still at a high level. As an example, a software development project will start off with a detailed plan for Requirements Gathering phase, but other plans, such as testing plans, may not yet have the same amount of detail. Rolling wave simply means that you put in detail as the detail becomes available. It may also be that a particular task is absolutely necessary in order to execute a later task in the project schedule, and so you detail it immediately.

Q. When using decomposition in activity definition, the final output is:

❑ A. Deliverables ❑ B. Work packages

❑ C. Activities or action steps ❑ D. Schedule

The answer is C.

Q. Updates to the WBS during activity definition are often called:

❑ A. Supporting detail ❑ B. Refinements

❑ C. Updates ❑ D. Activities

The answer is B. These refinements tend to occur with riskier projects.

Q. A form of progressive planning is called:

❑ A. Scheduling ❑ B. Charting

❑ C. Expanded trial ❑ D. Rolling wave

The answer is D. As detail becomes known or it is necessary to put in detail in order to progress on the project, you do rolling wave planning.

Q. The major output from activity definition is:

❑ A. The schedule ❑ B. The activity list

❑ C. WBS ❑ D. SOW

The answer is B. The activity list is used for further work on the scheduling aspects of the project. It is the first document to be done in the Project Time Management process.

Q. Other outputs from activity definition are:

❑ A. Activity attributes, milestone lists

❑ B. WBS, SOW

❑ C. Technical requirements and the WBS

❑ D. Activity costs, schedule costs

The answer is A. Activity attributes identify "multiple attributes associated with each schedule activity" (PMBOK, p. 130). Milestone lists record whether or not each milestone is required by the contract (mandatory) or based on project requirements.

Activity Sequencing

Now that we have a list of activities, we need to put them into some sort of logical order, which is called activity sequencing. Many factors influence how you order your activities, such as the product characteristics, dependencies that can be mandatory, discretionary, or external, and milestones that have been agreed upon in activity definition.

Mandatory dependencies are called hard logic. Mandatory dependencies often occur because of physical limitations. An example of this would be in construction, where you must complete the framing before you can hang the drywall. However, in IT, there are fewer of these dependencies than you might think at first glance. Most project managers confuse these mandatory dependencies with discretionary dependencies out of habit. Let's discuss the differences.

Discretionary dependencies are preferred sequence of activities, sometimes called "Best Practices." In Information Technology, most project managers plan to wait until design is complete before starting coding. But in reality, you can start coding about half way through design. Discretionary dependencies are also known as preferred, preferential, or soft logic.

Q. Milestones are:

- ❑ A. Activities with durations
- ❑ B. Significant events in the project life cycle
- ❑ C. Cost measurements
- ❑ D. Denote start and finish of all activities

The answer is B. Milestones are significant events in the project life cycle with zero duration. Milestones show completion of deliverables, phases, and other events you want highlighted. One last dependency to discuss is external dependencies. These are stakeholders' or outside parties' desired sequence of activities (e.g., government, suppliers, etc.).

> **Q. Three types of dependencies are mandatory, discretionary, and _____.**
>
> ❏ A. Easy ❏ B. Planned
>
> ❏ C. Internal ❏ D. External

The answer is D. External dependencies occur because something outside of the project itself causes the need for a task to be done. For instance, a government regulation might require that you report a certain type of information as the first part of a new software package you are writing.

> **Q. How long is the duration for a milestone?**
>
> ❏ A. 0 days ❏ B. 3 days
>
> ❏ C. It depends ❏ D. 5 days

The answer is A. There is no duration for a milestone when you are doing your scheduling.

Network Diagrams

Learning the different network diagram methods is important. These network diagrams will be on the test, and there are several questions concerning this area. The Precedence Diagramming Method (PDM) uses boxes or nodes as activities and arrows as dependencies between the nodes. PDM is also known as Activity On Nodes (AON). Most project management software uses this method (see Figure 10-1). Four different dependency relationship types make up the PDM network:

- Finish-to-start—An activity must finish before the next activity begins.

- Finish-to-finish—An activity must finish before the next activity can finish.

- Start-to-start—An activity must start before the next activity can start.

- Start-to-finish—An activity must start before the next activity can finish.

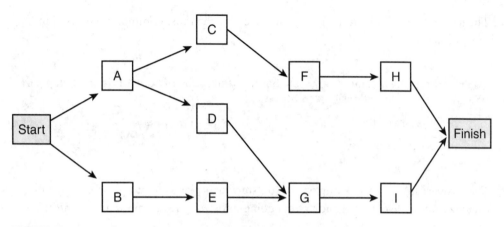

FIGURE 10-1: Precedence Diagramming Method (PDM).

The finish-to-start dependency is the most common one, and it is used in Microsoft Project. An example of this dependency would be having to finish buying paint before you can begin to paint a room. The painting of the room is dependent on purchasing the paint.

The finish-to-finish dependency occurs when one task must be completed before another task can be completed. For instance, you must finish sanding all the walls before you can finish painting all the walls.

The start-to-start dependency means that you must begin a task before another task begins. An example of this dependency would be that you have to start prepping the walls before you can start painting them.

The start-to-finish dependency occurs when something must be started before finishing another task. This dependency often occurs when you are installing a new phone system. You must start the new phone system running before you can finish with the old system. It is very difficult to get a perfect switch, so you need to have redundant activities to make sure you can still have a working phone system.

Q. The type of dependency that is used by Microsoft Project is a _____ dependency.

❑ A. Start-to-finish   ❑ B. End-to-end

❑ C. Finish-to-start   ❑ D. Start-to-end

The answer is C. Finish-to-start dependencies are the most common types used in most projects.

Q. Starting a new computer system before turning the old one off is an example of a _____ dependency.

   ❑ A. Start-to-finish   ❑ B. End-to-end

   ❑ C. Finish-to-start   ❑ D. Natural

The answer is A. In this example, you are starting a new system but protecting your organization by leaving the old system going until you are certain that a comfortable switchover can be made.

Arrow Diagramming Method (ADM) uses arrows as activities, and nodes are used to connect and show dependencies. In other words, the lines in between nodes are where you place the task name. Thus this method is also called Activity On Arrows (AOA). Though it's not used much in the real world, you still need to understand the method. The important concepts are that with the PDM method, dummy activities are used to show complete relationships between tasks, and the fact that ADM uses only finish-to-start dependences.

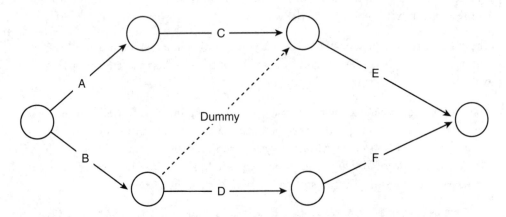

FIGURE 10-2: Arrow Diagramming Method (ADM).

The next methods allow conditional branches (i.e., if–then–else condition) and loops (i.e., an activity repeated more than once). Graphical Evaluation and Review Technique (GERT) and System Dynamics are examples of this method. Conditional branches are not used in PDM and ADM.

Network templates are useful to speed up network diagramming. Parts of standardized templates can be used in building project networks for repeatable or identical parts of the network, such as coding several programs in software development or imitation and closing phases of projects. These are called subnets or fragnets.

> **Q.** **Which network diagramming method uses dummy activities?**
>
> ❑ A. PDM   ❑ B. GERT
>
> ❑ C. PERT   ❑ D. ADM

The answer is D. ADM (Arrow Diagramming Method) or activities on arrows uses dummy activities to correctly show all logical relationships.

> **Q.** **PDM is also known as what?**
>
> ❑ A. Activities on nodes   ❑ B. Activities dependencies
>
> ❑ C. Activities on arrows   ❑ D. Activities sequencing

The answer is A. The names of the activities are placed in the boxes on the diagram that are known as nodes.

> **Q.** **PDM stands for:**
>
> ❑ A. Positive Daily Mechanisms
>
> ❑ B. Process Diagramming Method
>
> ❑ C. Precedence Daily Management
>
> ❑ D. Precedence Diagramming Method

The answer is D. This is the most commonly used method.

> **Q.** **Conditional branches can be found in:**
>
> ❑ A. GERT   ❑ B. PERT
>
> ❑ C. PDM   ❑ D. AON

The answer is A. The graphical evaluation and review technique can show conditional branches that reflect what happens if a certain action is taken.

After finishing activity sequencing, you will have a project network diagram. The PMBOK describes project network diagrams as "schematic displays of the project's activities and the logical relationships (dependencies) among them" (PMBOK, p. 135). Most project managers use computers to draw network diagrams, but network diagrams can also be constructed manually. I like to use sticky note pads in some cases so that I can move the activities around on a board and have a visual sense of the relationships.

Network diagrams can contain one or more summary tasks. PMBOK also calls these summary tasks hammocks, meaning that they span the beginning and end of the tasks somewhat like a hammock. Summary tasks are a high-level compilation of the tasks below them. You might have to add to or subdivide your activity list during sequencing to establish the correct relationships. Network diagrams also assess resources and time requirements and tradeoffs, in addition to facilitating "what if" exercises and highlighting critical activities.

> **Q. A schematic display of the project's activities and the logical relationships among them is a(n) _____.**
>
> ❑ A. Technically difficult process   ❑ B. Working schedule
>
> ❑ C. Project network diagram   ❑ D. Schedule diagram

The answer is C. This is an output from activity sequencing.

> **Q. _____ are a high-level compilation of the tasks below them.**
>
> ❑ A. WBS   ❑ B. Summary tasks
>
> ❑ C. Schedules   ❑ D. PDM

The answer is B. The summary tasks do not show detail of all the tasks below them.

Activity Resource Estimating

Activity resource estimating is the process of defining resources (people, equipment, material) needed for the schedule activities. This includes what, when, and how many resources are needed for the various project activities. The activities attributes are the main input for this information.

Activities attributes, an output of activity definition, are descriptive terms and definitions used to describe codes, predecessors, successors, constraints, person responsible, geographical location, level of effort, lead and lag, imposed dates, assumptions, and so on. Organizational process and environmental factors influence resource estimating by limiting and controlling how you acquire and use resources.

Most project managers will use a combination of techniques to develop the resource estimates. Two of the most used are bottom-up estimating and expert judgment. Bottom-up takes the lowest level of the decomposed WBS and rolls up these tasks to the next level. For example, if you have only two tasks on a lower level that both take two days to complete, the summary task at the next higher level will take four days because it sums the numbers below it. Mature industries may have published estimating data that contains extensive data on all sorts of metrics for capabilities, type of machines, different tools, and so on. Some examples are feet of pipe laid per hour or the standard time it takes to do a brake job for a Ford Taurus. Of course, most project managers use some type of project management software to help with this estimating because it can help organize all the resource inputs.

The resource estimates are useful for identification and documentation of resource requirements used for each activity and any specialized knowledge and level needed. Resource calendars describe resource availability and allocation allowed. Resource Breakdown Structure (RBS) is a hierarchical structure of the identified resource by category and type (PMBOK, p. 138).

Activity Duration Estimating

One of the hardest areas for project managers to accomplish is estimating duration of activities. First, each project is a unique endeavor, so there isn't always a lot of historical information available. Second, estimating is more of an art than a science because it gives you inconsistent results. Let's discuss what PMI considers important for activity duration estimating.

According to PMI, "The Activity Duration Estimating process requires that the amount of work effort required to complete the schedule activity is estimated, the assumed amount of resources to be applied to complete the schedule activity is estimated, and the number of work periods needed to complete the scheduled activity is determined" (PMBOK, p. 139). The person who is most familiar with the tasks or who is going to do the work should provide the estimates or check them because that person will be most qualified to make estimations.

> **Q.** **The project plan is developed by:**
>
> ❏ A. The manager of project managers
>
> ❏ B. Executive management
>
> ❏ C. The project team and manager
>
> ❏ D. Sponsors

The answer is C. We hire people for their expertise; we should let them use it. Allowing the project team to help with duration estimating will build buy-in from the team at the same time. PMBOK refers to this as "expert judgment" (PMBOK, p. 141).

These estimates become better as the project team gains more knowledge of the project requirements. Most project management software allows adjustment to remaining work by the resource assigned to the activity or task. Thus, the project manager can go in the program and change the estimate as the requirements become clearer. This process is referred to as progressively elaborated estimates. Over time, your work estimates should converge with the actual hours used.

> **Q.** **The project schedule is developed in the _____ phase.**
>
> ❏ A. Execution   ❏ B. Initiation
>
> ❏ C. Planning   ❏ D. Conceptual

The answer is C. You then work off this schedule for the rest of the project.

Determining who your resources are or at least what roles and experience you need on your project will influence your duration estimating. For example, an experienced senior coder should take less time than a junior coder to develop a software program. These resource roles are documented in the activity resource requirements from the activity resource estimating process. As we work with resource requirements, we must remember the Law of Diminishing Returns as applied to the efficiency of adding resources to activities in order to reduce the activity duration. For example, if it takes one painter 40 hours to paint a room, then if you add a second painter, it should take 20 hours. However, the efficiency of the two painters is 50% less, according to the Law of Diminishing Returns. More communication is needed, and they might bump into each other, causing lower efficiency. Although some programs allow you to put several people on a task and show that the time needed for the task is reduced, in reality, having too many people on a task will usually cause it to take longer.

The organization that you work with or for may have some organizational assets available to help with your estimating. Estimating databases and other historical data are examples of organizational assets that might be helpful. Remember that these are guidelines, not exact values for all tasks in the new project. Records of previous projects also might be helpful for estimating. It is also important to note if the estimate missed the actual value by a great deal, which may be shown by looking at past records of similar work. At the very least, you will have a project calendar from past schedules of the organization.

When project managers are faced with a similar project but have very few specific requirements, they typically will use top-down or analogous estimating. This process is usually done in the initial phases of the project. It is a form of expert judgment where past experience is used as a basis for estimating a similar new project. Another widely used method is Quantitatively Based Durations or parametric estimating. This method uses some form of parameter measurement to estimate activity durations. For example, the parameter may be lines of code per hour or feet of pipe installed per hour. One additional adjustment to activity duration that most project managers incorporate is a contingency reserve. This is additional time within the schedule of the overall project. This added time, which is based on risk, is called a time reserve or buffer.

Q. **Estimating databases and other historical data are examples of _____ that might be helpful in estimating durations.**

   ❑ A. Records   ❑ B. Organizational assets

   ❑ C. Written data   ❑ D. Electronic information

The answer is B. Organizational process assets are useful if the information contained in the asset is close to the information you will need to successfully plan and execute a new project.

Q. **Top-down estimating is also known as _____ estimating.**

   ❑ A. Organizational   ❑ B. Simple

   ❑ C. Analogous   ❑ D. Primary

The answer is C. Analogous estimating is often used to give the first overview of potential costs and schedule for a project that is similar to a previous one.

Three-Point Estimates, once called Program Evaluation and Review Technique (PERT), is a more mathematical approach to estimating activities and developing the schedule. This method uses a weighted average duration estimate to calculate activity durations. I like to use this to help team members come up with time estimates when brainstorming. These estimates have a built-in risk factor. Let's look at the formula.

Each task has three estimates:

- Pessimistic (P)
- Most Likely (M)
- Optimistic (O)

Mean formula = (P + 4M + O) / 6

Standard deviation formula = (P – O) / 6

Standard Deviation is used to calculate confidence of success:

- 1 Standard deviation = 68%
- 2 Standard deviation = 95%
- 3 Standard deviation = 99.7%
- 6 Standard deviation = 99.9% (This is known as six sig)

Example:

Task A Duration:

- Pessimistic (P) = 35
- Most Likely (M) = 26
- Optimistic (O) = 20

Mean: 35 + (4 × 26) + 20 / 6 = 35 + 104 + 20 / 6 = 159/6 = 26.5

Standard Deviation:

35 – 20 / 6 = 2.5

To be 96% confident of completing this task on time:

26.5 + (2 × 2.5) = 31.5

The final activity estimate should be described in a range of durations, such as days or weeks, or in a percentage. Documentation of the "basis of estimates" or the methods and assumptions used to compute activity estimates should be included in the final activity duration estimates. Don't forget to update any activity changes that result from estimating activity durations.

Q. **Task Z Duration:**
- **Pessimistic (P) = 60**
- **Most Likely (M) = 40**
- **Optimistic (O) = 32**

Given Task Z estimates, calculate the activity duration:

❑ A. 45   ❑ B. 54.5

❑ C. 42   ❑ D. 40

The answer is C. $60 + 4 \times 40 + 32 / 6 = 252 / 6 = 42$.

Schedule Development

Schedule development is the process of determining a project's realistic start and finish dates. This does not mean that the resulting schedule will please the project sponsor, but at least this is the starting point. The schedule development is an iterative process that brings together all the previous steps plus some additional input integrated from the other areas such as cost estimating. Most project managers do the previous steps in time management at the same time as schedule development. The use of project management software, such as Microsoft Project, makes combining steps much easier.

Understanding Lag and Lead is important to schedule development and thus is important for the PMP exam. Lag and Lead fine-tune task dependencies by offsetting or overlapping tasks. Lag is a delay in the schedule that is out of your control or that may simply be part of the nature of the activities. For example, you may have a two-week delay between ordering application servers and installing them because of shipping. Other important factors are resource pools within the organization, personal calendars, and constraints that are already listed as organizational process assets or in the project Scope Statement. Understanding your available resource capabilities and experience will affect the schedule, as will holidays and resource vacation. Imposed dates and key events can limit scheduling flexibility.

The tools and techniques in PMBOK for putting these inputs together to develop the schedule include the Critical Path Method (CPM), schedule compression, what-if scenario analysis, and resource leveling. These tools will be covered on the exam. Let's look at them in detail.

The PMBOK describes CPM as "a method that calculates the theoretical early start and finish dates, and the late start and finish dates, for all schedule activities without regard for any resource limitations" (PMBOK, p. 145).

CPM examines start and finish dates to calculate the activity and dependencies path with the least scheduling flexibility. The Forward Pass Through Network determines Early Start for each activity. Early Start defines the earliest an activity can start based on the defined schedule logic. Backward Pass Through Network determines Late Start for each activity. Late Start defines the latest an activity can start without delaying the project completion date, based on the defined schedule logic.

Forward Pass Through Network Logic: starting with the project start date, this is defined as the Early Start (ES) date for the first network activity.

- For the first activity, ES (project start date) + duration = Early Finish (EF) date of first activity.

- For each subsequent activity, ES + duration of first activity = ES date of subsequent activity.

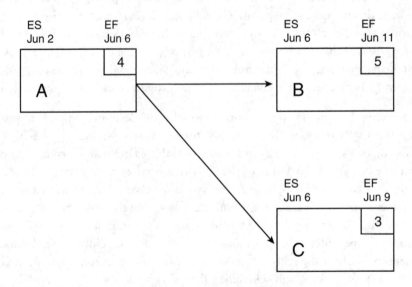

FIGURE 10-3: Forward pass example 1.

When activity has multiple predecessors, the Early Start (ES) of the successor activity is the latest of the Early Finish (EF) dates of the predecessor activities.

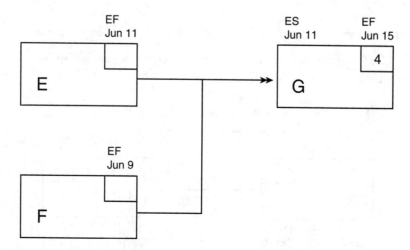

FIGURE 10-4: Forward pass example 2.

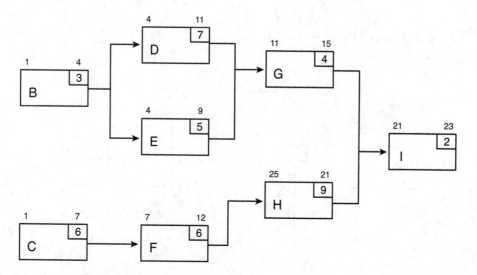

FIGURE 10-5: Forward pass example 3.

Backward Pass Through Network is similar to a Forward Pass. Backward Pass Through Network Logic: starting with the project Late Finish (LF) date from the Forward Pass through Network.

- For the last activity, LF – duration = Late Start (LS) date of last activity.
- For each prior activity, Late Start (LS) of last activity = Late Finish (LF) date of prior activity.

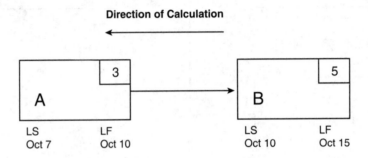

FIGURE 10-6: Backward pass example 1.

When activity has multiple successors, use the earliest Late Start (LS) of the successor activities.

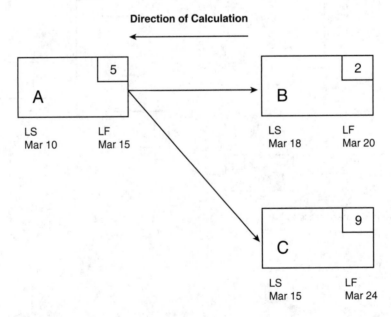

FIGURE 10-7: Backward pass example 2.

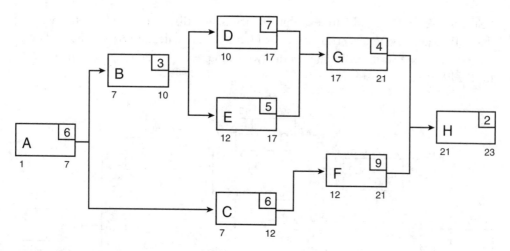

FIGURE 10-8: Backward pass example 3.

For CPM, these passes through the network are used to calculate Float or Slack. Float is defined as:

- Float = Late Finish – Early Finish
- Float = Late Start – Early Start

From this calculation, you can see that you have scheduling flexibility if Float is greater than zero (0). If Float is less than zero (0), then the schedule cannot be met without re-planning. Finally, the Critical Path is defined as the total Float of the activities on the Critical Path equaling zero.

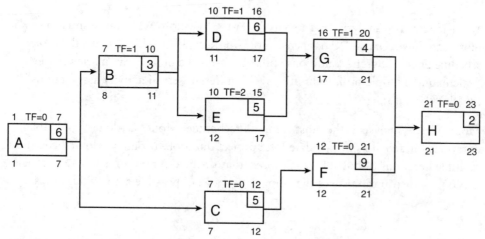

FIGURE 10-9: Critical Path example.

Below is a second Critical Path example, which is slightly more complex. However, the PMP exam has simple, straightforward Critical Path calculations. By recalculating the early and late start/finish dates in the two examples, you can prepare yourself for the PMP exam questions.

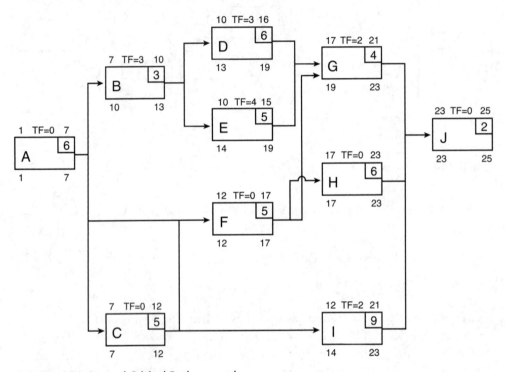

FIGURE 10-10: Second Critical Path example.

What-If Scenario Analysis "is an analysis for the question 'What if the situation represented by scenario 'X' happens?'" (PMBOK, p. 146). This will test the project schedule under different conditions and help assess the impact. Simulation involves "calculating multiple project durations with different sets of activity assumptions" (PMBOK, p. 146).

Monte Carlo Analysis is the most common technique. Monte Carlo uses probable durations for activities to calculate total project duration. Monte Carlo involves doing multiple iterations of possible scenarios so that the final output of a Monte Carlo simulation is a distribution curve that shows the range of possible activity durations.

Q. Which technique below is the most common simulation technique?

❏ A. GERT

❏ B. Monte Carlo

❏ C. Linear Analysis

❏ D. Decompression

The answer is B.

Resource Leveling is another tool in schedule development. Resource Leveling removes the peaks and valleys of resource allocation. This technique also examines resource over-allocation and critical resource allocation. This technique lets the schedule and cost slip. Leveling Heuristics are rules of thumb and are often used to level or allocate resources. Some examples of Leveling Heuristics are the 80/20 rule and the assigning of critical resources first to Critical Path activities.

It is possible to extend working hours and work on weekends to reduce critical duration. However, planning overtime before the start of the project removes the most effective project management tool available to pull the schedule back when those unknowns surface. You should also be careful to consider tiring the project team. It is possible to do extra work for a short period of time, but after that, the work quality level will go down, and the team will be put under great stress. Long durations of stress are certain to cause problems on the project.

Q. Rules of thumb are known as _____.

❏ A. Leveling Heuristics

❏ B. Common sense

❏ C. Problem solvers

❏ D. Monte Carlo Analysis

The answer is A. These are rules that occur naturally and can sometimes be used to level resources on a project schedule.

Q. Monte Carlo simulation is done using _____ scenarios.

❏ A. Simple

❏ B. Technical

❏ C. Common

❏ D. Multiple

The answer is D. By using multiple scenarios, the Monte Carlo simulation technique shows a range of possible events.

Productivity measures, such as using different technologies and machinery, can also shorten duration with increases in resource's productivity. Project Management Software can produce an optimal project schedule by addressing Critical Path activities with resource allocation. "This technique is sometimes called the resource-based method" (PMBOK, p. 147).

A relatively new technique is the Critical Chain Method. Critical Chain combines calculating Critical Path and applying resource availability. The Critical Chain Method adds duration buffers throughout the schedule instead of at one point in the schedule.

Schedule Compression is used to shorten the schedule. The two main techniques are Crashing and Fast Tracking. Crashing involves adding more resources to the Critical Path activities to shorten these activities' durations. Although Crashing may save time, it almost always results in increased costs. Doing more activities in parallel is Fast Tracking. This often results in rework and usually increases risk. Many project managers will shorten the schedule by arbitrarily reducing every task by 20%. This is not an appropriate project management technique, so expect it as an answer on the exam. Why, you ask? It is more effective to shorten tasks on the Critical Path. It is best to see all the alternatives before selecting the one with the least impact.

Q. **What tasks would you Fast Track to shorten the project duration in the Critical Path in Figure 10-9?**

☐ A. E & G ☐ B. B, D, & E

☐ C. C & F ☐ D. C & G

The answer is C. By Fast Tracking on the Critical Path, you compress the longest path and gain duration.

Q. **Doing more activities in parallel is called _____.**

☐ A. Fast Tracking ☐ B. Schedule clearing

☐ C. Compressed work ☐ D. Planning compression

The answer is A. Be aware that doing Fast Tracking may save some time but almost always results in rework, which may negate the time savings.

The output of schedule development is the project schedule. The project schedule can be displayed in different ways, such as Bar (Gantt) Charts, Network Diagrams (CPM & PDM), and Milestone Charts. Let's look at the differences and when to use each:

Bar Charts

- Good to show progress and controlling tool
- Does not display task dependencies
- Does not help with project organization

Network Diagram

- Displays task dependencies
- Effective in planning and organizing the work
- Provides for project control

Milestone Charts

- Displays major events (e.g., software coding completed)
- Used for management and customer reporting

Schedule supporting data is developed and updated. This documentation includes but is not limited to activity attributes, assumptions and constraints, and resource requirements. The approved project schedule from the alternatives available is called the schedule baseline.

Q. Bar charts do not show _____.
- ❑ A. Time constraints
- ❑ B. Dependencies
- ❑ C. Partial tasks
- ❑ D. All of the above

The answer is D. Bar charts show progress and are useful tools, but they do not show any of the answers listed above.

Schedule Control

Schedule Control involves understanding what influences a schedule change, knowing that the schedule has changed, and managing schedule changes, and it is "a portion of the Integrated Change Control process" (PMBOK, p. 152). After the project schedule has been approved, the project manager can baseline the schedule, which results in the "schedule baseline." This sets the performance measurement for the project. As execution begins, this is what you are measured against.

The approved project schedule must be technically realistic and realistic in terms of resources. I know as an experienced project manager that you are usually given a due date you must meet. Your job is to come up with alternative schedules to meet this deadline but also to explain the risks involved with meeting an aggressive due date. Your sponsor then will approve the schedule with the risk threshold that he or she can handle.

> **Q. The approved project schedule is called the:**
> - A. Sponsored schedule
> - B. Performance schedule
> - C. Baseline schedule
> - D. Approved schedule

The answer is C.

During project execution, you will post progress to the project schedule, and your performance reporting will show variance. As you know, no project runs exactly according to the baseline schedule. Your project management software is helpful to quickly identify variances of dates, work, or costs.

The way you decide how to handle variances is called variances analysis. If you see variances between what was expected and the actual results, then you need to decide whether corrective action is necessary. You should pay attention to critical and sub-critical tasks first when examining variances. Corrective actions could include additional planning to revise duration estimates, activity dependencies, and maybe alternative schedules.

Other changes might come from change requests, which can be both internal and external. Your schedule change control system should determine how you will identify, analyze, and approve these changes. The schedule change control system may already be a part of your organizational process assets, and it should certainly be a part of your overall project change control system.

After you gather these data on project progress variances, the variances may make it necessary to do schedule updates or corrective actions. Corrective actions are anything done to bring expected future schedule performance in line with the project plan (PMBOK, p. 155). To put it another way, corrective actions are anything done to meet the current finish date. Overtime, Fast Tracking and Crashing are examples of time management corrective actions.

Updates or modifications to project schedule information are schedule updates. Scope changes or changes to estimates usually require a special type of schedule update called *revisions*. Revisions are changes to the schedule start and finish dates in the approved project schedule (PMBOK, p. 155). The project sponsor must approve all schedule updates.

Q. Anything done to bring expected future schedule performance in line with the project plan is known as _____.

☐ A. Replanning   ☐ B. Schedule arrangement

☐ C. Corrective actions   ☐ D. Rebaselining

The answer is C. Fast Tracking and Crashing are examples of corrective actions that can be taken.

Q. If you update the schedule, the updates must be approved by the _____.

☐ A. Project manager   ☐ B. Project team

☐ C. Line management   ☐ D. Sponsor

The answer is D. The sponsor must be told that schedule changes have occurred as soon as they occur.

When schedule changes or variances happen, some project managers want to *rebaseline* the project schedule. This will certainly make the project look good, but rebaselining should only occur if the variances are so severe that the current performance measurements (baselines) make no sense. Variances are not evil by themselves. They serve a purpose of identifying areas that need improvement in similar and maybe all future projects. When a project is rebaselined, all historical data is lost, making it impossible to note in the lessons learned why this variance happened. In the lessons learned documentation, you explain not only variances but also corrective actions and other schedule control updates.

> **Q.** Revisions are a special type of schedule updates that make changes to:
>
> ☐ A. Costs ☐ B. Resources
>
> ☐ C. Same as Fast Tracking ☐ D. Start/Finish Dates

The answer is D.

> **Q.** Rebaselining should occur only if the current baselines _____.
>
> ☐ A. Are off by 10% ☐ B. Are off by 20%
>
> ☐ C. Make no sense ☐ D. Are bad

The answer is C. You should rebaseline only if the actual project progress has little to do with the original baseline.

Questions from Chapter Ten   ?

1. The _____ is the document that starts the entire Project Time Management process.

- ❑ A. Charter
- ❑ B. SOW
- ❑ C. RFP
- ❑ D. Scope Statement

2. Decomposition of the Scope Statement results in the _____.

- ❑ A. Project plan
- ❑ B. WBS
- ❑ C. SOW
- ❑ D. Schedule

3. You break down the WBS into smaller _____ to get detail so that you can construct a schedule.

- ❑ A. Work packages
- ❑ B. Time components
- ❑ C. Sections
- ❑ D. Issues

4. When using decomposition in activity definition, the final output is:

- ❑ A. Deliverables
- ❑ B. Work packages
- ❑ C. Activities or action steps
- ❑ D. Schedule

5. Updates to the WBS during activity definition are often called:

- ❑ A. Supporting detail
- ❑ B. Refinements
- ❑ C. Updates
- ❑ D. Activities

6. A form of progressive planning is called:

- ❑ A. Scheduling
- ❑ B. Charting
- ❑ C. Expanded trial
- ❑ D. Rolling wave

7. The major output from activity definition is:

- ❑ A. The schedule
- ❑ B. The activity list
- ❑ C. WBS
- ❑ D. SOW

8. Other outputs from activity definition are:

❑ A. Activity attributes, Milestone lists

❑ B. WBS, SOW

❑ C. Technical requirements, and the WBS

❑ D. Activity costs, schedule costs

9. Milestones are:

❑ A. Activities with durations

❑ B. Significant events in the project life cycle

❑ C. Cost measurements

❑ D. Denote start and finish of all activities

10. Three types of dependencies are mandatory, discretionary, and _____.

❑ A. Easy

❑ B. Planned

❑ C. Internal

❑ D. External

11. How long is the duration for a milestone?

❑ A. 0 days

❑ B. 3 days

❑ C. It depends

❑ D. 5 days

12. The type of dependency that is used by Microsoft Project is a _____ dependency.

❑ A. Start-to-finish

❑ B. End-to-end

❑ C. Finish-to-start

❑ D. Start-to-end

13. Starting a new computer system before turning the old one off is an example of a(n) _____ dependency.

❑ A. Start-to-finish

❑ B. End-to-end

❑ C. Finish-to-start

❑ D. Natural

14. Which Network Diagramming Method uses dummy activities?

❑ A. PDM

❑ B. GERT

❑ C. PERT

❑ D. ADM

15. **PDM is also known as what?**

- ❏ A. Activities on nodes
- ❏ B. Activities dependencies
- ❏ C. Activities on arrows
- ❏ D. Activities sequencing

16. **PDM stands for:**

- ❏ A. Positive Daily Mechanisms
- ❏ B. Process Diagramming Method
- ❏ C. Precedence Daily Management
- ❏ D. Precedence Diagramming Method

17. **Conditional branches can be found in:**

- ❏ A. GERT
- ❏ B. PERT
- ❏ C. PDM
- ❏ D. AON

18. **A schematic display of the project's activities and the logical relationships among them is a(n) _____.**

- ❏ A. Technically difficult process
- ❏ B. Working Schedule
- ❏ C. Project network diagram
- ❏ D. Schedule diagram

19. **_____ are a high-level compilation of the tasks below them.**

- ❏ A. WBS
- ❏ B. Summary tasks
- ❏ C. Schedules
- ❏ D. PDM

20. **The project plan is developed by:**

- ❏ A. The manager of project managers
- ❏ B. Executive management
- ❏ C. The project team and manager
- ❏ D. Sponsors

21. **The project schedule is developed in the _____ phase.**

- ❏ A. Execution
- ❏ B. Initiation
- ❏ C. Planning
- ❏ D. Conceptual

22. **Estimating databases and other historical data are examples of _____ that might be helpful in estimating durations.**

- ❏ A. Records
- ❏ B. Organizational assets
- ❏ C. Written data
- ❏ D. Electronic information

23. Top-down estimating is also known as _____ estimating.

- ❑ A. Organizational
- ❑ B. Simple
- ❑ C. Analogous
- ❑ D. Primary

24. Which technique below is the most common simulation technique?

- ❑ A. GERT
- ❑ B. Monte Carlo
- ❑ C. Linear Analysis
- ❑ D. Decompression

25. Rules of thumb are known as _____.

- ❑ A. Leveling Heuristics
- ❑ B. Common sense
- ❑ C. Problem solvers
- ❑ D. Monte Carlo analysis

26. Monte Carlo simulation is done using _____ scenarios.

- ❑ A. Simple
- ❑ B. Technical
- ❑ C. Common
- ❑ D. Multiple

27. What tasks would you Fast Track to shorten the project duration in the Critical Path in Figure 10-9?

- ❑ A. E & G
- ❑ B. B, D, & E
- ❑ C. C & F
- ❑ D. C & G

28. Doing more activities in parallel is called _____.

- ❑ A. Fast Tracking
- ❑ B. Schedule clearing
- ❑ C. Compressed work
- ❑ D. Planning compression

29. Bar charts do not show _____.

- ❑ A. Time constraints
- ❑ B. Dependencies
- ❑ C. Partial tasks
- ❑ D. All of the above

30. The approved project schedule is called the:

- ❑ A. Sponsored schedule
- ❑ B. Performance schedule
- ❑ C. Baseline schedule
- ❑ D. Approved schedule

31. **Anything done to bring expected future schedule performance in line with the project plan is known as _____.**

- ❑ A. Replanning
- ❑ B. Schedule arrangement
- ❑ C. Corrective actions
- ❑ D. Rebaselining

32. **If you update the schedule, the updates must be approved by the _____.**

- ❑ A. Project manager
- ❑ B. Project Team
- ❑ C. Line management
- ❑ D. Sponsor

33. **Revisions are a special type of schedule updates that make changes to:**

- ❑ A. Costs
- ❑ B. Resources
- ❑ C. Same as Fast Tracking
- ❑ D. Start/Finish Dates

34. **Rebaselining should occur only if the current baselines _____.**

- ❑ A. Are off by 10%
- ❑ B. Are off by 20%
- ❑ C. Make no sense
- ❑ D. Are bad

Answers from Chapter Ten

1. **The answer is D**. The Scope Statement is the base for all decisions you make about acquiring and utilizing resources during the execution of the project.

2. **The answer is B**. The WBS is the document that you use to begin the definition of activities that you will need to do in order to successfully complete the project.

3. **The answer is A**. The work packages give you the detail you need to construct a schedule.

4. **The answer is C**. Many companies have a collection of templates that contain historical information about a previous project. Templates can help you get started with your activities list, especially with historical information about similar projects.

5. **The answer is B**. These refinements tend to occur with riskier projects.

6. **The answer is D**. Rolling wave planning is done when new detail is available or you must put in detail in order to progress on the project..

7. **The answer is B**. The activity list is what is used for further work on the scheduling aspects of the project. It is the first document to be done in the Project Time Management process.

8. **The answer is A**. Activity attributes identify "multiple attributes associated with each schedule activity" (PMBOK, p. 130). Milestone lists record whether the milestone is required by the contract (mandatory) or based on project requirements.

9. **The answer is B**. Milestones are significant events in the project life cycle with zero duration. Milestones show completion of deliverables, phases, and other events you want highlighted.

10. **The answer is D**. External dependencies occur because something outside of the project itself causes the need for a task to be done. For instance, a government regulation requires that you report a certain type of information as the first part of a new software package you are writing.

11. **The answer is A**. There is no duration for a milestone when you are doing your scheduling.

12. **The answer is C**. Finish-to-start dependencies are the most common types used in most projects.

13. **The answer is A**. In this example, you are starting a new system but protecting your organization by leaving the old system going until you are certain that a comfortable switchover can be made.

14. **The answer is D**. ADM (Arrow Diagramming Method) or activities on arrows uses dummy activities to correctly show all logical relationships.

15. **The answer is A**. The names of the activities are placed in the boxes on the diagram that are known as nodes.

16. **The answer is D**. This is the most commonly used method.

17. **The answer is A**. The graphical evaluation and review technique can show conditional branches that reflect what happens if a certain action is taken.

18. **The answer is C**. This is an output from activity sequencing.

19. **The answer is B**. The summary tasks do not show the details of all the tasks below them.

20. **The answer is C**. We hire people for their expertise; we should let them use it. Allowing the project team to help with duration estimating will build buy-in from the team at the same time. PMBOK refers to this as "expert judgment" (PMBOK, p. 141).

21. **The answer is C**. You then work off this schedule for the rest of the project.

22. **The answer is B**. Organizational process assets are useful if the information contained in the assets is close to the information you will need to successfully plan and execute a new project.

23. **The answer is C**. Analogous estimating is often used to give the first overview of potential costs and schedule for a project that is similar to a previous one.

24. **The answer is B**.

25. **The answer is A**. These are rules that occur naturally and that can sometimes be used to level resources on a project schedule.

26. **The answer is D**. By using multiple scenarios, the Monte Carlo simulation technique shows a range of possible events.

27. **The answer is C**. By Fast Tracking on Critical Path, you compress the longest path and gain duration.

28. **The answer is A**. Be aware that doing Fast Tracking may save some time but almost always results in rework that may negate the time savings.

29. **The answer is D**. Bar charts show progress and are useful tools, but they do not show any of the answers listed here.

30. **The answer is C**.

31. **The answer is C**. Fast Tracking and Crashing are examples of corrective actions that can be taken.

32. **The answer is D.** The sponsor must be told that schedule changes have occurred as soon as they do occur.

33. **The answer is D.**

34. **The answer is C.** You should rebaseline only if the actual project progress has little to do with the original baseline.

CHAPTER ELEVEN

Project Cost Management

The PMBOK describes project cost management as "the processes involved in planning, estimating, budgeting, and controlling costs so that the project can be completed within the approved budget." As one of the triple constraints, cost is often the single most important indicator for the sponsor. (The triple constraints are cost, time, and quality.) When beginning a project, it is always a good idea to understand the mindset of the sponsor. The sponsor is likely to value one of the triple constraints more than another, and often cost will be the most important of the three constraints. If cost is the most important constraint for the sponsor, you should be sure to give status reports that show how close you are to the budget; keeping the sponsor informed of his/her major concern is important for the success of any project.

There are also times when you have little or no control over the cost of the project, such as when you are an internal project manager and all the resource costs are supplied and monitored by the organization in which you work. You do not have a great deal of control over whom you use on the project or the wages they are paid if you are working within an organization.

The opposite of this is the contracted project manager who comes from an outside organization to run a project. In this case, the project manager will be expected to run the budget that he or she has been given by the contracted organization. There are cases where you will bring your project team with you, which gives you a good mechanism for controlling your costs. There are also situations where you come in as a project manager to manage a specific project and use resources from the contracting organization. This does not happen often, but it is possible. In any case, knowing how to establish a baseline for costs is an important factor in project management success. The PMBOK shows three processes through which you need to go in order to establish your budget.

> **Q.   Cost, time, and quality are known as:**
>
> ❑   A.   Triple constraints   ❑   B.   Three chapters of PMBOK
>
> ❑   C.   Tactical measurements   ❑   D.   Project indicators

The answer is A. Although these are also three chapter headings in PMBOK, they are known together as the triple constraints.

The three processes in Project Cost Management are Cost Estimating, Cost Budgeting, and Cost Control. In each process, it is important to construct a realistic budget. As with all of the knowledge areas, the various processes overlap and interact during the project. They should not be thought of as discrete processes without interaction with the others.

Life cycle costing and value engineering techniques are ways of looking at projects that are not included in the three processes mentioned earlier. The life cycle costing techniques look at a broad overview of the project rather than the narrower views that are shown in the four processes of this knowledge area. There are trades that can be made in the cost of the project, which are done in life cycle costing. For instance, if you decide not to run tests on every iteration of an IT project, you will cut the cost of the project. However, that cost may be shifted to the customer because the product of the project may not perform as anticipated. Life cycle can also look at costs that occur after the project has been completed. Costs can be incurred or left out of the project that will affect the maintenance phase of the project. Quality issues such as testing may be included in this life cycle analysis. In this case, the customer may require that you do rework to handle any omissions that happen because of lack of complete testing. But this example shows how life cycle costing is a broader consideration in project cost management than those we are about to explore.

Value engineering techniques are done to give the project manager the best possible engineering tasks to reduce cost during the project, to improve the quality of the work as well as the final performance of the project's product, and to optimize decision making. Value engineering is also called value analysis or value management.

> **Q.   Looking at a broad overview of the project costs is known as:**
>
> ❑   A.   Auditing   ❑   B.   Life cycle engineering
>
> ❑   C.   Life cycle costing   ❑   D.   Value engineering

The answer is C. Life cycle costing looks at the entire project and is a technique that helps determine the most cost-effective ways of managing the project.

Q. **Value analysis and value management are other names for:**

❑ A. Profitability

❑ B. Life cycle management

❑ C. Life cycle costing

❑ D. Value engineering

The answer is D. The planning of engineering tasks to reduce cost, improve quality, and maximize product performance is value engineering. Value engineering also helps to give clear data from which good decisions can be made.

As we look at the three processes in depth, keep in mind that you need some basic understanding of general management cost evaluation techniques such as ROI, discounted cash flow, and others for the exam. These will be discussed later in this chapter. Although it is not the purpose of the PMP certification to make you a CPA, the various cost techniques are useful to know because sponsoring organizations use these techniques to help decide whether to go forward with projects. The general management cost techniques are also helpful because they provide potential results against which a project manager can manage. Get to know them, and they will be helpful on more than just the examination.

Q. **ROI and discounted cash flow are two examples of:**

❑ A. General management cost evaluation

❑ B. Value management cost techniques

❑ C. Project management cost evaluation

❑ D. General cost techniques

The answer is A. Various techniques are used in general management to make decisions about the use of capital; these are two of them.

Another factor that a project manager should consider in project cost management is the concept of direct and indirect costs. If you are being rewarded for bringing the budget under control, you need to know which costs you have control over and which costs are not within your control. Costs that result from the execution of the project are called direct costs. These costs are directly related to the project being run. For instance, any hardware that is specifically used for the project is a direct cost to the project because money would not be spent on the hardware if the project were not being done. As you are doing your budgeting for the project, be aware of the costs that will be directly linked to the execution of the project. This is particularly important if you are being compensated based on your ability to finish the project within budget. You can control direct costs in most cases; you cannot control indirect costs, so your compensation should be linked only to direct costs.

The indirect costs on a project are costs that would occur whether the project was being done or not. For instance, you are not responsible for the electricity bills if you are doing the project in your organization's facilities. You have no control over these (other than making sure you turn out the lights at night), but it is a cost to the company. Heating is another example. The heating of the building is not something that occurs because of a specific project. It is an indirect cost because it is not linked directly to the project. The project manager has no control over indirect costs and should not be rewarded or penalized because of these costs.

> **Q. Heating and electricity are examples of _____ costs.**
>
> ❏ A. Strategic ❏ B. Tactical
>
> ❏ C. Direct ❏ D. Indirect

The answer is D. The costs of heating are not controllable by the project manager and do not occur because the project is being executed. This makes them indirect costs.

> **Q. The project manager can have control over _____ costs.**
>
> ❏ A. Strategic ❏ B. Tactical
>
> ❏ C. Direct ❏ D. Indirect

The answer is C. Costs that are directly incurred because the project is being executed are directs costs. In some cases the project manager has control over the costs, and in some cases the organization itself will control the costs. In any case, the costs occur only when the project is going on.

The processes that we are about to discuss may overlap on smaller projects. Cost estimating and cost budgeting are very closely linked and for some projects may be seen as a single process. PMBOK presents them as separate processes so that all of the inputs, tools and techniques, and outputs of each breakdown can be seen and managed.

The control of costs is made easier when early planning is done well. All of the major documents such as a requirements document will give the project manager a clearer look at the potential costs of the project. A good scope definition and WBS are critical components in controlling costs because they show the overall scope of the project as well as the tasks that need to be done to complete the project.

> **Q.** **Cost control is easiest to do _____ the project.**
>
> ❑ A. Early in ❑ B. Late in
>
> ❑ C. In the middle of ❑ D. After

The answer is A. The earlier you have good plans from which to work, the easier it is to control your costs and perform good cost planning. If there is no clarity about the work to be done, there will be no clarity about the costs to be incurred.

Resource Planning

This topic is not in the project cost management section of the 3rd edition of the PMBOK, but it is still a very important factor in determining the costs of the project. This process is closely linked to both cost estimating and cost budgeting.

Remember that in many organizations, resources may be assigned to several projects at once, particularly if they are specialty resources. In the case of multiple assignments, it is absolutely critical for costing that detail is given in the WBS that will allow a project manager to correctly budget for the resources needed. If the task time is too large, this is not possible, and rather than estimating, you will be guessing.

> **Q.** **The _____ gives the detail you need to correctly estimate costs for the project.**
>
> ❑ A. Scope Statement ❑ B. Project Charter
>
> ❑ C. SOW ❑ D. WBS

The answer is D. This is the document where the Scope Statement is decomposed, and it will give you the task detail necessary to make resource planning possible.

> **Q.** **In the WBS, _____ hours is the suggested longest task duration.**
>
> ☐ A. 20 ☐ B. 8
>
> ☐ C. 40 ☐ D. 60

The answer is C. If you have a task that will take longer than this, it is very difficult to assess resources needed to execute the task. You can certainly have tasks that are shorter than this; they will be useful for many of the resource planning activities. But you will not be able to plan well if a given task is over 40 hours in length. There are too many unknowns in a task over 40 hours to do good resource planning.

Historical information in the resource planning process has the same caveats as it does in all the other processes. You can look at previous projects to determine what resource needs occurred, but you must be careful to examine each piece of information as it relates to the current project. Because all projects are unique, it is possible to have resource information that is correct for previous projects but just slightly off for the current one. However, if historical information is available, particularly if you can talk to the previous project's manager and he or she is a PMP, you will get a great deal of valuable information that can help you in your current planning.

One other word of caution: It is highly likely that you will not have exactly the same personnel from project to project. By changing personnel, you will change the dynamics on the project team. The new resources may work differently or have skills that were not available from your previous team. Certainly new resources will change the amount of time you need to complete tasks.

You should also evaluate the skill level and work output level of your current team for each project. This is particularly true when using historical data as a part of the inputs to your planning process. These data are a guideline, not a finished blueprint. People make the difference on the project team's performance, and so does the project manager. The time it takes a team to do a task will vary when other people are added to the team. The timeline may increase or decrease. Whatever occurs, change in personnel means change in resource utilization.

> **Q. Historical information is a _____, not a _____.**
>
> ☐ A. Nuisance, fact ☐ B. Guideline, blueprint
>
> ☐ C. Fact, guess ☐ D. Panacea, problem

The answer is B. Historical information will not be the exact blueprint you need for your current project. People change, technologies change, situations change. All of these factors mean that although you can look at historical information as a guide, do not use it as your plan.

Q. **Historical information can be used as a guide, not as a blueprint because each project is _____.**

  ❑ A. Tactical   ❑ B. Important

  ❑ C. Unique   ❑ D. Planned

The answer is C. The basic definition of a project includes the fact that each project is unique. Something (often many things) is always different between projects, so do not accept historical information as your final plan. It can guide you, but historical information should not be the only data you look at to do your planning.

The Scope Statement is another input to resource planning. As with all the documents in the inputs to resource planning, the more clarity you have in the Scope Statement, the better the chance that you will effectively allocate resources to tasks. If the Scope Statement is unclear in any way, you will be unable to give accurate estimates of the resource needs for the project.

The Scope Statement also contains the justification for the project as well as the project objectives. The justification for the project will generally give you clues as to the importance of the project to the organization. For instance, if you are managing a project that must be finished to avoid a government fine of $500K per day, you will most certainly be able to access all of the resources you need to finish the project with all due haste. If, on the other hand, your project is to change email servers, there will not be the same urgency, and you are not nearly as likely to get all the resources you want or need with as much speed as a project that will cost the company millions of dollars per month if neglected. So, be aware of the justification as you go through your resource planning and make sure that reality is a large part of planning.

The resource pool description is a very important part of the inputs to resource planning. The equipment you have available will determine how long your project will take. So too will the people you can engage to execute the project. The resource pool description can vary greatly from organization to organization. In some organizations, the description of a worker may simply say "coder," whereas in others, a full description of what languages the coder is competent in and how much experience the coder has had on similar projects may be available.

There may be code words for certain organizations in the resource pool description that you will need to know in order to make choices about whom you want to be on your project. The words "senior" and "junior" when used as modifiers for any position give information that is specific to the organization in which you are working. For instance, how long does it take a "senior" coder to write a module of code? Can two "junior" coders do the same work in the same time as one "senior" coder? You'll have to answer these types of questions when looking at a resource pool.

It should be noted that in many cases, looking at a resource pool is a luxury. Very few organizations can offer unlimited resources to the project manager; this usually happens only if neglecting the project may cause a failure of the organization. Your decision as a project manager deals with the resources you are given and the best way to help them execute the plan. If you can pick and choose from a large list, you can be assured that your project will be under close scrutiny because for most organizations, resources are a major constraint. If the project is important enough to the organization to allow the project manager to choose anyone he or she wants, be aware that you will be watched very, very closely.

Q. Equipment, materials, and people are three types of choices in _____.

  ❑ A. Scope Statements   ❑ B. WBS

  ❑ C. SOW   ❑ D. Resource pool description

The answer is D. All three of these elements are choices you will have to make to successfully plan the project.

Q. _____ of resources play(s) an important part in how you choose people and materials for your project.

  ❑ A. Descriptions   ❑ B. Firing

  ❑ C. Cost   ❑ D. Quality

The answer is A. If you receive a list of resources, be sure you understand what they are and that you have a description in your mind that matches the description of the organization giving you the resource pool. For instance, the words "heavy duty" may mean different things to different organizations. Asking what the words mean, especially if the words are descriptors, is something you should do for your own project.

Organizational policies will also affect your resource planning. You need to know whether outsourcing is permitted and if so, what organizations or countries you are permitted to outsource to. You might have to consider whether the organization wants to buy new equipment or to lease or rent it. You may have to consider whether the organization wants to put people on its own payroll or always have contractors working with them. The organization may have assembled a list of preferred vendors. Someone, perhaps many people, in the organization will set all of these policies, and you should consider these policies when you are doing resource planning.

Q. Determining whether you should choose to do a task in house or to outsource it is an example of a(n) _____.

❑ A. Tactical decision ❑ B. Strategic decision

❑ C. Management decision ❑ D. Organizational policy

The answer is D. The organization will often have policies that are used to determine how resources are selected. As a professional project manager, you should make every effort to be aware of any organizational policies that will affect your resource planning.

Finally, you will look at activity durations in resource planning. The major key to doing these is that you often trade skills, efficiency, and time for cost. If you choose to get more expensive, faster equipment, you are deciding that time is more valuable than cost. The same is true with people. The more skilled the people, the higher the cost is to use them on your project. However, if you are up against a looming deadline, changing the input into the task can change activity durations. (Activity durations are also discussed in the previous chapter.)

Q. When you are choosing a certain level of skills or mechanical efficiency, you are trading _____ for time.

❑ A. Cost ❑ B. Quality

❑ C. People ❑ D. Ideas

The answer is A. The triple constraints of cost, quality, and time are always in play in a project. You must choose between the three constantly as you go through resource planning. You will probably not be the final arbiter of who to use or what equipment to use on the project because those choices will be made in organizational meetings leading to organizational policy. You should know that there are tradeoffs to be made between the triple constraints, and you should give good information to sponsors and stakeholders about your decisions in choosing resources.

Another source for expert judgment is professional and technical associations. These can be excellent sources for your planning. Many associations keep databases on average costs for their members. This information is extremely valuable and gives you a large amount of data from which to work. One thing to note if you are using a database from an association: If the data to be used are averages, you should consider how many cases the association used to get these numbers. If, for instance, the association was only able to get a few organizations to respond to questionnaires concerning costs, then the data may be skewed. It is valuable to know how many organizations were surveyed in order to determine how accurate the data are. The larger the number of organizations included in the survey, generally the better the numbers are. One large company in an expensive city can change the average costs for resources, so be certain of how the numbers were reached and then use them to help you in your resource planning.

One other type of organization that can give you expert judgment is industry groups. These are often very useful and can give you good information about the industry as a whole. Once again, note who the members are. The groups that include organizations like yours will give you the best information.

Q. To determine the final number of resources needed for a large task, you _____ the _____ levels in the WBS to get the next higher level.

❑ A. Sum, lower ❑ B. Divide, average

❑ C. Multiply, higher ❑ D. Sum, higher

The answer is A. You sum up the lower levels of the WBS to get the final number for the resources needed in the summary task at the top.

Cost Estimating

This process is directly related to resource planning. One cannot be done without the other. Cost estimating involves "developing an approximation of the costs of the resources needed to complete each schedule activity" (PMBOK). Developing an approximation (estimate) is both a skill and an art. An estimate is a rough determination. It is not intended as a final usable number but rather is used to forecast, within certain parameters, what the actual number may be.

Estimating classes often begin with the instructor asking someone in the class how long it will take to go from the classroom to a place downtown. When this is asked, almost everyone in the room will be very accurate with their estimate because they are familiar with the mileage and routes. The next estimate required is between the classroom and Phoenix, Arizona. Unless someone in the class is familiar with that trip, it is likely that the estimates will be much rougher because the people giving the estimate will be less sure of the amount of time the trip takes.

In the first case, because of the students' familiarity with the trip, their estimates were accurate. Although they were still estimates, the estimates were based on commonly known facts. In the second case, the students knew where Phoenix was but did not have the experience of traveling to it from the current location, so their estimates were not as accurate as those given for the first trip.

In all estimating, it is best to find people or documents that can give actual numbers instead of guessing what the correct number is. In cost estimating, it is important that you find some estimating tools, documents, or expert judgment that will make the estimate the closest it can possibly be to the actual cost.

Three types of estimates are listed in the PMBOK. Each has a range of accuracy. The first type is:

- **Order of magnitude estimate.** This estimate has the range of –25% to +75% accuracy. An example would be if you had made an estimate of $100 for the cost. The range of cost in an order of magnitude estimate would be from $75 to $175. As you can see, this is a rather large range and is usually the first type of estimate that is done.

The second estimate type is:

- **Budget estimate.** This estimate has a range of –10% to +25%. Again, if you had an estimate of $100, the actual cost range in a budget estimate would be $90 to $125. As you can see, the range is narrowing from the order of magnitude estimate.

The third estimate type is:

- **Definitive estimate.** This has a very small range, from –5% to +10%. Using the $100 estimate, the range would be small, from $95 to $110.

These types of estimates show ranges that you may have when cost estimating. A project manager should always try to give a definitive estimate because that estimate is the closest a project manager can get to the actual cost. Project managers are often plagued with estimates that are not accurate enough to do a true budget. The better the estimate, the better the final budget and the greater the chance of bringing the project in on budget.

> **Q. An estimate that has the range of –25% to +75 is called a(n) _____ estimate.**
>
> ❏ A. Definitive ❏ B. Budget
>
> ❏ C. Order of magnitude ❏ D. Strategic

The answer is C. This is the estimate with the largest variance and is often the first estimate done.

> **Q. The estimate that has the range of –5% to +10% is called a(n) _____ estimate.**
>
> ❏ A. Capital ❏ B. Order of magnitude
>
> ❏ C. Budget ❏ D. Definitive

The answer is D. This is the final estimate that you will use when executing the project. Although it is extremely difficult to have estimates that are this exact, it is a best practice to try to make the final estimate as close as possible to the actual cost.

> **Q. The estimate that has the range of –10% to +25% is called a(n) _____ estimate.**
>
> ❏ A. Budget ❏ B. Order of magnitude
>
> ❏ C. Definitive ❏ D. Capital

The answer is A. This is the middle of the three estimates, and it gives a smaller range than the order of magnitude but a larger range than the definitive estimate.

> **Q. Developing an approximation of the costs of the resources needed to complete project activity is _____.**
>
> ❏ A. Accounting ❏ B. Cost control
>
> ❏ C. Cost estimating ❏ D. Budgeting

The answer is C. It is sometimes difficult to remember that the final approximation of cost is just that: an approximation or estimate.

There are six inputs into cost estimating: enterprise environmental factors, organizational process assets, project Scope Statement, WBS, WBS dictionary, and the project management plan. These have been discussed in detail elsewhere.

The tools and techniques found in cost estimating include: analogous estimating, determining resource rate costs, bottom-up estimating, parametric estimating, project management software, vendor bid analysis, reserve analysis, and the cost of quality.

Analogous estimating is also known as top-down estimating. This is simply using another project's cost to estimate the new project's cost. You use an analogous project (one that is like the current one) to do the estimating. This technique is used often when you want a "big picture" of the costs of your project. It does not include much detail, but it can be useful for getting a reasonable idea of cost. As with anything that uses past history to predict the future, make sure that the unique parts of your project are reflected in the estimate. There is no one-to-one correlation between older projects and newer projects, so remember that analogous estimating gives you an idea, not complete detail.

One of the reasons to use analogous estimating is that it is almost cost-free. Simply looking up a past project and examining the costs that were incurred is all that needs to be done. Analogous estimating is not considered the most accurate tool in cost estimating, but it is one of the lowest-cost tools.

Determining resource cost rates was discussed previously. In the past, this was a major process in itself. Rates must be established at the beginning of the project and used to calculate the costs of doing the project. These rates will be a major input into the overall cost estimate and include both human and mechanical resources.

Bottom-up estimating involves estimating the individual work packages and summing the individual numbers to arrive at the final number. The better the breakdown of the work packages, the better the bottom-up estimating will be. This is the most accurate of the estimating tools if the WBS is done in detail. The more detail in the tasks, the more it will cost to estimate because you will have more tasks to look at in the estimating process. There is a tradeoff between detail and cost that should be considered before you begin to estimate.

Parametric estimating is one of the tools listed in the cost estimating process. To use parametric estimating, you take characteristics of the project (parameters) and use a mathematical model to predict costs. For instance, if you are going to build a hospital, then you will look at parameters that pertain only to hospitals. By using a parametric model, the accuracy is increased if the information going into the model is as accurate as possible, the parameters are measurable, and the model works at any size.

Q. Estimating cost by looking at previous projects is known as _____ estimating.

☐ A. Analytical ☐ B. Analogous

☐ C. Strategic ☐ D. Bid

The answer is B. Analogous estimating is used when previous projects are used as a benchmark for estimating cost.

Q. Analogous estimating is also known as _____ estimating.

☐ A. Bottom-up ☐ B. Parametric

☐ C. Top-down ☐ D. Top-to-bottom

The answer is C. This type of estimating looks at the large picture first and gives an overall view of the potential costs.

Q. Summing the total of WBS tasks to find the total cost is known as _____ estimating.

☐ A. Top-down ☐ B. Analytical

☐ C. Parametric ☐ D. Bottom-up

The answer is D. By starting with the lowest tasks and then rolling up the costs, you will arrive at the final cost estimate.

Q. If you are using models that look at project characteristics to do cost estimating, you are doing _____.

☐ A. Parametric estimating ☐ B. Analytical thinking

☐ C. Acute cost analysis ☐ D. Model characterization

The answer is A. Parametric estimating looks at parameters specific to your project and measures the new project against ones that have been done in the past.

Q. In general, _____ estimating gives the most accurate picture of costs for doing cost estimating.

❑ A. Analogous

❑ B. Parametric modeling

❑ C. Bottom-up

❑ D. Top-down

The answer is C. This is true because you start with a breakdown that gives you the most accurate cost estimate possible.

Vendor bid analysis begins when you request proposals from the vendors for the execution and completion of your project. The responses to these proposals should give you a good idea of the actual costs of the project you are about to execute. Something to note is that the lowest costs do not always indicate the best "deal" for the project manager and the organization. It is extremely important to analyze the response to your requests so that the quotes from various vendors are estimating the same amount of work and cost to execute what you want in the project. The better you are at writing detailed requests, the easier it is for the vendors to respond to you.

Reserve analysis includes contingency allowances that are also called reserves. These are funds that *may* be used as the project goes on. The obvious problem is that these reserves can inflate the original cost estimates. These costs are called "known unknowns" because you know that they might be incurred, but you are not certain whether they actually will.

The cost of quality is discussed at length in the project quality knowledge section.

Q. The best way to get a good bid from the vendor is to write a good _____ document.

❑ A. Letter

❑ B. Request

❑ C. Risk Statement

❑ D. Quality

The answer is B. The better you are at framing the requirements of the project, the better the vendor should be in giving you a response.

Q. Costs that are expected to occur but the time when this will happen is not known are called:

❏ A. Indirect

❏ B. Tactical

❏ C. Direct

❏ D. Known unknowns

The answer is D. You expect that there is a high probability that a cost will occur, but you are not sure when it will happen.

The outputs from cost estimating are cost estimates, activity cost estimate detail, change requests, and updates of the cost management plan. When doing cost estimates, it is very important that the people seeing them understand whether they are order of magnitude or definitive. The first budget that most people see is the budget that they remember the longest. Even if you have stamped "order of magnitude" all over the estimate, many people take the first estimate as the final. Remember also that many people have no idea what "order of magnitude" means, so some explanation of the term is needed. When you are going to show cost estimates to others, be sure that they know how accurate the estimates are. Even if you are careful, someone will probably consider your first estimate to be cast in stone.

You should be able to refine your estimates as the project progresses because you will acquire more and more detail as the execution of the project goes on. The detail associated with cost estimates will grow as the tasks are better understood and documented. As with any project document, make sure that you put estimates under version control. Any change in the estimate means that a new version number should be assigned. No matter how small the change, you should revise the version number. Failure to do this will result in major problems if different versions of the cost estimates are used by different people to justify costs in the project.

Q. It is likely that the _____ estimate is the one that people remember most.

❏ A. Last

❏ B. First

❏ C. Summary

❏ D. Capital

The answer is B. The first estimate that people see is often the one that they remember the most. Even if you explain the major caveat that you are simply showing a first estimate, it always seems that people remember the first information they receive.

Q. _____ **is a major part of keeping track of a string of estimates.**

☐ A. Cost estimating

☐ B. Version control

☐ C. Summary tracking

☐ D. Line item identification

The answer is B. Version control is a vitally important part of project management. No more so than in cost estimates. These documents must be kept under version control, and any changes to the estimate necessitate a new version number.

The supporting detail used in cost estimating includes a work description, information about how the cost estimate was developed, documentation of assumptions, and a range of possible results. This last item can be done as a numerical explanation, such as estimating a cost at $200 and showing a plus-minus range of +/– $40. You can also show the range by using the types of estimates explained previously, such as order of magnitude, budget, or definitive. If you are using these words, it is a good idea to make sure that you note what they mean in terms of range.

Resource calendars are pertinent for a cost estimator, especially when you are using people that will be used on more than one project. Look for overlaps in assignments that will be problematic as the project progresses. Also, it is extremely important to get blocks of uninterrupted time. It is much easier for a coder to work straight through a module than it is for him or her to work on the code for one week, stop for a week, and then come back to the original work. Although this type of schedule may work in theory, it does not work in practice. People need blocks of time to do their best work. When you are doing cost budgeting, you should expect costs to rise if you cannot get the resources sufficient lengths of time to finish tasks.

The cost management plan describes how cost variances will be managed. This means that you may choose to manage major variances differently from minor differences in the estimate. How you will handle variances should be explained in your cost management plan.

As with many documents and actions in project management, the cost management plan may be formal or informal, highly detailed or broadly discussed. The choice of whether to make the cost management plan a formal document will be determined by the needs of the shareholders. This could be a piece of the communication plan because you will be asking what the stakeholders need you to report in terms of the status of the cost estimates.

> **Q.** **The description of how cost variances are to be handled is found in the _____.**
>
> ❑ A. Accounting system   ❑ B. Cost management plan
>
> ❑ C. Accompanying detail   ❑ D. Scope Statement

The answer is B. This is the PMBOK definition of a cost management plan.

> **Q.** **The cost management plan may be formal or informal, detailed or sparse, depending on the needs of the _____.**
>
> ❑ A. Stakeholders   ❑ B. Office staff
>
> ❑ C. Project manager   ❑ D. Program manager

The answer is A. Any of the plans that are used in project management should be useful to stakeholders. They will tell you how much detail they need.

Cost Budgeting

Cost budgeting is closely tied to the previous section. It involves establishing a cost baseline by allocating costs to activities or work packages. This baseline is used to measure performance during the execution of the project. A key point to remember is that even though you may turn in a final budget, the numbers with which you are working are still estimates because they measure actions to be taken in the future. They are not accounting numbers that give accurate measurement to past occurrences; they are approximations (in some cases accurate approximations) of what is to come.

The inputs to cost budgeting are the project Scope Statement, the WBS, a WBS dictionary, cost estimates, cost estimate supporting detail, project schedule, resource calendars, contracts, and the cost management plan. The project Scope Statement becomes the document upon which all budgeting decisions are based. The project manager will use the project Scope Statement and its decomposed cousin, the WBS, to make sure that the costs are estimated as carefully as possible. In the budgeting process, allocation of limited resources occurs as the funding for the entire project is considered when doing the final budgeting. Resources, whether they are capital or people, are always limited in some way in all organizations. The WBS dictionary gives details that are not in the WBS itself. By using the dictionary, you can get a level of detail that will help you put your budget together.

Q. **Detail of the WBS for doing your budgeting is found in the _____.**

❑ A. SOW

❑ B. WBS dictionary

❑ C. Schedule

❑ D. Charter

The answer is B. Use the dictionary as a tool to look at detail in the overall project task system. This will help give you better figures for use in your cost budgeting.

The project schedule that was discussed in the previous chapter shows planned start and finish dates for the various tasks needed to complete the project. Particularly if you are doing a very complex project that will take more than six months, you will need to estimate when costs will occur so that budgeting is done to match the expected times for capital outlay.

Q. **The planned start and finish dates for the tasks in the project are shown in the:**

❑ A. Scope Statement

❑ B. Charter

❑ C. Project schedule

❑ D. Risk management plan

The answer is C. The project schedule is your measurement tool to use when determining when you will need to make expenditures to get the various parts of the project done.

Q. **Risk events that occur that were totally unexpected are called:**

❑ A. Tactical problems

❑ B. Unknown unknowns

❑ C. Known unknowns

❑ D. Glaring mistakes

The answer is B. Unknown unknowns are events that occur that are unexpected. You can plan for their cost by putting together a budget specifically linked to these types of events.

Q. **When you allocate a budget to risk events that you expect to occur but are not sure when they will occur, you are dealing with:**

❑ A. Known unknowns

❑ B. Unknown unknowns

❑ C. Capital issues

❑ D. Forced expenditure

The answer is A. You know about the possibility of the risk event occurring but cannot pinpoint when it will occur.

The various tools and techniques described in the cost budgeting section are cost aggregation, reserve analysis, parametric estimating, and funding limit reconciliation. The concept of cost aggregation simply means that you aggregate all the costs in one level of task in the WBS, and this will be the cost of the task above. An example of this would be four tasks on the third level of the WBS that each have a cost of $10,000. The second level of the WBS thus would show $40,000.

Reserve analysis has been discussed before but deserves another look. Contingency reserves are those set aside for unplanned but potentially required changes. These are called unknown unknowns because the project manager doesn't know when the change will occur or whether it will occur at all.

The outputs from cost budgeting are the cost baseline, project funding requirements, updates on the cost management plan, and change requests. The cost baseline is the measurement you use throughout the project that measures the cost performance on the project. To show a cost baseline, which usually is represented as an S curve (see Figure 11-1), you sum all the costs for the time period you want to measure and show that as a baseline. Your actual costs are shown against the baseline and show how well you are performing against the plan. The baseline is your standard. Any variations from your baseline should go through some type of change control to note that the baseline has been altered.

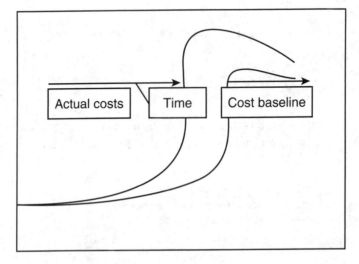

FIGURE 11-1: Cost baseline represented as an S curve.

You will be showing the funding requirements for the project when you finish with cost budgeting. It is still an estimate, but it should be as close to the actual cost as you can possibly get it. During this part of project planning, you should work to make sure that the numbers shown are accurate, not just educated guesses.

Q. The major output of cost budgeting is the _____.

    ❑ A. Summary of costs   ❑ B. Capital budget

    ❑ C. Cost baseline   ❑ D. Capital baseline

The answer is C. The cost baseline is the budget that will be your measurement of costs for the project. It is usually time-phased so that you can look at a specific point in time and measure how you are doing against the baseline for that particular time.

Cost Control

Cost control is the last process area in project cost management. Cost control is concerned with influencing the factors that create changes to the cost baseline to ensure that changes are agreed upon, determining that the cost baseline has changed, managing the actual changes as they occur, recording all changes against the baseline, communicating changes to the stakeholders, and acting to bring cost overruns within acceptable project limits. Clearly, there must be a mechanism to make everyone involved in a cost change aware of the change and to ensure that everyone is in agreement that the change must occur. This is a key for effectively managing as a project manager. You should have documentation that the changes in costs have been agreed upon. However, some changes may be outside of your control. For instance, if you are doing a construction project that involves many vehicles and the price of gasoline rises precipitously, you do not need to go to anyone except to note that the prices have changed.

If a price change occurs, you need to document how much it was and when it occurred. This is part of showing people what cost changes have occurred. A great deal of this process involves getting information to stakeholders who are outlined in the communication plan. You should immediately notify the appropriate people when the cost baseline has changed.

Finally, you should act as quickly as possible to control the changes. The sponsor may allow certain levels of cost change to be accepted without requiring immediate communication. Usually, if this is true, there is a threshold for the changes that is often expressed as a percentage of the original baseline. For example, you may have consent from the sponsor to accept changes of no more than 5% from the original baseline without needing his or her written approval. No matter what the circumstances, your job is to react to changes and note them quickly. The changes that make major differences in the cost of the project are the ones that you must control first. Smaller changes are still important but are not as important as larger ones.

You should use cost control no matter whether the change is positive or negative. The job of the project manager is not to bring a project in under budget. His or her job is to bring the project in on budget. Being under budget can be just as problematic as being over budget. Project management deals with getting accurate plans and then executing them. As with other types of change control, such as scope change control and quality control, you should be able to explain why costs changed.

Q. **The project manager's job is to bring the project in _____ budget.**

   ❏ A. Over   ❏ B. Under

   ❏ C. On   ❏ D. Close to

The answer is C. Your job as a project manager is to give accurate assessments of what the project will cost. Coming in below cost is not recommended because your cost estimating should give you a correct picture of the overall budget.

Q. **When a cost change occurs, be sure to document _____ and _____ it occurs.**

   ❏ A. How and where   ❏ B. Where and when

   ❏ C. When and how   ❏ D. When and why

The answer is D. You should document when the cost changed occurred and as much as possible the reasons for its occurrence.

The inputs to cost control are the cost baseline, project funding requirements, performance reports, change requests, and the cost management plan. Cost baseline as a concept is covered in the cost budgeting section of this chapter. The performance reports for cost are treated the same as any of the other cost reports. What you are looking for is variance from the plan based on what has actually occurred. Variance management works as well as the information in the performance reports, so it is necessary to be certain of the accuracy of detail in the reports. The performance reports in cost control can also be used to alert project members about problems and issues that may surface in the future.

Change requests for cost control are much the same as change requests in scope control, quality control, or in fact any of the control areas of the nine knowledge areas. The change requests in cost control usually increase the budget. In some cases, you may actually decrease the budget, particularly if you are downsizing the project. Although change requests can come in non-permanent form such as oral requests, your job as project manager is to make certain that the changes are noted and put into a permanent part of the project file. No matter whether the requests come from someone who bumps into you in the hall or through a complex change request system, you should note all requests and what happens to them. Even if the request is turned down, make a note of it. It is possible that the same request will be resubmitted later, and you may want to look at how the change request was handled the first time it was submitted. This can often save a great deal of time.

Q. Change requests should be noted _____ when they occur and become a part of the project record.

☐ A. Often   ☐ B. Tactically

☐ C. Permanently   ☐ D. Orally

The answer is C. You want to keep permanent records of every change made from the original approved plan. This is just as true in cost control as it is in any other type of control in a project.

The tool and techniques in cost control are the cost change control system, performance measurement, forecasting, performance reviews, project management software, and variance management. The cost change control system is actually just one part of the integrated control systems, and like all of the other change control systems, it outlines the procedures by which the cost baseline may be changed.

Performance measurement shows variations from the baseline planning. Earned value management is one of the types of performance measurement. This has been explained in detail in Chapter 4, "Execution and Control." Because there are usually four or five questions on earned value, it is a good idea to reread that section. Simply put, Earned Value Management is an accounting concept that is used only in projects. Earned Value Management matches the planned value (PV) against the earned value (EV) to determine how your project projections match what you predicted. The other acronym that you must know is actual cost (AC). It would be good to take a few minutes to reread the topic in Chapter 4.

Earned Value

This topic was discussed in Chapter 4. If you do not need this topic explained again, skip to the next section. However, this time I will use only the new abbreviations without worrying about the old ones. There are still three values for each activity that we will be measuring.

1. The first value is called the planned value (PV). This is the cost that was estimated for activities during the project—what you estimated and planned.

2. The second value is called actual cost (AC). This is the money amount that was actually spent on activities for the project.

3. The third value is called the earned value (EV). This is the value of the work that has been completed on the project.

Using these three values in various combinations gives us information about how the work is going compared to how we thought the work would go. Variance management is a standard for project management, and earned value is no exception. There are two variances that we look at: cost and schedule. Cost Variance (CV) is calculated by taking earned value and subtracting actual costs. The formula for this reads CV=EV–AC.

Cost Variance

CV=EV–AC

Schedule Variance (SV) is calculated by subtracting planned value from earned value. The formula reads SV=EV–PV.

Schedule Variance

SV=EV–PV

Note that in both types of variance, you subtract something from earned value (EV).

Q. **The abbreviation for the portion of the approved cost estimate that is to be spent on tasks during a given measured period is:**

❑ A. EV   ❑ B. AC

❑ C. PV   ❑ D. DC

The answer is C. The two letters stand for "planned value," which means that the estimates you used to put together your cost plan are represented by planned value. At any point in the project, you should be able to calculate how much you planned for the activities to cost up to that time. Planned value is a future value. It is your best estimate of what things *will* cost in the future.

Q. The abbreviation for the amount that was budgeted for work to be performed is:

❑ A. EV   ❑ B. AC

❑ C. PV   ❑ D. DC

The answer is C, planned value.

Q. The abbreviation for costs actually incurred is:

❑ A. EV   ❑ B. AC

❑ C. PV   ❑ D. DC

The answer is B. The letters stand for "actual costs," which are the real costs that have been incurred during the project. Your accounting department may give this number to you.

After looking at the two main types of variance information, the next step is to look at two performance indices. These are efficiency indicators that can be used to show how the cost and schedule parts of the project are progressing. As with most of the tools used in performance reporting, the performance indices show performance as a variance from plan. If your costs are exactly what you planned at the beginning of the project, your cost performance index will be 1.0. If your schedule is going exactly as you planned, your schedule performance index will be 1.0.

Cost performance index (CPI)

$$CPI = EV/AC$$

The cost performance index equals earned value divided by actual costs.

Q. What is your CPI if EV = 5 and AC = 4?

❑ A. .80 ❑ B. 1.0

❑ C. 1.25 ❑ D. 2.0

The answer is C. EV = 5, AC = 4, and the formula reads CPI = 5/4, which is 1.25.

Q. What is your CPI if AC = 10 and EV = 8?

❑ A. .80 ❑ B. 80

❑ C. 1.25 ❑ D. 2.0

The answer is A. EV = 8, AC = 4, and the formula reads CPI = 8/10, which is .80.

Q. What is your CPI if EV = 20 and AC = 20?

❑ A. 4.0 ❑ B. 1.0

❑ C. 2.0 ❑ D. 1.25

The answer is B. AC = 20, EV = 20, and the formula reads CPI = 20/20, which is 1.

With this formula, the best possible outcome is 1.0. If your cost performance index is above 1.0, it indicates that you have costs that are less then estimated. Some people think that this is a good thing to do, but a professional project manager knows that any variance from the estimate means that incorrect assumptions were made in the planning. A second factor occurs if you bring a project in under budget where your CPI was above 1.0. Bringing a project in under budget will often mean that your budgets are challenged for each subsequent project. Being as close as you can to budget is the optimum for CPI.

Schedule Variance Index (SPI)

$$SPI=EV/PV$$

The second performance index is the schedule variance index, or SPI. The SPI equals the earned value divided by the planned value.

Q. What is your SPI if EV = 8 and PV = 6?

☐ A. 1.33 ☐ B. .66

☐ C. 1.0 ☐ D. .75

The answer is A. EV = 8 and PV = 6, and the formula reads SPI=8/6, which is 1.33.

Q. What is your SPI if PV = 8 and EV = 6?

☐ A. 1.0 ☐ B. .75

☐ C. 1.33 ☐ D. 2.0

The answer is B. EV = 6 and PV = 8, and the formula reads SPI=6/8, which is .75.

As with the cost performance index, you should be looking for 1.0 as the answer to the formula. Any variance from 1.0 means that you should be looking at what caused the variance to determine whether there is something you can do in the future to bring the project back in line.

This concludes the section on earned value analysis. The concept is simple, and the formulas are simple. One thing to remember for either the variance formulas of the performance formulas in earned value analysis is that the earned value (EV) is always the first number in the formula.

CV=EV–AC

SV=EV–PV

CPI=EV/AC

SPI=EV/PV

Project closeout is also an output from cost control. In the project closeout, it is helpful if the organization has specific processes to use. If projects are closing or being canceled, it is a good idea to have a standard set of procedures for all projects.

Lessons learned are an important part of analyzing cost performance of a project. As discussed previously, lessons learned should be kept from the beginning of the project and discussed at regular intervals, not only when the project is over. Lessons learned should show why there were variances in the costs of the project from the original plan and how the various actions taken to correct the problems were chosen. The lessons learned for the cost portion of the project are only one part of the larger lessons learned database kept for the entire project.

The majority of the outputs for cost control are updates of some kind. Cost estimates, cost baseline, organizational process assets, and the project management plan are examples of these updates.

You will also have change requests in cost that have occurred as you go through the entire budgeting process. These need to be documented and will be kept throughout the project to show who requested the changes and the outcome of each request.

Any corrective actions done in costs will pertain to adjusting schedule budgets. These corrective actions should be tracked as much as any of the changes done during the project so that the project manager can always look at them and see why they were done.

Not in the PMBOK but on the Examination

There are questions on cost on the PMI examination that are not included in the PMBOK. There are not very many of them, and you only have to know one or two of the formulas for the following. For the most part, you simply have to know what they mean. Remember that you are not sitting for a CPA examination but for a PMP certification. You do not have to be an accountant to pass this examination; far from it. Here are some of the terms to know. If you want more information, Harold Kerzner's sections on cost in his book *Project Management: A Systems Approach to Planning, Controlling, and Scheduling* are excellent. You can also Google the words you see here for much more information.

Present Value(PV): The current value of a given future cash flow stream, discounted at a given rate. This formula is one you should know to calculate a present value.

$$PV = \frac{FV}{(1+r)n}$$

FV = Future value, which is divided by 1 plus the interest rate (r) multiplied by the number of time periods (n).

The examples on the exam almost always use .10 as the interest rate. An example would be to find what the value of $6000 received three years from now would be today. To do that, you apply the formula, 6,000 (1 + .1)3 equals 6,000/1.331, which equals $4,507. So $4,507 today would equal $6,000 three years from now.

Internal rate of return (IRR): A method that determines the discount rate at which the present value of future cash flows will exactly equal investment outlay. Before you go any further, know that a formula for this is not on the exam. In order to do an IRR, you need a computer program. The better the IRR, the more likely the project will be chosen if the only criterion is return. An example where this may not be true is where the government requires a new accounting system to be in place by a certain date. The value of the project will not be determined by figuring the return that will be made on cost because the project must be done in order to comply with the law.

Payback period: The amount of time it takes to recover the expenditure for the project before you begin to actually generate revenue.

Opportunity cost: When you make the choice of one project over another, you can look at opportunity cost. "This is the cost of doing one project instead of another which ties up capital and usually means that the organizational management feels that the project chosen gives a better chance of return." RKM

Sunk costs: Money that has been spent on the project that will never be recovered. It is a good idea to know that sunk costs are not recoverable so that when someone says to you, "Can you recover the costs already expended on this project?" you can look at them and say, "No." Sunk costs are gone, never to be recovered.

Depreciation: There are two types of depreciation: straight line and accelerated. Straight line means you take the same amount of depreciation each year. Accelerated depreciation means that variable amounts of depreciation are taken each year, and at the beginning of the depreciation, you take more than at the end. This would be especially useful if you were depreciating computers, which often obsolesce much faster than other pieces of equipment.

You can go from straight line depreciation to accelerated depreciation in your books, but you cannot go in reverse. You are not allowed to start depreciating something using accelerated depreciation the first year and then go to straight line for following years.

As you have probably figured out by now, most of these formulas are useful primarily to an accountant. On the exam, you may be asked one or two questions about these accounting terms, but you certainly do not have to use the formulas or even know what the formulas are.

Q. _____ are costs that are not recoverable.

❑ A. Capital costs ❑ B. Real costs

❑ C. Sunk costs ❑ D. Overhead costs

The answer is C. You cannot recover sunk costs, as much as many organizations would like to do so.

Q. The amount of time it takes to recover the expenditure for the project before you begin to actually generate revenue is known as the _____.

❑ A. Return on investment ❑ B. Payback period

❑ C. Selection period ❑ D. Return period

The answer is B. Some projects are chosen because the payback period is shorter than on other projects being considered.

Q. You can go from _____ to accelerated depreciation from one year to the following year but not the reverse.

❑ A. Straight line depreciation

❑ B. Capital expenditure methodology

❑ C. Direct cost capitalization

❑ D. Intermediate depreciation

The answer is A. You can switch from straight line depreciation as your means of accounting to accelerated depreciation the next year, but you cannot do the reverse.

Questions from Chapter Eleven   ?

1. Cost, time, and quality are known as:

- ❏ A. Triple constraints
- ❏ B. Three chapters of PMBOK
- ❏ C. Tactical measurements
- ❏ D. Project indicators

2. Looking at a broad overview of the project costs is known as:

- ❏ A. Auditing
- ❏ B. Life cycle engineering
- ❏ C. Life cycle costing
- ❏ D. Value engineering

3. Value analysis and value management are other names for:

- ❏ A. Profitability
- ❏ B. Life cycle management
- ❏ C. Life cycle costing
- ❏ D. Value engineering

4. ROI and discounted cash flow are two examples of:

- ❏ A. General management cost evaluation
- ❏ B. Value management cost techniques
- ❏ C. Project management cost evaluation
- ❏ D. General cost techniques

5. Heating and electricity are examples of _____ costs.

- ❏ A. Strategic
- ❏ B. Tactical
- ❏ C. Direct
- ❏ D. Indirect

6. The project manager can have control over _____ costs.

- ❏ A. Strategic
- ❏ B. Tactical
- ❏ C. Direct
- ❏ D. Indirect

7. Cost control is easiest to do _____ the project.

- ❏ A. Early in
- ❏ B. Late in
- ❏ C. In the middle of
- ❏ D. After

8. The _____ gives the detail you need to correctly estimate costs for the project.

❑ A. Scope Statement   ❑ B. Charter

❑ C. SOW   ❑ D. WBS

9. In the WBS, _____ hours is the suggested longest task duration.

❑ A. 20   ❑ B. 8

❑ C. 40   ❑ D. 60

10. Historical information is a _____, not a _____.

❑ A. Nuisance, fact   ❑ B. Guideline, blueprint

❑ C. Fact, guess   ❑ D. Panacea, problem

11. Historical information can be used as a guide, not as a blueprint because each project is _____.

❑ A. Tactical   ❑ B. Important

❑ C. Unique   ❑ D. Planned

12. Equipment, materials, and people are three types of choices in _____.

❑ A. Scope Statements   ❑ B. WBS

❑ C. SOW   ❑ D. Resource pool description

13. _____ of resources play(s) an important part in how you choose people and materials for your project.

❑ A. Descriptions   ❑ B. Firing

❑ C. Cost   ❑ D. Quality

14. Choosing to do a task in house or to outsource it may be an example of a(n) _____.

❑ A. Tactical decision   ❑ B. Strategic decision

❑ C. Management decision   ❑ D. Organizational policy

15. When you are choosing a certain level of skills or mechanical efficiency, you are trading _____ for time.

❑ A. Cost   ❑ B. Quality

❑ C. People   ❑ D. Ideas

16. The first place to look for expert judgment is often in _____.

❑ A. PMI ❑ B. Relatives

❑ C. Your own organization ❑ D. A vendor's organization

17. In order to use a consultant well, you need to have your own _____ and _____ clearly understood as you engage the consultants.

❑ A. People, managers ❑ B. Expectations, requirements

❑ C. Tasks, strategy ❑ D. Requirements, hopes

18. When using either associations or industry groups, it is always important to know what _____ went into the final numbers.

❑ A. Thinking ❑ B. Data

❑ C. Tactics ❑ D. Skills

19. To determine the final number of resources needed for a large task, you _____ the _____ levels to get the next level higher.

❑ A. Sum, lower ❑ B. Divide, average

❑ C. Multiply, higher ❑ D. Sum, higher

20. An estimate that has the range of –25% to +75 is called a(n) _____ estimate.

❑ A. Definitive ❑ B. Budget

❑ C. Order of magnitude ❑ D. Strategic

21. The budget that has the range of –5% to +10% is called a(n) _____ estimate.

❑ A. Capital ❑ B. Order of magnitude

❑ C. Budget ❑ D. Definitive

22. The budget that has the range of –10% to +25% is called a(n) _____ estimate.

❑ A. Budget ❑ B. Order of magnitude

❑ C. Definitive ❑ D. Capital

23. Developing an approximation of the costs of the resources needed to complete project activity is _____.

❑ A. Accounting ❑ B. Cost control

❑ C. Cost estimating ❑ D. Budgeting

24. Project team knowledge, commercial cost-estimating databases, and project files are all part of _____ used as an input into cost estimating.

    ❏ A. Resource requirements
    ❏ B. Estimating software
    ❏ C. Historical information
    ❏ D. Public information

25. The document that shows the correct accounting category to list various cost estimates is called the _____.

    ❏ A. Accounting system
    ❏ B. Chart of accounts
    ❏ C. Accounting method
    ❏ D. Standard accounts

26. Evaluating _____ is part of cost estimating.

    ❏ A. Schedules
    ❏ B. Personnel
    ❏ C. Assignments
    ❏ D. Risks

27. Estimating cost by looking at previous projects is known as _____ estimating.

    ❏ A. Analytical
    ❏ B. Analogous
    ❏ C. Strategic
    ❏ D. Bid

28. Analogous estimating is also known as _____ estimating.

    ❏ A. Bottom-up
    ❏ B. Parametric
    ❏ C. Top-down
    ❏ D. Top-to-bottom

29. Summing the total of WBS tasks to find the total cost is known as _____ estimating.

    ❏ A. Top-down
    ❏ B. Analytical
    ❏ C. Parametric
    ❏ D. Bottom-up

30. If you are using models that look at project characteristics to do cost estimating, you are doing _____.

    ❏ A. Parametric modeling
    ❏ B. Analytical thinking
    ❏ C. Acute cost analysis
    ❏ D. Model characterization

31. In general, _____ estimating gives the most accurate picture of costs for doing cost estimating.

    ❏ A. Analogous
    ❏ B. Parametric modeling
    ❏ C. Bottom-up
    ❏ D. Top-down

32. It is likely that the _____ estimate is the one that people remember most.

   ❑ A. Last   ❑ B. First

   ❑ C. Summary   ❑ D. Capital

33. _____ is a major part of keeping track of a string of estimates.

   ❑ A. Cost estimating   ❑ B. Version control

   ❑ C. Summary tracking   ❑ D. Line item identification

34. The major output of cost budgeting is the _____.

   ❑ A. Summary of costs   ❑ B. Capital budget

   ❑ C. Cost baseline   ❑ D. Capital baseline

35. Change requests should be noted _____ when they occur and become a part of the project record.

   ❑ A. Often   ❑ B. Tactically

   ❑ C. Permanently   ❑ D. Orally

36. If you think that the costs you have incurred up to now are in some way atypical of the project and that the rest of the project will cost the original estimate, the formula for finding the EAC is:

   ❑ A. EAC = (AC + (BAC-EV)/CPI)

   ❑ B. EAC=AC + ETC

   ❑ C. EAC=AC + BAC-EV.

   ❑ D. EAC=AC + EV

37. If you think that the costs you have incurred up to now are an indicator of what will happen for the rest of the project your formula for finding the EAC is:

   ❑ A. EAC = (AC + (BAC-EV)/CPI)

   ❑ B. EAC=AC + ETC

   ❑ C. EAC=AC + BAC-EV.

   ❑ D. EAC=AC + EV

38. The CPI used in the above formula is a(n) _____.

   ❑ A. Actual cost   ❑ B. Cost control

   ❑ C. Cost schedule   ❑ D. Performance factor

39. If you think that the costs to be incurred for the rest of the project were incorrectly estimated and use a new estimate for your EAC, the formula is:

❑ A. EAC = (AC + (BAC-EV)/CPI)

❑ B. EAC=AC + ETC

❑ C. EAC=AC + BAC-EV.

❑ D. EAC=AC +EV

40. The abbreviation for the amount that was budgeted in order for work to be performed is:

❑ A. EV   ❑ B. AC

❑ C. PV   ❑ D. DC

41. The abbreviation for costs actually incurred is:

❑ A. EV   ❑ B. AC

❑ C. PV   ❑ D. DC

42. _____ are costs that are not recoverable.

❑ A. Capital costs   ❑ B. Real costs

❑ C. Sunk costs   ❑ D. Overhead costs

43. The amount of time it takes to recover the expenditure for the project before you begin to actually generate revenue is known as the _____.

❑ A. Return on investment   ❑ B. Payback period

❑ C. Selection period   ❑ D. Return period

44. You can go from _____ to accelerated depreciation from one year to the following year but not the reverse.

❑ A. Straight line depreciation   ❑ B. Capital expenditure methodology

❑ C. Direct cost capitalization   ❑ D. Intermediate depreciation

45. The best way to get a good bid from the vendor is to write a good _____ document.

❑ A. Letter   ❑ B. Request

❑ C. Risk Statement   ❑ D. Quality

46. Detail of the WBS for doing your budgeting is found in the _____.

    ❏ A. SOW   ❏ B. WBS dictionary

    ❏ C. Schedule   ❏ D. Charter

47. Costs that are expected to occur but the time when they will occur is not known are called?

    ❏ A. Indirect   ❏ B. Tactical

    ❏ C. Direct   ❏ D. Known unknowns

48. What is your SPI if EV = 8 and PV = 6?

    ❏ A. 1.33   ❏ B. .66

    ❏ C. 1.0   ❏ D. .75

49. What is your SPI if PV = 8 and EV = 6?

    ❏ A. 1.0   ❏ B. .75

    ❏ C. 1.33   ❏ D. 2.0

Answers from Chapter Eleven

1. **The answer is A.** Although these are also three chapter headings in PMBOK, they are known together as the triple constraints.

2. **The answer is C.** Life cycle costing looks at the entire project and is a technique that helps determine the most cost effective ways of managing the project.

3. **The answer is D.** The planning of the engineering tasks to reduce cost, improve quality and maximize performance of the product is value engineering. Value engineering also helps to give clear data from which good decisions can be made.

4. **The answer is A.** There are other techniques used in general management to make decisions about use of capital. These techniques are two of them.

5. **The answer is D.** The costs of heating are not controllable by the project manager and do not occur because the project is begin executed. This makes them indirect costs.

6. **The answer is C.** Costs that are directly incurred because the project is being executed are directs costs. In some cases the project manager has control over the costs and in some cases the organization itself will control the costs. In any case, the costs occur only when the project is going on.

7. **The answer is A.** The earlier you have good plans from which to work the easier it is to control your costs and get good cost planning. If there is no clarity about the work to be done, there will be no clarity about the costs to be incurred.

8. **The answer is D.** This is the document where the Scope Statement is decomposed and will give you the task detail necessary to make resource planning possible.

9. **The answer is C.** If you have a task that is larger than this is terms of time, it is very difficult to assess resources needed to execute the task. You can certainly have tasks that are shorter than this; they will be useful for many of the resource planning activities. But you will not be able to plan well if the task is over 40 hours in length. There are too many unknowns in a task over the 40 hours to do good resource planning.

10. **The answer is B.** Historical information will not be the exact blueprint you need for your current project. People change, technologies change, situations change. All of these factors mean that although you can look at historical information as a guide, do not use it as your plan.

11. **The answer is C.** The basic definition of a project includes the fact that each project is unique. Something, often times many things, will be different between projects. So do not accept historical information as your final plan. It can guide you to get there, but it is not the final answer.

12. **The answer is D**. All three of these elements are choices you will have to make to successfully plan the project.

13. **The answer is A**. If you receive a list of resources, be sure you understand what they are and that you have a description in your mind that matches the description of the organization giving you the resource pool. For instance, the words "heavy duty" may mean different things to different organizations. Asking what the words mean, especially if the words are descriptions is something you should do for your own project.

14. **The answer is D**. The organization will often have policies that are used to determine how resources are selected. As a professional project manager you should make every effort to be aware of any organizational policies that will affect you resource planning.

15. **The answer is A**. The triple constraints of cost, quality, and time are always in play in a project. You must choose between the three constantly as you go through resource planning. You will probably not be the final arbiter of who to use or what equipment to use on the project because those choices will be made in organizational meetings leading to organizational policy. You should know that there are tradeoffs to be made between the triple constraints, and you should give good information to sponsors and stakeholders about your decisions in choosing resources.

16. **The answer is C**. If someone in your organization has been through a project similar to yours, that person can be an excellent source of information. In addition, that person will have the same constraints on him or her that you have and will have made decisions on resources based on those constraints.

17. **The answer is B**. The clearer you are concerning your own expectations and requirements, the better you will be at engaging consultants effectively.

18. **The answer is B**. The data are only useful to you when you know how they were derived. It is possible that one case in the data may be so far away from the average data that in fact the entire set of information is not truly useful. This would be the case when a very large company's data was blended in with several companies that were less than one tenth the size of the big company. Ask how the data were derived, and you can save yourself a lot of grief later.

19. **The answer is A**. You sum up the lower levels of the WBS to get the final number for the resources needed in the summary task at the top.

20. **The answer is C**. This is the estimate with the largest variance and is often the first budget done.

21. **The answer is D**. This is the final estimate you will use when executing the project. Although it is extremely difficult to create estimates that are this exact, it is a best practice to try to make the final estimate as close as possible to the actual cost.

22. **The answer is A.** This is the middle of the three estimates, and it gives a smaller range than the order of magnitude but a large range than the definitive estimate.

23. **The answer is C.** This is the directly from the PMBOK.

24. **The answer is C.** All three of these can be used to help estimate cost.

25. **The answer is B.** If the organization has a chart of accounts, the various estimates should be assigned to the correct category.

26. **The answer is D.** The occurrence of risks within a project will change the cost of the project. It is important for the project manager to calculate as well as possible the costs involved in managing the various risk events that might occur on a project. These costs are as critical as any of the other costs.

27. **The answer is B.** Analogous estimating uses previous projects as a benchmark for estimating cost.

28. **The answer is C.** This type of estimating looks at the large picture first and gives an overall view of the potential costs.

29. **The answer is D.** By starting with the lowest tasks and then rolling up the costs, you will arrive at the final cost estimate.

30. **The answer is A.** Parametric modeling looks at parameters specific to your project and measures the new project against ones that have been done in the past.

31. **The answer is C.** This is true because you start with a breakdown that gives you the most accurate cost estimate possible.

32. **The answer is B.** The first estimate that people see is often the one that they remember the most. Even if you explain the major caveat that you are simply showing a first estimate, it always seems that people remember the first information they receive.

33. **The answer is B.** Version control is a vitally important part of project management. No more so than in cost estimates. These documents must be kept under version control, and any changes to the estimate necessitate a new version number.

34. **The answer is C.** The cost baseline is the budget that will be your measurement of costs for the project. It is usually time-phased so that you can look at a specific point in time and measure how you are doing against the baseline for that particular time.

35. **The answer is C.** You should keep permanent records of every change made from the original approved plan. This is just as true in cost control as it is in any other type of control in a project.

36. **The answer is C**. You take the actual costs of the project and add the original estimate at completion to that number to get your estimate at completion.

37. **The answer is A**. You use a cost performance index to determine what your final estimate at completion will be.

38. **The answer is D**. The cost performance index is used in this case as an indicator of how the rest of the project will progress in terms of cost. This leads to an estimate at completion.

39. **The answer is B**. You take the actual costs and add your new estimates to that to get your new estimate at completion.

40. **The answer is A**. Earned value is the value of work that you have already done on the project. This is the concept that is not used in standard accounting and one that you will have to explain to management if you want to report using the earned value analysis technique.

41. **The answer is B**. The letters stand for "actual costs," which are the real costs that have been incurred during the project. Your accounting department may give this number to you.

42. **The answer is C**. You cannot recover sunk costs, as much as many organizations would like to do so.

43. **The answer is B**. Some projects are chosen because the payback period is shorter than on other projects being considered.

44. **The answer is A**. You can switch from straight line depreciation as your means of accounting to accelerated depreciation the next year, but you cannot do the reverse.

45. **The answer is B**. The better you are at framing the requirements of the project, the better the vendor should be in giving you a response.

46. **The answer is B**. Use the dictionary as a tool to look at detail in the overall project task system. This will help give you better figures for use in your cost budgeting.

47. **The answer is D**. You expect that there is a high probability that a cost will occur but you are not sure when it will happen.

48. **The answer is A**. EV = 8 and PV = 6, and the formula reads SPI=8/6, which is 1.33.

49. **The answer is B**. EV = 6 and PV = 8, and the formula reads SPI=6/8, which is .75.

CHAPTER TWELVE

Project Quality Management

T he PMBOK states that Project Quality Management must "address both the management and the product of a project." This applies no matter what the nature of the project is or the subject matter it addresses. Project Quality Management includes "all the activities of the performing organization that determine quality policies, objectives, and responsibilities so that the project will satisfy the needs for which it was undertaken" (PMBOK, 3rd ed). The three major processes within Project Quality Management are Quality Planning, Perform Quality Assurance, and Perform Quality Control. The three processes interact with each of the other knowledge areas, and they interact and overlap with one another, frequently being done at the same time.

Quality management in the PMBOK is written to be compatible with the International Organization for Standardization (ISO). The ISO has published a series of guidelines and standards for quality, which are numbered as the ISO 9000 and ISO 10000 series of standards. Project Quality Management is used in the management of the project itself and the output of the project's product or service.

Q. The organization that controls the standards for quality is the _____.

- ❏ A. ISO
- ❏ B. INA
- ❏ C. PMI
- ❏ D. IIQ

The answer is A. The ISO is the international organization that controls the standards for quality.

Quality is "the totality of characteristics of an entity that bear on its ability to satisfy stated or implied needs" (PMBOK). Another way to say this is that quality is conformance to requirements. One of the standard questions used to explain quality is, "Which offers higher quality, McDonald's or the Four Seasons in New York?" The answer surprises many people when it turns out that both have high-quality food. The difference is not in the quality level but in the grade. McDonald's consistently turns out food that meets high quality standards. Those standards are the requirements that are set for the food they offer. The Four Seasons also has high quality standards as well as having higher-grade food. But both work on the principle of high-quality food. Both have quality as one of the facets of their offerings to the public. Price is not a key in quality; conformance to standards is.

It is important to remember the concept of grade in discussing quality. You can certainly have high quality and low grade as a combination of features. Grade is defined as "a category or ranking given to entities that have the same functional use but different technical characteristics" (PMBOK). When ranking a project, low quality is always seen as a problem, whereas low grade may not be. As an example, suppose that Wendy's offered catsup as a condiment for its sandwiches, whereas Spago's offered pureed fresh tomatoes with balsamic vinegar and rock salt as a condiment for one of its sandwiches. Both offer quality based upon requirements, but the grade difference between the two is large and certainly more costly at Spago's. Thus, making the distinction between quality and grade is important for the project manager.

Q. Conformance to specifications is one description of _____.

  ❑ A. Grade   ❑ B. Scope

  ❑ C. Quality   ❑ D. Technical information

The answer is C. Quality on a project means that you are conforming to a standard that is set before you begin the project.

Q. The food at Wendy's and Spago's are both high-quality but differ in _____.

  ❑ A. Objectivity   ❑ B. Conception

  ❑ C. Scope   ❑ D. Grade

The answer is D, grade. Both restaurants set standards and meet them, so they have good quality food. The difference between the two is in the grade of the food they offer.

It is equally important to understand the difference between precision and accuracy because they are not the same thing. Precision denotes measurements that show little variation from each other, whereas accuracy is the degree to which measurements approach the true value. It is possible to have precise measurements that are not accurate, and it is also possible to have accurate measurements that are not precise.

Q. **In which of the following sets does the first term denote measurements that show little variation from each other whereas the second term is the degree to which measurements approach the true value?**

☐ A. Accuracy, precision   ☐ B. Precision, accuracy

☐ C. Consistency, accuracy   ☐ D. Quality, quantity

The answer is B. Knowing the difference between these two will help greatly in the managing of quality for any project.

Quality is one of the three key constraints in any project, with the other two being cost and schedule. Quality in itself is not a new concept by any stretch of the imagination. It has been around in one form or another in the U.S. since the mid-1800s. In its beginnings, quality was mostly concentrated on finding problems as opposed to preventing them.

Q. **Prior to World War I, what was the focus of quality?**

☐ A. Statistical process control

☐ B. Inspection and identification of problems

☐ C. Appearance

☐ D. There was no quality focus

The answer is B because quality in that time period was focused on finding and identifying problems through inspection. However, it became apparent in the ensuing years that quality could not be "inspected in" after the fact and that some sort of control had to be established earlier in the process before the product was complete.

> **Q.** **After World War I and continuing until after World War II, what quality concept was developed?**
>
> ❑ A. Rigorous inspection standards
>
> ❑ B. Quality Assurance
>
> ❑ C. Quality Control
>
> ❑ D. Six Sigma

The answer is C, Quality Control, which included the development of most of the charting and mathematical procedures for measuring quality. Most of these techniques are still being used today.

After World War II, the quality movement really moved into high gear as one after another "quality guru" appeared and greatly changed the quality landscape. Once again, the focus changed to move the quality aspects further up in the process chain so that quality problems could be circumvented rather than corrected.

> **Q.** **After Quality Control, the succeeding process was:**
>
> ❑ A. Quality Concepts ❑ B. Six Sigma
>
> ❑ C. Quality Assurance ❑ D. Quality Circles

The answer is C, Quality Assurance. Quality Assurance moved more into the realm of avoiding problems rather than correcting them. This movement commenced in the 1950s and, led by the aforementioned "quality gurus," continued for more than 20 years. Among the most recognized names was that of Dr. W. Edwards Deming, who was largely ignored when he first spoke out with his ideas on quality. Other notable names were Crosby, Juran, Ishikawa, and Baldridge.

> **Q.** **The first recognized expert in quality, who is considered by many to be the "Father of the Quality Movement," was:**
>
> ❑ A. Deming ❑ B. Baldridge
>
> ❑ C. Juran ❑ D. Crosby

The answer is A, Dr. W. Edwards Deming, although he had to offer his services to a foreign country in the throes of reconstruction.

Q. What is the act of avoiding quality problems rather than inspecting for them?

☐ A. Quality Control   ☐ B. Quality System Work

☐ C. Quality Assurance   ☐ D. Quality Managing

The answer is C.

Q. As a direct result of Deming's work overseas, the Deming Prize is offered by:

☐ A. Germany   ☐ B. France

☐ C. England   ☐ D. Japan

The answer is D, Japan, because that is where Deming's thinking on quality was first recognized, accepted, and applied, to the great advantage of the post-war reconstruction effort in that country. After Deming came a series of recognized names, each with his/her own take on quality, and each enjoyed a wide following.

Q. Philip Crosby asserted:

☐ A. Quality costs are sometimes too much.

☐ B. Quality is free.

☐ C. Zero defects is unachievable.

☐ D. Always use statistical process control.

The answer is B, quality is free. In fact, that was the title of a book Crosby wrote in which he held that the cost of quality is always less than what defects will cost you when everything is taken into account.

Q. Ishikawa is best known for:

☐ A. The 85/15 Rule

☐ B. The Fishbone Diagram

☐ C. Japanese application of Deming's theories

☐ D. The quality movement in the automobile industry

The answer is B, the Fishbone Diagram, which is used to graph the sources of quality problems. It is called this because of its structure, which resembles the skeleton of a fish. As a matter of interest, Deming was the one who asserted that 85% of quality problems required management involvement whereas only 15% were solvable by workers, whereas Crosby believed management was the entire key to quality.

Q. Deming gave us a revision to the Shewhart Cycle, which is:

☐ A. Plan, Act, Do, Check   ☐ B. Plan, Do, Check, Act

☐ C. Plan, Check, Do, Act   ☐ D. Plan, Act, Check, Do

The answer is B, Plan, Do, Check, Act, which is sometimes simply called the PDCA cycle, by which continuous improvement is achieved.

Despite the preponderance of evidence of the value of quality being pursued early in any project, the U.S. was slow to embrace the quality movement. In fact, it was well after Deming was working in Japan, which began to export quality products, that anyone took notice. Quality products being produced in Japan was in complete contrast to the cheap and faulty imitations that marked Japanese-produced items immediately following World War II.

Q. When did the U.S. wake up to the benefits of Quality Assurance?

☐ A. The 1970s

☐ B. The 1980s

☐ C. The 1990s

☐ D. Not until the introduction of Six Sigma

The answer is B, the 1980s, some 30 years after Deming's work in Japan. However, when the U.S. did wake up, it began to catch up to the rest of the world. In fact, the U.S. now offers a very prestigious national award for quality.

Q. The most sought-after quality award offered in the United States is:

□ A. The Malcolm Baldridge National Quality Award

□ B. The Philip Crosby Award

□ C. The U.S. Chamber of Commerce Quality Award

□ D. The Juran Award

The answer is A, the Malcolm Baldridge National Quality Award, named for a former Secretary of Commerce. Some of the winners include Corning, Inc., GTE, AT&T, and Eastman Chemical. The award has seven areas, which are graded and have a total of 1,000 possible points, and the largest area is Business Results, which accounts for 450 points.

There are as many definitions of quality as there are writers on the subject because each had a slightly different approach to achieving quality performance.

Q. Which quality guru advocated conformance to requirements in his definition of quality?

□ A. Baldridge   □ B. Juran

□ C. Deming   □ D. Crosby

The answer is D, Crosby, who maintained that the key to quality was getting a measurable definition of quality in the requirements at the outset and making sure the final product conformed to that definition. The PMBOK from PMI has its own definition of Project Quality Management. The PMBOK definition of Project Quality Management has elements of Deming, Crosby, Juran, and Total Quality Management (TQM).

Q. The PMBOK definition of Project Quality Management does not include:

□ A. Planning   □ B. Control

□ C. Assurance   □ D. Confirmation

If you read carefully, you will note that this question asked what was not included, rather than what was included. The answer is D, Confirmation. The PMBOK states that Project Quality Management is "the policy, procedures, and processes of Quality

Planning, Quality Assurance, and Quality Control, with continuous process improvement activities conducted throughout, as appropriate."

Of course quality in project management did not stop there. The modern version centered first on Total Quality Management (TQM), which is not attributed solely to one person. It is more of a consensus approach that contends that quality is achieved by a total organizational approach, where everyone is involved in quality. That includes not only the organization in question but their suppliers as well. It also espouses the ideas of continual improvement, employee empowerment, and benchmarking. TQM had such an influence that the Malcolm Baldridge National Quality Award had as its underlying principles the growth of TQM. Following TQM, the notion that quality could have strategic implications for the growth of businesses was an easy step, and that is the direction it took. For the first time, quality was really being looked at from the consumer point of view more than that of the supplier. The most recent arrival in the quality arena is Six Sigma. Using the tools of Statistical Process Control, which will be discussed later, and the idea of unending improvement, Six Sigma pushes the concept that the accuracy rate should be 99.9997%.

Q.   Who defines quality according to the modern concept?

☐   A. The engineering staff   ☐   B. The marketing staff

☐   C. The CEO   ☐   D. The customer

The answer is D, the customer. Companies are discovering that managing quality assists them in doing the things that differentiate them from their competitors in the eyes of consumers. Thus, project management quality means that not only must projects be managed in a quality environment, but also their products or outcomes must reflect that quality in their final form. The ISO 9000 definition of quality says that it is "the totality of features and characteristics of a product or service that bears on its ability to satisfy stated or implied needs."

The notion that "implied needs" are considered in the equation has a direct impact on the project manager's ability to control scope, and the first point to gain control of that aspect is in Quality Planning. It is during that time that standards, regulations, and definitions can be put in the requirements so that quality can be defined in an objective, measurable way.

Quality Planning

Like the other disciplines of project management, the PMBOK discusses Quality Planning, Perform Quality Control, and Perform Quality Assurance using what it refers to as inputs, tools and techniques, and outputs.

Under Quality Planning, the PMBOK lists as inputs Enterprise Environmental Factors, Organization Process Assets, Project Scope Statement, and Project Management Plan. The Enterprise Environmental Factors are frequently the result of federal, state, and local regulations, procedures, and so on that bear on the subject matter the project is dealing with. Organizational Process Assets include such things as quality policy, lessons learned, quality-related programs and processes, and organizational standards. Ideally each organization should have a quality policy that would direct or influence project quality policy.

> **Q. An organization's quality policy should come from:**
>   - ❑ A. The project manager
>   - ❑ B. The customers
>   - ❑ C. Top management
>   - ❑ D. Accounting

The answer is C, top management. In fact, the policy should reflect the top management view of quality and its importance in the strategic planning processes.

> **Q. The project quality policy should be written by:**
>   - ❑ A. The customer for each project
>   - ❑ B. The project team for each project
>   - ❑ C. Top management for each project
>   - ❑ D. Accounting for each project

The answer is B, the project team for each project. The project team, led by the project manager, puts together the quality policy for each project using what is known about the customer's desires in terms of quality in order to conform to the quality policy of the company, which comes from top management.

Organizational Process Assets could be a database or file of lessons learned and best practices that relate directly to the project application as well as a chosen set of quality processes and procedures such as Six Sigma, the Crosby Quality Education System, and so on.

Q. Organizational Process Assets do not include:

- ❑ A. Lessons learned
- ❑ B. Quality methodology
- ❑ C. Federal regulations
- ❑ D. Best practices

The answer is C. Federal regulations fall under the category of Enterprise Environmental Factors.

The next input to a Project Quality Plan is the Scope Statement. If properly crafted, it should circumscribe the project, making its boundaries quite clear to every stakeholder and to the project team.

Q. The Scope Statement for a project is written during Initiation as a part of:

- ❑ A. Project Scope Planning
- ❑ B. Project Quality Planning
- ❑ C. Project Policy Guidance
- ❑ D. Project Boundary Definition

The answer is A, Project Scope Planning.

The Scope Statement includes justification for the project, objectives of the project, a list of deliverables, and a description of the product that will result on completion of the project. The product should reflect the defined requirements, which are derived from the stakeholders' needs, wants, and expectations. In addition, the Scope Statement covers the defined thresholds and acceptance criteria for the project. Thresholds generally relate to cost, time, and resource parameters for the project, whereas acceptance criteria address how well the product meets the stakeholders' requirements.

The actual product (or process in the case of a service) is further defined in the Product Description and may include technical descriptions and details, which often have a direct bearing on the manner in which quality is approached in the Project Quality Plan.

> **Q. How many of the other eight processes called out in the PMBOK are considered to potentially have an input to Project Quality Planning?**
>
> ❑ A. All of them
>
> ❑ B. All except Project Risk Management
>
> ❑ C. All except Project Human Resources Management
>
> ❑ D. All except Project Integration Management

The answer is A. All the other processes can have an influence on Project Quality Planning, which is an indication of how interdependent every process in the PMBOK is on the other eight processes during the Planning phase. Therefore, it should be no surprise that the PMBOK lists the project plan as a major input to Project Quality Planning.

> **Q. The manner in which the inputs to quality are handled is referred to by the PMBOK as:**
>
> ❑ A. Definitions   ❑ B. Guidelines
>
> ❑ C. Tools and techniques   ❑ D. Descriptions

The answer is C, tools and techniques, which include Cost/Benefit Analyses, Benchmarking, Design of Experiments, Calculation of the Cost of Quality, and what the PMBOK refers to as "additional quality tools." Such tools may be brainstorming techniques like the Crawford Slip, flowcharting, affinity diagramming, and various matrix constructs. The PMBOK says that the outputs of all these processes are the Quality Management Plan, Quality Metrics, Quality Checklists, Process Improvement Plan, the Quality Baseline, and Updates to the Project Management Plan.

> **Q. The Quality Management Plan describes:**
>
> ❑ A. How quality policy will be implemented
>
> ❑ B. Where in the project quality is important
>
> ❑ C. Why there is a need for quality
>
> ❑ D. When to apply quality

The answer is A, how quality policy will be implemented. One of the other outputs in Quality Management Planning is called Quality Metrics.

Q. Another term for a Metric is:

☐ A. Standards and regulations ☐ B. Operational definition

☐ C. Product appearance ☐ D. Fitness for use

The answer is B, operational definition, because these definitions are used to measure the degree to which quality is being obtained.

The PMBOK lists yet another output of the Quality Management Planning process as Checklists. These are useful to make sure no steps are skipped, and when generalized for use in other projects, they may be subject to constant improvements through the lessons learned processes. Such generalized checklists can be a handy reference for project managers to carry with them just to make sure they are asking the right quality-related questions of team members.

The fourth output of Quality Management Planning is the Process Improvement Plan, although it is actually a subset of the Project Management Plan. The Process Improvement Plan is aimed at better satisfying the stakeholders by increasing the customer value of the product. It includes Process Boundaries, Configurations, and Metrics as well as identifying Targets for Improved Performance.

Q. The Process Improvement Plan does not include which of the following:

☐ A. Process Metrics

☐ B. Process Configurations

☐ C. Targets for Improved Performance

☐ D. The Project Management Plan

The answer is D, the Project Management Plan. The Process Improvement Plan is part of the Project Management Plan. The next output of Project Quality Planning is the Quality Baseline. As a baseline, this output facilitates the measuring of the degree of quality being achieved as the project progresses.

Finally, there are the updates to the project plan. These must pass through the Integrated Change Control Process so that their effects on the project plan are correctly recorded and implemented by the project team.

Performing Quality Assurance

After the Quality Management Planning is completed and implemented, attention can be turned to Performing Quality Assurance, the second of the three processes needed to guide the project in producing quality results. According to the definition found in the PMBOK, "Quality Assurance (QA) is the application of planned systematic quality activities to ensure that the project will employ all processes needed to meet requirements."

Q. The PMBOK treats Perform Quality Assurance with:

❑ A. Inputs

❑ B. Tools and techniques

❑ C. Outputs

❑ D. All of the above

The answer is D, all of the above. In fact, the PMBOK lists ten inputs to the Perform Quality Assurance process.

Q. One of the inputs to Quality Assurance according to the PMBOK is:

❑ A. Statement of Scope

❑ B. Quality Policy

❑ C. Quality Management Plan

❑ D. Checklists

The answer is C. The Quality Management Plan is the first of the ten inputs listed.

The other inputs to Quality Assurance are Quality Metrics, Process Improvement Plan, Work Performance Information, Approved Change Requests, Quality Control Measurements, Implemented Change Requests, Corrective Action, Defect Repair, and Preventive Actions. Quality Control Measurements are documented in such things as Statistical Process Control charting and Inspection Reports such as Pass/Fail reporting and Corrective Action reports that detail each discrepancy and the action taken to fix it. Operational Definitions or Metrics establish what will be measured that is related to the quality of the project and its products.

Q. Another term for Operational Definitions is:

❑ A. Project Measurements

❑ B. Metrics

❑ C. Quality Definitions

❑ D. Quality Policies

The answer is B, Metrics, which can be used interchangeably with Operational Definitions. Generally speaking, Operational Definitions include product attributes, performance criteria, and the methods and processes that are used to measure quality.

The PMBOK says that the tools and techniques used in Quality Assurance are Quality Planning tools and techniques, Quality Audits, Process Analysis, and Quality Control tools and techniques. Among the Quality Planning tools and techniques are benchmarking, flowcharting, designing experiments, and conducting cost/benefit analyses. Benchmarking involves picking a practice, process, product, service, cost, etc. that sets the standard for all others. This gives you a standard against which you can measure your present position, and it can help you track progress toward attaining or even exceeding the standard you have selected.

Q. Benchmarking is useful for:

- A. Measuring your level of quality against a standard
- B. Determining your major quality problems
- C. Engineering quality only
- D. Software quality only

The answer is A, measuring your level of quality against a standard.

Quality audits are mostly conducted as an independent, objective review rather than as an internal review by members of the project team. Generally, quality audits use recognized standards against which performance is measured.

Q. One of the tools used by a quality audit team is:

- A. Trick questions
- B. Checklists
- C. Status Reports
- D. None of the above

The answer is B, Checklists. This ensures that the audit will cover all areas of concern in a standard manner for every project.

The outputs from Perform Quality Assurance are Requested Changes, Recommended Corrective Actions, Organizations Process Assets Updates, and Project Management Plan Updates. As can be seen from the outputs described, Quality Assurance involves continuous improvement rather than a one-time effort.

> **Q.** **The idea for continuous improvement in quality is a theme of:**
>
> ❑ A. TQM   ❑ B. Deming
>
> ❑ C. Crosby   ❑ D. All of the above

The answer is D, all of the above. Actually, all three were very clear on the importance of continual improvement of quality by any organization.

Performing Quality Control

The third element of Project Quality Management is Perform Quality Control. The PMBOK 3rd ed. describes Perform Quality Control as "monitoring specific project results to determine if they comply with relevant quality standards and identifying ways of eliminating causes of unsatisfactory results."

> **Q.** **Quality Control is performed:**
>
> ❑ A. At the start of a project   ❑ B. When defects are identified
>
> ❑ C. For the life of the project   ❑ D. After the project is accepted

The answer is C: for the life of the project. The PMBOK goes on to list seven inputs, ten tools and techniques, and ten outputs involved in Quality Control.

> **Q.** **The seven inputs to Quality Control are the Metrics, the Quality Management Plan, Checklists, Work Performance Information, Approved Change Requests, Organizational Assets, and:**
>
> ❑ A. Deliverables   ❑ B. Ishikawa Diagrams
>
> ❑ C. Flowcharts   ❑ D. Quality audits

The answer is A, deliverables, which, after all, are the very purpose of undertaking the project from the outset.

Specifically, the PMBOK says the ten tools and techniques used in Quality Control are Cause and Effect Diagrams, Histograms, Run Charts, Scatter Diagrams, Control Charts, Pareto Diagrams, Statistical Sampling, Flowcharting, Defect Repair Review, and Inspection. We already have seen that quality cannot be "inspected into" a product or process; however, that does not imply that we should not use inspection.

Q. What should be the role of inspection in Quality Control?

☐ A. To determine the level of performance against standards

☐ B. To prove that you are producing a quality product

☐ C. To satisfy upper management and the customer

☐ D. Minimally useful because quality cannot be inspected in

The answer is A, to determine the level of performance against standards. Although one could argue that elements of B and C have some value, A is the best answer. We inspect to see where we are in terms of quality. Inspection can take many forms, including visual examination, precise measurements with instruments, tasting, and testing. In some instances, the testing can include destructive testing, which renders the tested item useless. An example of this might be the collision testing of prototype automobiles to determine their resistance to damage or ability to protect occupants.

Q. Another term for Cause and Effect Diagrams is:

☐ A. Trend Analysis   ☐ B. Ishikawa Diagrams

☐ C. Scatter Diagrams   ☐ D. Metrics

The answer is B, Ishikawa Diagrams, or as they are sometimes called, Fishbone Diagrams because of their physical structure. Figure 12-1 is an example of a Cause and Effect Diagram.

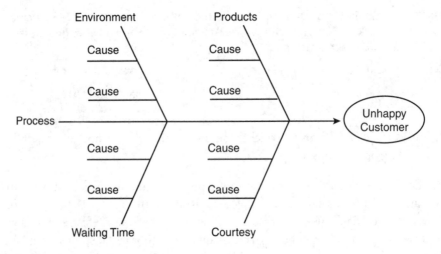

FIGURE 12-1: Cause and Effect Diagram.

Yet another type of charting is known as Scatter Diagrams, which are used to track one variable against another. Examples are tracking operation speed of equipment vs. breakdowns or age of automobile drivers vs. number of accidents. The PMBOK lists a tool known as Trend Analysis to analyze such charts. This tool predicts, mostly through extrapolation, what the future results will be, given the historical data.

Control Charts are a category under a statistical technique known as Statistical Process Control or SPC. Control Charts are useful in Quality Control in that they offer a graphical picture of data over a specific time period for a process. This usually is plotted with time on the horizontal axis and the data values at specific times on the vertical axis. The diagram in Figure 12-2 is an example of a Control Chart that plots data around a mean value. Note that there are zones on either side of the expected average or mean value that are labeled LCL and UCL, which stand for Lower Control Limit and Upper Control Limit. Data that falls within the LCL and UCL is considered normal variation in the process, whereas data outside those limits is considered abnormal and worth investigating to determine what caused the variation. Note also that data plotted outside the control limits of the chart are labeled as out of control.

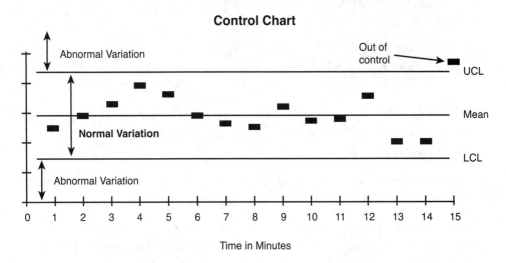

FIGURE 12-2: Plotting data around a mean value.

Defect Repair, or as it is sometimes called, Rework, involves bringing the rejected items to a level that makes them acceptable, and it is frequently an expensive but necessary action. Defect Repair is, therefore, something that should be continually examined to determine the causes for the failures so they may be avoided in the future. From a project management viewpoint, every instance of Rework should be included in the "lessons learned" artifacts of the project to assist those who engage in similar future projects.

Another useful charting technique uses histograms, often called Pareto Diagrams. These diagrams were named for Vilfredo Pareto (1848–1923), an Italian economist who advanced several economic theories on society among which were that 80% of the wealth is controlled by 20% of society. This was by no means intended to be a precise measure, but his mathematical formula for this theory gave rise to the heuristic known as the 80/20 Rule. This rule says that 80% of problems are the result of 20% of assignable causes. These bar charts are useful in that they allow you to group errors, defects, and other problems into logical groups so that you can focus on solving the most frequent problems first. You should not expect that every time you use a Pareto Diagram, you will come up with an 80/20 breakdown, but that in no way diminishes their value as a Quality Control tool.

> **Q.** **Recording of the causes for Rework could best be done by:**
> - A. Pareto Charts
> - B. Changes to the project schedule
> - C. Project Status Reports
> - D. The Comptroller

The answer is A, Pareto Charts, which allow you to look at not only the causes of failure but also their frequency so that you can target the ones that offer the most improvement if corrected.

Flowcharting allows you to get a picture of processes so that they can be analyzed for possible areas of errors or disconnects that can cause quality problems.

Checklists are used to prove that all steps detailed in the Quality Assurance outputs were completed. Completed Checklists should be included in the historical record of the project and can be useful artifacts in the event of a project audit.

> **Q.** **Quality Checklists are used to:**
> - A. Ensure that Quality Assurance steps were followed
> - B. Keep quality inspectors busy
> - C. Inform upper management where failures occur
> - D. Prevent project audits

The answer is A, Ensure that Quality Assurance steps were followed.

According to the PMBOK, the outputs from Quality Control are QC Measurements; Validated Defect Repair; Updates of the Quality Baseline, the Organization Process Assets and the Project Management Plan; Recommended Corrective and Preventive Actions and Defect Repair; Requested Changes; and Validated Deliverables.

QC Measurements are outputs in the sense that they are fed back to Quality Assurance for use in the revision and refinement of standards, processes, and procedures in the organization. Upon completion of repair of defective items, the items are inspected using the same standard as before, so either the repair action is validated or the item is again rejected and either repair is attempted again or the item is scrapped. QC measurements provide feedback for the updating of the Quality Baseline, the Organization Process Assets, and ultimately the Project Management Plan. Similarly, measurements taken in performing the QC function lead to recommendations for corrective and preventive actions, in addition to recommendations for the repair of defects. Most importantly, QC measurements are used to validate deliverables for the project and assure they are correct and fit for the use intended.

Q. QC measurements play an important role in improving project quality if they are:

❑ A. Kept in a safe location in the QC organization

❑ B. Part of a feedback system to improve quality

❑ C. Reported to the customer only in the event of a dispute

❑ D. Recorded in the project archives as lessons learned

The answer is B because the measurements, when fed back properly, are key in instituting continuous quality improvement.

As we have seen, quality is an important facet of project management and plays directly with the other eight processes that contribute to managing projects of various sizes and complexity. Although all of the nine processes discussed in the PMBOK have their place in projects, quality is one that is intimately involved in every project, no matter the subject, size, or complexity.

Questions from Chapter Twelve ?

1. The three most important aspects of a project to stakeholders are:

- ❏ A. Cost, Schedule, Strategy
- ❏ B. Schedule, Quality, Risk
- ❏ C. Quality, Cost, Risk
- ❏ D. Cost, Schedule, Quality

2. Quality in the U.S. dates back to:

- ❏ A. 1970s
- ❏ B. World War II
- ❏ C. World War I
- ❏ D. Mid-1800s

3. Quality checklists are used to:

- ❏ A. Ensure that Quality Assurance steps were followed
- ❏ B. Keep quality inspectors busy
- ❏ C. Inform upper management where failures occur
- ❏ D. Prevent project audits

4. QC measurements play an important role in improving project quality if they are:

- ❏ A. Kept in a safe location in the QC organization
- ❏ B. Part of a feedback system to improve quality
- ❏ C. Reported to the customer only in the event of a dispute
- ❏ D. Recorded in the project archives as lessons learned

5. The organization that controls the standards for quality is the _____.

- ❏ A. ISO
- ❏ B. INA
- ❏ C. PMI
- ❏ D. IIQ

6. Which is not true?

- ❏ A. Quality is important to products
- ❏ B. Quality can be inspected into any product
- ❏ C. Quality can be influenced by cost
- ❏ D. Quality can be influenced by schedule

7. Quality Assurance was preceded by:

- ❏ A. Quality Circles
- ❏ B. Employee Empowerment
- ❏ C. Quality Control
- ❏ D. Inspection

8. Conformance to specifications is one description of _____.

- ❏ A. Grade
- ❏ B. Scope
- ❏ C. Quality
- ❏ D. Technical information

9. The food at Wendy's and Spago's are both high-quality but differ in _____.

- ❏ A. Objectivity
- ❏ B. Conception
- ❏ C. Scope
- ❏ D. Grade

10. Prior to World War I, what was the focus of quality?

- ❏ A. Statistical process control
- ❏ B. Inspection and identification of problems
- ❏ C. Appearance
- ❏ D. There was no quality focus

11. Who is credited with the concept of "Zero Defects"?

- ❏ A. Deming
- ❏ B. Crosby
- ❏ C. Ishikawa
- ❏ D. Juran

12. Pareto's Law is sometimes called:

- ❏ A. The 85/15 Rule
- ❏ B. The 90/10 Rule
- ❏ C. Pareto's Folly
- ❏ D. The 80/20 Rule

13. After World War I and continuing until after World War II, what quality concept was developed?

- ❏ A. Rigorous inspection standards
- ❏ B. Quality Assurance
- ❏ C. Quality Control
- ❏ D. Six Sigma

14. After Quality Control, the succeeding process was:

- ❏ A. Quality Concepts
- ❏ B. Six Sigma
- ❏ C. Quality Assurance
- ❏ D. Quality Circles

15. The first recognized expert in quality, who is considered by many to be the "Father of the Quality Movement," was:

☐ A. Deming

☐ B. Baldridge

☐ C. Juran

☐ D. Crosby

16. What is the act of avoiding quality problems rather than inspecting for them?

☐ A. Quality Control

☐ B. Quality System Work

☐ C. Quality Assurance

☐ D. Quality Managing

17. A Pareto Analysis often uses:

☐ A. Bar Charts

☐ B. Statistical Process Control Charts

☐ C. Normal Distribution Curves

☐ D. Linear programming

18. Deming advocated:

☐ A. Continuous improvement

☐ B. Zero defects

☐ C. Pareto Analyses

☐ D. None of the above

19. As a direct result of Deming's work overseas, the Deming Prize is offered by:

☐ A. Germany

☐ B. France

☐ C. England

☐ D. Japan

20. Philip Crosby asserted:

☐ A. Quality costs are sometimes too much.

☐ B. Quality is free.

☐ C. Zero defects is unachievable.

☐ D. Always use statistical process control.

21. Ishikawa is best known for:

☐ A. The 85/15 Rule

☐ B. The Fishbone Diagram

☐ C. Japanese application of Deming's theories

☐ D. The quality movement in the automobile industry

22. **After Quality Assurance came:**

- ❑ A. Quality Control
- ❑ B. Quality Improvement
- ❑ C. Quality Inspection
- ❑ D. Quality Planning

23. **The PMBOK definition of quality includes:**

- ❑ A. Control
- ❑ B. Assurance
- ❑ C. Planning
- ❑ D. All of the above

24. **Deming gave us a revision to the Shewhart Cycle, which is:**

- ❑ A. Plan, Act, Do, Check
- ❑ B. Plan, Do, Check, Act
- ❑ C. Plan, Check, Do, Act
- ❑ D. Plan, Act, Check, Do

25. **When did the U.S. wake up to the benefits of Quality Assurance?**

- ❑ A. The 1970s
- ❑ B. The 1980s
- ❑ C. The 1990s
- ❑ D. Not until the introduction of Six Sigma

26. **The most sought-after quality award offered in the United States is:**

- ❑ A. The Malcolm Baldridge National Quality Award
- ❑ B. The Philip Crosby Award
- ❑ C. The U.S. Chamber of Commerce Quality Award
- ❑ D. The Juran Award

27. **Which quality guru advocated conformance to requirements in his definition of quality?**

- ❑ A. Baldridge
- ❑ B. Juran
- ❑ C. Deming
- ❑ D. Crosby

28. **TQM is attributed to:**

- ❑ A. Juran
- ❑ B. Deming
- ❑ C. Crosby
- ❑ D. No single person

29. Six Sigma advocates an accuracy rate of:

- ❏ A. 99.999%
- ❏ B. 100%
- ❏ C. 99.9997%
- ❏ D. 99.9999%

30. Who defines quality according to the modern concept?

- ❏ A. The engineering staff
- ❏ B. The marketing staff
- ❏ C. The CEO
- ❏ D. The customer

31. The project quality policy should be written by:

- ❏ A. The customer for each project
- ❏ B. The project team for each project
- ❏ C. Top management for each project
- ❏ D. Accounting for each project

32. How many of the other eight processes discussed in the PMBOK are considered to potentially have an input to Project Quality Planning?

- ❏ A. All of them
- ❏ B. All except Project Risk Management
- ❏ C. All except Project Human Resources Management
- ❏ D. All except Project Integration Management

33. The ISO 9000 definition of quality includes:

- ❏ A. Ability to supply stated and implied needs
- ❏ B. Only stated needs
- ❏ C. Differentiation of companies by quality
- ❏ D. Only clearly defined needs

34. The Scope Statement for a project is written during:

- ❏ A. First status meeting
- ❏ B. Project initiation
- ❏ C. Quality planning
- ❏ D. Project planning

35. The manner in which the inputs to quality are handled is referred to by the PMBOK as:

- ❏ A. Definitions
- ❏ B. Guidelines
- ❏ C. Tools and techniques
- ❏ D. Descriptions

36. **Another term for a Metric is:**

- ❑ A. Standards and regulations
- ❑ B. Operational definition
- ❑ C. Product appearance
- ❑ D. Fitness for use

37. **Benchmarking is useful for:**

- ❑ A. Measuring your level of quality against a standard
- ❑ B. Determining your major quality problems
- ❑ C. Engineering quality only
- ❑ D. Software quality only

38. **According to the PMBOK, which of the following is not an input to Quality Planning?**

- ❑ A. Scope Statement
- ❑ B. Quality policy
- ❑ C. Other process inputs
- ❑ D. Fishbone Diagrams

39. **Quality Assurance is influenced by:**

- ❑ A. Quality Planning
- ❑ B. Stakeholder Risk Tolerance
- ❑ C. Nothing from outside the project
- ❑ D. Solely by the customer

40. **The idea for continuous improvement in quality is a theme of:**

- ❑ A. TQM
- ❑ B. Deming
- ❑ C. Crosby
- ❑ D. All of the above

41. **What should be the role of inspection in Quality Control?**

- ❑ A. To determine the level of performance against standards
- ❑ B. To prove you are producing a quality product
- ❑ C. To satisfy upper management and the customer
- ❑ D. Minimally useful because quality cannot be inspected in

42. **Recording of the causes for Rework could best be done by:**

- ❑ A. Pareto Charts
- ❑ B. Changes to the project schedule
- ❑ C. Project Status Reports
- ❑ D. The Comptroller

43. **Measuring quality of a product against a standard is called:**

❑ A. Pareto Analysis
❑ B. Benchmarking
❑ C. Lessons learned
❑ D. Auditing

44. **Quality Control inputs according to the PMBOK include:**

❑ A. Metrics and Checklists
❑ B. Work Process Results
❑ C. Quality Management Plan
❑ D. All of the above

45. **In Quality Control, in order to determine the level of quality against a standard, you should use:**

❑ A. Inspection
❑ B. The quality policy of the organization
❑ C. Risk Analysis
❑ D. Pareto's Law

46. **The mathematics of probability are used in:**

❑ A. Histograms associated with Pareto Analyses
❑ B. Statistical Sampling
❑ C. Ishikawa Diagramming
❑ D. None of the above

47. **Process adjustments are an output from Quality Control and are the outcome of:**

❑ A. Measuring the cause of failures
❑ B. Making necessary changes to processes
❑ C. Analysis of Rework
❑ D. All of the above

Answers from Chapter Twelve

1. **The answer is D**. These are known as the "triple constraints" within a project.

2. **The answer is D**. It was during this time that quality became important as a discipline.

3. **The answer is A**. Ensure that Quality Assurance steps were followed.

4. **The answer is B** because the measurements, when fed back properly, are key in instituting continuous quality improvement.

5. **The answer is A**. The ISO is the international organization that controls the standards for quality.

6. **The answer is B**. Quality cannot be inspected in because inspection takes place after the production of the service or product.

7. **The answer is C**. This process was in place before the idea of Quality Assurance became important.

8. **The answer is C**. Quality on a project means that you are conforming to a standard that is set before you begin the project.

9. **The answer is D**, grade. Both restaurants set standards and meet them, so they have good quality food. The difference between the two is in the grade of food they offer.

10. **The answer is B** because quality in that time period was focused on finding and identifying problems through inspection. However, it became apparent in the ensuing years that quality could not be "inspected in" after the fact and that some sort of control had to be established earlier in the process before the product was complete.

11. **The answer is B**. In his book *Quality is Free*, Crosby talks about the possibility of using zero defects as a goal.

12. **The answer is D**. Pareto suggested that 80% of the wealth was controlled by 20% of the population. This ratio is often used in business to describe the ratio of income to customers. Often, 80% of the income to the organization is controlled by only 20% of the customers. This is a common ratio.

13. **The answer is C**, Quality Control, which included the development of most of the charting and mathematical procedures for measuring quality. Most of these techniques are still being used today.

14. **The answer is C**, Quality Assurance. Quality Assurance moved more into the realm of avoiding problems rather than correcting them. This movement commenced in the 1950s and, led by the aforementioned "quality gurus," continued for more than 20 years. Among the most recognized names was that of Dr. W. Edwards Deming, who was largely ignored when he first spoke out with his ideas on quality. Other notable names were Crosby, Juran, Ishikawa, and Baldridge.

15. **The answer is A**, Dr. W. Edwards Deming, although he had to offer his services to a foreign country in the throes of reconstruction.

16. **The answer is C**. The main idea is that preventive actions are better than corrective ones.

17. **The answer is A**. This is the main visual form for Pareto Charts.

18. **The answer is A**. Continuous improvement is also the keystone of the Kaizen philosophy of many Japanese companies.

19. **The answer is D**, Japan, because that is where Deming's thinking on quality was first recognized, accepted, and applied, to the great advantage of the post-war reconstruction effort in that country. After Deming came a series of recognized names, each with his own take on quality. Each had his own slant on quality, but each enjoyed a wide following.

20. **The answer is B**, quality is free. In fact, that was the title of a book Crosby wrote in which he held that the cost of quality is always less that what defects will cost you when everything is taken into account.

21. **The answer is B**, the Fishbone Diagram, which is used to graph the sources of quality problems. It is called this because of its structure, which resembles the skeleton of a fish. As a matter of interest, Deming was the one who asserted that 85% of quality problems required management involvement whereas only 15% were solvable by workers, whereas Crosby believed management was the entire key to quality.

22. **The answer is D**. This is now the common process used in companies and projects throughout the world.

23. **The answer is D**.

24. **The answer is B**, Plan, Do, Check, Act, which is sometimes simply called the PDCA cycle, by which continuous improvement is achieved.

25. **The answer is B**, the 1980s, some thirty years after Deming's work in Japan. However, when the U.S. did wake up, it began to catch up to the rest of the world. In fact, the U.S. now offers a very prestigious national award for quality.

26. **The answer is A**, the Malcolm Baldridge National Quality Award, named for a former Secretary of Commerce. Some of the winners include Corning, Inc., GTE, AT&T,

and Eastman Chemical. The award has seven areas, which are graded and have a total of 1,000 possible points; the largest area is Business Results, which accounts for 450 points.

27. **The answer is D**, Crosby, who maintained that the key to quality was getting a measurable definition of quality in the requirements at the outset and making sure the final product conformed to that definition. The PMBOK from PMI has its own definition of Project Quality Management. The PMBOK definition of Project Quality Management has elements of Deming, Crosby, Juran, and Total Quality Management (TQM).

28. **The answer is D**.

29. **The answer is C**. This has become well known as a quality practice used by the Motorola Corporation.

30. **The answer is D**, the customer. Companies are discovering that managing quality assists them in doing the things that differentiate them from their competitors in the eyes of consumers. Thus, project management quality means that not only must projects be managed in a quality environment, but also their products or outcomes must reflect that quality in their final form. The ISO 9000 definition of quality says that it is "the totality of features and characteristics of a product or service that bears on its ability to satisfy stated or implied needs."

31. **The answer is B**, the project team for each project. The project team, led by the project manager, puts together the quality policy for each project using what is known about the customer's desires in terms of quality in order to conform to the quality policy of the company, which comes from top management.

32. **The answer is A**. All the other processes can have an influence on Project Quality Planning, which is an indication of how interdependent every process in the PMBOK is on the other eight processes during the planning phase. Therefore, it should be no surprise that the PMBOK lists the project plan as a major input to Project Quality Planning.

33. **The answer is A**.

34. **The answer is B**. This will become the guiding document for most of the work done on the project.

35. **The answer is C**, tools and techniques, which include Cost/Benefit Analyses, Benchmarking, Design of Experiments, Calculation of the Cost of Quality, and what the PMBOK refers to as "additional quality tools." Such tools may be brainstorming techniques like the Crawford Slip, flowcharting, affinity diagramming, and various matrix constructs. The PMBOK says that the outputs of all these processes are the Quality Management Plan, Quality Metrics, Quality Checklists, Process Improvement Plan, the Quality Baseline and Updates to the Project Management Plan.

36. **The answer is B**, operational definition, because these definitions are used to measure the degree to which quality is obtained.

37. **The answer is A**, measuring your level of quality against a standard.

38. **The answer is D**. When taking the examination, make sure you note when a question is asked in the negative.

39. **The answer is A**. The planning done in quality will influence all aspects of Project Quality Management.

40. **The answer is D**, all of the above. Actually, all three were very clear on the importance of continual improvement of quality by any organization.

41. **The answer is A**, to determine the level of performance against standards. Although one could argue that elements of B and C have some value, A is the best answer. We inspect to see where we are in terms of quality. Inspection can take many forms including visual examination, precise measurements with instruments, tasting, and testing. In some instances, the testing can include destructive testing, which renders the tested item useless. An example of this might be the collision testing of prototype automobiles to determine their resistance to damage or ability to protect occupants.

42. **The answer is A**, Pareto Charts, which allow you to look at not only the causes of failure but their frequency so you can target which ones offer the most improvement if corrected.

43. **The answer is B**. The benchmarks give a guide for the project manager. They come from previous projects and can be used to construct plans for a new project. In addition, they can be used as measuring devices.

44. **The answer is D**.

45. **The answer is A**. This was the first attempt in quality management to get better quality. However, inspection means that you wait until the product or service is complete to check it, so other ways of managing quality have been added to inspection.

46. **The answer is B**. As the discipline of statistics became more rigid, statistics became a major help in controlling and producing quality products and services.

47. **The answer is D**.

CHAPTER THIRTEEN

Project Human Resources Management

The human resources management questions on the examination generally are the simplest and easiest. You can answer most of the questions based on your work experience. Although this knowledge area is not stressed on the examination, it is an important one to know because you will be using the principles all the time when working in project management.

According to the PMBOK, this knowledge area includes the "processes that organize and manage the project team." As such, human resources management deals with all the project team, the sponsors/customer, and anyone who is working in support of the project and the project team. If you are in a large organization, you will have an expanded set of people with whom you work, although they will not be directly related to work you do on specific projects.

Chapter 2 of the PMBOK includes some discussion of a variety of topics that are found in general management literature. The literature on this topic is extensive, and courses are offered on this topic up through the PhD level at many colleges. So the Human Resources chapter in the PMBOK is not intended as an in-depth look at managerial skills. The topics in this chapter give you a start in this area, one on which you can and should build.

Several topics are listed: leading, communicating, negotiating, problem solving, and influencing organizational behavior. Each of these topics has significant research behind it, and these topics and skills are useful to any manager. However, these topics are not solely used in a single type of management such as general management. The professional project manager must interact with his or her project team using all of these skills, so the more the project manager knows about them, the higher the chance for project success.

A second set of skills deals with the manager and individuals. These are delegating, motivating, coaching, and mentoring, which tend to be more individually focused than the previously described skills. However, both the first set of skills and the ones listed in this paragraph can be used for more than one person as well as when dealing only with the individual.

Q. **Leading, communicating, and problem solving are examples of _____ management skills.**

❑ A. Project ❑ B. General

❑ C. Senior ❑ D. HR

The answer is B. These are general skills that managers of any type will need to use in order to perform successfully for the organization.

Q. **According to the PMBOK, delegating, motivating, coaching, and mentoring are skills used to manage the _____.**

❑ A. Organization ❑ B. Project team

❑ C. Individual ❑ D. Personal relations

The answer is C. These are discussed in the PMBOK as skills that deal with the individual for the most part. However, these skills also can be used in situations with more than one person.

Another set of skills deals with team building and dealing with conflict, which are used in both group and individual management. Finally, there are skills such as performance appraisal, recruitment, retention, regulatory issues, and labor relations that are generally considered more administrative than management-oriented. This is in contrast with the other topics listed earlier, which are found in the behavioral management context.

Q. **Recruitment, regulatory issues, performance appraisal, and labor relations are skills generally used more in the _____ area.**

❑ A. Tactical ❑ B. General management

❑ C. Accounting ❑ D. Administrative

The answer is D. These are generally thought of as administrative skills and often are not done by the project manager if the organization has experts in these skills within the personnel of the company.

However, a project manager has to understand that although all of these skills are used to manage people on projects, there are also other considerations that pertain only to projects and project management. These considerations are a direct result of the definition of a project.

The first consideration is that by nature, all projects are temporary and are used to create a new product or service. Thus, the relationships in a project are very different from the ongoing relationships that one finds in standard organizational life. The project team is unique to the project you are managing, and although you may use the same project team members on several projects in a row, the projects themselves will be slightly different. This means that you should work to make the general management skill sets fit into the project management arena because these skills relate to any type of organizational setting.

The second consideration is that the project team may expand and contract as the project is executed. The number of people on the project may change as different phases are carried out. So techniques that are useful in one phase may not be useful in the next.

Q. The _____ of the team may contract and expand depending on the phase of the project.

❑ A. Abilities ❑ B. Capabilities

❑ C. Size ❑ D. Concept

The answer is C. The size of the team may change as people are added or let go to meet the requirements of certain phases of the project.

Finally, although we will talk about administrative issues, they are often not the province of the project manager or his or her team. The HR department in most organizations will handle many of the administrative issues, and the HR department should be made up of people who have skill sets that can be used by the project manager, but are skill sets that are not the primary responsibility of the project manager.

Human Resource Planning

The first of the process groups in project human resource management is human resource planning. According to PMBOK, this determines "roles, responsibilities, and reporting relationships, and creates the staff management plan." The roles and responsibilities can be for either a group of people or an individual. The groups may be internal, or they may be a contracted project management firm. In the case of the latter, it is absolutely necessary that the roles of the people as well as their responsibilities be documented before beginning the project.

With internal groups, the overall organizational policies and structures apply. So too do the roles and responsibilities and the reporting relationships that the team members have within the organization. The structure of reporting lines is extremely important for the project manager to consider because this will determine how the project manager handles the team.

For the most part, an internal project manager does not have complete control over the project team. The various team members with their variety of skill sets usually report to managers in the functional area they represent. As we discuss types of power later in this chapter, you will see how important this issue is for the project manager to consider and manage. Often the external or contracted project manager, if he or she is running his or her own contracted project team, will have control over the entire function of the team. This is one of the major differences in a project manager's span of control.

Communications planning and organizational planning interact as planning processes. The project's final structure will determine the communication requirements of the project, and the communication planning will follow the organizational planning.

> **Q.** A(n) _____ does not generally have complete control over the team.
>
> ❑ A. Internal project manager   ❑ B. Contracted project manager
>
> ❑ C. Internal project lead   ❑ D. External project lead

The answer is A. The various members of the project team that is built within an organization will have reporting lines to their functional managers and will not report directly to the project manager.

The inputs to organizational planning are enterprise environmental factors, organizational process assets, and the project management plan that includes the activity resource requirements (PMBOK). Organizational culture and structure are the major topics within the input of enterprise environmental factors. Some of the factors involving organizational culture and structure are organizational, technical, interpersonal, logistical, and political.

The organizational factor includes information about the departments that will be involved in the project, the current working relationships between the various departments, and the relationships, formal and informal, that exist between the departments that will be used to execute the project.

Q. A reporting line to a manager is an example of a(n) _____ interface.

- ❏ A. Tactical
- ❏ B. Simple
- ❏ C. Formal
- ❏ D. Informal

The answer is C. A reporting relationship is a formal relationship that is designed by the organization.

There will be many relationships and reporting lines within an organization, and as a project manager, you will be expected to know these in order to better manage the project. The issue of current working relationships is also a major one for a project manager. If there is a history of either good or bad relationships between departments, you should be aware of it. Although past relationships between departments do not always indicate future behavior with respect to your project, they can be used as guidelines and can give you a "heads up" on potential issues.

The second type of relationship deals with the formality of the relationship. The formal relationships will be shown in organizational charts and are easy to ascertain. The informal relationships are ones that will determine the overall dynamics of the project team and as such are something that the project manager must monitor constantly.

The technical interfaces will be between various technical disciplines or functions. The interpersonal interfaces will be between various individuals working on the project and may be formal, as in the case of a reporting line to a manager, or informal, as in the relationship between two people who are on the project team and need to communicate to complete their tasks. In addition, you need to know the job descriptions of the various team members, which will help determine choices of personnel. Finally, the trust levels between the various project team members are very important dynamics for the project manager to manage. At least it would be good to know whether there are any questions about trust between potential team members so that issues may be brought forward and handled early in the project.

The logistical part of the enterprise environmental factors consists of the working spaces and the distances between people on the team. If your team is multinational, and several members of the team are working in other countries, you must work to make sure that you can accommodate issues such as time changes, lack of interpersonal communication, and various local customs that will impact the work of the project team. Collocation is usually recommended for making the best project team. Collocation means having the entire project team in the same building, either with adjoining facilities or housed in one large room. (This almost never happens during the complete duration of the project.)

> **Q.** The distances between people on the team are managed as a part of the _____ of the team.
>
> ❑ A. Problems ❑ B. Structure
>
> ❑ C. Tactics ❑ D. Logistics

The answer is D. The logistics can get very complicated if you are using a multinational team with members in various far-flung places.

Finally, the political aspects of the organizational culture will have an impact on how the project team works. Not political in terms of national parties, but rather in terms of smaller groups. The only time national parties may enter into project management might be when the politics of a certain country factor into the completion of the project. Permits and licenses may be a part of this issue. Project team politics may include informal power that some department has within a given organization. For instance, in many IT organizations, the development department has the greatest organizational power because that department is the one that actually creates the product or service.

> **Q.** The structure of the organization, collective bargaining agreements, and the overall economic conditions of the organization itself are examples of _____.
>
> ❑ A. Documents ❑ B. Constraints
>
> ❑ C. Control issues ❑ D. Organizational issues

The answer is B. All of these are constraints that may affect the project and the project manager. The key for the project manager is to check at the beginning of the project to determine whether any of these constraints will affect the project as it is executed.

The second input into human resources planning is organizational process assets, which are sets of processes in an organization that are useful for performing the project. Two of the major process assets listed in PMBOK are templates and checklists. These two give guidelines to the project manager and, if in fact they already exist, will make it easier to reduce the amount of planning time because processes are already in place for certain tasks in the organization. Even though the current project will not exactly mirror a past project, the templates and checklists used before may be extremely helpful. Be sure to monitor these two assets to make sure that your current project's checklist content is taken care of, and do not assume that the past checklists or templates are carbon copies of what you need currently.

> **Q.** **Templates and checklists are examples of _____.**
> - ❏ A. Organizational design
> - ❏ B. Organizational culture
> - ❏ C. Process assets
> - ❏ D. Process tactics

The answer is C. These two are process assets that can be used to help reduce the amount of time needed in the planning process if used correctly.

The project plan is the last of the inputs to human resource planning. The project plan has a variety of information useful to the new project manager. First, the activity resource requirements have been detailed so that planning flows from available information. Second, there are a variety of project management activities such as risk management and procurement that are listed in the overall project plan that can help the project manager assess and assign people to various tasks that are needed in the project.

> **Q.** **The list of people needed for the project team is refined as part of _____.**
> - ❏ A. The WBS
> - ❏ B. Human resource planning
> - ❏ C. Organizational charts
> - ❏ D. Tactical planning

The answer is B. Human resource planning is the area where required people are identified.

Three tools and techniques for human resource planning are found in the 3rd edition of the PMBOK. They are organization charts and position descriptions, networking, and organizational theory. There are a variety of formats used to document the team members' roles, responsibilities, and relationships. According to the PMBOK, most of the formats fall into three types: hierarchical, matrix, and text-oriented.

The Work Breakdown Structure is an example of a hierarchical chart. It shows relationships of the various tasks and people in a top-down, graphic format. The WBS looks like a family tree and is common in organizational control.

In addition to the WBS, PMBOK lists two other types of breakdown structures. The first is the Organization Breakdown Structure, or OBS. The difference between the WBS and the OBS is that the OBS shows departments or units of the organization and is not organized along the lines of deliverables.

The next breakdown structure type is the Resource Breakdown Structure, or RBS. This type of hierarchical chart breaks down the project by resource types so that the project manager can see quickly which resources can be grouped together. For instance, quality testers may be listed together, although they may be used at different times during the project for different areas of quality testing. The RBS does not have to be only for human resources and may include materials, communication technologies, and other types of resources needed to execute the project.

Q. The OBS, WBS, and RBS are all examples of _____.

❑ A. Control charts ❑ B. Project standards

❑ C. Tactical controls ❑ D. Hierarchical charts

The answer is D. All of them have a graphic, top-down, "family tree" orientation.

Q. The breakdown structure that shows departments or units of the organization is the _____.

❑ A. WBS ❑ B. OBS

❑ C. RBS ❑ D. CBS

The answer is B. The Organizational Breakdown Structure shows the organization's units and departments as a top-down graph.

Q. The hierarchical chart that shows resources is the _____.

❑ A. RBS ❑ B. CBS

❑ C. OBS ❑ D. ABC

The answer is A. The Resource Breakdown Structure details the various resources, both human and mechanical, that are needed to successfully execute the project.

Q. The breakdown structure that shows a hierarchical list of required project tasks is the _____.

   ❑ A. CBS   ❑ B. OBS

   ❑ C. RBS   ❑ D. WBS

The answer is D. The Work Breakdown Structure is one of the principal documents that a project manager uses to manage the project.

The second format type that is mentioned in the PMBOK is the matrix format.

TABLE 13-1: Matrix Format

Name	Drew	Al	Nancy
Development	X		X
Testing	X	X	
Documentation		X	X

Table 13-1 is an example of a matrix format that shows usage of personnel on three tasks that need to be done in an IT project. The Responsibility Assignment Matrix (RAM) details the different tasks for the people listed in the matrix chart. You can see quickly which people have overlapping tasks and which are used on specific tasks. This will help you as you schedule the project.

Q. The _____ details tasks for people in the project.

   ❑ A. WBS   ❑ B. RAM

   ❑ C. SOW   ❑ D. CBS

The answer is B. The Responsibility Assignment Matrix is used to give an overview of personnel responsibility for particular tasks.

The text-oriented format is generally a written file that describes the roles and responsibilities of a person on the project. This type of format allows for greater detail than others, but it is not used for quick analysis of personnel needs.

The outputs to the human resource planning are roles and responsibilities, project organization charts, and the staffing management plan. PMBOK suggests that four items should be considered when listing the roles and responsibilities of a person on the project. In addition to roles and responsibilities themselves, the other items are authority and competency.

Authority is defined as "the right to apply project resources, make decisions, and sign approvals." Authority is generally assigned in the organizational structure, although there may be projects where there will be matrixed authority. It is best when the responsibilities of the individual are matched with the authority to get tasks done. It is extremely frustrating to be given the responsibility for a task without the necessary authority to see it through.

The competency item in roles and responsibilities deals with the skills of the project member to complete project tasks and responsibilities. People are occasionally assigned to a project who do not have the requisite skills to get particular tasks done or who are not sufficiently trained to do the tasks in a timely manner. Knowing the skill levels of project team members is important when planning human resources for any type of project.

Q. **The right to apply project resources, sign approvals, and make decisions is known organizationally as _____.**

   ❏ A. Leadership   ❏ B. Authority

   ❏ C. General management   ❏ D. Project management

The answer is B. This authority will most often come from the organization.

Q. **Skills to do the project activities and tasks are defined as _____.**

   ❏ A. Necessary   ❏ B. Necessities

   ❏ C. Timely   ❏ D. Competencies

The answer is D. The project manager must know the skill sets and skill levels of potential project team members to do effective human resource planning.

The project organization chart is a graphic display of the various members of the project team and the managers to whom they report. This chart can help the project manager to gain an understanding of the communication lines needed to run the project.

The staffing management plan is a subset of the project management plan. This plan details the resources needed for the project. Depending on the size and complexity of the project, this plan will be formal or informal, detailed or broadly stated. The more complex the project, the more detail is included. In a large DoD project, this type of plan will almost always be formal. On a project with a smaller scope, the plan may be informal. The detail and formality of the staffing management plan depends on the needs of the project.

A variety of information can be captured in the staffing management plan. Some items are optional. These include staff acquisition, a timetable, release criteria, training needs, recognition and rewards, compliance, and safety. Each of these items can be detailed or even left out if the project warrants it.

> **Q. Whether a staffing management plan is formal or informal may depend on the _____.**
>
> ❑ A. Sponsor's wishes
>
> ❑ B. Size and complexity of the project
>
> ❑ C. Project team members' skills
>
> ❑ D. Tactical considerations.

The answer is B. The size and complexity of the project will be one of the determining factors as to whether to make the staffing management plan formal or informal.

Staff acquisition includes several questions that must be answered in order to have good human resource planning. Among these questions are whether to keep your HR search in-house or go to outsourcing for resources. Team logistics is another topic that may be included in the staff acquisition plan, although this topic might be found in other places in planning. The logistics issues include the various locations of team members and the ways the team may work from off-site offices.

Costs are another issue in staff acquisition. After you have determined the level of skills needed to complete the project, you will have to compute the costs associated with the necessary skills. This type of management decision is often a tradeoff between time and cost, although in the best of all possible projects, you will not have to worry about skimping at all.

The timetable for the project can be part of the staffing management plan. You can depict the necessary resource usage using a variety of illustrations. If you look in the

PMBOK 3rd ed. at Figure 9-6, you will see a resource histogram that is useful in determining how much time is expected from the various team members and/or functions. Many types of charts are available to show the information. You choose the one with which you are the most comfortable and that gives you manageable information.

The release criteria include both the timing of the release of team members and the method in which you will release them. The cost involved with retaining people who are not needed to continue the project can be a major one. This and the fact that orderly transitions to new projects are desirable make the use of release criteria important.

Yet another item to be considered in the staffing management plan is the need for training. In some projects, training is needed because the people assigned to the project do not have complete information on the tasks that are required of them. A training plan can be a great help in shoring up the skill levels needed on the project.

> **Q. The timing and method of letting team members go is known as _____.**
>
>   ❑ A. HR policy   ❑ B. Project team management
>
>   ❑ C. Release criteria   ❑ D. Project management

The answer is C. These criteria should be determined early in the project.

Although not listed by PMBOK at this point, training for end users is important to consider early in the project. If you are installing a new AR system and want end users to understand and use the new software quickly and effectively, it is a good idea to detail the planning that will make this happen. End-user training can make or break the final outcome of the project, so it should be a part of the overall staffing plan because you will need to assign a person or people to actually conduct the training.

Recognition and rewards are major parts of the motivation of a project team. In order to make sure that everyone is on the same page, there must be clear criteria for team member rewards and a system to obtain these rewards. In order to be effective, the rewards should be linked directly to something under the project member's control. Frustration can occur if the team member has no control over his or her own rewards. The key to all of this is to make the reasons for rewards clear and to get agreement from various team members concerning what they will be rewarded for during the execution of their particular set of required project tasks.

The compliance part of the staffing management plan deals with tactics for complying with contracts, government regulations, and any other applicable policies that the organization has put in place. Usually, these policies will be available through the human resources department, and it is a good idea to check for any compliance issues before beginning the project.

Q. A major part of project team motivation is (are) _____.

☐ A. Perks   ☐ B. Rewards and recognition

☐ C. Strictness   ☐ D. Documentation

The answer is B. Rewards and recognition are among the most important factors in project team motivation.

Another area of compliance is that of legal requirements. Legal requirements may constrain how you choose projects and how projects are executed. An example of this would be a project to shut down support for a previous version of software and to migrate all users to a new version. You should check first with the legal department to make sure that no contracts have been written that would stop you from discontinuing help desk service. This is not an unusual issue, and you should examine it at the beginning of the project.

Finally, safety can be a major issue within a staffing management plan. The organization should set policies and procedures concerning the safety of all people involved in the project, which can be included in the staffing management plan. Many construction companies consider safety to be *the* major issue on a project. It is a good idea to make sure that the policies are in place and then to carry them out.

Q. Release criteria, safety policies, compliance, and training can all be found in the _____.

☐ A. SOW   ☐ B. WBS

☐ C. Staffing management plan   ☐ D. Corporate general plan

The answer is C. All of these can be found in a staffing management plan, although this will depend on where the organization prefers to cover these topics.

> **Q.** Government regulations, union contracts, and legal requirements are all examples of the need for _____ when executing a project.
>
> ❑ A. Safety ❑ B. Documents
>
> ❑ C. Oversight ❑ D. Compliance

The answer is D. Compliance with both external and internal regulatory issues is necessary for a project to run smoothly.

> **Q.** For many companies, _____ is the primary concern.
>
> ❑ A. Quality control ❑ B. Procurement policy
>
> ❑ C. Safety ❑ D. Structure

The answer is C. Keeping the project team safe, particularly in construction projects, should be a major concern for organizations.

> **Q.** The correct time to let team members go and determining how to do so is known as _____.
>
> ❑ A. Hiring and firing ❑ B. Staff acquisition
>
> ❑ C. Corrective action ❑ D. Release criteria

The answer is D. If this is planned at the beginning of the project, it will make running the project much simpler and will prevent potential issues with personnel.

Acquire Project Team

Acquiring a project team is the process of getting the resources necessary to execute the project. There are five inputs into acquiring the project team: enterprise environmental factors, organizational process assets, roles and responsibilities, project organization charts, and the staffing management plan. All of these were discussed in the last section.

The only topic that has been expanded upon is that of the enterprise environmental facts. The areas of discussion are now labeled:

Availability—When are people available, and who are they?

Ability—What skill sets do these people have?

Experience—How much experience do the people assigned to the project have?

Interests—Are the project team members interested in their assigned tasks?

Costs—How much will the project team members be paid?

The tools and techniques used in acquiring the project team include pre-assignment, negotiation, acquisition, and virtual teams. Pre-assignment simply means that some members of the project team were selected before the project started. This can happen because of a contract or because a special skill set is needed.

Negotiation is a very important part of the project manager's daily duties. The project manager may have to negotiate with the line managers for his or her project team in order to make certain that they will be available when it will fit best for project execution. He or she may also have to negotiate with other project teams, particularly if special skill sets are used in both the projects and resources for these skills are scarce.

Acquisition of project team members will occur when there are no in-house resources that have the skills necessary to complete tasks within the project. In this case, the organization will use outsourcing to fill the needs.

Virtual teams are defined by the PMBOK as teams who fulfill their roles with little or no time spent meeting face-to-face. There are many different ways virtual teams occur in organizational life. The first will be if the members of the project team are not located in the same area. Multinational projects are an example. Another reason for a virtual team can be that someone with a special skill works in another place geographically but communicates electronically. There may be issues for handicapped personnel that prevent them from working on-site. And finally, projects that would normally be discontinued because of travel costs can be done using virtual teams.

Q. Getting project team members assigned when there is no one in-house with the necessary skill sets is known as _____.

❑ A. Acquisition ❑ B. Contract supervision

❑ C. Management details ❑ D. Actual reporting

The answer is A. This is the act of acquiring those skills needed to complete a project.

> **Q.** **A project team with members located in the U.S., India, and Germany would be called a _____.**
>
> ❑ **A.** Perfect team ❑ **B.** Virtual team
>
> ❑ **C.** Scattered team ❑ **D.** Difficult team

The answer is B. In a virtual team, not all team members are in the same geographical location.

> **Q.** **Working with a line manager to get a skilled person on the project team would be an example of _____.**
>
> ❑ **A.** Decision making ❑ **B.** Team building
>
> ❑ **C.** Trouble ❑ **D.** Negotiation

The answer is D. Negotiation is a significant skill required to run a project. The project manager will constantly be negotiating with other managers for resources during the execution of a project.

Developing the Project Team

The definition of developing a project team is that it "improves the competencies and interaction of team members to enhance project performance" (PMBOK). The objectives include improving the skill sets of project team members so that future work will be done more effectively and efficiently and building trust between members of the team so that teamwork is improved. The first objective, improving skill sets, should be done systematically. The skills that need to be improved should be defined so that progress can be seen. It is particularly helpful to write down various milestones in skill development because this will be a part of the recognition of the professional growth of the team member.

The second of these objectives, building trust and cohesiveness, does not have a standard way of operating. There are so many issues involved in getting trust between project team members that the topics could have a separate chapter or even a separate book. It must be said that simply doing a few team exercises will not make the project team better. Building trust and cohesiveness is a lengthy process that does not happen on each project.

Q. **In order to provide rewards and recognition for the bettering of skill sets by the members of the project team, the expected outcome of skill training should be _____.**

❑ A. Formal and informal   ❑ B. Written and measurable

❑ C. Tactical and strategic   ❑ D. Long and complex

The answer is B. Writing down expectations for skill set growth and having measurable milestones is necessary for successful project management.

The inputs to developing a project team are project staff assignments, staffing management plans, and resource availability. All of these have been discussed earlier in the chapter.

The tools and techniques used in developing a project team are general management skills, training, team-building activities, ground rules, collocation, and recognition and rewards.

For some reason, general management skills are styled "soft skills" in section 9.3.2 of the PMBOK. I am not certain what makes these skills (discussed at length earlier) "soft." These are usually the skill sets that determine the success of the project. The so-called "hard" skills often concern mathematical or statistical skills. I have yet to meet a person who can look me in the eye and say that getting a person to perform over a period of time is easier than getting a machine to do the same thing. Time to get rid of the pejorative term "soft skills" and start using "people skills" as the alternative.

Training includes activities used to make the project team members better at their project tasks. This can include online training, classroom work, computer-based training, and on-the-job training. The training may be formal, as when an instructor or teacher leads the training, or it may be informal, as when a colleague or mentor does it. In order to see the outcomes of the training, you should first measure the skills you are about to train and then measure them again at the end of the training to be sure that the people have gained something from the training.

Team-building activities are often very difficult to relate to the current project. Being able to do exercises together is not the same as being a good team. It is usually advisable to have professional facilitation.

Ground rules are the baseline rules by which the project will be run. Some of these will be formal, backed by the organization. Others may be informal but may have been put in place by the project team over a period of time or over several different projects. Usually the important ground rules about how to treat each other are not written down but instead are passed down from project to project. The project manager must set an example to make the ground rules work.

Collocation is advisable if at all possible. Having your people in the same place gives face-to-face communication opportunities that are not possible with project team members in different geographical locations. The place where collocated people meet is sometimes call the war room, although recent events in our country make these words a little insignificant compared to the dangers and perils facing our armed services.

> **Q. Having your project team meet in a single location where they can work in a face-to-face environment is known as _____.**
>
> ❏ A. Collocation   ❏ B. Team structure
>
> ❏ C. Team dynamics   ❏ D. Location construction

The answer is A. If at all possible, it is generally best to have the whole team in the same space at the same time. In international projects, this will not be possible.

The output from developing a project team is the team performance assessment. The project manager and the project management team should do assessments of the project team's performance and focus on the team as a whole. Although it is important to do individual reviews, it is just as important to reward and recognize the team as a whole. Dwight Eisenhower once said, "It does not matter who gets the credit, as long as the team wins."

> **Q. Online, classroom, computer-based, and on-the-job are all examples of types of _____.**
>
> ❏ A. Ideas   ❏ B. Training
>
> ❏ C. Tactics   ❏ D. Communication

The answer is B. These, and other types of training, will help raise the skill standards of individuals and the whole team.

> **Q. Ground rules may be _____ and _____.**
>
> ❏ A. Hard, long   ❏ B. Simple, repetitive
>
> ❏ C. Formal, informal   ❏ D. Complex, reflexive

The answer is C. Both types of ground rules, informal and formal, are important to manage as a project manager. Often the informal ground rules determine how the overall project will be run and how successful the project will be if all the project team members follow them.

> **Q. The _____ skills of general management are often the _____ to do.**
>
> ❏ A. Soft, hardest   ❏ B. General, last
>
> ❏ C. Hard, easiest   ❏ D. Tactical, hardest

The answer is A. People skills are almost always the hardest to learn and to master. Mathematical and technical skills are learned early. Handling people well is hard.

Managing the Project Team

Managing the project team involves "tracking team member performance, providing feedback, resolving issues, and coordinating changes to enhance project performance" (PMBOK). As a result of managing the project team, the staffing management plan is updated, issues are resolved, change requests are submitted, and lessons learned are added to the organization's database if one is available. This topic is as complex and "hard" as any that the project manager has to face.

The inputs to managing the project team are organizational process assets, project staff assignments, roles and responsibilities, project organization charts, the staffing management plan, team performance assessment, work performance information, and performance reports, according to the PMBOK. All of these have been discussed earlier.

The tools and techniques for managing the project team are observation and conversation, project performance appraisals, conflict management, and the issue log. As with all types of management, it is important to work directly with project members and to have personal interaction with them instead of just waiting for reports. Observation and conversation are two important parts of managing the project team. In fact, these are a major part of the management style known as MBWA, Management by Walking Around. As your project progresses, interpersonal management will keep you informed of how your team members are feeling and the ways in which you can help them be better at their jobs. No job is more important than this in project management.

How complex or simple the performance appraisals are will depend on the complexity of the project, labor contract requirements, any organizational policies that apply, and the length of the project. Some may be formal. These will generally be structured by the organization itself to get information about your project team. Other appraisals may be informal, particularly if the appraisals are ad hoc as you are doing MBWA.

If your performance appraisals are formal, you should begin with a set of objectives for the appraisal. Written documents are used for the most part in formal appraisals, and these documents should help you reach the objectives you set for the appraisal. During formal appraisals, you should give feedback to the team member. This feedback can be negative or positive, depending on performance. A management technique that works well is to give positive feedback before and after the negative. This is known as the "sandwich" technique, where you put negative feedback in between positive feedback. Do not be worried about negative feedback. Most people know when they have done something that is negative. Just make sure that you have it documented and can deliver the criticism without making it personal. Try to have positive ways to correct the actions when you do a performance report. In fact, this would be a good time to set personal objectives for the team member. Write these down and bring them up again when you have your next formal appraisal meeting.

Conflict management, if successful, can result in a better team performance. The more formal the ground rules and role definition are, the less conflict there may be. At first, it is a good idea to have the team members try to work out their own differences. If this is not possible, you should address the problem early and use a collaborative approach. It is important that you do not compromise when working on a conflict. Compromise is likely to make all parties unhappy and will not solve the conflict; it will merely keep it going until a later date. If you have continuing conflicts, you may have to use disciplinary actions or actions suggested by the organization for conflict resolution.

An issues log has been discussed before. The key to the log is to keep it as a written document and make it a permanent part of the overall project records. This means that you note the conflict, detail actions taken to deal with the conflict, and note the final outcome of the conflict. The more you record, the better off you will be in the future.

Q. The first way to solve a conflict is to let the _____ work it out.

❑ A. Team members ❑ B. Top management

❑ C. Project manager ❑ D. Sponsor

The answer is A. If possible, let the people involved in the conflict work it out in a collaborative manner.

Q. One way of resolving conflict that rarely works is a _____ style.

- ❑ A. Team
- ❑ C. Collaborative
- ❑ B. Strategic
- ❑ D. Compromising

The answer is D. Compromising while solving conflict results in the continuation of the conflict and seldom brings resolution.

Q. The issues log should be _____.

- ❑ A. Short
- ❑ C. Written
- ❑ B. Interesting
- ❑ D. Informal

The answer is C. By writing issues down, you create a permanent record of how issues were handled and resolved.

Q. When doing a performance appraisal, it is helpful to set _____ for the upcoming period.

- ❑ A. Compromises
- ❑ C. Issues
- ❑ B. Objectives
- ❑ D. Schedules

The answer is B. If you set clear objectives, you can use them as discussion points in the next performance appraisal.

Q. Conflict management will be easier if _____ ground rules are set before the project begins.

- ❑ A. Formal
- ❑ C. Strategic
- ❑ B. Tactical
- ❑ D. Informal

The answer is A. If formal ground rules are set at the beginning of the project, it may be possible to avoid conflicts by referring to the established ground rules.

Q. **A standard management practice that will help you observe and communicate with your project team is known as _____.**

☐ A. MBO   ☐ B. MBA

☐ C. MBWA   ☐ D. NBA

The answer is C. The acronym means Management by Walking Around, and it describes a practice that should be a standard for any type of manager. If you want to get your team to work closely with you, be sure to let them see you and in turn make sure that you communicate in person with them.

The outputs for managing the project team are requested changes, recommended corrective actions, recommended preventive actions, organizational process assets updates, and updated project management plans.

The requested changes listed as an output for managing the project team are changes in personnel. Sometimes you will be forced to make changes because of events out of your control. Other times you will choose to make changes because of something you believe will make the project work more effectively. When making a staffing change request, you should use the same standard change control process that is used for other areas of managing the project.

The recommended corrective actions in this section deal with human resource issues such as staffing changes (reductions or additions), additional training, and disciplinary actions. The disciplinary actions should be done in accordance with organizational policy. Disciplinary actions should be kept in written form in an organizational guide. If they are not, you should question the HR department for guidelines. Do not do your own version of disciplinary actions. The organization decides how to discipline.

Recommended preventive actions are those actions that are taken to avoid problems in the future. If possible, it is a good idea to take preventive action before a problem or conflict occurs. If you see a potential problem or some actions that you are certain will lead to problems in the future, you should try to forestall these problems.

The updates of the organizational process assets center around lessons learned documentation. As far as possible, document knowledge that has been learned during the project so that the information is available for future reference. If you have a historical database in place, lessons learned will go into it. For projects that do not have a complete database, you can save lessons learned as a separate file for future information.

Some of the lessons learned in the HR area are organization charts, positions, descriptions, ground rules, useful recognition events, skills or competencies of the team members that were uncovered during the execution of the project, and issues and solutions as found in the issues log.

Finally, updating the project plan will finish the output for managing the project team. Change requests and approved change requests should both be kept. In addition, you should note corrective actions to see if they result in updates to the staffing management plan.

Q. The term "requested changes" as it refers to managing the project team deals with _____ changes.

☐ A. Computer ☐ B. Schedule

☐ C. Staffing ☐ D. WBS

The answer is C. Requested staffing changes are an output of managing the project team.

Q. Disciplinary actions should be done in accordance with _____ policy.

☐ A. Project team ☐ B. Sponsor

☐ C. Government ☐ D. Organizational

The answer is D. The organization should set policies concerning disciplinary actions. You should contact the HR department to make sure you are in compliance with the organizational policy.

Q. Organization charts, position, descriptions, ground rules, and useful recognition events are all examples of _____.

☐ A. Project behavior ☐ B. Lessons learned

☐ C. HR control ☐ D. Project activity

The answer is B. These, and others, are examples of information that may be contained in your lessons learned.

Q. Actions that are taken to avoid problems in the future are called _____ actions.

❑ A. Management   ❑ B. Control

❑ C. Standard   ❑ D. Preventive

The answer is D. These types of actions should be taken when you have reason to believe that some type of problem may occur in the future. It is always better to anticipate problems and deal with them than it is to react to them after they have occurred.

Questions from Chapter Thirteen ?

1. Leading, communicating, and problem solving are examples of _____ management skills.

- ❑ A. Project
- ❑ B. General
- ❑ C. Senior
- ❑ D. HR

2. According to the PMBOK, delegating, motivating, coaching, and mentoring skills are used to manage the _____.

- ❑ A. Organization
- ❑ B. Project team
- ❑ C. Individual
- ❑ D. Personal relations

3. Recruitment, regulatory issues, performance appraisal, and labor relations are skills generally used more in the _____ area.

- ❑ A. Tactical
- ❑ B. General management
- ❑ C. Accounting
- ❑ D. Administrative

4. The _____ of the team may contract and expand depending on the phase of the project.

- ❑ A. Abilities
- ❑ B. Capabilities
- ❑ C. Size
- ❑ D. Concept

5. A(n) _____ does not generally have complete control over the team.

- ❑ A. Internal project manager
- ❑ B. Contracted project manager
- ❑ C. Internal project lead
- ❑ D. External project lead

6. A reporting line to a manager is an example of a(n) _____ interface.

- ❑ A. Tactical
- ❑ B. Simple
- ❑ C. Formal
- ❑ D. Informal

7. The people needed for the project team are defined as part of the _____.

- ❑ A. WBS
- ❑ B. Human resource planning
- ❑ C. Organizational charts
- ❑ D. Tactical planning

8. The distances between people on the team are managed as a part of the _____ of the team.

   ❑ A. Problems   ❑ B. Structure

   ❑ C. Tactics   ❑ D. Logistics

9. The structure of the organization, collective bargaining agreements, and the overall economic conditions of the organization itself are examples of _____.

   ❑ A. Documents   ❑ B. Constraints

   ❑ C. Control issues   ❑ D. Organizational issues

10. Templates and checklists are examples of _____.

    ❑ A. Organizational design   ❑ B. Organizational culture

    ❑ C. Process assets   ❑ D. Process tactics

11. The OBS, WBS, and RBS are all examples of a _____.

    ❑ A. Control chart   ❑ B. Project standard

    ❑ C. Tactical controls   ❑ D. Hierarchical charts

12. The breakdown structure that shows departments or units of the organization is the _____.

    ❑ A. WBS   ❑ B. OBS

    ❑ C. RBS   ❑ D. CBS

13. The hierarchical chart that shows resources is the _____.

    ❑ A. RBS   ❑ B. CBS

    ❑ C. OBS   ❑ D. ABC

14. The breakdown structure that shows a hierarchical list of required project tasks is the _____.

    ❑ A. CBS   ❑ B. OBS

    ❑ C. RBS   ❑ D. WBS

15. The _____ details tasks for people in the project.

    ❑ A. WBS   ❑ B. RAM

    ❑ C. SOW   ❑ D. CBS

16. The right to apply project resources, sign approvals, and make decisions is known organizationally as _____.

   ❑ A. Leadership   ❑ B. Authority
   ❑ C. General Management   ❑ D. Project Management

17. Skills to do the project activities and tasks are defined as _____.

   ❑ A. Necessary   ❑ B. Necessities
   ❑ C. Timely   ❑ D. Competencies

18. Whether a staffing management plan is formal or informal may depend on the _____.

   ❑ A. Sponsor's wishes   ❑ B. Size and complexity of the project
   ❑ C. Project team members' skills ❑ D. Tactical considerations

19. The timing and method of letting team members go is known as _____.

   ❑ A. HR policy   ❑ B. Project team management
   ❑ C. Release criteria   ❑ D. Project management

20. A major part of project team motivation is (are) _____.

   ❑ A. Perks   ❑ B. Rewards and recognition
   ❑ C. Strictness   ❑ D. Documentation

21. Release criteria, safety policies, compliance, and training can all be found in the _____.

   ❑ A. SOW   ❑ B. WBS
   ❑ C. Staffing management plan   ❑ D. Corporate general plan

22. Government regulations, union contracts, and legal requirements are all examples of the need for _____ when executing a project.

   ❑ A. Safety   ❑ B. Documents
   ❑ C. Oversight   ❑ D. Compliance

23. For many companies, _____ is the primary concern.

   ❑ A. Quality control   ❑ B. Procurement policy
   ❑ C. Safety   ❑ D. Structure

24. The correct time to let team members go and determining how to do so is known as _____.

    ❏ A. Hiring and firing
    ❏ B. Staff acquisition
    ❏ C. Corrective action
    ❏ D. Release criteria

25. Getting project team members assigned when there is no one in-house with the necessary skill sets is known as _____.

    ❏ A. Acquisition
    ❏ B. Contract supervision
    ❏ C. Management details
    ❏ D. Actual reporting

26. A project team with members located in the U.S., India, and Germany would be called a _____.

    ❏ A. Perfect team
    ❏ B. Virtual team
    ❏ C. Scattered team
    ❏ D. Difficult team

27. Working with a line manager to get a skilled person on the project team would be an example of _____.

    ❏ A. Decision making
    ❏ B. Team building
    ❏ C. Trouble
    ❏ D. Negotiation

28. In order to provide rewards and recognition for the bettering of skill sets by the members of the project team, the expected outcome of skill training should be _____.

    ❏ A. Formal and informal
    ❏ B. Written and measurable
    ❏ C. Tactical and strategic
    ❏ D. Long and complex

29. Having your project team meet in a single location where they can work in a face-to-face environment is known as _____.

    ❏ A. Collocation
    ❏ B. Team structure
    ❏ C. Team dynamics
    ❏ D. Location construction

30. Online, classroom, computer-based, and on-the-job are all examples of types of _____.

    ❏ A. Ideas
    ❏ B. Training
    ❏ C. Tactics
    ❏ D. Communication

31. Ground rules may be _____ and _____.

☐ A. Hard, long
☐ B. Simple, repetitive
☐ C. Formal, informal
☐ D. Complex, reflexive

32. The _____ skills of general management are often the _____ to do.

☐ A. Soft, hardest
☐ B. General, last
☐ C. Hard, easiest
☐ D. Tactical, hardest

33. The first way to solve a conflict is to let the _____ work it out.

☐ A. Team members
☐ B. Top management
☐ C. Project manager
☐ D. Sponsor

34. One way of resolving conflict that rarely works is a _____ style.

☐ A. Team
☐ B. Strategic
☐ C. Collaborative
☐ D. Compromising

35. The issues log should be _____.

☐ A. Short
☐ B. Interesting
☐ C. Written
☐ D. Informal

36. When doing a performance appraisal, it is helpful to set _____ for the upcoming period.

☐ A. Compromises
☐ B. Objectives
☐ C. Issues
☐ D. Schedules

37. Conflict management will be easier if _____ ground rules are set before the project begins.

☐ A. Formal
☐ B. Tactical
☐ C. Strategic
☐ D. Informal

38. A standard management practice that will help you observe and communicate with your project team is known as _____.

☐ A. MBO
☐ B. MBA
☐ C. MBWA
☐ D. NBA

39. The term "requested changes" as it refers to managing the project team deals with _____ changes.

- ❑ A. Computer
- ❑ B. Schedule
- ❑ C. Staffing
- ❑ D. WBS

40. Disciplinary actions should be done in accordance with _____ policy.

- ❑ A. Project team
- ❑ B. Sponsor
- ❑ C. Government
- ❑ D. Organizational

41. Organization charts, positions, descriptions, ground rules, and useful recognition events are all examples of _____.

- ❑ A. Project behavior
- ❑ B. Lessons learned
- ❑ C. HR control
- ❑ D. Project activity

42. Actions that are taken to avoid problems in the future are called _____ actions.

- ❑ A. Management
- ❑ B. Control
- ❑ C. Standard
- ❑ D. Preventive

Answers from Chapter Thirteen

1. **The answer is B.** These are general skills that managers of any type will need to use in order to perform successfully for the organization.

2. **The answer is C.** These are discussed in the PMBOK as skills that deal with the individual for the most part. However, these skills also can be used in situations with more than one person.

3. **The answer is D.** These are generally thought of as administrative skills and often are not done by the project manager if the organization has experts in these skills on staff.

4. **The answer is C.** The size of the team may change as people are added or let go to meet the requirements of certain phases of the project.

5. **The answer is A.** The various members of the project team that is built within an organization will have reporting lines to their functional managers and will not report directly to the project manager.

6. **The answer is C.** A reporting relationship is a formal relationship that is designed by the organization.

7. **The answer is B.** Human resource planning is the area where required people are identified.

8. **The answer is D.** The logistics can get very complicated if you are using a multinational team with members in various far-flung places.

9. **The answer is B.** All of these are constraints that may affect the project and the project manager. The key for the project manager is to check at the beginning of the project to determine whether any of these constraints will affect the project as it is executed.

10. **The answer is C.** These two process assets can be used to help reduce the amount of time needed in the planning process if used correctly.

11. **The answer is D.** All of them have a graphic, top-down, "family tree" orientation.

12. **The answer is B.** The Organizational Breakdown Structure shows the organization's units and departments as a top-down graph.

13. **The answer is A.** The Resource Breakdown Structure details the various resources, both human and mechanical, that are needed to successfully execute the project.

14. **The answer is D.** The Work Breakdown Structure is one of the principal documents that a project manager uses to manage the project.

15. **The answer is B.** The Responsibility Assignment Matrix is used to give an overview of personnel responsibility for particular tasks.

16. **The answer is B.** This authority will most often come from the organization.

17. **The answer is D.** The project manager must know the skill sets and skill levels of potential project team members to do effective human resource planning.

18. **The answer is B.** The size and complexity of the project will be one of the determining factors as to whether to make the staffing management plan formal or informal.

19. **The answer is C.** These criteria should be determined early in the project.

20. **The answer is B.** Rewards and recognition are among the most important factors in project team motivation.

21. **The answer is C.** All of these can be found in a staffing management plan, although this will depend on where the organization prefers to cover these topics.

22. **The answer is D.** Compliance with both external and internal regulatory issues is necessary for a project to run smoothly.

23. **The answer is C.** Keeping the project team safe, particularly in construction projects, should be a major concern for organizations.

24. **The answer is D.** If this is planned at the beginning of the project, it will make running the project much simpler and will prevent potential issues with personnel.

25. **The answer is A.** This is the act of acquiring those skills needed to complete a project.

26. **The answer is B.** In a virtual team, not all team members are in the same geographical location.

27. **The answer is D.** Negotiation is a significant skill required to run a project. The project manager will constantly be negotiating with other managers for resources during the execution of a project.

28. **The answer is B.** Writing down expectations for skill set growth and having measurable milestones is necessary for successful project management.

29. **The answer is A.** If at all possible, it is generally best to have the whole team in the same space at the same time. In international projects, this will not be possible.

30. **The answer is B.** These, and other types of training, will help raise the skill standards of the individuals and the whole team.

31. **The answer is C.** Both types of ground rules, informal and formal, are important to manage as a project manager. Often the informal ground rules are the ones that determine how the overall project will be run and how successful the project will be if all the project team members follow the informal rules.

32. **The answer is A.** People skills are almost always the hardest to learn and to master. Mathematical and technical skills are learned early. Handling people well is hard.

33. **The answer is A.** If possible, let the people involved in the conflict work it out in a collaborative manner.

34. **The answer is D.** Compromising while solving conflict results in the continuation of the conflict and seldom brings resolution.

35. **The answer is C.** By writing issues down, you create a permanent record of how issues were handled and resolved.

36. **The answer is B.** If you set clear objectives, you can use them as discussion points in the next performance appraisal.

37. **The answer is A.** If formal ground rules are set at the beginning of the project, it may be possible to avoid conflicts by referring to the established ground rules.

38. **The answer is C.** The acronym means Management by Walking Around, and it describes a practice that should be a standard for any type of manager. If you want to get your team to work closely with you, be sure to let them see you and in turn make sure you communicate in person with them.

39. **The answer is C.** Requested staffing changes are an output of managing the project team.

40. **The answer is D.** The organization should set policies concerning disciplinary actions. You should contact the HR department to make sure you are in compliance with the organizational policy.

41. **The answer is B.** These, and others, are examples of information that may be contained in your lessons learned.

42. **The answer is D.** These types of actions should be taken when you have reason to believe that some type of problem may occur in the future. It is always better to anticipate problems and deal with them than it is to react to them after they have occurred.

CHAPTER FOURTEEN

Project Communications Management

T he topic of project communications management is interesting because although it gets little focus on the examination (there are less than eight questions on this topic), it almost always ranks as one of the management areas students and professionals consider the most important for the success of a project. Although there may be few questions that are directly from this chapter, there will be other topics in other knowledge areas that can be found under the heading of communication. (For instance, lessons learned are a form of written historical communication.) Although there are certainly several topic areas on the examination and in the text that are valuable, it must be noted that the area of management and organizational communication is much deeper and more researched than the short chapter included in the PMBOK. Most of the people who have taken the examination noted that the communications questions were among the easiest on the examination.

The PMBOK states that project communications management includes "the processes required to ensure timely and appropriate generation, collection, dissemination, storage, retrieval, and ultimate disposition of project information. It provides critical links among people and information that are necessary for project success." As with any form of management, the ability to receive and understand information, send clear and correct information, analyze incoming information, and get data in a form where the data can become useful information are key parts of a manager's function in any capacity, be it project or general management. The professional manager will always have critical tasks that involve communication. As a matter of fact, there are very, very few tasks that a manager does that do not have a component of communication in them.

Q. Information is not useful to the receiver if it is not _____.

❑ A. Timely   ❑ B. Interesting

❑ C. Complex   ❑ D. Scarce

The answer is A. In order for information to be useful, it must come at the correct time.

The PMBOK shows four processes in project communications management: communications planning, information distribution, performance reporting, and manag(ing) stakeholders. Again, the processes overlap each other, and in many cases, it is difficult if not impossible to see where one process begins and another ends. It should be noted that my degree is in communication, not communication*s*. Departments in various universities around the country use the singular form; they are communication departments.

Communication Planning

This process involves "determining the information and communications needs of the stakeholders" (PMBOK). The questions to answer are who gets the information, when they get it, what channels will be used to get it to them, who will the sender be, and what the content of the communication is. We will look at each of these questions separately.

Who gets the information is specifically stated in PMBOK. The people who receive the information are defined in the communication plan. Not everyone on the project will be expected to receive every piece of information that you, the project manager, will have. If this were done, there would be such a glut of information that nothing would be communicated.

When the information is sent is critical. There are many studies showing the importance of the timing of communication. If the communication is done too early, it may be misplaced or ignored. If it is too late, problems certainly will occur. This can be seen when a person sends a massive amount of communication at the beginning of the project and expects project team members to remember what was contained in the communication and when the best time to use the information is. This is obviously a major management problem, which you will alleviate by going through communication planning.

The channels through which information will be sent are as important as any other part of the communications planning process. You can communicate information by mail, by email, in person, in meetings, by phone, by fax, and so on; the list of channel types is enormous. None of these channels is the best. The type of channel used should be matched with the way in which the communication will be used. You should also be aware that there are always assumptions about clarity in communication that are generally not true. For instance, the use of email has become more and more prevalent. Unfortunately, email has many problems that can cause communication disconnect. Sometimes the information contained in email is not well written. Other times, the email is one of hundreds that the receiver is getting every day, so it gets lost under an avalanche of other messages. In addition, with email, there is no immediate feedback such as you have when you communicate in person. Each channel of communication brings both good and bad factors. This is not the place to discuss all of them, but there are extensive research articles on the Internet, in scholarly journals, and in libraries that you can reference.

> **Q.** The people who get specific types of information from the project manager are _____.
>
> ❑ A. Project team members
>
> ❑ B. Stakeholders
>
> ❑ C. Project administrators
>
> ❑ D. People in the communication plan

The answer is D. Although all of the other people may get communication at some time, the people in the communication plan are the ones that will get specific types of information. This is why the planning of your communication process is done early in the process of managing a project. If the list of people who need to get information changes, then change your communication plan.

> **Q.** Which type of channel is the best for good communication?
>
> ❑ A. Email   ❑ B. Phone
>
> ❑ C. FAX   ❑ D. All of them

The answer is D. There is no one best channel of communication. Each channel has specific properties that make it unique. The best communication comes from a combination of channels. Using only one channel all the time will result in bad communication some of the time. Choose the channel to fit the communication need.

The inputs to communications planning are enterprise environmental factors, organizational process assets, the project Scope Statement, constraints, and assumptions (PMBOK). The first of these inputs, enterprise environmental factors, was described earlier. In order to have good communication during the project, you need to question the various stakeholders to find what their expectations are for the output of the project and the type of communication that they expect to have during the project. Failure to do this will always result in a lack of project cohesion. If you make assumptions about what a specific stakeholder needs without asking him or her, there is an increased likelihood of communication problems. Asking what kind of information a stakeholder needs is the first step to avoiding these problems.

The organizational process assets may well include some type of expected communication system for projects done within the organization. There are certainly times when stakeholders do not know all of the information they need to perform well. A communication system may well already be in place as a process, and if it is, it is imperative that you use it during the project. You must also be certain to let the stakeholders know what information you think they will need, and you must ask them for their communication requirements. By doing both of these communication actions, you will be able to meet all communication requirements, yours and theirs.

Q. How do you get the communications requirements for stakeholders?

❑ A. Prayer ❑ B. Ask them

❑ C. Meetings ❑ D. Osmosis

The answer is B. Questioning people about their communication requirements for the project is the first step in getting these requirements.

Q. In addition to stakeholder needs, who else's needs should be considered when establishing communication requirements?

❑ A. The sponsor ❑ B. The advisory board

❑ C. The customer ❑ D. The project manager

The answer is D. The project manager should consider what information he or she believes will be important to the stakeholders and should be sure to include that information in the communication requirements.

The tools and techniques for communications planning are limited to two entries. The first is a communication requirements analysis that is also titled stakeholder analysis. This consists of interviewing the various stakeholders to determine their communication needs. The information needs and the timing of that information are closely linked, so you should be certain to inquire about both aspects of these needs. The technology used for various project team communications should be determined by the specific type of information that is to be transferred. Doing this will support project team performance.

A quick word about stakeholders. Although members of the project team are the stakeholders that will execute the project, the sponsor is the one who gives authorization for expenditures. It would seem rather obvious that the sponsor is the one person who should receive timely information about the progress of the project. However, there are some organizations where the sponsor is not given up-to-the-minute information. This is unfortunate because the sponsor is the person who originally made the project possible. The sponsor is the first person you should interview for your stakeholder analysis because he or she is the one who has taken responsibility for the project.

There is one other consideration that is becoming more and more important in the IT world. The version of the software that is to be used should be standardized. The software side of communication technology is just as important as the hardware. People who send information that needs special software to be read are causing unnecessary problems in communication. The project manager who fails to tell the project team which version of the software will be used in common will find that frustration sets in if several people cannot read the communication with their current software because it is a different version than the sender's.

Q. The _____ is the most important stakeholder to keep current on the project execution.

- ❑ A. Advisory board
- ❑ B. Project member
- ❑ C. Sponsor
- ❑ D. Consultant

The answer is C. Because the sponsor started the entire process and is ultimately responsible for the outcome of the project, he or she is the single most important stakeholder to keep informed.

> **Q.** It is important to control the _____ of the software just as much as the hardware technologies.
>
> ❑ A. Version   ❑ B. Amount
>
> ❑ C. Brand   ❑ D. Concept

The answer is A. If people use different versions of the software, this is certain to delay communication and frustrate project team members.

The second tool to consider is the technology. The types of communication technologies used should always match the scope of the project. For instance, if the project is a large one with a multinational project team, it is possible that a website will be the best way to continuously have information available for the project team. This would scarcely be the case on a one-week project where you are trying to get out the quarterly newsletter with only three people on the project team. In this case, the technology might be email or the phone. In fact, there might be so much face-to-face communication that interpersonal communication replaces any type of technology.

When choosing technology for communication, there are several questions to consider. Do you need the information on a real-time basis? If you do, then you will not be using standard mail to get information to people on the project team. What technology is available to the entire team? For instance, does everyone on the project team have access to email? Remember that if your team agrees on one type of technology as the major communication technology for the project, then everyone on the team needs to have access. Leaving one or two project members out of the communication loop is a mistake that will always cause delays in the execution of the project.

The use of cell phones is growing as a project communication technology, and I have been on project teams that use cell phones as their major communication device. In fact, some companies will give out cell phones to their project teams so that communication in that form is always available.

The use of a specific technology will depend on the volume of information to be sent and received, the type of information, the need for speed of dispersal, and the best use of the team's time when communicating. The time for determining the type of technology to be used is when the communications planning is beginning. This will help the project team know how to reach each other and how the team will communicate.

> **Q.** You need to know the volume and type of information that will be communicated when considering the best _____ for communication during the project.
>
> ❑ A. Technology ❑ B. Encoding
>
> ❑ C. Places ❑ D. People

The answer is A. Choosing the best technology for communication requires as much planning as choosing the timing of communication.

Communications planning has one output: a communications management plan. This plan has several dimensions, some of which have already been described. First, it will describe who will get the information needed to successfully execute the project. Second, the communications management plan will describe what information is necessary to be successful. Third, the communications management plan will describe when information is needed. Finally, the communications management plan will describe how the information is to be passed. As you can see, a great deal of effort can be expended in creating the communications plan.

However, I have worked on many projects that didn't have a formal communications plan. There should be a formal plan, but it does not have to be very detailed. Keep the essentials in mind when writing the communications plan, and the project team is likely to read the plan and use it as a guideline. If the plan becomes too complex and tries to forecast every possible communication issue, it will be of little use.

Information Distribution

The information distribution process is clearly intertwined with communication planning. The same quartet of questions applies for distribution as it did in the communication planning process—who, what, when, and how are the questions that need to be answered. Focus on these when determining information distribution needs.

The input to information distribution is the communication management plan. This was described earlier in this chapter.

According to the PMBOK, the tools and techniques used in information distribution are communication skills, information gathering retrieval systems, information distribution methods, and the lessons learned process. The term "communication skills" has many meanings and dimensions, all of them depending on the context of the communication. In the PMBOK, the dimensions that are listed are the ability to write and communicate orally, formal and informal reports, and internal and external communication. Another listed dimension is the direction of the communication. This is described as including upward and downward communication as well as horizontal communication. (Horizontal, or lateral, communication occurs between people of equivalent level, such as equal-ranking members of the project team.) Massive amounts of information are available concerning the best ways in which to handle these topics. This is not the place to deliver that information.

Q. The three directions of communication listed in the PMBOK are upward, downward, and _____ communication.

   ❑ A. Outward   ❑ B. Lateral

   ❑ C. Distant   ❑ D. Inward

The answer is B. Lateral communication occurs between team members and all stakeholders who are peers.

The information gathering and retrieval systems may be paper systems, such as filing systems, which are done manually. In this day and age, it is likely that you will have electronic systems available, which will give access to both non-technical information, such as the status of the project, and technical information, such as design specifications and test plans. It is important that all people who should have access to information can actually get to it.

The distribution methods will include any type of channel that will help the project team successfully complete the project. Status meetings are one of the most important means of distributing information. You can determine in advance what needs to be distributed, and having the whole team at the meeting, or at least everyone represented, will give you a way to communicate with all stakeholders at once. You can have paper copies of information to send as well as electronic copies. In addition, you can have databases that can be accessed by appropriate team members that contain information necessary to execute the project. Voice mail may be used, but if it is, be sure not to assume that just because you have left a voice mail, the other party has received and understood it. If you are working with an international team, you may have videoconferencing. This technology does not take the place of having people in the same room, but it can be very helpful if you have information to pass, want to do it in real time, and do not want to spend time traveling. All of the distribution methods should be related to the best way to get information to the project team members so that they can successfully work on the project.

The outputs from information distribution are updates to organizational process assets and requested changes. The changes cited here are changes to the information distribution process. The two outputs have been discussed at length elsewhere in this book.

Performance Reporting

Performance reporting "involves the collection of all baseline data, and distribution of performance information to stakeholders" (PMBOK). The inputs into performance reporting according to the PMBOK include performance information, performance measurements, forecasted completion, QC measurements, the project management plan, approved change requests, and deliverables. All of these have been discussed earlier in this book.

Project records are a special type of performance reporting that will include important communication on the execution of the project. They must be permanent, so they will be either electronic in form or on paper. You may want to record important verbal interchanges, but for the most part, the project records must be in some form that can be put under version control. The important point is that the project records should be organized so that you can refer to the various records separately. This means, for instance, that all emails should be kept unless they had nothing to do with the project itself. You can order emails by date or topic, but it is always surprising how many times in a project you will refer to some document or communication that at first did not seem very important, so keep them.

Project reports are the various status reports or issues reports. For the most part, these should be kept chronologically. These will show the progress of the project as it was presented in various project status meetings.

Q. Project records must be _____.

- ❑ A. Lengthy
- ❑ B. Detailed
- ❑ C. Permanent
- ❑ D. Tactical

The answer is C. The records must be permanent so that they can be referred to after they have been sent and received. This means that you will not use verbal communications as project records unless someone wrote down the conversation. In that case, the notes of the conversation or meeting should be circulated to get agreement that what was captured is what was actually said.

Performance reporting involves reporting how resources are being used to execute the project and reporting the project's status. There are three distinct parts to performance reporting. The first is status reporting. This type of reporting gives information about where the project is currently. Cost (or budget) and schedule compliance are the two main pieces of information in status reports.

> **Q.** **The part of performance reporting that is an estimate of the future is _____.**
>
>   ❑ **A.** Progress reporting   ❑ **B.** Schedule
>
>   ❑ **C.** WBS   ❑ **D.** Forecasting

The answer is D. Forecasting is a form of estimate that describes the potential needs of a project.

> **Q.** **If performance reporting shows a completion percentage, you are doing _____.**
>
>   ❑ **A.** Forecasting   ❑ **B.** Scheduling
>
>   ❑ **C.** Progress reporting   ❑ **D.** Status reporting

The answer is C. When completion percentage is used in performance reporting, you are doing progress reporting.

> **Q.** **The report that explains the current condition of the project is _____.**
>
>   ❑ **A.** Progress reporting   ❑ **B.** Status reporting
>
>   ❑ **C.** Forecasting   ❑ **D.** Schedule analysis

The answer is B. Status reporting shows the current condition of the project, usually using at least the schedule conformance and the budget conformance as two main pieces of information.

Other project records include any of the other project documents that contain information about how the project is being executed. They can be from any of the knowledge areas, such as quality, risk, cost, or time.

The tools and techniques for performance reporting include information presentation tools, performance information gathering, status review meetings, and time and cost reporting systems.

Project presentations are simply any reports that were made formally to stakeholders of the project. These may be on paper, but PowerPoint presentations are becoming the most common method of presentation. Either way, these presentations will present ideas and concepts that were important enough to show the stakeholders in a formal presentation.

Performance reviews are done in meetings to assess how the project is progressing and the current status of the project. Variance analysis is one of the techniques used to describe the current status. Because you will begin the execution of the project with a baseline, you will be able to see how the estimated baseline compares to the actual performance. In variance analysis, you are trying to find the amount of variance from the plan and the causes of the variance. As with most project reporting, time and cost will be key parts of variance analysis. You can also do variance analysis on any of the knowledge area reports, such as scope, quality, and risk. If there is any type of plan with a baseline, you can do variance analysis on it.

The output from performance reporting is the performance reports themselves. Performance reports are used to explain the performance of the project. The level of detail and information in the report will depend on the people who are going to see and use the report. Stakeholders will have varied needs for information, and the reports they receive should reflect this. In other words, "one report fits all" is not the case. The reports, in any form, will often discuss the variances between what was expected and what happened. The typical report of this type will be the earned value analysis that was discussed in Chapter 11, "Project Cost Management."

Change requests as an output are those requests that are the result of communicating a specific report to a stakeholder. As analysis is done on the project, it shows there may be some need for a change to be made. The potential changes come in the form of a change request, which will be handled through the use of various change control processes, such as cost change control and schedule change control.

Q. Performance reports usually discuss _____ between estimated and actual performance on the project.

☐ A. Variances   ☐ B. Differences

☐ C. Relationships   ☐ D. Connections

The answer is A. Variance management consists of comparing the actual performance of the project to the baseline. The project manager manages variances and looks for the reasons why the variances occurred.

Stakeholder Management

The final process in project communications management is managing the stakeholders. The inputs into managing stakeholders are the communication management plan and organizational process assets. The communication plan will show the stakeholder goals and objectives. In addition, the type and level of communication to be executed during the project will be a topic in the stakeholder management plan.

The tools and techniques of managing stakeholders are communication methods and issue logs.

There are dozens of possible communication methods for managing stakeholders. These will depend on the needs of the stakeholders. In addition, different methods will be used if all the project team members are not located in the same place (collocated). The first choice in communicating information with stakeholders will always be face-to-face. In-person meetings should be used as much as possible. However, there are times when these are not practical. For instance, some of your team may be in Europe, some in the U.S., and some in Asia. Obviously, face-to-face meetings with the whole team in this case will be a problem. It is always a good policy, if not always possible or practical, to have at least one meeting with all the stakeholders present. This is sometimes bypassed through the use of videoconferencing. Although videoconferencing is not as good as face-to-face communication, it can be very useful.

If face-to-face, in-person meetings are not practical, all sorts of choices are available for communicating between project team members. Cell phones, email, websites, and written communication sent by snail mail are just some of the available methods. You need to balance the practicality of the communication method with the usefulness of the method to make the communication system work.

Issue logs constitute an extremely important tool in project management. As each issue occurs, as it will on any project, you should list it in the log and then number it. After this, state what can be done about the issue and if necessary who can resolve the issue. This last part, which is called escalating the issue, is an extremely important part of the issue log. Issues between two people with lateral positions may continue to remain unresolved unless you note that someone in the organization has the authority to solve the issue. Listing this person will help you control issues and bring them to closure.

If the issue is resolved, note that but still keep the issue in the log. Do not erase any issues that have occurred. These are as much a part of the lessons learned of the project as any other information. Do not reuse any numbers for issues. After an issue has been given an ID number, that number cannot be used again. By doing this, you will avoid confusion.

> **Q. The best type of communication method for passing information to stake-holders is _____.**
>
> ❑ A. Smoke signals   ❑ B. Face-to-face
>
> ❑ C. Email   ❑ D. Telephone

The answer is B. Although this type of communication is not always possible or practical, it remains the best possible way to communicate to stakeholders.

> **Q. The key factor in closing issues is the person to whom you will _____ the issue in order to resolve it.**
>
> ❑ A. Communicate   ❑ B. Write
>
> ❑ C. Send   ❑ D. Escalate

The answer is D. You must have a person that can resolve the issue between two laterals. That person must have the authority to make a decision, and in order to get that decision, you escalate the issue to him or her.

The outputs from managing stakeholders are resolved issues, approved change requests, updates of organizational process assets, and updates on the project management plan. The issues log is where the resolved issues are archived. Whether these issues are internal to the organization or involve outside people, the log must be kept so that the resolution of issues is permanently kept on record.

Administrative Closure

This is a topic that is left out of the PMBOK 3rd edition section on project communications management, but it is a very useful concept for a practicing project manager. Whether a project comes to an end because of reaching the originally established deliverables or because it is stopped in the middle, every project requires closure. Formal acceptance of the product of the project by the sponsor or customer is done during Administrative Closure when the output of the project is documented. Logging and retention of all project records, adherence to specifications, analysis of project success and/or failure, and saving lessons learned are all parts of the Administrative Closure process. When the project is finished, this type of information is archived for use either in reviewing the project or as guidelines for new projects.

Ideally, you should have Administrative Closure for each phase of the project if possible. (This is much like lessons learned.) The longer you wait to do Administrative Closure, the more likely it is that usable information will be lost.

Q. _____ acceptance of the product of the project is done during Administrative Closure.

❏ A. Formal   ❏ B. Written

❏ C. Oral   ❏ D. Electronic

The answer is A. The sponsor or customer should formally accept the final product of the project at this time.

Q. You should do Administrative Closure at the end of each _____ of the project.

❏ A. Deliverable   ❏ B. Month

❏ C. Phase   ❏ D. Week

The answer is C. Waiting until the end of the project to do Administrative Closure may result in loss of important information. The end of each phase is a natural time for gathering and archiving documentation.

The inputs to Administrative Closure are performance measurement documentation, product documentation, and other project records (PMBOK). When doing Administrative Closure, all documentation pertaining to the execution of the project by the project team should be made available. This should include not only performance reports but also the original plans against which performance is measured.

Product documentation such as specifications, drawings, blueprints, technical documentation, and other varieties of documentation should also be available for Administrative Closure as well as any other project records that will help make Administrative Closure go efficiently.

The tools and techniques found in Administrative Closure have all been discussed elsewhere in this chapter.

Finally, the outputs from Administrative Closure are project archives, project closure, and lessons learned. The project archives should be indexed. This makes it easier to go through the project records and find specific topic areas. Putting all the project files in a cabinet without an index can result in more time being spent on simply finding the documentation to be reviewed than in actually reviewing the documents. Each project archive should be prepared for archiving by the appropriate party on the project team. After receiving the archives from the appropriate people, make sure that databases containing materials that are being archived are updated.

PMBOK points out that when projects are done under contract as opposed to in-house, it is extremely important to focus on financial records. Years after the project has been finished, it is still possible that various people will want to look through data such as cost. The specific data that are often the most important years later are costs and their control during the project.

Q. **Project archives need to be _____ to be most useful.**

  ❑ A. Written   ❑ B. Oral

  ❑ C. Controlled   ❑ D. Indexed

The answer is D. In order to search for materials after Administrative Closure has occurred and the project is finished, indexing archives helps make searching for information much faster and simpler.

Project closure as an output of Administrative Closure means that the customer or sponsor of the project has accepted the final output of the project. The requirements for the project, the deliverables for the project, and the results of doing the project are all used to get customer acceptance. This acceptance should be formal and written. It is not sufficient to simply get verbal acceptance when doing project closure.

Lessons learned have been discussed several times elsewhere in the book. The key part is that when Administrative Closure is done, there should be some type of lessons learned database that future project managers can search for information on how the project was run. Lessons learned are one of the most valuable of all the pieces of information available after a project is finished. Often they are not done, but to be of help to other project managers, you should work hard to see that lessons learned are done during Administrative Closure.

> **Q.** **Acceptance of the output of the project by the sponsor or customer should be _____.**
>
> ❑ A. Early
>
> ❑ B. Oral
>
> ❑ C. Formal
>
> ❑ D. Indexed

The answer is C. It is extremely important to have formal acceptance when the project is being brought to Administrative Closure. If the acceptance is formal, you will have a record of it. You can refer to this record at any later time, and it forestalls any arguments about whether the project was done correctly.

Channels of Communication

This is discussed in the phase section of the book, but because this is one of the few communication questions that always seems to be on the PMI examination, here it is once again.

The formula for determining how many channels there are between a given number of people is:

N (N–1)/2, where N = the number of people on the project.

If you have four people on the project, the formula looks like this:

4 (4–1)/2

The answer is that six channels of communication exist when there are four people on the project. Learn this formula and how to use it. It will be on the examination.

Questions from Chapter Fourteen ?

1. Information is not useful to the receiver if it is not _____.

   ❏ A. Timely
   ❏ B. Interesting
   ❏ C. Complex
   ❏ D. Scarce

2. The people who get specific types of information from the project manager are _____.

   ❏ A. Project team members
   ❏ B. Stakeholders
   ❏ C. Project administrators
   ❏ D. People in the communication plan

3. Which type of channel is the best for good communication?

   ❏ A. Email
   ❏ B. Phone
   ❏ C. FAX
   ❏ D. All of them

4. How do you get the communications requirements for stakeholders?

   ❏ A. Prayer
   ❏ B. Ask them
   ❏ C. Meetings
   ❏ D. Osmosis

5. In addition to the stakeholder needs, who else's needs should also be considered in communication requirements?

   ❏ A. The sponsor
   ❏ B. The advisory board
   ❏ C. The customer
   ❏ D. The project manager

6. The _____ is the most important stakeholder to keep current on the project execution.

   ❏ A. Advisory board
   ❏ B. Project member
   ❏ C. Sponsor
   ❏ D. Consultant

7. It is important to control the _____ of the software just as much as the hardware technologies.

   ❏ A. Version
   ❏ B. Amount
   ❏ C. Brand
   ❏ D. Concept

8. The three directions of communication listed in the PMBOK are upward, down-ward, and _____ communication.

   ❑ A. Outward   ❑ B. Lateral

   ❑ C. Distant   ❑ D. Inward

9. Project records must be _____.

   ❑ A. Lengthy   ❑ B. Detailed

   ❑ C. Permanent   ❑ D. Tactical

10. The part of performance reporting that is an estimate of the future is _____.

    ❑ A. Progress reporting   ❑ B. Schedule

    ❑ C. WBS   ❑ D. Forecasting

11. If the performance reporting shows a completion percentage, you are doing _____.

    ❑ A. Forecasting   ❑ B. Scheduling

    ❑ C. Progress reporting   ❑ D. Status reporting

12. The report that explains the current condition of the project is _____.

    ❑ A. Progress reporting   ❑ B. Status reporting

    ❑ C. Forecasting   ❑ D. Schedule analysis

13. The abbreviation for the portion of the approved cost estimate that is to be spent on tasks during a given, measured period is:

    ❑ A. EV   ❑ B. AC

    ❑ C. PV   ❑ D. DC

14. The abbreviation for the amount that was budgeted for work to be performed is:

    ❑ A. EV   ❑ B. AC

    ❑ C. PV   ❑ D. DC

15. The abbreviation for costs actually incurred is:

    ❑ A. EV   ❑ B. AC

    ❑ C. PV   ❑ D. DC

16. What is your CPI if EV = 5 and AC = 4?

- ❑ A. .80
- ❑ B. 1.0
- ❑ C. 1.25
- ❑ D. 2.0

17. What is your CPI if AC = 10 and EV = 8?

- ❑ A. .80
- ❑ B. 80
- ❑ C. 1.25
- ❑ D. 2.0.

18. What is your CPI if EV = 20 and AC = 20?

- ❑ A. 4.0
- ❑ B. 1.0
- ❑ C. 2.0
- ❑ D. 1.25

19. What is your SPI if EV = 8 and PV = 6?

- ❑ A. 1.33
- ❑ B. .66
- ❑ C. 1.0
- ❑ D. .75

20. What is your SPI if PV=8 and EV = 6?

- ❑ A. 1.0
- ❑ B. .75
- ❑ C. 1.33
- ❑ D. 2.0

21. Performance reports usually discuss _____ between estimated and actual performance on the project.

- ❑ A. Variances
- ❑ B. Differences
- ❑ C. Relationships
- ❑ D. Connections

22. _____ acceptance of the product of the project is done during Administrative Closure.

- ❑ A. Formal
- ❑ B. Written
- ❑ C. Oral
- ❑ D. Electronic

23. You should do Administrative Closure at the end of each _____ of the project.

- ❑ A. Deliverable
- ❑ B. Month
- ❑ C. Phase
- ❑ D. Week

24. Project archives need to be _____ to be most useful.

- ❏ A. Written
- ❏ B. Oral
- ❏ C. Controlled
- ❏ D. Indexed

25. Acceptance of the output of the project by the sponsor or customer should be _____.

- ❏ A. Early
- ❏ B. Oral
- ❏ C. Formal
- ❏ D. Indexed

26. N (N-1)/2 is the formula for:

- ❏ A. Industrial estimation
- ❏ B. Channels of communication
- ❏ C. Risk assessment
- ❏ D. Quality levels

27. The best type of communication method for passing information to stakeholders is _____.

- ❏ A. Smoke signals
- ❏ B. Face-to-face
- ❏ C. Emails
- ❏ D. Telephone

28. The key factor in closing issues is the person to whom you will _____ the issue in order to resolve it.

- ❏ A. Communicate
- ❏ B. Write
- ❏ C. Send
- ❏ D. Escalate

Answers from Chapter Fourteen

1. **The answer is A**. In order for information to be useful, it must come at the correct time.

2. **The answer is D**. Although all of the other people may get communication at some time, the people in the communication plan are the ones who will get specific types of information. This is why the planning of your communication process is done early in the process of managing a project. If the list of people who need to get information changes, then change your communication plan.

3. **The answer is D**. There is no one best channel of communication. Each channel has specific properties that make it unique. The best communication comes from a combination of channels. Using only one channel all the time will result in bad communication some of the time. Choose the channel to fit the communication need.

4. **The answer is B**. Questioning people about their communication requirements for the project is the first step in getting these requirements.

5. **The answer is D**. The project manager should consider what information he or she believes will be important to the stakeholders and be sure to include that information in the communication requirements.

6. **The answer is C**. Because the sponsor started the entire process and is ultimately responsible for the outcome of the project, he or she is the single most important stakeholder to keep informed.

7. **The answer is A**. If people use different versions of the software, this is certain to delay communication and frustrate project team members.

8. **The answer is B**. Lateral communication occurs between team members and all stakeholders who are peers.

9. **The answer is C**. The records must be permanent so that they can be referred to after they have been sent and received. This means that you will not use verbal communications as project records unless someone writes down the conversation. In that case, the notes of the conversation or meeting should be circulated to get agreement that what is captured is what was actually said.

10. **The answer is D**. Forecasting is a form of estimate that describes the potential needs of a project.

11. **The answer is C**. When percentage of completion is used in performance reporting, you are doing progress reporting.

12. **The answer is B**. Status reporting shows the current condition of the project, usually using at least the schedule conformance and the budget conformance as two main pieces of information.

13. **The answer is C.** The two letters stand for planned value, which means that the estimates you used to put together your cost plan are represented by planned value. At any point in the project, you should be able to calculate how much you planned for the activities to cost up to that point. Planned value is a future value. It is your best estimate of what things *will* cost in the future.

14. **The answer is C,** Planned value.

15. **The answer is B.** The letters stand for actual costs and are the real costs that have been incurred during the project. Your accounting department may give this number to you.

16. **The answer is C.** EV = 5, AC = 4, and the formula reads CPI=5/4, which is 1.25.

17. **The answer is A.** EV = 8, AC = 4, and the formula reads CPI = 8/10, which is .80.

18. The answer is B. AC = 20, EV = 20, and the formula reads CPI = 20/20, which is 1.

19. **The answer is A.** EV = 8 and PV = 6, and the formula reads SPI=8/6, which is 1.33.

20. **The answer is B.** EV = 6 and PV = 8, and the formula reads SPI=6/8, which is .75.

21. **The answer is A.** Variance management consists of comparing the actual performance of the project to the baseline. The project manager manages variances and looks for the reasons the variances occurred.

22. **The answer is A.** The sponsor or customer should formally accept the final product of the project at this time.

23. **The answer is C.** Waiting until the end of the project to do Administrative Closure may result in loss of important information. The end of each phase is a natural time to gather and archive documentation.

24. **The answer is D.** In order to search for materials after Administrative Closure has occurred and the project is finished, indexing archives helps make searching for information much faster and simpler.

25. **The answer is C.** It's extremely important to have formal acceptance when the project is being brought to Administrative Closure. If the acceptance is formal, you will have a record of it. You can refer to this record at any later time, and it forestalls any arguments about whether the project was done correctly.

26. **The answer is B.** Learn the formula. It will be on the test.

27. **The answer is B.** Although this type of communication is not always possible or practical, it remains the best possible way to communicate to stakeholders.

28. **The answer is D.** You must have a person who can resolve the issue between two laterals. That person must have the authority to make a decision, and in order to get that decision, you escalate the issue to him or her.

CHAPTER FIFTEEN

Project Risk Management

Accordingto the PMBOK, 3rd edition, project risk management includes the
processes of conducting Risk Management Planning, identification, analysis,
responses, and monitoring and control on a project. In this chapter, you will
learn how the project risk management processes increase the chance of meeting project objectives. When practiced on a project, risk management increases the potential
of success and decreases the potential negative impacts the risk events may have if
they occur. This planning also guides the team to develop appropriate responses. To
be most effective, the project team must also continually monitor risk occurrences and
take appropriate action throughout the project life cycle.

The Project Risk Management Processes

There are six Project Risk Management processes:

Risk Management Planning

Risk Identification

Qualitative Risk Analysis

Quantitative Risk Analysis

Risk Response Planning

Risk Monitoring and Control

Some of these processes are designed to guide the project team through a complete
and robust analysis of risks and opportunities. Others assist the team in managing,
monitoring, and controlling risks and opportunities. Cost overruns and schedule

delays on projects are often attributed to unexpected events (risk events) that were not taken into account.

Risks are either known, meaning that they are identified and analyzed, or unknown, meaning that they are non-specific but expected while at the same time being unidentified and not analyzed. Because of this, schedule and budget contingency cannot be quantified but are part of a general contingency. For example, some projects use a standard amount of contingency for these unknowns, ranging from 10% to 25% of the total budget, with more for higher risk projects and less for more predictable projects. If the project team discusses and focuses on risk frequently, more risks can be identified and responses can be developed.

Q. Project risk is the uncertainty that an event or condition that affects _____ will be realized.

❑ A. Project performance as measured by the functional managers

❑ B. Project impact on the organization

❑ C. Opportunities the project could realize

❑ D. At least one of the project objectives such as cost, scope, time, or quality

The correct answer is D. Project risks affect the ability of the project team to meet its commitments of time, costs, scope, or quality.

Q. True or False? Risks may have one or more causes and one or more impacts.

The correct answer is true. Risk events such as a delay in receiving a customer's approval to proceed on a design may have multiple causes. For example, a delay in the delivery of documents to a customer for their approval and incomplete information on the documents could cause the approval to be delayed. As a result of the delay, the project schedule, deliverable quality, and project cost all may be negatively impacted.

Risk Management Planning

Risk Management Planning is the process of developing an approach and executing risk management activities for a project.

Q. Risk Management Planning should be completed _____ in the project planning phase.

   ❑ A. Sometime   ❑ B. Late

   ❑ C. Early   ❑ D. Never

The correct answer is C. Other risk management processes are driven by and dependent on the Risk Management Plan.

Inputs to Project Risk Management Planning

The inputs to Risk Management Planning include:

Environmental factors,

Organizational process assets,

Project Scope Statement, and

Project management plan, as described in earlier sections of this book.

Project Risk Management Planning Tools and Techniques

Meetings for planning and analysis are the primary tools for creating the Risk Management Plan, which is the output of this process. One of the ways that a project team can begin to define the types and sources of risk events is to create a Risk Breakdown Structure (RBS). An example of an RBS is shown in Table 15-1.

TABLE 15-1: Example Risk Breakdown Structure

Project			
Technical	External	Organizational	Project Management
Requirements	Suppliers	Resources	Estimating
Technology	Regulatory	Funding	Planning
Quality	Market	Prioritization	Controlling
Performance and Reliability	Weather	Customer	Documentation

The Risk Breakdown Structure is one way to identify risks in a structured manner. It assists the team in conducting a systematic review of risks and development of responses to risks.

> **Q.   What is a Risk Breakdown Structure (RBS)?**
>
> ❑   A.   Flowchart of risks
>
> ❑   B.   Risk impacts on the organization
>
> ❑   C.   List or diagram of risks by category
>
> ❑   D.   Risk management activities that are on the schedule

The best answer is C. An RBS is optional but may assist the team in identifying risks and opportunities by looking at the sources of risks or the areas where risks may occur.

The Risk Management Plan can include a Probability and/or Impact Matrix for organizing the information that will be used during the Risk Identification process to prioritize and quantify risks, and it may in some cases show opportunities for the project as well. Common information in the matrix includes numerical and/or descriptive definitions of impact, negative and positive, and the probability of occurrence. The combination of probability and impact determines whether a risk is rated high, moderate, or low. These descriptors are rank ordered in a relative scale. Numerical scales can also be used.

> **Q.   Which of the following would be used to describe the significance of the negative impact of threats or the positive impact of opportunities?**
>
> ❑   A.   Cost, time, scope, and quality
>
> ❑   B.   Sources of the risk events
>
> ❑   C.   Types of risk responses
>
> ❑   D.   Very Low, Low, Moderate, High

The correct answer is D. Relative scales of impact are rank ordered to differentiate risks that require special attention from lesser risks. Numerical scales such as 0.1, 0.5, and 0.9 can also be used to assign values to the impact of the risks.

Outputs of Risk Management Planning

In summary, the Risk Management Plan should describe the entire risk management process, including auditing of the process. It should also define the content and format of the Risk Register, reporting, and risk tracking.

- Methodology—Describes how risk management will be done on the project

- Roles and responsibilities—Defines the risk management team and their responsibilities for risk management activities

- Budgeting—Assigns budget for risk management activities to be included into the project cost baseline (project budget)

- Timing—Specifies when and how often the risk management activities appear in the project schedule

- Risk categories—Defines types and sources of risks to guide the Risk Identification process

- Definitions—Operational definitions for the project team to use to ensure consistency in the assessment of risks and opportunities

- Probability and Impact Matrix—Specific combinations of impact and probability, which lead to risk ratings such as high, medium, or low

- Revised thresholds—Revised or validated descriptions that trigger taking action; scope, quality, cost, and time thresholds may be different from each other

- Reporting formats—How to communicate risk activities and their results

- Tracking—How to document risk monitoring and management activities

TABLE 15-2: Sample Definitions of Impact on Project Objectives

Project Objective	Relative Scale for Impact				
	Very Low	**Low**	**Moderate**	**High**	**Very High**
Cost—Budget	Insignificant increase	< 10% increase	10%–20% increase	20%–40% increase	> 40% increase
Time—Schedule	Insignificant increase	< 5% increase	5%–10% increase	10%–20% increase	> 20% increase
Scope—Deliverable(s)	Scope decrease barely noticeable	Minor areas of scope are affected	Major areas of scope are affected	Reduction in quality is unacceptable	End item has limited use if any
Quality—Deliverable(s)	Quality decrease barely noticeable	Only very demanding applications are affected	Reduction in quality to this level requires approval	Reduction in quality is unacceptable	End item has limited use if any

Table 15-2 shows the operational definitions of Impact on Project Objectives. This creates alignment and improved communication by the team when identifying and analyzing risks.

The Risk Management Plan will be used throughout the life cycle of the project. As the team moves through the subsequent Risk Management Processes, the plan will be revised, updated, and improved.

Q. According to Table 15-2, the impact of a risk to the project schedule will be classified as _____ if the delay to the project (as a result of the risk event) will be one week to a 20-week project schedule.

❑ A. Low   ❑ B. High

❑ C. Very Low   ❑ D. Moderate

The correct answer is A. If there is a delay of one week over a 20-week time period, that is the equivalent of a 5% increase. According to the matrix, that is a Low impact to the Time objective of the project.

Risk Identification Process

Risk Identification is the way project teams determine the risks that affect the project so that analysis and risk response can be performed. Risk Identification is an iterative process and continues throughout the life of the project.

Inputs to the Risk Identification Process

Risk Identification uses the Risk Management Plan as an input, whereas the Quantitative and Qualitative Risk Analysis processes use the Risk Register as an input. The inputs to Risk Identification are similar to the inputs to the Risk Management Planning process with the addition of the Risk Management Plan.

To identify risks, teams often enlist the aid of risk and technical experts, stakeholders, customers, and others, both inside and outside of the project team and organization, to identify risks. Involving the team increases accuracy and ownership as well as commitment to the project. In order to have an effective Risk Identification meeting, several conditions must be met.

First, it is important to *create an atmosphere where team members are comfortable bringing up potential risks.* Some organizations have a culture of "shooting the messenger" or emphasizing optimism over realistic risk assessment. A thorough examination of all possible risks can only occur in an environment that is perceived as safe and fair.

Second, the team must be able to *identify potential risk events without evaluation.* Brainstorming is a good way to do this. Some groups think that brainstorming occurs when they take turns sharing ideas and writing them down or even discussing them as they are brought up. This is *not* brainstorming. True brainstorming occurs without analysis or censorship, and when people have a free flow of ideas without defending, explaining, or evaluating their ideas. In the best brainstorming sessions, team members are participating fully and equally, writing their own ideas on Post-it Notes, then saying them out loud as they are "slapped" on a piece of flip chart paper. This method is called "Write It, Say It, Slap It" and uses auditory, visual, and kinesthetic modes for whole brain thinking. Remember, brainstorming is for generating ideas for identification of risks. Evaluation comes later during Qualitative Risk Analysis.

Third, *all ideas should belong to the team, not to an individual.* When the team puts forth an idea, especially an unpopular one, it carries more weight than a single individual, and no single individual is "blamed" for the bad news. Some team members may have less credibility than others, and the credibility of the team as a whole will generally outweigh the credibility of a lone team member.

Fourth, *include the "right" people.* Make sure you have technical, political, and organizational expertise in the meeting. Non-supporters, potential saboteurs, stakeholders, key functional managers, suppliers, and other project managers can greatly enhance the quality of the potential Risk Identification or opportunities when invited to participate.

A project team can sometimes skip Qualitative Risk Analysis when they have enough expertise and experience with previous projects and risk responses.

Q. _____ usually follows the Risk Identification process, but sometimes _____ directly follows the Risk Identification process when an experienced risk manager is involved.

- ❑ A. Risk Management Planning, Quantitative Risk Analysis
- ❑ B. Qualitative Risk Analysis, Quantitative Risk Analysis
- ❑ C. Quantitative Risk Analysis, Qualitative Risk Analysis
- ❑ D. Risk Monitoring and Control, Risk Response Planning

The correct answer is B. Risk Identification must precede Risk Analysis. A person who is experienced in risk management may be able to skip the Quantitative and Qualitative Risk Analysis and determine the risk response solely upon identification of the risks and previous experience.

Q. **The inputs to Risk Identification are similar to the inputs to the Risk Management Planning process with the addition of the _____.**

   ❑ A. Scope Statement   ❑ B. Risk Management Plan

   ❑ C. Risk Identification method   ❑ D. WBS

The answer is B.

Tools and Techniques of Risk Identification

During planning meetings, the project team will conduct documentation reviews or use checklists and/or diagramming techniques to identify risks. A number of information gathering techniques, assumptions analyses, and diagramming techniques may be employed as part of the identification process. Diagramming techniques commonly used by project teams are cause and effect diagrams, flow charts, and influence diagrams.

Information Gathering Techniques

- Brainstorming—Using the project team and other experts to generate a list of risk events

- Delphi technique—Developing consensus through a polling technique in multiple rounds, moderated by a facilitator

- Interviewing—Interviewing subject matter experts or others experienced in projects

- Root Cause Identification—Inquiry into the causes of a project's risks

- Strengths, weaknesses, opportunities, and threats (SWOT) analysis—Using a SWOT analysis to identify risk events

Risk checklists, often developed from knowledge gained on previous projects and historical information, should be reviewed at project closeout for continuous improvement. As with brainstorming, when using risk tools and techniques, remember that if the project team participates fully, there will be more ownership for the outcome, in addition to greater accuracy.

> **Q. Which of the following is NOT an information gathering technique for risk management?**
>
> ❏ A. Interviews   ❏ B. Probability and Impact Matrix
>
> ❏ C. Delphi technique   ❏ D. Root cause analysis

The correct answer is B. The Probability and Impact Matrix is a component of the Risk Management Plan, used as an input to the Risk Identification process.

Outputs of the Risk Identification Process

The outputs of the Risk Identification process are contained in the Risk Register, a comprehensive document that includes:

Risks

Root causes

Potential risk responses (optional)

An updated list of risk categories from the RBS

The number of meetings required to complete the Risk Identification process is dependent on the complexity of the project. There may be a separate meeting for each project deliverable, risk category, or subproject, with the appropriate participants. The results of these meetings are transferred to the Risk Register, which is updated and used as a basis for Risk Monitoring and Control.

> **Q. The Risk Register consists of:**
>
> ❏ A. Qualitative Risk Analysis, Quantitative Risk Analysis, and Risk Management Plan
>
> ❏ B. Qualitative Risk Analysis, Risk Response Plan, list of identified risks
>
> ❏ C. List of identified risks, potential responses, root causes, and updated risk categories
>
> ❏ D. Risk Responses, Risk Categories, Risk Management Plan

The correct answer is C. The Risk Register is a comprehensive document that lists the risks, root causes, potential responses (optional), and an updated list of risk categories from the RBS. It uses the Risk Management Plan as an input, and the Quantitative and Qualitative Risk Analysis processes use the Risk Register as an input.

For teams that do not choose to use a formal Risk Register, the project risks may be tracked with an issues list or an open items list. Frequent and disciplined reviews of risks are an essential part of successful risk management.

Qualitative Risk Analysis Process

The Qualitative Risk Analysis process sorts and prioritizes risk events by evaluating the probability and impact of risk events. The project team will use the Risk Management Plan to guide the process, and the items on the Risk Register will be evaluated. Many factors influence the approach to and the type of qualitative analysis that will be performed. These factors include the project status and type, the quality and accuracy of data, and assumptions about the project.

In performing a qualitative analysis, the project team will assign risk probability and impact. A probability/impact risk rating matrix is a common tool for evaluation of risks, and assumptions testing may be used to evaluate the strength and accuracy of the information that will be used. Qualitative analysis will lead to an overall risk ranking for the project and a list of prioritized risks.

There generally is not enough time or money to address every risk event that may be identified, so the project team should expend its effort on the most important risk events—the ones that have the greatest return impact on the project. This return can be in the form of negative impacts that are prevented or minimized, or positive impacts where the probability is increased. Qualitative Risk Analysis allows the team to prioritize the identified risks.

Inputs to the Qualitative Risk Analysis Process

The project team will use the Risk Management Plan to guide the process, and the items on the Risk Register will be evaluated. The inputs to the Qualitative Risk Analysis process are similar to Risk Identification with the exception of Enterprise Environmental Factors and the Project Management Plan and the addition of the Risk Register.

Q. Inputs to the Qualitative Risk Analysis process include:

- ❑ A. Risk Register
- ❑ B. Project Scope Statement
- ❑ C. Risk Management Plan
- ❑ D. Organizational Process Assets
- ❑ E. Probability and Impact Matrix
- ❑ F. All of the above
- ❑ G. A, B, C, and E
- ❑ H. A, B, C, and D

The correct answer is H. The completed Probability and Impact Matrix is not an input to the Qualitative Risk Analysis. The Risk Register is an output of the Risk Identification process, and the Risk Management Plan is an output of the Risk Management process. The Project Scope Statement and the Organizational Process Assets affect all the Project Risk Management processes.

Qualitative Risk Analysis Process Tools and Techniques

The primary tools and techniques used for Qualitative Risk Analysis are:

- Risk Probability and Impact Assessment—Investigates the likelihood and effect on project objectives for each risk

- Probability and Impact Matrix—A look-up table that integrates probability and impact combinations into risk ratings such as high, medium, or low

- Risk Data Quality Assessment—Examining the data used to evaluate risks to determine whether it is accurate and reliable, including the distinction between fact and opinion

- Risk Categorization—Sources and locations of project risks

- Risk Urgency Assessment—Designation of the critical nature of a risk for warning signs, severity, and time to implement a response

Q. _____ and _____ are assessed for each identified risk in the Qualitative Risk Analysis process.

- ❑ A. Probability, impact
- ❑ B. Impact, priority
- ❑ C. Probability, costs
- ❑ D. None of the above

The correct answer is A. The purpose of this process is to sort and prioritize risk events using the likelihood that the risk event will occur as well as the consequences of the risk event.

The risk probability assessment determines the chance that a risk event will come to pass. Attempting to prevent a risk event with a very low probability or a low impact may not be the best use of project resources if the negative effect on meeting any of the project objectives is less than the impact of the occurrence. The impact assessment examines the risk events' effects on the project objectives. Each risk event is evaluated in order to prioritize the risks and determine an appropriate range of responses. For example, if the impact of a risk event to the project is limited to $1,000, it would not make sense to spend $1,000 to prevent the risk event. If the probability of occurrence of the risk event is very low, the team may decide to take their chances and do nothing, hoping that the risk event will not happen. In order to determine the probabilities and impact on the project objectives, the project team will need the operational definitions from the Risk Management Plan.

To prevent the team from using exclusively anecdotal data or unstructured discussions, it is best to use a structured process. Informal discussions in meetings are convenient but are not as robust as a disciplined process. Good decision-making processes should be used as well, ones that differentiate between opinion and data.

The outputs of the Qualitative Risk Analysis include the updated Risk Register with some or all of the following factors (see Table 15-3):

- Priority—Each individual risk is ranked according to significance and increased chance of meeting project objectives (scope, cost, time, or quality) from a risk response

- Category—Looking at the cause or location of risks can lead to an understanding of root cause and hence more effective risk responses

- Near-term response—Risks that require an immediate response are grouped so that they can be addressed in a timely fashion

- Additional analysis—Risks that require more analysis and response

- Low priority risks for watch lists—Risks that are low priority but that should be watched

- Trends in Qualitative Risk Analysis—Trends that require additional analysis that may point the team to a potential problem area

Q. The _____ section of the Risk Register can be used to ensure that some risk events are not overlooked during the project life cycle.

☐ A. Priority

☐ B. Watch List

☐ C. Qualitative Risk Analysis

☐ D. None of the above

The correct answer is B. The Risk Register not only prioritizes the risk events but also focuses attention on lower-priority risks that, if ignored during the project, could become very high-priority. Monitoring lower-priority risks could prevent them from growing. It is said, "That which is measured, improves."

TABLE 15-3: Risk Register Example—Qualitative Risk Analysis

Risk Event Description	Priority (High, Medium, Low)	Category of Risk	Near-Term Response	Additional Analysis Required	Watch List	Trends
Equipment vendor delivers late	High	External—Suppliers	Expediting activities	Yes—explore alternatives for implementation	If the inspection date is delayed by the vendors' schedules this must be noted in the status reports	Other purchase orders are delayed—examine the project procurement process for improvements
Project personnel reassigned before end of project	Low	Organizational	None	No	Communicate with functional managers on a monthly basis	Ask sponsor for additional observations

The Risk Register is a comprehensive document that lists the components of the risks for the purpose of developing responses, further analysis, or other actions by the project team.

> **Q.** **The Risk Register is updated periodically throughout the project life cycle. The Risk Register is initiated during _____ and further updated based on the information developed in the _____.**
>
> ❑ A. Risk Management Planning, Qualitative Risk Analysis
>
> ❑ B. Risk Identification, Quantitative Risk Analysis
>
> ❑ C. Risk Identification, Qualitative Risk Analysis
>
> ❑ D. Risk Management Planning, Risk Identification

The correct answer is C. The Risk Register cannot be developed before risk events are identified, and the information from the Qualitative Risk Analysis is needed to prioritize the risks for further action.

Quantitative Risk Analysis

Quantitative Risk Analysis applies interviewing and statistical techniques to evaluate the effect of risk events on the project objectives. Quantitative Risk Analysis helps the project manager to determine appropriate amounts of management reserve or contingency to be used in the project cost and schedule objectives. Because Quantitative Risk Analysis uses numerical data and statistical techniques, it has more credibility than the Qualitative Risk Analysis, which is primarily based on expert judgment. The sensible risk response decision(s) and contingency reserve amounts will be based on the information from the Quantitative Risk Analysis.

Quantitative Risk Analysis Inputs

The inputs for the Quantitative Risk Analysis are the same as the Qualitative Risk Analysis with the exception of the updated Risk Register and the project plan. Because the Risk Register is updated during Qualitative Analysis, this information is usually needed for Quantitative Analysis. The components of the project plan that are important for this Quantitative Analysis are the project cost management plan and the project schedule management plan.

Q. The inputs to the Quantitative Risk Analysis process are the Project Management Plan, Risk Register, Risk Management Plan, _____, and _____.

❑ A. Organizational Process Assets, Project Scope Statement

❑ B. Impact and Probability Matrix, Project Scope Management Plan

❑ C. Risk Probability, Impact Assessment

❑ D. Project Scope Management Plan, Organizational Process Assets

The correct answer is A. The Project Scope Statement and Organizational Process Assets are inputs to all of the risk management processes.

Quantitative Risk Analysis should be revisited after Risk Response Planning has been completed to ensure that the risk responses are adequate.

Quantitative Risk Analysis Tools and Techniques

The are seven tools of Quantitative Risk Analysis, which include data gathering, risk analysis and modeling techniques:

- Interviewing—Used to obtain information to quantify probability and impact

- Probability Distributions—Statistical distributions used to represent uncertainty in durations of schedules or costs

- Expert Judgment—Subject matter experts internal or external to the organization

- Sensitivity Analysis—Method for determining which risks have the most potential impact on the project

- Expected Monetary Value (EMV)—Statistical concept that calculates outcomes, such as decision tree analysis, modeling, and simulation

- Decision Tree Analysis—Quantifies the EMV of possible scenarios

- Modeling and Simulation—Model that translates uncertainty into potential impact on project objectives

Decision Tree Analysis

Decision Tree Analysis multiplies the outcome (usually expressed in monetary terms) by the probability, which produces a number that can be used to compare outcomes. For example, if there is a 50% chance that the risk event will occur and the cost of the risk event is estimated to be U.S. $10,000, then the expected outcome is $5,000, although the real outcome would be either U.S. $0 or U.S. $10,000. However, for evaluation purposes, the expected value of this risk is U.S. $5,000. Each option is converted to its expected value, using the same process (probability multiplied by the amount of time or money).

Q. Name the two tools and techniques of the Quantitative Analysis that are most subjective, i.e., that are based on opinions.

❑ A. Interviewing, Decision Tree Analysis

❑ B. Probability Distributions

❑ C. Expert judgment, Interviewing

❑ D. Expert judgment, Sensitivity Analysis

The best answer is C. Decision Tree Analysis, Probability Distributions, Modeling and Simulation, Expected Monetary Value, and Sensitivity Analysis are numerically based statistical tools.

Quantitative Risk Analysis Outputs

The Risk Register is again the primary output of the Quantitative Risk Analysis, updated by the Quantitative Risk Analysis with:

- Estimates of cost and schedule outcomes—Used to calculate contingency reserves
- Probabilities of achieving project objectives—Cost and time objectives
- Prioritized list of quantified risks—List of greatest risks, that is, threats and opportunities
- Trends in Quantitative Risk Analysis —Trends that may affect risk responses

Q. What parts of the Risk Register are added during Quantitative Risk Analysis?

❑ A. Trends in Quantitative Risk Analysis results

❑ B. Probabilities of achieving project objectives

❑ C. Estimates of cost and schedule outcomes

❑ D. B and C

❑ E. A and B

The correct answer is D. Probabilities of achieving project objectives and estimates of cost and schedule outcomes are both added during the Quantitative Risk Analysis process. The other outputs were developed during Risk Identification and Qualitative Risk Analysis.

Risk Response Planning

Risk Response Planning provides options for reducing threats to project objectives and enhancing opportunities. In this process, the responsibilities for implementing these responses must be assigned and incorporated into the project budgets (cost and time).

The inputs are:

- Risk Management Plan—Roles, responsibilities, definitions, budgets, and risk thresholds

- Risk Register—Including risk priority, the near-term risks, those that need more analysis, watch list, and trends

Risk Response Planning Inputs

Without the discipline of previous risk management processes, project teams may be tempted to rush into developing responses for risks that are identified but not evaluated and analyzed. Risk responses utilize resources, so these responses should deliver value to the project. Minus an understanding of the causes and impact of each risk, the selected risk responses may not be adequate or may be unnecessary. If Risk Identification is not performed well, some risk events may be missed. When resources are scarce and potential risks are numerous, Quantitative Risk Analysis will ensure that project resources are directed to the most effective risk responses.

Each identified risk that is significant enough to affect project objectives will need at least one risk response. There are several categories of responses. Some are intended to prevent risks, some are intended to protect the project objectives from risk, and some are reactive. These categories are sorted by negative risks or threats, positive risks or opportunities, and both threats and opportunities. The choice of response may also be influenced by other factors, such as the organization's culture, regulations, and industry standards, for example.

Options for dealing with negative risks or threats include:

- Avoid—There are many ways to avoid risks:
  - Change the project plan to eliminate the risk
  - Change the project plan to protect the project objectives from its impact
  - Relax the project objective(s) that are at risk
  - Change the project plan (scope) by clarifying requirements
  - Improve performance through better communication and acquiring expertise and information
- Transfer—Shift the consequence of a risk and ownership of the response to a third party. Insurance policies and outsourcing are examples of transference. This option is commonly used if the risk is too great or if outside experts are needed to manage the risk.
- Mitigate—Reduce the probability and/or consequences of an adverse risk event to an acceptable threshold. Some of the activities for mitigation may end up on the project schedule and as such can cause a change to the original project schedule and project budget. This is one reason why it is a good idea to start the risk management processes early.

Options for dealing with positive risks or threats include:

- Exploit—Directly exploit risks with positive impacts to take advantage of an opportunity for improved project performance.
- Share—Allocate ownership of the risk to a third party more capable of capturing the positive risk or opportunity. Incentives are built into the partnership to encourage this.
- Enhance—Identify and maximize key drivers for opportunities, thereby strengthening the impact or increasing the probability of the positive risk event.

Strategies for both threats and opportunities include:

- Accept—Do nothing; used when there is no possibility of elimination or when the costs are prohibitive.
- Contingency—Do nothing until certain predetermined conditions (risk triggers) are met. Contingency plans are created in advance and activated when these conditions are met.

Q. Name the strategies for negative risks.

❑ A. Avoid, Mitigate, Transfer, Contingency, Accept

❑ B. Avoid, Transfer, Mitigate

❑ C. Avoid, Transfer, Accept, Mitigate

❑ D. None of the above

The best answer is A. Contingency and Accept are for both positive and negative risk events and should be considered in addition to the negative risk responses.

TABLE 15-4: Examples of Risk Response Strategies

Strategy	Type of Risk	Example
Avoid	Negative, Threat	Revise the schedule so that if the risk occurs, the project completion date is not missed
Transfer	Negative, Threat	Insurance policy
Mitigate	Negative, Threat	In-process inspection or review
Exploit	Positive, Opportunity	Shorten the project duration by increasing resources or level of talent
Share	Positive, Opportunity	Joint venture
Enhance	Positive, Opportunity	Increase probability of a positive risk event
Accept	Positive or Negative	Add enough time or money into contingency reserve to handle the risk if it occurs
Contingency	Positive or Negative	Additional oversight of a vendor if certain schedule or quality objectives are missed

Risk Response Planning Outputs

Again, the updated Risk Register and the updated Risk Management Plan are the primary outputs for this Risk Management Process. The level of detail in the register should be appropriate for the risk priority and the risk responses that have been approved and selected.

The components of the Risk Register are:

- Identified risks

- Risk owners

- Outputs from Qualitative and Quantitative Analyses

- Approved response strategies

- Budget and schedule activities

- Contingency reserves

- Contingency plans and triggers

- Secondary risks

- Project Management Plan updates

- Risk response activities

- Risk Related Contractual Agreement

TABLE 15-5: Updated Risk Register—Risk Responses

Risk Event Description	Priority (High, Medium, Low)	Risk Owner	Category of Risk	Approved Response Strategy	Contingency Reserve	Contingency Plan and Triggers	Secondary Risks
Equipment vendor delivers late	High	Mary	External—Suppliers	Contingency	3 weeks to the schedule $3000 for additional effort, travel, and expedited shipping	Additional meetings (at vendor's site) with vendor if intermediate milestones are missed and expedited shipping	Taking an active part in managing the vendor may decrease vendor's ownership of meeting the delivery date

Q. True or False? Mitigation as a response strategy will always add time and/or money to the project.

The correct answer is false. Adding items to the project plan may not change the project costs or scheduled completion date if the mitigation activity is a modification of something that is already planned, such as contacting the vendor in the example in Table 15-5 to check on the status of the order by phone on a weekly or daily basis and asking for verification of progress.

Risk Monitoring and Control (RM&C)

The purpose of Risk Monitoring and Control is to monitor the risk management plan and to identify, analyze, and plan for new risks while keeping track of existing risks and risk responses. Risk Monitoring and Control activities include:

- Testing project assumptions
- Identifying risk changes and their trends
- Verifying compliance with Risk Management policies
- Updating and modifying contingency reserves as needed

Just as it is critical to keep the project plan up to date and to continuously monitor project performance, the Risk Management Plan and the Risk Register must be frequently reviewed and periodically updated to realize the benefits of the prior Risk Management Processes: Risk Management Planning, Risk Identification, Qualitative Risk Analysis, Quantitative Risk Analysis, and Risk Response Planning. It is especially important to update the Risk Management Plan when:

- There are large variances between the project plan or Risk Management Plan and the actual project performance,
- There are surprises (both good and bad),
- Significant changes are made to scope or schedule or budget,
- There is a change in the external and/or internal environment—regulatory, legal, market, etc., or
- A change in one or more key project personnel has occurred—a key team member, project customer, project sponsor, or key stakeholder.

Why would these situations trigger a close look at the Project Management and Risk Management Plans? Because any of these events could affect project risks and/or be an indicator that:

- Things are different than previously believed,

- Assumptions in the Project and Risk Management Plans are no longer valid, or

- There is an increased chance of changes to the project objectives due to new players on the project. (No matter how well project deliverables and acceptance criteria have been documented, different interpretations can occur when new people turn up.)

In a project where there are a lot of changes, or toward the end of a project implementation when there are frequent small changes or rapid workarounds, it is a good idea for the project manager to raise the project team's awareness and sensitivity to identify changes that affect or change project risk.

Risk Monitoring and Control Inputs

Inputs include:

- Risk Management Plan—Updated from the Risk Response Plan

- Risk Register—Also updated from the Risk Response Plan

- Approved Change Requests that may affect the original plans

- Work Performance Information—Actual performance, such as costs and completion dates, and the need for corrective action when substandard performance is discovered

Risk Monitoring and Control Tools and Techniques

Throughout the project life cycle, the project team should have an awareness of risks and how they can change over time.

- Risk Reassessment—As mentioned earlier in this chapter, reassessing risk should occur as often as needed based on the volatility of environment or "surprises."

- Risk Audits—An examination of the effectiveness of the risk responses. This data is needed for future projects and adjustments to the current project.

- Variance and Trend Analysis—Tools such as earned value analysis can uncover future potential threats to the cost and schedule objectives.

- Technical Performance Measurement—Similar to earned value analysis, this tool can help forecast success against functionality by comparing technical accomplishments to the project schedule.

- Reserve Analysis—Comparing the amount of contingency reserves that remain during various points of execution to the upcoming risks to determine if the current reserve amount is too large or too small.

Most project teams will reassess the risk management plan periodically during execution and review the Risk Register at project team meetings. Proactive project managers do not wait for problems to look at these items. They are proactively looking ahead and evaluating the impact of changes to the project environment as they occur. Change management impact should also consider the change to the risk status as well as schedule and budget.

Risk Monitoring and Control Outputs

Outputs of Risk Monitoring and Control include:

- Updated Risk Register—Outcomes of the risk activities and updated values or data used to revise the selected risk responses or identified risks as needed.

- Agreed upon Changes—Responding to risks may require changes to the project plan using the Integrated Change Control Process.

- Recommended Corrective Actions—Contingency plans and workaround plans that are needed to address risks that were not previously identified and those unknowns that were acknowledged in the contingency reserves.

- Recommended Preventive Actions—Actions that bring the project back into line with the project management plan. Reassessing risk on a routine basis may uncover emerging risks before the obvious problems (impacts) are visible.

- Updated Organizational Process Assets—Documentation of the results of all the Project Risk Management Processes can be converted to lessons learned, templates, processes, and other tools that can be used on future projects.

- Updated Project Management Plan—Approval of changes submitted to the Integrated Change Control Process will be revised to reflect changes as needed.

Conclusion

Risk management is important and should be done no matter the size or complexity of the project. Less complex, less risky, or smaller projects will require much less effort to review, evaluate, and manage risks. More complex projects will take more time, especially because complexity in itself is generally a risk. However, if the risk analysis takes more time, it is probably worth it. The first time this is done, it may be time-consuming. Remember, there is a learning curve, so the second and third times will be quicker. Bottom line—risk management is a good investment, and it more than pays for itself because problems are prevented that may have otherwise happened.

Questions from Chapter Fifteen   ?

1. Project risk is the uncertainty that an event or condition that affects _____ will be realized.

   ❑ A. Project performance as measured by the functional managers

   ❑ B. Project impact on the organization

   ❑ C. Opportunities the project could realize

   ❑ D. At least one of the project objectives such as cost, scope, time, or quality

2. True or False? Risks may have one or more causes and one or more impacts.

3. Risk Management Planning should be completed _____ in the project planning phase.

   ❑ A. Sometime   ❑ B. Late

   ❑ C. Early   ❑ D. Never

4. What is a Risk Breakdown Structure (RBS)?

   ❑ A. Flowchart of risks

   ❑ B. Risk impacts on the organization

   ❑ C. List or diagram of risks by category

   ❑ D. Risk management activities that are on the schedule

5. Which of the following would be used to describe the significance of the negative impact of threats or the positive impact of opportunities?

   ❑ A. Cost, time, scope, and quality

   ❑ B. Sources of the risk events

   ❑ C. Types of risk responses

   ❑ D. Very Low, Low, Moderate, High

6. According to Table 15-2, the impact of a risk to the project schedule will be classified as _____ if the delay to the project (as a result of the risk event) will be one week to a 20-week project schedule.

   ❑ A. Low   ❑ B. High

   ❑ C. Very Low   ❑ D. Moderate

7. _____ usually follows the Risk Identification process, but sometimes _____ directly follows the Risk Identification process when an experienced risk manager is involved.

❏ A. Risk Management Planning, Quantitative Risk Analysis

❏ B. Qualitative Risk Analysis, Quantitative Risk Analysis

❏ C. Quantitative Risk Analysis, Qualitative Risk Analysis

❏ D. Risk Monitoring and Control, Risk Response Planning

8. The inputs to Risk Identification are similar to the inputs to the Risk Management Planning process with the addition of the _____.

❏ A. Scope Statement   ❏ B. Risk Management Plan

❏ C. Risk Identification method   ❏ D. WBS

9. Which of the following is NOT an information gathering technique for risk management?

❏ A. Interviews   ❏ B. Probability and Impact Matrix

❏ C. Delphi technique   ❏ D. Root cause analysis

10. The Risk Register consists of:

❏ A. Qualitative Risk Analysis, Quantitative Risk Analysis, and Risk Management Plan

❏ B. Qualitative Risk Analysis, Risk Response Plan, list of identified risks

❏ C. List of identified risks, potential responses, root causes, and updated risk categories

❏ D. Risk Responses, Risk Categories, Risk Management Plan

11. _____ and _____ are assessed for each identified risk in the Qualitative Risk Analysis process.

❏ A. Probability, impact

❏ B. Impact, priority

❏ C. Probability, costs

❏ D. None of the above

12. The _____ section of the Risk Register can be used to ensure that some risk events are not overlooked during the project life cycle.

- ❑ A. Priority
- ❑ B. Watch List
- ❑ C. Qualitative Risk Analysis
- ❑ D. None of the above

13. The Risk Register is updated periodically throughout the project life cycle. The Risk Register is initiated during _____ and further updated based on the information developed in the _____.

- ❑ A. Risk Management Planning, Qualitative Risk Analysis
- ❑ B. Risk Identification, Quantitative Risk Analysis
- ❑ C. Risk Identification, Qualitative Risk Analysis
- ❑ D. Risk Management Planning, Risk Identification

14. The inputs to the Quantitative Risk Analysis process are the Project Management Plan, Risk Register, Risk Management Plan, _____, and _____.

- ❑ A. Organizational Process Assets, Project Scope Statement
- ❑ B. Impact and Probability Matrix, Project Scope Management Plan
- ❑ C. Risk Probability, Impact Assessment
- ❑ D. Project Scope Management Plan, Organizational Process Assets

15. Name the two tools and techniques of the Quantitative Analysis that are most subjective, i.e., based on opinions.

- ❑ A. Interviewing, Decision Tree Analysis.
- ❑ B. Probability distributions
- ❑ C. Expert judgment, Interviewing
- ❑ D. Expert judgment, Sensitivity Analysis

16. What parts of the Risk Register are added during Quantitative Risk Analysis?

- ❑ A. Trends in Quantitative Risk Analysis results
- ❑ B. Probabilities of achieving project objectives
- ❑ C. Estimates of cost and schedule outcomes
- ❑ D. B and C
- ❑ E. A and B

17. Name the strategies for negative risks.

    ❏ A. Avoid, Mitigate, Transfer, Contingency, Accept

    ❏ B. Avoid, Transfer, Mitigate

    ❏ C. Avoid, Transfer, Accept, Mitigate

    ❏ D. None of the above

18. True or False? Mitigation as a response strategy will always add time and/or money to the project.

Answers from Chapter Fifteen

1. **The correct answer is D**. Project risks affect the ability of the project team to meet its commitments of time, costs, scope, or quality.

2. **The correct answer is true**. Risk events such as a delay in receiving a customer's approval to proceed on a design may have multiple causes. For example, a delay in the delivery of documents to a customer for their approval and incomplete information on the documents could cause the approval to be delayed. As a result of the delay, the project schedule, deliverable quality, and project cost all may be negatively impacted.

3. **The correct answer is C**. Other risk management processes are driven by and are dependent on the Risk Management Plan.

4. **The best answer is C**. An RBS is optional but may assist the team in its identification of risks and opportunities by looking at the sources of risks or the areas where risks may occur.

5. **The correct answer is D**. Relative scales of impact are rank ordered to differentiate risks that require special attention from lesser risks. Numerical scales such as 0.1, 0.5, and 0.9 can be used to assign values to the impact of the risks.

6. **The correct answer is A**. If there is a delay of one week over a 20-week time period, that is the equivalent of a 5% increase. According to the matrix, that will be a Low impact to the Time objective of the project.

7. **The correct answer is B**. Risk Identification must precede Risk Analysis. A person who is experienced in risk management may be able to skip the Quantitative and Qualitative Risk Analysis and determine the risk response solely upon identification of the risks and previous experience.

8. **The answer is B**.

9. **The correct answer is B**. The Probability and Impact Matrix is a component of the Risk Management Plan, used as an input to the Risk Identification process.

10. **The correct answer is C**. The Risk Register is a comprehensive document that lists the risks, root causes, potential responses (optional), and an updated list of risk categories from the RBS. It uses the Risk Management Plan as an input, and the Quantitative and Qualitative Risk Analysis processes use the Risk Register as an input.

11. **The correct answer is A**. The purpose of this process is to sort and prioritize risk events using the likelihood that the risk event will occur as well as the consequences of the risk event.

12. **The correct answer is B.** The Risk Register not only prioritizes the risk events but also focuses attention on lower-priority risks that, if ignored during the project, could become very high-priority. Monitoring lower-priority risks could prevent them from growing. It is said, "That which is measured, improves."

13. **The correct answer is C.** The Risk Register cannot be developed before risk events are identified, and the information from the Qualitative Risk Analysis is needed to prioritize the risks for further action.

14. **The correct answer is A.** The Project Scope Statement and Organizational Process Assets are inputs to all of the risk management processes.

15. **The best answer is C.** Decision Tree Analysis, Probability Distributions, Modeling and Simulation, Expected Monetary Value, and Sensitivity Analysis are numerically based statistical tools.

16. **The correct answer is D.** Probabilities of achieving project objectives and estimates of cost and schedule outcomes are both added during the Quantitative Risk Analysis process. The other outputs were developed during Risk Identification and Qualitative Risk Analysis.

17. **The best answer is A.** Contingency and Accept are for both positive and negative risk events and should be considered in addition to the negative risk responses.

18. **The correct answer is false.** Adding items to the project plan may not change the project costs or scheduled completion date if the mitigation activity is a modification of something that is already planned, such as contacting the vendor in Table 15-5 to check on the status of the order by phone on a weekly or daily basis and asking for verification of progress.

CHAPTER SIXTEEN

Project Procurement Management

According to the PMBOK, project procurement management includes "the processes to purchase or acquire the products, service, or results needed from outside the project team to perform the work." Procurement management also includes contract management and administration of contracts. The contracts in question generally come from a vendor.

There are six project procurement management processes shown in PMBOK. They are planning purchases and acquisitions, planning contracting, request for seller responses, selecting sellers, contract administration, and contract closure. As with all the rest of the knowledge areas, the various processes interact and overlap with one another.

According to the PMBOK, "A contract is a mutually binding agreement that obligates the seller to provide the specified product/service and obligates the buyer to pay for it." A contract binds both parties, buyer and seller. The seller agrees to provide specific products or services, and the buyer agrees to provide consideration for the service or good. The consideration may be monetary, but it does not have to be. In project management, there are many occasions when the project manager must be aware of how a variety of contracts are structured, and in some cases, the project manager will be the administrator of the contract. In the PMBOK, procurement management is discussed using the buyer-seller relationship. As the various contract types are delineated, the buyer-seller relationship is a key focus of this knowledge area. The assumption used in the PMBOK for the discussion of procurement management is that the buyer of the items for the project is internal to the project team and that the seller is external to the project team.

> **Q.** In a standard contract, _____ are bound.
>
>   ❑ A. Buyer and seller   ❑ B. Project manager and sponsor
>
>   ❑ C. Seller and sponsor   ❑ D. Buyer and project manager

The answer is A. Both the buyer and seller are bound by the contract.

> **Q.** The seller agrees to furnish products/services, and the buyer agrees to provide _____.
>
>   ❑ A. Time   ❑ B. Effort
>
>   ❑ C. Consideration   ❑ D. Facilities

The answer is C. Consideration may be monetary, but it does not have to be.

> **Q.** For the examination, procurement is discussed using the _____ relationship.
>
>   ❑ A. Technical   ❑ B. Buyer/seller
>
>   ❑ C. Vendor/seller   ❑ D. Purchasing

The answer is B. PMI discusses procurement focusing on the buyer/seller relationship.

> **Q.** In PMBOK, the buyer is _____ to the project team, and the seller is _____ to the project team.
>
>   ❑ A. Assigned, allocated   ❑ B. Important, secondary
>
>   ❑ C. Related, outside   ❑ D. Internal, external

The answer is D. For the purposes of this chapter, this is the configuration of buyer and seller.

Planning Purchases and Acquisitions

The process for planning purchases and acquisitions can include external purchasing of products or services as well as those tasks that can be performed within the organization by the project team. At the end of the process, the project manager should be able to determine whether or not to buy, what to buy, and the quantity to purchase. The planning for purchase and acquisitions also includes identifying potential sellers. Depending on the type of project, permits and licenses may be required to perform certain types of tasks leading to the execution of the project. This is more likely to happen in construction projects than in IT projects.

The question of when to acquire will be affected by the project schedule. There are many significant financial considerations concerning planning purchases, not the least of which is tying up capital that could be used for other purposes within the organization. These issues will be discussed in this chapter.

Finally, each make-or-buy decision will involve risk. The evaluation of the risks involved will always be a part of a detailed planning of purchases and acquisitions for the organization. Reviewing contract types will be a part of this evaluation, and mitigation of risk exposure should be a part of the planning as it relates to different types of contracts and the risk exposure of each.

The inputs into planning purchases and acquisitions are enterprise environmental factors, organizational process assets, project Scope Statement, Work Breakdown Structure, a WBS dictionary, and the project management plan.

The enterprise environmental factors in procurement include the market conditions in which the project is to be done and the products/services that are available in the market, from whom they can be procured, and under what terms and conditions. If the organization itself does not have formal purchasing or contracting groups, then people on the project team will have to do all the tasks necessary for procurement of products/services to execute the project. There may be times when the project team will need to engage subject matter experts in order to do procurement of various products/services that are not within the scope of knowledge of members of the project team.

Organizational process assets include any formal or informal policies that already exist within the organization that pertain specifically to procurement. An example of an organizational policy would be to have a set sum above which purchases must be made with a contract. Under the sum, the purchases may be made with a purchase order. This may be standard for all projects, or it may vary as the size of projects varies. In any case, the organization will set constraints on how purchases can be done and may also have constraints on the size of vendors that can be used for specific types of projects. A qualified vendor list would also be a part of the process assets of the organization as well as a constraint in procurement.

Within the project Scope Statement, there will be constraints on procurement such as needed delivery dates, availability of resources, and other organizational policies. The project Scope Statement is the document that will start the procurement planning because it explains the needs for the project as a list of deliverables. The project Scope Statement may also include acceptance criteria that will be used to validate each of the deliverables as they are finished. Detail in the Scope Statement may also show technical requirements and concerns that need to be managed when going through the procurement process.

The Work Breakdown Structure and the WBS dictionary are outputs of decomposition of the Scope Statement. The WBS lists tasks necessary to execute the project, and the dictionary provides detail about these tasks.

The project management plan as an input into planning purchases and acquisitions includes the overall plan for managing the project as well as subsidiary plans such as risk management, quality management, and procurement management plans. If a Risk Register is available in the project management plan, it can be a valuable tool in planning purchasing. There may also be a component of the plan that deals with risk-related contracts, such as insurance. These risk-related contracts should specify each party's responsibility for risks defined in the contract if and when they occur. The other inputs into planning purchases and acquisition are discussed in depth elsewhere.

Q. Market conditions are a part of _____.

   ☐ A. Organizational process assets

   ☐ B. Project management concerns

   ☐ C. Enterprise environmental factors

   ☐ D. General management concerns

The answer is C. Market conditions will influence almost all factors of procurement.

Q. Formal or informal policies that pertain to procurement are part of the _____.

   ☐ A. Organizational process assets

   ☐ B. Project management concerns

   ☐ C. Enterprise environmental factors

   ☐ D. General management concerns

The answer is A. The processes already delineated within the organization will determine how procurement is done.

Q. **Needed delivery dates and availability of resources can be found in the details of the _____.**

   ❑ A. WBS   ❑ B. SOW

   ❑ C. Project Scope Statement   ❑ D. Project Charter

The answer is A. These two factors are included in the detail done when decomposing the Scope Statement.

Q. **A Risk Register is a detailed part of the _____.**

   ❑ A. Project Scope Statement   ❑ B. Project management plan

   ❑ C. Project scheduling plan   ❑ D. Project Charter

The answer is B. The Risk Register will generally include owners of and responses to risks that are identified at the time of writing the project management plan.

The tools and techniques used in planning purchases and acquisitions are make-or-buy analysis, expert judgment, and contract types. Make-or-buy analysis is used to determine whether the organization has the capacity to make or offer a specific product/service or whether the organization will need to procure the product/service from a vendor. It is possible that an organization may be able to make a product for use in the project but that doing so would be considerably more expensive than buying it. It may also be that a vendor will have product/service availability that is not present in the organization, even though the organization might be able to provide the product/service if given enough time.

Make-or-buy decisions measure the costs of both options. When doing this analysis, it should include both direct and indirect costs so that the final decision is based on comparisons that are equal. For instance, if the buy decision is made, you need to factor in the costs of managing the purchasing process. Although these types of costs are not hidden, they are sometimes ignored, although not by companies that want to stay in business. Another consideration is whether the product/service can be reused in other projects. For instance, a computer that is bought for a specific project may not be cost justified for just that one project, but it may be justified if the cost is spread over several projects on which the computer can be used.

Expert judgment can be found both internally and externally. Most often this type of judgment will come from a subject matter expert who can assist the project manager in making sure that the requirement for purchasing is clearly stated. Expert judgment also includes professionals such as accountants and attorneys. Each of these types of experts could be used in analyzing materials before purchasing. Before going outside of the project team or even the organization, it is a good idea to check for organizational assets who have the requisite information and expertise. These people may be available to you at little or no cost and may have some background in how the organization runs its procurement processes.

Q. When doing make-or-buy analysis, you should make sure that both _____ and _____ costs are included so that the comparisons are equal.

   ❑ A. Tactical, strategic   ❑ B. Management, project

   ❑ C. Delayed, sunk   ❑ D. Direct, indirect

The answer is D. Every effort must be made to ensure that comparisons include all applicable costs.

Q. Technical judgments made to assess inputs and outputs of the planning of purchases and acquisition are an example of using _____.

   ❑ A. Expert judgment   ❑ B. External assets

   ❑ C. Internal assets   ❑ D. Computers

The answer is A. These people may be technical subject matter experts or professionals such as attorneys or accountants. Expert judgment is useful all throughout the procurement process.

Contract Types

Contract types are tools in planning purchases and acquisitions that are important for the examination as well as for professional management. There will be several questions on the exam about the different types. One of the important facts to know is the degree of risk for the seller and the buyer that each type of contract contains. This graphic shows the risk levels for each of these types of contract.

HIGH   LOW

Fixed Price (FP)
FP With Economic Adjustment
Fixed Price Incentive Fee (FPIF)
Cost and Cost Sharing
Cost Plus Incentive Fee (CPIF)
Cost Plus Fee (CPF)
Cost Plus Fixed Fee (CPFF)
Time and Materials

Seller Risk   Buyer Risk

LOW   HIGH

FIGURE 16-1: Risk levels for contract types.

Each of the contract types has risk attached to it. As we go through these contract types, you need to learn who assumes the most risk, the buyer or the seller.

Fixed price/lump-sum contracts—In this type of contract, the seller assumes the greatest risk because the price is set. This means that the seller must comply with the contract and provide the service/product for a specific price. If the time it takes to deliver the service/product expands, the seller cannot charge for the extra time. The same would be true if extra materials were needed to deliver the service/product. If this occurs, the seller cannot charge for the extra materials because the price for the contract is already fixed.

Incentives can be used with a fixed price contract based on meeting project deliverables or exceeding them. These deliverables could include schedules and costs as two of the measurements for incentives. In addition, some economic adjustment such as cost-of-living increases could be written into a fixed price contract.

Cost-reimbursable contracts—These contracts involve paying for the actual costs that the seller incurs plus an agreed upon fee that will represent the profit for the seller. For the most part, the buyer is buying direct costs, costs that are incurred because the project is being done. Indirect costs are often called either overhead or general and administrative costs. These are costs that occur no matter whether the project is progressing or not, and a short negotiation may be necessary to have indirect costs included in the total cost package. There are several types of cost-reimbursable contracts to consider.

The cost-reimbursable contract has risk for both sides. If the contract is well written and specifies what costs can be included and those that are excluded, then the buyer is protected. If the allowable costs are not well defined, the buyer takes the risk of having the seller incur costs that are not expected. The key, as with all contracts, is clarity regarding what costs are allowable.

Cost-Plus-Fee (CPF) or Cost-Plus-Percentage of Cost (CPPC)—When the contract is cost-plus-percentage of cost, the seller is reimbursed for costs that are incurred for performing the contract work, and then the seller receives a percentage of the cost that is agreed upon before beginning work. In this case, the fee varies with the actual cost.

Note that in this type of contract, you have a variable cost contract and you need to manage the costs as the seller incurs them. It is necessary in any type of cost-reimbursable contract to determine the costs that will be allowed and have these written in the contract. This type of contract puts most of the risk on the buyer.

Cost-Plus-Fixed-Fee (CPFF)—In this type of contract, the seller is reimbursed for allowable costs and then receives a fee that is agreed upon before beginning the work. The fee will be the profit for the seller, so the seller should try to maximize the fee while the buyer tries to lower it. With good-faith negotiating, it is expected that both sides will come to an agreement on the fee quickly. The main part of writing this type of contract, as it is with all cost plus contracts, is to make sure that allowable costs are specified in the contract. Rather than having to go to formal arbitration or some other form of arbitration, it is most effective to have agreement by both parties to the contract as to what is allowable.

Cost-Plus-Incentive-Fee (CPIF)—The seller is reimbursed for costs as with all cost plus contracts. In the case of the incentive fee, it is a predetermined fee that is paid if certain conditions of the contract are met or bettered. There will also be cases where both parties, buyer and seller, will benefit from producing above expectations.

Time and Material contracts (T&M)—These types of contracts are a cross between cost-reimbursable and fixed price contracts. These contracts contain the highest risk for the buyer because they are open-ended. The seller simply charges for what is done to produce the product/service in the contract. This can be a problem if the time scheduled for the production is greatly underestimated. Because the contract simply states that time and materials will be paid for, the seller can charge for time that is needed, no matter whether it exceeds estimates. In the cases where time or material greatly exceeds the estimates, there may be a need for arbitration to determine the correct fee. The fixed price component of a T&M contract comes with agreement between the seller and buyer as to the types of materials that can be used and the amount of time that is expected. For instance, the buyer may require that standard versions of products be used in the building of a house rather than custom-made products.

The greatest risk to the buyer is the T&M contract. The greatest risk to the seller is the firm fixed price contract. Often, buyer and seller will negotiate aspects of both types so that the risk is spread between both the seller and the buyer.

Q. There are three general types of contracts: cost reimbursable, time and materials, and _____.

☐ A. Cost required   ☐ B. Fixed price

☐ C. Simple cost   ☐ D. Reimbursed time

The answer is B. The third type of contract is the fixed price, often called the firm fixed price contract.

Q. Which type of contract has the highest risk for the buyer?

☐ A. Fixed price   ☐ B. Reimbursed time

☐ C. Time and materials   ☐ D. Cost plus

The answer is C. There may be major variations between the estimated amount of time and the actual amount of time spent. In a time and materials contract, the buyer agrees to pay for time used by the seller, which creates the risk.

Q. In the cost plus contract with the initials CPFF, the FF stands for _____.

☐ A. Formula foundation   ☐ B. Free fixed

☐ C. Founded fixed   ☐ D. Fixed fee

The answer is D.

Q. Which type of contract has the highest risk for the seller?

☐ A. Fixed price   ☐ B. Reimbursed time

☐ C. Time and materials   ☐ D. Cost plus

The answer is A. Because the price is fixed in the contract, the seller must absorb any costs that are not covered in the initial contract.

Q. The type of contract where the buyer and seller share in the savings is _____.

❏ A. Fixed Price

❏ B. Cost reimbursable with incentive fee

❏ C. Cost reimbursable with fixed fee

❏ D. Time and materials

The answer is B. The percentage of the savings that will go to the seller and buyer is negotiated at the time of writing the contract.

Q. Which type of contract uses a percentage of cost as a part of the agreed upon contract?

❏ A. T&M   ❏ B. CPFF

❏ C. CPIF   ❏ D. CPPC

The answer is D. The acronym reads "cost plus percentage of cost."

Here is an example of a question that uses the cost plus incentive fee contract.

Q. A buyer negotiates a fixed-price incentive contract with the seller. The target cost is $200,000, the target profit is $35,000, and the target price is $250,000. The buyer negotiates a ceiling price of $280,000 and a share ratio of 70/30. If the contract is completed with actual costs of $180,000, how much profit will the buyer pay the seller?

❏ A. $49,000   ❏ B. $41,000

❏ C. $38,000   ❏ D. $29,000

The answer is B. This is how to work this problem out. The numbers that you need to be concerned with are the target cost, $200,000, the target profit, $35,000, the share ratio of 70/30, and the actual costs of $180,000. (In a share ratio, the first percentage goes to the buyer and the second number is the percentage that the seller will get.) Using these numbers, the calculation goes like this. You subtract the actual costs from the target cost, which gives you $20,000. Seventy percent of that goes to the buyer, whereas thirty percent goes to the seller. In this case, that would be 30% of $20,000 or $6,000. Add $6,000 to the target profit of $35,000, and you have your answer, which is $41,000.

The outputs of planning purchases and acquisitions are the procurement management plan, the contract statement of work, make-or-buy decisions, and requested changes. The procurement management plan can be simple or very complex depending on the type and size of the project. Some of the parts of a procurement management plan are:

- Definition of the contract types to be used
- What actions the project team can take by itself if the organization already has a purchasing, legal, or procurement department
- Document types to be used
- Constraints and assumptions
- How to estimate and handle lead times for procurement
- Mitigation of project risk through insurance or performance bonds
- Identifying pre-qualified sellers
- Metrics used to manage contracts and evaluate seller offers

(There are other parts of the procurement management plan in the PMBOK. These can be found on page 279 of the 3rd edition.)

The contract statement of work describes the various procurement items in sufficient detail to give prospective sellers a guideline to see whether they can provide the item or items. This contract statement of work (CSOW) is a subset of the SOW. A CSOW may include specifications, quantities, quality levels, requested performance measurements and data, the work location, and the amount of time expected to fulfill the contract.

Q. Definition of contract types to be used, how to handle lead times for procurement, and metrics used to manage contracts are all found in the _____.

   ❑ A. SOW   ❑ B. Procurement management plan

   ❑ C. WBS   ❑ D. Scope Statement

The answer is B.

> **Q.** **The document that gives detail to prospective sellers concerning item or items to be purchased is the _____.**
>
> ❑ A. SOW ❑ B. Charter
>
> ❑ C. WBS ❑ D. CSOW

The answer is D. The contract statement of work is the place where detail is given, not the SOW. The CSOW is considered a subset of the SOW.

The make-or-buy decisions, which have been made by going through the make-or-buy analysis, will also be listed as an output of the planning for purchasing and acquisition. The main point is that the decisions (and why they were made) have been documented so that they can be examined if necessary.

The final output is the requested changes that have been made to the overall project management plan because of the planning of purchases and acquisition.

Plan Contracting

The documents needed to support the request seller responses process and select sellers process are written in this process area.

The inputs to plan contract are the procurement management plan, the contract statement of work, the make-or-buy decisions, and the project management plan itself. The first three of these have been discussed earlier. The project management plan provides the scheduled delivery dates in the project schedule. These dates will be used in planning the contracts and in developing procurement documentation. Some of the parts are:

- **The Risk Register**—Contains information relating to risk management such as identified risks, risk owners, risk analysis, risk prioritization, risk level, and risk responses.

- **Contractual services**—These are risk-related services that may include insurance and other forms of risk mitigation.

- Activity resource requirement

- The project schedule

- Activity cost estimates

- Cost baseline

The tools and techniques used in plan contracting are standard forms and expert judgment. The standard forms may be standardized contracts, non-disclosure agreements, checklists, and any documents needed for bid management. They may be a part of the organizational process assets or available from outside sources. The expert judgment can also come from internal assets or external sources.

> **Q. The document that contains information such as identified risks and risk owners is called a _____.**
>
> ❑ A. Risk Register   ❑ B. SOW
>
> ❑ C. WBS   ❑ D. Risk locator

The answer is A. A Risk Register can also contain risk analysis, risk level, and risk responses.

The outputs of planning the contracting are procurement documents, evaluation criteria, and updates to the contract statement of work. Procurement documents are sent to prospective sellers to obtain proposals. The buyer should make the procurement documents as clear and complete as possible so that the sellers' response is usable and clearly responds to the buyers' needs. The documents may be very complex or relatively simple depending on the project needs for procurement. The procurement documents may be called request for bid, request for proposal, request for quotation, or several other titles. In all cases, these documents are seeking information from the seller as to how the seller will meet the needs of the project.

The amount of detail in the procurement documents will depend in large part on the complexity of the project and also on the amount of risk that the planned purchases and acquisitions will have; the greater the risk, the more detail. The documents need to be both concise and flexible—concise because all sellers will work from it, and flexible because the seller may see opportunities for both parties to have better buying solutions than those written in the procurement document.

Depending on the type of organization and the size of the project, requests for procurement documents can include letters to pre-approved sellers and publication in newspapers, in magazines, and on the Internet. The Internet is becoming a major source for proposals in many cases. An interactive website where emails can be sent to ask for clarification of procurement documents is the norm for many organizations and is used as one of the primary sources for many governmental departments, both state and national. It is also used extensively in the private sector.

The second output from planning the contracting is the evaluation criteria. Ideally, the project team has a set of criteria used to measure the responses to the procurement documents. In many cases, the seller will not even be eligible for consideration unless a fixed set of criteria is met. (The seller must be able to post a million dollar bond, for example.) In very simple procurement situations, the only factor may be the price if the material or service is easily available from several sources.

Other selection criteria can include technical capability of the seller, technical approach to the project, financial capability, business size, references, and intellectual property rights. On page 283 of the PMBOK 3rd edition, you will find other selection criteria listed. Remember that the criteria should help you determine the correct seller for your project needs and that the better you are at documenting your needs for the project, the better the responses will be from the sellers.

> **Q.** **The evaluation criteria are determined by the _____.**
>
> ❑ A. Seller   ❑ B. Project manager
>
> ❑ C. Buyer   ❑ D. Sponsor

The answer is C. The buyer determines what requirements are needed and then documents these needs. The evaluation criteria will often determine whether a seller is even eligible to participate in the proposal process.

> **Q.** **Procurement documents are documents seeking information from the _____.**
>
> ❑ A. Seller   ❑ B. Project manager
>
> ❑ C. Buyer   ❑ D. Accountant

The answer is A. The specific purpose of a procurement document is to get information from the seller as to how the requirements of the project can be met through purchasing and acquisition.

Request Seller Responses

This is the process where bids and proposals are obtained from the prospective sellers. The sellers are responsible for these responses and are the ones putting forth the time and effort to respond.

Inputs to requesting seller responses include organizational process assets, the procurement management plan, and procurement documents. The organizational assets may include information on past performance of sellers that will be relevant to the choosing of a seller for the new project. Some organizations keep this information, and it often helps to pre-select qualified sellers.

The tools and techniques of requesting bidder responses are bidder conferences, advertising, and developing a qualified sellers list. Bidder conferences are meetings with prospective sellers to ensure that they have a clear understanding of the procurement requirements. During these bidder conferences, which are also called vendor or contractor conferences, all potential sellers are invited to bring questions about procurement requirements and discuss them. In some projects, any questions asked in these meetings must be posted to an Internet site so that any vendors not present at the conference will have the same information as those who were at the conference.

Advertising can build the number of potential sellers by getting information out to a large number of vendors. In some government jurisdictions, certain types of procurement items must be advertised publicly. Some government jurisdictions require that any pending government contracts be made public, usually through newspapers, but more and more through websites on which sellers may search for all current open projects.

A qualified sellers list can be developed in many ways. If the organization has lists of current qualified sellers, this list will be the basis for new projects. One thing to remember is that new companies may be offering solutions to your procurement requirements but may not be on your qualified sellers list. In many cases, it is hard to get on this type of list, which can discourage some companies that are highly qualified. Other places to get names for a qualified sellers list can be the Internet, associations, trade catalogues, and directories available in libraries. It is always a good idea to keep these lists updated both by looking at new potential sellers and by weeding out old lists. This will give you a good chance to get the best possible procurement for your organization.

The outputs from requesting seller responses are the qualified sellers list, the procurement document package, and proposals. The proposals are done by the seller and give information that describes the way in which the seller will be able to supply items requested. The seller's proposal is a formal legal offer in response to the buyer's request. There may also be a round of oral explanation. The information given orally is also binding.

Q. **Meetings with prospective sellers to ensure they have a clear understanding of the requirements are known as _____.**

   ❑ A. Bidder conferences   ❑ B. Vendor conferences

   ❑ C. Contract conferences   ❑ D. All of the above

The answer is D. All of these are names for conferences where the perspective sellers can ask questions concerning requirements so that they get a clear outlook on what is expected of them.

The procurement document package is the entire package of materials sent to the sellers by the buyer. The procurement document package is the document set that guides the seller in responding to the buyer's needs.

Select Sellers

Selecting sellers is the process where sellers are chosen based on the responses that have been made to requests by the buyer. The sellers' responses are filtered through evaluation criteria that are selected by the buyer, and the final award, which may go to one or several sellers, is made based on these criteria. Often the criteria are weighted so that certain criteria are more important than others. Price is always a criterion unless the project is in response to a massive emergency. In certain types of projects, the technical solutions offered as well as the skill sets of the vendors may be a major factor in determining who will get the contract.

Inputs to selecting sellers include organizational process assets, the procurement management plan, evaluation criteria, procurement document package, proposals, qualified sellers list, and the project management plan. All of these were discussed earlier in the chapter.

The tools and techniques for selecting sellers may include a weighting system, independent estimates, a screening system, contract negotiation, seller rating systems, expert judgment, and proposal evaluation techniques. The weighting system usually assigns a value to each of the evaluation criteria. By summing all of the criteria ratings, you will have a number that gives you one of the major tools for determining who will be the vendor of choice.

Independent estimates are done either by the buyer or by another independent organization. The independent estimates can be compared to the sellers' estimates when responding to the buyer's proposal.

A screening system is tied to the weighting system. In the screening system, go/no-go criteria are established so that a minimum standard is set for the seller. This screens out the sellers that do not have the prerequisites necessary to bid for the project.

Contract negotiation occurs before the final contract is approved and signed. During contract negotiation, various aspects of the contract may be negotiated. When agreement is reached, the final contract is the output of the process.

Rating systems for sellers are tied to both weighting systems and screening systems. The organization puts together its requirements and performance criteria and makes this into a rating system. All the sellers should be rated using the same metrics.

Expert judgment may be used when looking at proposals that contain specialized information. The subject matter expert looks at the portions of the contract that are within his or her specialty area and gives an opinion on the seller's proposal.

Proposal evaluation techniques are a blend of evaluation criteria, screening systems, rating systems, weighting systems, and possibly expert judgment. Various inputs can be used from reviewers of the proposal to build a proposal evaluation system that can be used for multiple projects.

The outputs from selecting sellers are the actual selected sellers, the contract, a contract management plan, issues of resource availability, updates to the procurement management plan, and requested changes. All of these have been discussed previously.

Q. The system that assigns a value to evaluation criteria is known as the _____.

   ❑ A. Weighting system   ❑ B. Screening system

   ❑ C. Expert judgment   ❑ D. Rating system

The answer is A. The weighting system is the basis for many of the other tools that are used in selecting sellers.

Contract Administration

Both buyer and seller administer contracts to make sure that the obligations set forth in the contract are met. Both must perform according to the terms of the contract. If you are on the project management team, you must be aware of the legal issues and implications as you administer the contract. Several project management processes are applied when administering the contract. Among them are performance reporting, quality control, integrated change control, and risk monitoring and control. Each one of these processes helps the project manager manage the contract.

During contract administration, performance by the seller is reviewed and documented so that any questions arising from the execution of the contract can be negotiated. Future relationships with the seller may also be determined to a great extent by how the current contract is fulfilled. The project manager should be certain that documentation concerning various aspects of the contract is saved and available as the project progresses. This documentation will be the basis for issue resolution if there are any questions concerning how the contract was fulfilled.

Q. Risk control, quality control, and performance reporting are all used in _____.

   ❑ A. Project management   ❑ B. Contract administration

   ❑ C. Reports   ❑ D. Sponsor communication

The answer is B. When administering a contract, the project manager should be certain to include processes specific to project management to get the best possible control of the project execution.

Q. Contracts are administered by the _____.

   ❑ A. Buyer   ❑ B. Seller

   ❑ C. Sponsor   ❑ D. Buyer and seller

The answer is D. Both the buyer and seller should administer the contract to make certain that the obligations in the contract are being met.

Q. Contracts can be amended prior to contract closure in accordance with the _____ of the contract.

   ❑ A. Requirements   ❑ B. Change control terms

   ❑ C. Sponsor regulations   ❑ D. Organizational requirements

The answer is B. Change control terms should be specified in the contract and used to manage any changes made prior to contract closure.

Inputs into contract administration include the contract itself, the contract management plan, selected sellers, performance reports, approved change requests, and work performance information. The performance reports are done by the seller and include technical documentation of work done on the project as well as the actual performance reports themselves. The buyer reviews these reports to ensure that the performance of the seller meets the obligations of the contract.

The tools and techniques used in contract administration are a contract change control system, buyer-conducted performance reviews, inspections and audits, performance reporting, the payment system, claims administration, records management system, and information technology. The change control system defines the process by which the contract can be changed. This process should be part of the contract itself, and all the necessary approval levels should be discussed in this part of the contract.

The seller will give the buyer performance reports, and the buyer will conduct performance reviews that show differences between the baseline of the project and the actual performance. This will include quality, cost, and schedule as the major parts of the review. Any contract non-compliance, as well as successes, will be noted during the buyer performance review.

Inspections and audits are a type of buyer performance review. The inspections and audits are used to identify variations from the original plan by the seller and are expected to help disclose any problems in the seller's work plan or execution of deliverables during the execution of the project.

The payment system controls payments to the seller and may be controlled by the accounts payable function of the buyer. On very large projects, the project itself may require the development of a payment system different from that of the organization. The project management team must review and approve payments made.

If the buyer and the seller cannot agree on what changes have been made, what the compensation is for the change, and even whether or not a change has occurred, claims will be made that must be settled either by the two parties or in accordance with procedures delineated in the contract. Contested claims may in some cases escalate into litigation, so the managing of claims administration is an extremely important facet of project management.

The records management system is a set of processes used by the project manager to manage contract documentation and records. As mentioned several times, it is imperative that contract administration be based on documentation. The records management system will be the system that controls the documentation for the project.

The outputs for contract administration include contract documentation, requested changes, recommended corrective actions, updates of organizational process assets, and updates to the project management plan. Contract documentation includes the contract itself, supporting information, and all change request information, both approved and unapproved. All documents relating to the contract are managed in this part of contract administration.

When changes are requested, it is just as important to save the changes that were not approved as those that were. This facet of contract administration will ensure that the project manager has complete records of all requests and the reasons for disallowing or allowing changes as they were requested. This information can be very valuable as the project goes on and may be reviewed if the same changes are requested at a later time in the project.

The recommended corrective actions are any actions that need to be taken to bring the seller into compliance with the terms of the contract. Note that the burden of performance in this area is on the seller. The recommended corrective actions can come from the seller himself or herself or from the buyer. In any case, the corrective actions deal with the contract and its fulfillment.

Updates to the organizational process assets will include saving any correspondence that has occurred between the buyer and seller. If the project has an external payment system, payment schedules and requests are a part of the updates. The seller performance evaluation documentation is also a part of the updates to organizational process assets.

The updates to the project management plan include the procurement management plan updates and also the contract management plan updates. As subsets of the overall project management plan, these two plans should be updated whenever changes are made.

Q. **The buyer will conduct performance reviews that show differences between the _____ of the project and the actual performance.**

  ❑ A. SOW   ❑ B. Baseline

  ❑ C. Charter   ❑ D. WBS

The answer is B. The baseline of the project is used when looking at variances between planned and actual performance.

Q. The _____ will offer performance reports concerning the work done on the project.

- ❏ A. Seller
- ❏ B. Buyer
- ❏ C. Sponsor
- ❏ D. Project manager

The answer is A. The seller must document work being done on the project, and this is done in performance reports.

Q. The _____ will conduct performance reviews that show differences between the baseline of the project and the actual performance.

- ❏ A. Sponsor
- ❏ B. Project manager
- ❏ C. Buyer
- ❏ D. Sponsor

The answer is C. The buyer conducts periodic performance reviews and rates the performance based on the differences between the baseline documents of the project and the actual performance of the project.

Q. _____ and _____ are both a type of buyer performance review.

- ❏ A. Inspections, audits
- ❏ B. Inspections, tours
- ❏ C. Questioning, tours
- ❏ D. Audits, tours

The answer is A. These are used to disclose variations from the original project plan.

Q. The payment system controls payments to the seller and may be controlled by the _____ function of the buyer.

- ❏ A. Accounts receivable
- ❏ B. Payment processing
- ❏ C. Accounts payable
- ❏ D. Check writing

The answer is C. If the organization has this type of function within it, it will control the payments to the seller. There will also be times when the payment system will be administered by someone within the project team.

Contract Closure

The final process in project procurement management is contract closure. This involves verification that the work and deliverables of the project are acceptable. Contract closure is used for all contracts that apply to the project. In projects that have several phases, contracts may apply only to one phase and not to the whole project.

Early termination of a contract is a unique type of contract closure. Early termination may result from mutual agreement of the contract parties that the contract should be terminated. It may also come about because the buyer or seller has defaulted on provisions in the contract. Even if early termination occurs, the seller may be paid for accepted and completed work that was done under the provisions of the contract up to the time of the termination.

The inputs into contract closure are the procurement management plan, the contract management plan, contract documentation, and contract closure procedure. All of these have been discussed.

The tools and techniques of contract closure include procurement audits and a records management system. Procurement audits are reviews of the procurement process, from planning the purchases and acquisitions through contract administration. The purpose of a procurement audit is to examine the procurements done during the project so that any discrepancies between the planning and the execution of the procurement process can be noted and documented for review.

The outputs from contract closure are closed contracts and updated organizational process assets. The buyer provides the seller with a formal written notice that the terms of the contract have been completed. In projects that have this type of formal procurement management, there will often be formal contract closure tasks that are defined in the original contract.

The organizational process assets updates will include a contract file, which is a set of indexed project contract documentation. Also included in updates of organizational process assets is formal written notice to the seller that the buyer has accepted the deliverables.

Finally, lessons learned are kept for future analysis and to help any future project managers look at past projects within the organization.

> **Q.** _____ involves verification that the work and deliverables of the project are acceptable.
>
> ❑ A. Contract closure ❑ B. Administrative closure
>
> ❑ C. Project schedule closure ❑ D. Management plan closure

The answer is A. The buyer notifies the seller that the deliverables and work done under the contract have been accepted.

> **Q.** Contract closure usually involves _____ notice that the contract has been completed.
>
> ❑ A. Legal ❑ B. Management
>
> ❑ C. Formal written ❑ D. Oral

The answer is C. The acceptance of the work done should be in written form. It is possible that the form of the acceptance will be outlined in the contract.

> **Q.** Early termination of a contract is a unique type of _____.
>
> ❑ A. Legal requirement ❑ B. Contract closure
>
> ❑ C. Contract fulfillment ❑ D. Contract management

The answer is B. The buyer may have to compensate the seller for work done up to that time by the seller.

> **Q.** A _____ is done to review all procurement processes done during the project.
>
> ❑ A. Project plan review ❑ B. Project management review
>
> ❑ C. Project performance review ❑ D. Procurement review

The answer is D. This is a structured review used to examine all of the procurement tasks done during the project.

Questions from Chapter Sixteen   **?**

1. In a standard contract, _____ are bound.

   ❑ A. Buyer and seller
   ❑ B. Project manager and sponsor
   ❑ C. Seller and sponsor
   ❑ D. Buyer and project manager

2. The seller agrees to furnish products/services, and the buyer agrees to provide _____.

   ❑ A. Time
   ❑ B. Effort
   ❑ C. Consideration
   ❑ D. Facilities

3. For the examination, procurement is discussed using the _____ relationship.

   ❑ A. Technical
   ❑ B. Buyer/seller
   ❑ C. Vendor/seller
   ❑ D. Purchasing

4. In PMBOK, the buyer is _____ to the project team, and the seller is _____ to the project team.

   ❑ A. Assigned, allocated
   ❑ B. Important, secondary
   ❑ C. Related, outside
   ❑ D. Internal, external

5. Market conditions are a part of _____.

   ❑ A. Organizational process assets
   ❑ B. Project management concerns
   ❑ C. Enterprise environmental factors
   ❑ D. General management concerns

6. Formal or informal policies that pertain to procurement are part of the _____.

   ❑ A. Organizational process assets
   ❑ B. Project management concerns
   ❑ C. Enterprise environmental factors
   ❑ D. General management concerns

7. Needed delivery dates and availability of resources can be found in the detail of the _____.

   ❑ A. WBS
   ❑ B. SOW
   ❑ C. Project Scope Statement
   ❑ D. Project Charter

8. **A Risk Register is a detailed part of the _____.**

   ❏ A. Project Scope Statement ❏ B. Project management plan

   ❏ C. Project scheduling plan ❏ D. Project Charter

9. **When doing make-or-buy analysis, you should make sure that both _____ and _____ costs are included so that the comparisons are equal.**

   ❏ A. Tactical, strategic ❏ B. Management, project

   ❏ C. Delayed, sunk ❏ D. Direct, indirect

10. **Technical judgments made to assess inputs and outputs of the planning of purchases and acquisition are an example of using _____.**

    ❏ A. Expert judgment ❏ B. External assets

    ❏ C. Internal assets ❏ D. Computers

11. **There are three general types of contracts: cost reimbursable, time and materials, and _____?**

    ❏ A. Cost required ❏ B. Fixed price

    ❏ C. Simple cost ❏ D. Reimbursed time

12. **Which type of contract has the highest risk for the buyer?**

    ❏ A. Fixed price ❏ B. Reimbursed time

    ❏ C. Time and materials ❏ D. Cost plus

13. **In the cost plus contract with the initials CPFF, the FF stands for _____.**

    ❏ A. Formula foundation ❏ B. Free fixed

    ❏ C. Founded fixed ❏ D. Fixed fee

14. **Which type of contract has the highest risk for the seller?**

    ❏ A. Fixed price ❏ B. Reimbursed time

    ❏ C. Time and materials ❏ D. Cost plus

15. **The type of contract where the buyer and seller share in the savings is _____.**

    ❏ A. Fixed Price

    ❏ B. Cost reimbursable with incentive fee

    ❏ C. Cost reimbursable with fixed fee

    ❏ D. Time and materials

16. Which type of contract uses a percentage of cost as a part of the agreed upon contract?

- ❑ A. T&M
- ❑ C. CPIF
- ❑ B. CPFF
- ❑ D. CPPC

17. A buyer negotiates a fixed-price incentive contract with the seller. The target cost is $200,000, the target profit is $35,000, and the target price is $250,000. The buyer negotiates a ceiling price of $280,000 and a share ratio of 70/30. If the contract is completed with actual costs of $180,000, how much profit will the buyer pay the seller?

- ❑ A. $49,000
- ❑ C. $38,000
- ❑ B. $41,000
- ❑ D. $29,000

18. Definition of contract types to be used, how to handle lead times for procurement, and metrics used to manage contracts are all found in the _____.

- ❑ A. SOW
- ❑ C. WBS
- ❑ B. Procurement management plan
- ❑ D. Scope Statement

19. The document that gives detail to prospective sellers concerning item or items to be purchased is the _____.

- ❑ A. SOW
- ❑ C. WBS
- ❑ B. Charter
- ❑ D. CSOW

20. The document that contains information such as identified risks and risk owners is called a _____.

- ❑ A. Risk Register
- ❑ C. WBS
- ❑ B. SOW
- ❑ D. Risk locator

21. The evaluation criteria are determined by the _____.

- ❑ A. Seller
- ❑ C. Buyer
- ❑ B. Project manager
- ❑ D. Sponsor

22. Procurement documents are documents seeking information from the _____.

- ❑ A. Seller
- ❑ C. Buyer
- ❑ B. Project manager
- ❑ D. Accountant

23. Meetings with prospective sellers to ensure that they have a clear understanding of the requirements are known as _____.

❑ A. Bidder conferences

❑ B. Vendor conferences

❑ C. Contract conferences

❑ D. All of the above

24. The system that assigns a value to evaluation criteria is known as _____.

❑ A. Weighting system

❑ B. Screening system

❑ C. Expert judgment

❑ D. Rating system

25. Risk control, quality control, and performance reporting are all used in _____.

❑ A. Project management

❑ B. Contract administration

❑ C. Reports

❑ D. Sponsor communication

26. Contracts are administered by the _____.

❑ A. Buyer

❑ B. Seller

❑ C. Sponsor

❑ D. Buyer and seller

27. Contracts can be amended prior to contract closure in accordance with the _____ of the contract.

❑ A. Requirements

❑ B. Change control terms

❑ C. Sponsor regulations

❑ D. Organizational requirements

28. The buyer will conduct performance reviews that show differences between the _____ of the project and the actual performance.

❑ A. SOW

❑ B. Baseline

❑ C. Charter

❑ D. WBS

29. The _____ will offer performance reports concerning the work done on the project.

❑ A. Seller

❑ B. Buyer

❑ C. Sponsor

❑ D. Project manager

30. The _____ will conduct performance reviews that show differences between the baseline of the project and the actual performance.

❑ A. Sponsor

❑ B. Project manager

❑ C. Buyer

❑ D. Sponsor

31. _____ and _____ are both a type of buyer performance review.

❑ A. Inspections, audits
❑ B. Inspections, tours
❑ C. Questioning, tours
❑ D. Audits, tours

32. The payment system controls payments to the seller and may be controlled by the _____ function of the buyer.

❑ A. Accounts receivable
❑ B. Payment processing
❑ C. Accounts payable
❑ D. Check writing

33. _____ involves verification that the work and deliverables of the project are acceptable.

❑ A. Contract closure
❑ B. Administrative closure
❑ C. Project schedule closure
❑ D. Management plan closure

34. Contract closure usually involves _____ notice that the contract has been completed.

❑ A. Legal
❑ B. Management
❑ C. Formal written
❑ D. Oral

35. Early termination of a contract is a unique type of _____.

❑ A. Legal requirement
❑ B. Contract closure
❑ C. Contract fulfillment
❑ D. Contract management

36. A _____ is done to review all procurement processes done during the project.

❑ A. Project plan review
❑ B. Project management review
❑ C. Project performance review
❑ D. Procurement review

Answers from Chapter Sixteen

1. **The answer is A.** Both the buyer and seller are bound by the contract.

2. **The answer is C.** Consideration may be monetary, but it does not have to be.

3. **The answer is B.** PMI discusses procurement focusing on the buyer/seller relationship.

4. **The answer is D.** For the purposes of this chapter, this is the configuration of buyer and seller.

5. **The answer is C.** Market conditions will influence almost all factors of procurement.

6. **The answer is A.** The processes already delineated within the organization will determine how procurement is done.

7. **The answer is A.** These two factors are included in the detail done when decomposing the Scope Statement.

8. **The answer is B.** The Risk Register will generally include owners of and responses to risks that are identified at the time of writing the project management plan.

9. **The answer is D.** Every effort must be made to ensure that comparisons include all applicable costs.

10. **The answer is A.** These people may be technical subject matter experts or professionals such as attorneys or accountants. Expert judgment is useful all throughout the procurement process.

11. **The answer is B.** The third type of contract is the fixed price, often called the firm fixed price contract.

12. **The answer is C.**

13. **The answer is D.**

14. **The answer is A.**

15. **The answer is B.**

16. **The answer is D.**

17. **The answer is B.** This is how to work this problem out. The numbers that you need to be concerned with are the target cost, $200,000, the target profit, $35,000, the share ratio of 70/30, and the actual costs of $180,000. (In a share ratio, the first percentage goes to the buyer and the second number is the percentage that the seller will get.) Using these numbers, the calculation goes like this. You subtract the actual costs from the target cost, which gives you $20,000. Seventy percent of that goes to

the buyer, whereas thirty percent goes to the seller. In this case, that would be 30% of $20,000 or $6,000. Add $6,000 to the target profit of $35,000, and you have your answer, which is $41,000.

18. **The answer is B**.

19. **The answer is D**. The contract statement of work is the place where detail is given, not the SOW. The CSOW is considered a subset of the SOW.

20. **The answer is A**. A Risk Register can also contain risk analysis, risk level, and risk responses.

21. **The answer is C**. The buyer determines what requirements are needed and then documents these needs. The evaluation criteria will often determine whether a seller is even eligible to participate in the proposal process.

22. **The answer is A**. The specific purpose of a procurement document is to get information from the seller as to how the requirements of the project can be meet through purchasing and acquisition.

23. **The answer is D**. All of these are names for conferences where the prospective sellers can ask questions concerning requirements so that they get a clear outlook on what is expected of them.

24. **The answer is A**. The weighting system is the basis for many of the other tools that are used in selecting sellers.

25. **The answer is B**. When administering a contract, the project manager should be certain to include processes specific to project management to get the best possible control of project execution.

26. **The answer is D**. Both the buyer and seller should administer the contract to make certain that the obligations in the contract are being met.

27. **The answer is B**. Change control terms should be specified in the contract and used to manage any changes made prior to contract closure.

28. **The answer is B**. The baseline of the project is used when looking at variances between planned and actual performance.

29. **The answer is A**. The seller must document work being done on the project, and this is done in performance reports.

30. **The answer is C**. The buyer conducts periodic performance reviews and rates the performance based on the differences between the baseline documents of the project and the actual performance of the project.

31. **The answer is A**. These are used to disclose variations from the original project plan.

32. **The answer is C.** If the organization has this type of function within it, it will control the payments to the seller. There will also be times when the payment system will be administered by someone within the project team.

33. **The answer is A.** The buyer notifies the seller that the deliverables and work done under the contract have been accepted.

34. **The answer is C.** The acceptance of the work done should be in written form. It is possible that the form of the acceptance will be outlined in the contract.

35. **The answer is B.** The buyer may have to compensate the seller for work done up to that time by the seller.

36. **The answer is D.** This is a structured review used to examine all of the procurement tasks done during the project.

APPENDIX A

Abbreviations

These are abbreviations that are used in this book and not found in the PMBOK. You should use the PMBOK for standard abbreviations.

ANSI—American National Standards Institute

AP—Accounts Payable

AR—Accounts Receivable

DoD—Department of Defense

FV—Future Value

GERT—Graphic Evaluation and Review

HIPPA—Health Insurance Portability and Accountability Act of 1996

IRR—Internal Rate of Return

ISO—International Organization for Standardization

IT—Information Technology

MBWA—Management By Walking Around

PDCA—Plan, Do, Check, Act

PERT—Program Evaluation and Review Technique

PMI—Project Management Institute

RM&C—Risk Monitoring and Control

ROI—Return on Investment

SPC—Statistical Process Control

T&M—Time and Material

TRB—Technical Review Board

Glossary

These are definitions that are not listed in the PMBOK. You should use the PMBOK for all other standard definitions.

Accounts Payable—Those accounts to which money is owed.

Accounts Receivable—Those accounts from which money is owed.

American National Standards Institute—The organization that sets engineering standards for America.

Closure—This is the project phase in which the organization or people who set up the requirements for the product of the project agree that the project team has delivered the product.

Deming—The first of the recognized experts in quality and considered by many to be the "Father of the Quality Movement" was Dr. H. Edwards Deming.

Department of Defense—The DoD was responsible in large part for formalizing project management processes.

Execution—The phase of the project in which all necessary resources are used to complete the project.

Feasibility—This is the process of determining the best usage of organizational resources depending on the perceived value of the project.

Fishbone Diagram—Introduced by Ishikawa, it is called so because of its structure, which resembles the skeleton of a fish.

Future Value—The value of a current sum at some date in the future.

Graphic Evaluation and Review Technique—This technique consists of showing various models in graphic form.

Health Insurance Portability and Accountability Act of 1996—This congressional act was enacted to help ensure standards for records keeping and transfer as well as privacy issues.

Information Technology—This all-encompassing term generally centers around computer hardware and software, although it also is used in conjunction with major communication tools such as the Internet.

Initiation—The time when someone or some organization specifically authorizes beginning and executing a project.

Internal Rate of Return—The method that determines the discount rate at which the present value of future cash flows will exactly equal investment outlay.

International Organization for Standardization—Worldwide federation of national standards bodies from 130 countries and non-governmental groups, promoting the development of standardization and related issues.

Knowledge Area approach—This is the way the PMBOK is structured. There are nine separate areas of study: Integration, Scope, Cost, Time, Quality, HR, Communications, Risk, and Procurement. Each of the knowledge areas is given a chapter in the PMBOK and explains the facts that PMI thinks are important in the study of the particular topic.

Lateral communication—The type of communication that occurs between team members and all stakeholders who are peers.

Leveling Heuristics—Rules of thumb.

Line management—This is the type of management in which the working person is in one group type, e.g. marketing or operations, and the members within that function report to single superiors who then report to their superiors and so on. It is the classic pyramid of business.

Management By Walking Around—The concept of managing by making yourself available to your people by actually showing up at their work areas is one that has been shown to help keep relationships in the organization comfortable.

Mean—The average of all the items in a sample.

Median—The value selected in a set of data so that roughly half of the data are smaller and roughly half of the data are larger.

Metric—An operational definition.

Mode—The most frequently occurring value in the data set.

Monte Carlo Simulation—An analytical method meant to imitate a real-life system, especially when other analyses are too mathematically complex or too difficult to reproduce. This is done by iterative passes through the information.

Phase Approach—The phase approach is one way of looking at the organization of a project. It includes the Initiation, Planning, Execution, Control, and Closing phases of a project.

Plan, Do, Check, Act—Sometimes simply called the PDCA cycle, by which continuous improvement is achieved.

Planning—The planning phase of a project is the phase where a project manager can utilize guidance from the PMBOK in order to professionally control the overall planning of the project.

Program Evaluation and Review Technique—This technique is a network model that allows for randomness in activity completion times. PERT was developed in the late 1950s for the U.S. Navy's Polaris project, which had thousands of contractors. It has the potential to reduce both the time and cost required to complete a project.

Project Management Institute—This is the organizational body that controls the Project Management Certification examination and is the only body recognized by ANSI as the standard in Project Management.

Project Plan—The actual plan that is the baseline you use to manage and complete the project.

Quality Assurance—The process of preventing problems rather than correcting them.

Responsibility to the Profession—This is the first section on the PMI website that deals with the professionalism and ethics of a project manager.

Responsibilities to Customers and the Public—This is the second section of the PMI website that deals with the professionalism and ethics of a project manager.

Return on Investment—This is a major form of investment analysis where the amount of return that will occur from an investment on a new project is calculated.

Risk Monitoring and Control—A continuous process of looking at risks on a project as the project is ongoing.

Scribe—The person writing down meeting notes for a project status meeting.

Self Actualization—In the Mazlow pyramid, this is the highest level.

Six Sigma—A disciplined data-driven approach and methodology for eliminating defects (driving towards six standard deviations between the mean and the nearest specification limit) in any process—from manufacturing to transactional and from product to service. The number used in six standard deviations is 99.99.

Statistical Process Control—A type of control that uses sampling methods so that large numbers of outputs can be monitored by using samples without having to look at each unit.

Technical Review Board—The technical review board consists of experts in a particular technical area and is used to determine whether the project team's performance is in keeping with expected technical limits.

Three-Point Estimates—Another name for PERT estimates.

Time and Material—A contract type in which the vendor suggests that the buyer be billed for time and materials as they occur during the project. This puts the risk on the buyer because the final price is variable.

Version Control—Keeping control of documents and other materials through the use of a numbering system. Any change to a current version creates a new version number.

Workarounds—Actions done in response to unexpected problems.

About the CD-ROM

The MeasureUp™ PMP Test Prep Exam

The main function of the MeasureUp PMP Test Prep Exam is test simulation—to prepare you to take the actual certification exam. This CD offers more than 400 multiple-choice questions. Under Study Mode, you can select the number of questions you want to run in a session—up to 200 questions at one time. In Certification Mode, the test exam is timed and includes 200 questions.

System Requirements

The following list includes the minimum system requirements for this application:

- Windows 95, Windows 98, or Windows NT 4.0 with the most recent service pack. Windows 3.1, Windows for Workgroups, UNIX, and Macintosh platforms are not supported

- 16 megabytes of RAM (32 or more recommended)

- 800 × 600 screen resolution, color depth of 256 colors or greater

- Pentium 120 processor or greater

- 15 megabytes of available hard disk space

Installation

1. Insert the CD-ROM into your CD-ROM drive. The Autorun feature should launch the software.

2. If Autorun is disabled, from the Start menu on the Microsoft Taskbar, choose "Run"

3. Type "d:\setup" and click OK (your drive letter may differ).

Starting the MeasureUp Practice Tests Application

Back up your important data files prior to doing any installation activities.

1. Select Start | Programs | Certification Preparation | Certification Preparation to start the application.

   The first time you start the application, you will be prompted to create a user profile.

2. Click Create User Profile to display the User Profile dialog box.

   If you already have a user profile, then the Logon dialog box displays when you start the MeasureUp Practice Tests application.

3. You must specify your username and password, if you specified a password when you created your user profile.

4. Click OK. If you do not want to start the MeasureUp Practice Test application, click Exit.

   If you do not have a user profile or want to create a new profile for another user, click Create New User Profile.

   Note that if the Auto-logon to this profile checkbox is selected on the User Profile dialog box, then the Logon dialog box will not display when the MeasureUp Practice Test application is started. Instead, the user is automatically logged on to the application with the selected user profile. This option should only be selected for single-user workstations

5. After you have successfully logged on to the MeasureUp Practice Tests application, the application displays the registered test available for use.

6. Click the PMPTestPrepV2.0....

7. From the test list window, you can choose to start a test, obtain test history, or logoff.

Taking a Test

After you select and start the test you want to take, the test questions for the selected exam are displayed.

The question text displays in the first section of the window and the available answer choices display in the second section of the window. To bookmark a question so that you can easily return to the question later during the test, select the Mark checkbox.

The Time Remaining box only displays if you are taking a test in Certification mode, or if you are taking a test in Custom mode and selected for the timer to be on. If you are taking a test in Custom mode and want to extend the amount of time you have remaining, click the Options button.

Navigating Through a Test

To navigate through the test questions, click the Previous, Next, and Go To buttons. You can also select these options from the Navigation Menu. Click Previous to move to a test question that you have previously viewed. Click Next to move to the next test question. You do not have to answer a question in order to move to the next question. Click Go To to view a specific test question, to jump to the first test question, to jump to the last test question, or to view the first unanswered question.

Sorting the Test Questions

Your test questions are sorted by question number by default. Each question's number is displayed in the upper left corner of the question window. If you select Navigate | Sort | by question, then the questions display in numerical order.

Displaying the Answer and Explanation

If you are taking a test in Study or Custom mode and want to view the correct answer(s), explanation, and reference(s) for a question as you take the test, click Explanation or select Navigation | Display Answer. The correct answer for the question is highlighted and the explanation and reference(s) for the question display.

Please note the Explanation button is not available in Certification mode; therefore, you can only view the correct answer(s), explanation, and reference(s) after you score the test.

If you select Do Not Display Any Answers Until the Test Is Complete from the Custom Mode tab or the Options dialog box, then you will not be able to view the answers, explanations, and references for the test questions until you score the test. You can also select to automatically display the answers to all of your responses or your incorrect responses from the Custom Mode tab or the Options dialog box.

Index

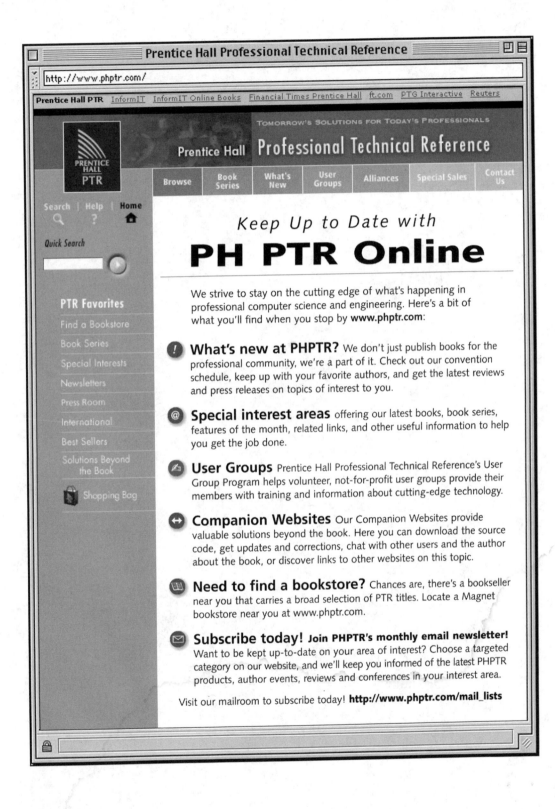

Wouldn't it be great

if the world's leading technical publishers joined forces to deliver their best tech books in a common digital reference platform?

They have. Introducing
InformIT Online Books
powered by Safari.

■ **Specific answers to specific questions.**
InformIT Online Books' powerful search engine gives you relevance-ranked results in a matter of seconds.

■ **Immediate results.**
With InformIT Online Books, you can select the book you want and view the chapter or section you need immediately.

■ **Cut, paste and annotate.**
Paste code to save time and eliminate typographical errors. Make notes on the material you find useful and choose whether or not to share them with your work group.

■ **Customized for your enterprise.**
Customize a library for you, your department or your entire organization. You only pay for what you need.

Get your first 14 days **FREE!**
For a limited time, InformIT Online Books is offering its members a 10 book subscription risk-free for 14 days. Visit **http://www.informit.com/online-books** for details.

POWERED BY
Safari
TECH BOOKS ONLINE

informit.com/onlinebooks

InformIT Online Books